In Search of
Vedic-Harappan Relationship

In Search of Vedic-Harappan Relationship

Edited by
Ashvini Agrawal

Aryan Books International
New Delhi

In Search of Vedic-Harappan Relationship

ISBN-81-7305-282-4

Published in **2005** by :
ARYAN BOOKS INTERNATIONAL
Pooja Apartments, 4B, Ansari Road, Darya Ganj, New Delhi-110 002 (India)
Tel.: 23287589, 23255799; Fax: 91-11-23270385; E-mail: aryanbooks@vsnl.com

Computer Typeset and Printed in India at
ABI Prints & Publishing Co., New Delhi

Preface

The search for a relationship between the Vedic and the Harappan Civilizations may be called a comparatively recent phenomenon though the modern writings of the Indian history started way back in the eighteenth century with the advent of the Europeans in India. The question never arose prior to that time as the very concept of *sanātana* remained the bedrock of the entire Indian civilization, culture and thought. The origin of this great civilization was never questioned simply because no one ever thought of calling it a 'borrowed culture' or its progenitors as migrants from some foreign land. Neither in memory nor in the vast ocean of its literature such an idea ever existed. However, the initial quest of the Westerners to know the history and culture of their newly conquered subjects led to the realization of their rich past that in its turn led to a well-calculated imperialist policy to rewrite Indian history, ascribing its earliest inhabitants as migrants from the West—Europe, Russian Steppes, Central Asia and whatever other places they could think of, except India itself, and also fixed the date of their imaginary migration in the middle of the second millennium BCE, albeit arbitrarily.

The early 1920s brought to light the sprawling cities of Mohenjo-daro in Sind and Harappa in Punjab, through the archaeological excavations, that by most conservative estimates belonged to the third millennium BCE. With these discoveries arose the problem of the authorship of this civilization and it was surmised, without any evidence, that its authors were Dravidians, the so-called original inhabitants of India, who were defeated and pushed towards the South by the Āryan invaders. But the credit for such an advanced urban civilization was not given to the Indians. John Marshall (1931), E. Mackay (1938), R. Mortimer Wheeler (1960), etc., attributed the urbanization in India to the Mesopotamian Civilization with terms like 'ideas have wings' that have been revived by scholars like M. Tosi (1993) with the terms like 'Turanian Cultural Shock'. The attempts of scholars like Sri Aurobindo, Lakshman Sarup and Madho Sarup Vats to relate the new discoveries with the Vedic Civilization were scoffed upon and the dictum of the Western scholars prevailed to be followed to this day by most of the Westerners and by their more vociferous Indian counterparts without ever caring to examine the evidence, old and new, afresh.

However, a section of scholars including archaeologists, Sankritists and historians brought to fore fresh evidence, both archaeological and literary, through their laborious investigations thus discarding the old theory given by the imperialists and their followers. Notions like the Āryan migration into India, their conflict with the inhabitants of the Indus Valley, the middle of the second millennium BCE as the date of composition of the *Ṛigveda* have been successfully challenged. At the same time the role of the Sarasvatī River in the Vedic vis-à-vis Harappan Civilization, the change of the nomenclature from the 'Indus Civilization' to the 'Sindhu-Sarasvatī Civilization' and the both being two phases of one and the same culture—the Vedic Civilization, have been proposed and highlighted. However, another section of scholars still remains opposed to these views, though without any justification.

In order to provide a common platform to all the scholars desirous of sorting out the matter, a seminar was organized by the Panjab University. Dealing with a single theme, *The Search for Vedic-Harappan Relationship,* the papers contained amazingly varied data, approach and subject matter yet convincingly leading to a consensus that the geographical horizons of the two coincide, that their chronological horizons overlap and that the mosaics of their cultural content have striking resemblance. It was felt that there is need to discard old views in the light of fresh evidence indicating the continuity of the Indian civilization from Ṛigvedic to the Harappan, the latter being the period of the *Atharvaveda* and the *Brāhmaṇas*.

Prof. B.B. Lal, Former Director-General, Archaeological Survey of India, led the discussion by presenting keynote address, dwelt upon the topic from every possible angle—the date of the *Ṛigveda,* the archaeological evidence of the Sindhu-Sarasvatī (Harappan) Civilization, the authors of the two, the role of the Sarasvatī, the views of the earlier writers like Max Müller, concluding that 'the often-touted objections against a Harappan-Vedic equation are groundless and there is enough circumstantial evidence to suggest that this equation is the most likely one'. He set the ball rolling by his remark—'It is time to rethink'.

Prof. B.P. Sinha, who presided over the inaugural session, also questioned the theory of the so-called Āryan migration and the very nomenclature Āryan for a race on the basis of literary as well as archaeological evidence. He strongly advocated the affinity of the Vedic and the Harappan Civilization and pleaded for the review of the entire evidence at our disposal in its totality.

The papers included in this volume represent almost every aspect of the theme, the major thrust being on the affinity between the archaeological and the literary evidence. The role of the Sarasvatī in the Vedic-Harappan Civilization with deep discussions on its identification, source and course, its place in the Vedic literature, Harappan sites on its ancient bed and their connotations, has drawn the attention of several scholars. The Sarasvatī which is eloquently praised in the Vedic literature as *nadītamā, ambītamā,* and *devītamā*, flowing from the Himalayas to the Arabian Sea as a perennial river, had more than a thousand Harappan settlements along its course till it disappeared due to geological-tectonic-volcanic changes forcing the inhabitants on its banks to migrate elsewhere. Its region, called Brahmāvarta, the most sacred land was not only home to the Vedic sages but it was here that Vedic-Harappan culture flourished from the beginning. The attempts to draw conclusions about the past on the basis of the present state of this great river are not only fallacious but also misleading.

The Āryan migration/invasion theory and the related questions like the date of the *Ṛigveda* vis-à-vis Harappan culture, the flow of ideas to or from the West, the date of the Mahābhārata War and the astronomical data, the archaeoastronomy and the like have been fruitfully discussed by an equally large number of scholars. Breaking the myth of the Āryan invasion/migration into the Saptasindhu land, it has been convincingly argued that the *Ṛigveda* must be dated prior to 3000 BCE and the Harappan culture reflects the age of the *Atharvaveda* and the *Brāhamaṇas*. The Mahābhārata War cannot be dated beyond the third millennium BCE and the literary and archaeological evidence point in the same direction without contradiction.

The relevance of the geographical references in the Vedic literature, especially to the ocean, rivers and Soma, their bearing on the present theme, significance and connotations have received due attention. Equally important are the articles correlating the material culture described in the Vedas and known from the remains of the Harappan cities, including art and architecture, town planning, pottery, trade and commerce, navigation, etc., along with an interesting article on the affinity of art motifs in the Vedic and Harappan Culture makes the connection between the two crystal clear. The religious affinity as discussed with the example of the significance of the *aśvattha* tree motif on the Harappan seals and pottery and the parallel references in the Vedic literature point in the same direction. The relation of the Harappan seals and the motifs thereon with the passages in the *Upanishads* and the *Saṃhitas* has also been dealt with. The presence of horse in the Harappan civilization that has been repeatedly questioned by the critics of the Vedic-Harappan relationship has also been convincingly established by more than one scholar.

The ethnic affinities, groups and relations, the connotations of the word *Ārya* have not escaped the attention of the scholars contributing to this volume. The discussion on the need of a new paradigm for the Ṛigvedic-Harappan relationship in the light of ethnic relationships and groupings leads to the same direction in a new way. The meaning of the word *Ārya* never denoted a race but was always used for cultured, noble, educated elite and that such people cannot be called barbarians by any stretch of imagination have been clearly established.

Rethinking and reinterpreting the oldest line of argument based on philology, that at one time had become the hallmark of the Āryan Migration Theory, it has been shown that the Dravidian origin of the Harappans is a myth. It has been convincingly pointed out that the Vedic Sanskrit is one of the Indo-European group of languages but its speakers have not descended from an Indo-European race. In fact there is no evidence that such a race ever existed.

The archaeological evidence brought to fore by recent excavations at Kunal in the Fatehabad district of Haryana, have brought to light the cultural remains from pre- to mature Harappan period shedding important light on the antiquity of the Harappans in Brahmāvarta and their affinity with the Vedic people. Though purely technical in nature, the paper serves as a base for further discussion on the topic clearly pointing to the Vedic-Harappan relationship.

The articles included in this Volume, based on deep research on scientific lines, help us clear a haze that was created around the earliest history of India, removing several wrong notions and clearing mental cobwebs. It was not possible to arrange them in any thematic order as the broad subject and approach of all the scholars has been the same as also their scholastic merit. Therefore, it was decided to put them in alphabetical order of the authors' names. This may not appear very scientific in itself but is an often-followed practice in such cases. Of course, the opinions expressed here remain open to further discussion and debate but may a consensus of opinion emerge on the issue as prayed in the *Rigveda*.

Samāno mantraḥ samiti samāni/
Samānam manaḥ saha chittamesham//

Ashvini Agrawal

Chandigarh
21 May, 2004

Contents

Acknowledgements

In the preparation of this Volume, comprising the results of discussions during the seminar, **The Search for Vedic Harappan Relationship**, all kinds of help came from various quarters. It is my bounden duty to acknowledge it. Prof B.B. Lal, Former Director-General, Archaeological Survey of India, has been very kind in accepting the invitation to deliver the keynote address, that forms the first chapter in this Volume, during the seminar and lead the discussions in spite of his very busy schedule. No word of thanks can be enough to repay his debt. The Late Prof B.P. Sinha, Former Professor and Head, Dept. of Ancient Indian History & Culture, Patna University, accepted the invitation to preside over the inaugural session of the seminar at a very short notice. Unfortunately he could not pen his ideas for this Volume as the cruel hands of death snatched him away shortly after the seminar. We bow our heads to his memory as a tribute to his scholarship.

Prof. O.P. Bharadwaj, Former Veda-Vyasa Professor of Indology and Director, Dept. of Indic Studies, Kurukshetra University, has been a constant source of inspiration, besides helping in planning and giving shape to the entire idea right from its inception. I am simply beholden to him for being a true friend, philosopher and guide.

All the participants of the seminar, those whose papers are in this Volume and also those who participated as discussants, deserve our special thanks. I must specifically mention Shri M.C. Joshi, Former Director-General, Archaeological Survey of India; Dr. S.P. Gupta, Former Director, Allahabad Museum; Prof. Shivaji Singh, Former Head, Dept. of AIHC & A, Gorakhpur University; Shri R.S. Bisht, Ex-Joint Director-General, Archaeological Survey of India; Prof. Ved Kumari Ghai, Former Head, Dept. of Sanskrit, Jammu University; Dr. I.K. Sarma, Former Director, Salar Jung Museum, Hyderabad; Prof. P.K. Agrawala, Dept. of AIHC & A, Banaras Hindu University; Dr. N.S. Rajaram, Bangalore; Shri Y. Krishan, New Delhi; Shri J.S. Khatri and Shri Madhav Acharya, Dept. of Archaeology, Haryana.

Prof. N. Kazanas, Athens, Dr. David Frawley, American Institute of Vedic Studies, Santa Fe, USA and Prof. Subhash Kak, Louisiana University, USA, obliged me with their learned articles for this Volume at a very short notice. I am personally grateful to all of them.

Shri Devendra Handa, Former Chairman, Dept. of AIHC & A, Panjab University, has been a constant guide for the activities of our Department. He always extends his ungrudging help, this time being no exception. He not only contributed to the seminar and this Volume but also helped in several ways to make the seminar a success for which I shall ever remain grateful to him. My colleagues in the University, Prof. N.K. Ojha, Dr. Mahesh Sharma, Dr. Suchi Dayal, Dr. Vipnesh Bharadwaj and Dr. R.P. Bhardwaj shouldered all the burden of arrangements for the seminar, keeping me free of all the worries. The entire credit of making the seminar a success goes to them. My office staff Ms. Varsha, Mr. Krishan Bisht, Mr. Ramesh and Mr. Sanjay carried out all the administrative responsibilities, putting in long hours in the office, yet remaining in the background. These silent workers deserve appreciation and special thanks.

It would not have been possible to arrange this seminar but for the generous financial help received from various quarters. Special mention may be made of Indian Council of Historical Research, New Delhi and the University Grants Commission, New Delhi, for providing sufficient funds for the seminar.

Shri Vikas Arya, the publisher, deserves special appreciation and thanks. He was able to extract a promise from me to edit this Volume for him more than a year ago and has ensured a meticulously neat work and beautiful get-up of the book. But for his personal interest and care the Volume may have delayed further.

List of Contributors

Shri M. Acharya
Dept. of Archaeology, Govt. of Haryana, Kurukshetra - 136 119.

Prof. Ashvini Agrawal
Professor, Department of Ancient Indian History, Culture & Archaeology & Dean, Faculty of Arts, Panjab University, Chandigarh - 160 014.

Prof. P.K. Agrawala
Professor, Dept. of Ancient Indian History, Culture & Archaeology, Banaras Hindu University, Varanasi.

B 1/54, Amethi Kothi, Nagwa, Varanasi – 221 005.

Prof. O.P. Bharadwaj
Ex-Veda Vyasa, Professor of Indology, Kurukshetra University. Former Director, Higher Education, Haryana.

'Vagvihara', # 465, Sector 7, Panchkula - 134 109.

Dr. David Frawley
Director, American Institute of Vedic Studies, PO Box 8357, Santa Fe NM 87504-8357.

Prof. Ved Kumari Ghai
Ex-Professor & Head, Dept. of Sanskrit, Jammu Unviersity, Jammu.

15/2, Trikuta Nagar, Jammu – 180 012.

Dr. S.P. Gupta
Chairman, Indian Archaeological Society, B - 17, Qutab Institutional Area, New Delhi - 110 016.

Prof. Devendra Handa
Former Chairman, Dept. of Ancient Indian History, Culture & Archaeology, Panjab University, Chandigarh.

1401, PUSHPAC Colony, Sector 49-B, Chandigarh.

Prof. Subhash Kak
Delaune Distinguished Professor of Electrical Engineering and Professor in the Asian Studies and Cognitive Studies Programs, Louisiana State University, Baton Rouge, LA 70803-5901 (USA).

Prof. N. Kazanas
Professor, Omilos Meleton, Pylarou 3 Str., Pangrati, Athens, GR 11635 (Greece).

Shri J.S. Khatri
Dept. of Archaeology, Govt. of Haryana, Kurukshetra - 136 119

Shri Yuvraj Krishan
D-1329, Vasant Kunj, New Delhi - 110 070.

Prof. B.B. Lal
Former Director General, Archaeological Survey of India.

F-7, Hauz Khas Enclave, New Delhi – 110 016.

Prof. N.K. Ojha
Chairman, Dept. of Ancient Indian History, Culture & Archaeology, Panjab University, Chandigarh – 160 014.

Prof. N.S. Rajaram
F2, Rajatha Manor, 42, Patalamma Temple Road, Southend Circle, Basavanagudi, Bangalore - 560 004.

Dr. Vasundhra Rehani
Dept. of Dayanand Chair for Vedic Studies, Panjab University, Chandigarh.

Dr. I.K. Sarma
Former Director, Archaeological Survey of India & Former Director, Salar Jung Museum, Hyderabad.

Flat No. 4, IInd Floor, Latha Apartments, Vidyanagar, Hyderabad – 500 044.

Prof. Shivaji Singh
Ex-Professor & Head, Dept. of Ancient Indian History, Culture & Archaeology, Gorakhpur University, Shivala Nagar (East), Mohaddipur, Gorakhpur – 273 008.

1

Search for Vedic-Harappan Relationship

New Perspectives

B.B. LAL

In the second half of the nineteenth century, a renowned German scholar, Max Müller, assigned to the *Veda*s a date around 1200 BC. This he did on a very ad hoc basis. While accepting the existence of the *Sūtra* literature around the 6th–5th centuries BC, he assigned a time-span of 200 years to each of the preceding literary periods, viz., those of the *Āraṇyaka*s, *Brāhmaṇa*s and *Veda*s. One might well ask: 'Why two hundred years and not one hundred, or say three hundred?' Evidently, ad hocism never worries about such questions. However, Max Müller's contemporaries, like Wilson, Whitney and Goldstucker, could not take the issue lying down. Thereupon, Max Müller somewhat cooled down and mentioned in his Preface to the *Ṛigveda,* as follows:

> I have repeatedly dwelt on the merely hypothetical character of the dates, which I have ventured to assign to the first periods of Vedic literature. All I have claimed for them has been that they are the minimum dates, and that the literary productions of each period which either still exist or which formerly existed could hardly be accounted for within shorter limits of time than those suggested.

Not feeling quite comfortable within himself even with the foregoing stand, Max Müller chose to lay down his arms. Thus, in 1890 came his final surrender in the following words:

> If now we ask as to how we can fix the dates of these periods, it is quite clear that we cannot hope to fix a *terminum a qua* [sic]. Whether the Vedic hymns were composed [in] 1000 or 2000 or 3000 years BC, no power on earth will ever determine.

The great irony of the whole episode, however, is that although the 'clergy' had long withdrawn his 'fatwa', his blind followers in India as well as abroad, still steadfastly cling to it. They do not dare cross this *lakshmaṇa rekhā.* Why? They alone know it best.

This was the scenario towards the end of the nineteenth century. The first quarter of the twentieth century, however, introduced another factor, which was not a literary one, but archaeological. In 1920s, a highly advanced urban civilization was brought to light as a result of the excavations at Harappa and Mohenjo-daro. (It goes variously by the names of the Harappan, Indus or Indus-Sarasvatī Civilization.) Some of the artefacts of this civilization had also been found in ancient cultural deposits in Mesopotamia, and since the latter had already been dated to the third millennium BC, the newly discovered Indian civilization could easily be assigned a comparable antiquity.

All this led to an interesting ready-made conclusion, as follows. Since, according to the 'fatwa' of Max Müller, the Vedas were as late as 1200 BC, whereas the Harappan Civilization belonged to third millennium BC, it was at once declared that this civilization could not have been that of the Vedic people. Further, since in India there are only two major language families, viz., the Sanskritic and the Dravidian, it became a natural corollary that the authors of the Harappan Civilization were a Dravidian-speaking people. And, since the Dravidian languages are spoken in southern India and not in the domain of the Harappan Civilization, it was further argued that the Āryans invaded the subcontinent from the north-west and pushed the Harappans all the way down to the south. To support this conclusion, which admittedly was circumstantial in nature, it was argued that the speakers of the Brahui language in a small pocket of Baluchistan are the survivors of the Harappan population.

The final seal on the theories of an Āryan invasion of India and a Harappan-Dravidian equation was put by Mortimer Wheeler who, on discovering a fortification wall around one of the mounds at Harappa, declared as follows (1947: 82):

> The Āryan invasion of the Land of Seven Rivers, the Panjab and its environs, constantly assumes the form of an onslaught upon the walled cities of the aborigines. For these cities the term used in the *Ṛigveda* is *pur,* meaning a 'rampart', 'fort' or 'stronghold'... Indra, the Āryan War-god, is *puraṁdara,* 'fort-destroyer'. He shatters 'ninety forts' for his Āryan protege Divodāsa....
>
> Where are—or were—these citadels? It has in the past been supposed that they were mythical, or were 'merely places of refuge against attack, ramparts of hardened earth with palisades and a ditch'. The recent excavation at Harappa may be thought to have changed the picture. Here, we have a highly evolved civilization of essentially non-Āryan type, now known to have employed massive fortifications, and known also to have dominated the river-system of north-western India at a time not too distant from the likely period of the early Āryan invasion of that region. What destroyed this firmly settled civilization? Climatic, economic, political deterioration may have weakened it, but its ultimate extinction is more likely to have been completed by deliberate and large-scale destruction. It may be no mere chance that at a late period of Mohenjo-daro men, women and children appear to have been massacred there. On circumstantial evidence, Indra stands accused.

With this second 'fatwa' by an archaeologist of Wheeler's eminence, it became 'a gospel truth' that the Harappans were a Dravidian-speaking people and that their civilization was destroyed by Āryan invaders, as a result of which it became 'extinct'. But, as it has been rightly said, you cannot keep on concealing the truth for long under the cover of darkness. Sooner or later the truth must come out. And indeed, it happened sooner than later. In less than two decades, an eminent western archaeologist, George F. Dales (1964), published a very scathing paper which he rightly labelled as 'The Mythical Massacre at Mohenjo-daro'. (Incidentally, had it been an Indian archaeologist to publish such a paper, he would have certainly been dubbed as being under the influence of 'Hindutva', in the unfortunate present-day politically surcharged academic climate in the country in which certain ideologues have lost all regards for truth.) The massacre theory has many a pit-fall. In nine seasons of excavations at Mohenjo-daro, altogether thirty-seven skeletons were found. While the number is not so vital, what is important is as follows. In the first place, all the skeletons came from the Lower Town and none from the Citadel. Are we then to believe that the invaders were interested in attacking only the common folks living in the Lower Town and not the rulers inhabiting the Citadel? Why were the latter consciously spared ? And even if we ignore this vital point, what is most incongruous in the massacre thesis is that these skeletons were recovered from different strata of the site: thus, while some came from the Intermediate and Late levels, quite a few were found in deposits which had accumulated after the abandonment of the site. If these deaths were due to the attack of invaders, the skeletons should have come only from the uppermost levels. How could these have penetrated into the earlier levels? Further, it must be mentioned that some of the skeletons bore cut-marks which had been duly healed. Had the deaths been the result of a massacre, on-the-spot killings would have left no time for the wounds to heal. Finally, there is yet another lacuna in the invasion-cum-massacre theory, viz. that no evidence of any warfare, in terms of weaponry, has been found at Mohenjo-daro, nor are there any vestiges of invaders in terms of any remains of an alien culture.

None of the sites of the Harappan Civilization, whether in the north or south or east or west, has yielded any evidence whatsoever of an invasion nor, contrary to what had been proposed by Wheeler, did the Harappan Civilization become extinct. What had really happened was that probably as a result of various factors, such as a fall in agricultural surplus because of the wearing out of the landscape owing to over-exploitation and climatic changes, and a substantial reduction in foreign trade, the economic prosperity witnessed during the Mature Harappan days was no longer there. An additional factor was the drying up of the Sarasvatī around this time. The population that had once settled firmly in its lush valley had per force to move north-eastwards in search of arable land and adequate water-supply. The inevitable outcome of it all was a sharp decline in the urban set-up and a reversal to the rural way of life. This kind of evidence is available throughout the length and breadth of the Harappan domain. Thus, with the breakdown of this overseeing urban authority, regional, but Harappan-derived, cultural facets began to mushroom, known, for example, as the Jhukar culture in Sindh, Cemetery H culture in Pakistani Punjab, the Hulas-Alamgirpur-Bhagwanpura complex in Haryana and Uttar Pradesh and the Rangpur culture in Gujarat. As I have fully demonstrated with comprehensive illustrations in *The Sarasvatī flows On,* there was no extinction of the Harappan Culture: a rurally oriented cultural phenomenon, basically derived from the Harappan, can be perceived in the country even today.

At this juncture, it may be well worth while to draw pointed attention to the biological evidence as well. After a thorough study of human skeletal remains from a large number of protohistoric sites, Hemphill and his colleagues have come to the following conclusion (1991: 137):

> As for the question of biological continuity within the Indus Valley, two discontinuities appear to exist. The first occurs between 6000 BC and 4500 BC and is reflected by strong separation in dental non-metric characters between neolithic and chalcolithic burials at Mehrgarh. The second occurs at some point after 800 BC and before 200 BC. In the intervening period, while there is dental non-metric, craniometric, and cranial non-metric evidence for a degree of internal biological continuity, statistical evaluation of cranial data reveals clear indication of an interaction with the West specifically with the Iranian Plateau.

Thus, while there may have been some interaction between Iran and India ('interaction' always means a two-way movement and not one way only), it should be abundantly clear that there was no mass intrusion of a new set of people into the Harappan matrix, as would be required in an 'Āryan-invasion' hypothesis. Hence, even on the biological turf, the Āryan-invasion theory is grounded.

Before discussing the issue of the Vedic-Harappan relationship, it may be well worth while to analyze if there is any real basis for the much-touted theory that the Harappans were a Dravidian-speaking people. As has already been indicated, the primary basis of this equation was that since, as per the 'fatwa' of Max Müller, the Vedas were as late as 1200 BC, and as the Harappan Civilization was ascribable to the third millennium BC, the latter could not be associated with the Vedic people. Under such an assumption, the only other possible claimants could have been the Dravidian-speaking people. This ready-made theory was given a further boost when it was noted that a section (even though it was very small) of the population of Baluchistan spoke a dialect attributed to the Dravidian family. It was thus argued that the Brahui-speakers were the residual Harappans when their main body was driven away to south India by the invading Āryans.

All scholars do not agree that Brahui belongs to the Dravidian family. Some are of the opinion that it is a form of the eastern Elamite. A more important point is that, it is held by many scholars that the Brahui-speaking people have not been living in that region since the third millennium BC but emigrated there much later—according to one view as late as the medieval times. To further support this, it may also be added that the Brahuis themselves have a tradition that they are migrants to the area where they live now. (Cf. Elfenbein 1987; Hock 1975; Sergent 1997). Thus, the Brahui-factor becomes redundant.

In this supposed Harappan-Dravidian equation, there is another major drawback. In entire South India, viz. in the States of Tamil Nadu, Karnataka, Andhra Pradesh and Kerala, there is not even a single Harappan site. All that we have in this region in the period concerned is what is known as the Southern Neolithic Culture. Are we then required to believe that the urban Harappan Civilization turned overnight into a Stone Age Neolithic Culture? I am sure that there would be no takers of such an unbelievable hypothesis.

Then there is yet another point that calls for attention. All over the world, it has been observed that when a region is overtaken by a people who speak a new language, the traces of the older language spoken in that region are always discernible in one form or another. Many of the towns, rivers and mountains in that area continue to retain the names given to them by the speakers of the earlier language. As for example, some American (Red) Indian names of rivers and places continue even today, even though most of North America has been run over by the Europeans. Such examples are the names of rivers like Mississippi and Missouri and towns like Chicago and Massachusetts. The same is the case in Europe where many pre-Indo-European names are still available. One thus expects that if the Harappans spoke the Dravidian language, the names at least of some of the rivers, towns, etc. in the region concerned should be of Dravidian affiliation. The hard fact is that there is no such evidence whatsoever. Thus, the very ground slips from underneath the feet of the Harappan-Dravidian equation.

There is one more point that requires to be straightened out in this context. It has been observed that there are some Dravidian words in the *Veda*s. The protagonists of the Harappan-Dravidian equation explain this phenomenon by saying that when the Āryans invaded the Harappans, they borrowed the Dravidian words concerned from the latter. While it is a fact that there do occur a few words of Dravidian affiliation in the Vedic texts, this feature is also explainable in another way. Just for argument's sake let it be assumed that the Harappans were a Sanskrit-speaking people. It is well known that the Harappans were not an insular people. Thus, they were in contact in varying degrees with their neighbours. They are known to have procured a part of their gold-supply from the Kolar mines, located in South India. In this way they did come in contact with the Southern Neolithic people. Since we do not know of any other language having been spoken in this region, it is only reasonable to hold that the Southern Neolithic folks spoke a Dravidian language. In such a scenario, it would have been but natural for the Sanskrit-speaking Harappans to have incorporated a few

Dravidian words in their own language.

Thus, the Harappan-Dravidian equation has no firm ground and needs to be given up. But that does not mean that the ground is automatically clear for a Harappan-Vedic equation. First consider the various arguments against such an equation. These are: (i) the Harappans were urbanites whereas the Vedic people were mere nomads; (ii) the Vedic people used spoked wheels in their vehicles whereas the Harappans knew no spoked wheels; (iii) that the horse was domesticated by the Vedic people whereas the Harappans did not know it; and (iv) that the *Veda*s were no older than 1200 BC, whereas the Harappan Civilization pertained to the third millennium BC. We shall now deal with these objections seriatim.

There cannot be a greater travesty of truth than to say that the Vedic people were nomads. They, like any other well-established society, had a very good system of governance. They had *sabhā*s and *samiti*s whose functions seem to have been both legislative and rendering advice to the rulers. And the rulers themselves enjoyed a series of hierarchcal status. Thus, some were at the peak and called *samrāṭ,* somewhat akin to an emperor. The next in gradation were *rājan,* i.e. kings. In a still lower category were *rājaka* or kinglings. Thus, Abhyāvartin Chāyamāna, who was a very powerful ruler, has been referred to as *Samrāṭ,* in *RV* 6.27.8. On the other hand, a ruler of lesser importance, namely Chitra, has been called *rājan,* a mere king (*RV* 8.21.18). The same verse speaks of still smaller chieftains, by using the term *rājaka.*

Staunch advocates of Vedic nomadism are sure to raise eyebrows over the above-mentioned distinction amongst the category of rulers, by saying that the texts do not imply what they state and that these distinctions are merely notional. Let them, however, know that this distinction was very much real. This is fully substantiated by what has been stated in the *Śatapatha Brāhmaṇa* (V.1.1.12–13).

> *Rājā vai Rājasūyena bhavati. Samrāḍ Vājapeyena. avaram hi Rājyaṁ paraṁ Sāmrājyam. Kāmayeta vai Rājā Samrāḍ bhavitum. avaram hi Rājyam paraṁ Sāmrājyaṁ. Na Smrāṭ Kāmayeta Rājā bhavitum. avaraṁ hi Rājyaṁ paraṁ Sāmrājyaṁ.*
>
> By offering the *Rājasūya* he becomes *Rājā* and by the *Vājapeya* he becomes *Samrāṭ*. The office of *Rājan* is lower, that of *Samrāṭ,* the higher; a *Rājan* might indeed wish to become *Samrāṭ,* for the office of *Rājan* is lower and that of *Samrāṭ* the higher, but the *Samrāṭ* would not wish to become a *Rājā,* for the office of *Rājan* is the lower and that of *Samrāṭ* the higher.

What better authority can there be to clinch the issue?

The Vedic Āryans were not nomads living in make-shift huts and moving from place to place, but had their own full-fledged settlements many of which were even fortified. The fortifications were made of stone and had even a hundred (i.e. a large number of) arms. The relevant expressions in the *Ṛigveda* are: *Śatamaśmanmayīnām purāmindro vyāsyat Divodāsāya dāduṣe* (*RV* 4.30.20); or *pūrbhavā śatabujiḥ* (*RV* 7.15.14).

Not only did the Vedic Āryans live in fortified towns but they were also well up in trade, whereby they achieved economic well-being. Besides land-trade, they were engaged even in sea-trade. This is amply clear from the following (*RV* 9.33.6):

> *rāyaḥ Samudrānśchaturo asmabhayam Soma viśvataḥ ā pavasva sahasriṇaḥ*
>
> From every side, O Soma, for our profit, pour thou forth four seas full of riches thousand fold.

Some of the boats used in this trade were very large. Sometimes as many as a hundred (i.e. a very large number of) oars were used: *śatāritram nāvamātasthivānsam* (*RV* 1.116.5).

Even the foregoing few quotations from the *Ṛigveda* should suffice to convince anyone that the allegation that the Vedic Āryans were 'nomads' is a pure myth, created by some Western scholars in the nineteenth century and blindly followed by many even to this day.

We may now pass on to the problem of the 'spoked wheel', which has been used to put a spoke in the wheel of a Harappan-Vedic equation. Those who say that the Harappans used only solid wheels and not spoked ones are either deliberately ignoring the evidence or have not kept themselves abreast of recent discoveries. Not one but at least three sites have provided evidence of the use of spoked wheels in the Mature Harappan levels. The sites concerned are: Kalibangan, Rakhigarhi and Banawali. The wheels are duly illustrated in *The Sarasvatī Flows On*. While the specimens from Kalibangan and Rakhigarhi (Pl. 1.1) delineate the spokes by means of a series of painted lines radiating from a central hub, in the case of the Banawali examples the spokes are shown in low relief (Pl. 1.2). This latter technique, continued to be used for depicting spokes on terracotta wheels right up to the historical times. This evidence takes care of the second objection raised.

Pl. 1.1 Rakhigarhi: Terracotta wheel. The painted lines represent the spokes. Mature Harappan.

Now, to the horse. Even as far back as 1938, E. Mackay had categorically stated that this animal was associated with the Harappan Civilization: 'Perhaps the most interesting of the model animals is one that I personally take to represent a horse' (Mackay 1938, Vol. I, p. 289; Vol. II, pl. LXXVIII, 11). Dealing with this very topic in 1968, Wheeler affirmed: 'One terracotta from a late level of Mohenjo-daro seems to represent a horse, reminding us that the jaw-bone of a horse is also recorded from the site, and that the horse was known at a considerably earlier period in northern Baluchistan,' (Wheeler 1968: 92).

Since then a lot of new evidence has poured in. For example, Lothal in Gujarat has yielded not only a terracotta figurine of the horse (Pl. 1.3) but also its faunal remains (Rao 1985). Another site in Gujarat, namely Surkotada, has also yielded horse bones (Joshi 1990). An internationally recognized authority on the skeletal remains of this animal, Sandor Bokonyi, Director of the Archaeological Institute, Budapest, Hungary, conveyed in 1993 through a letter to the then Director-General, Archaeological Survey of India, as follows:

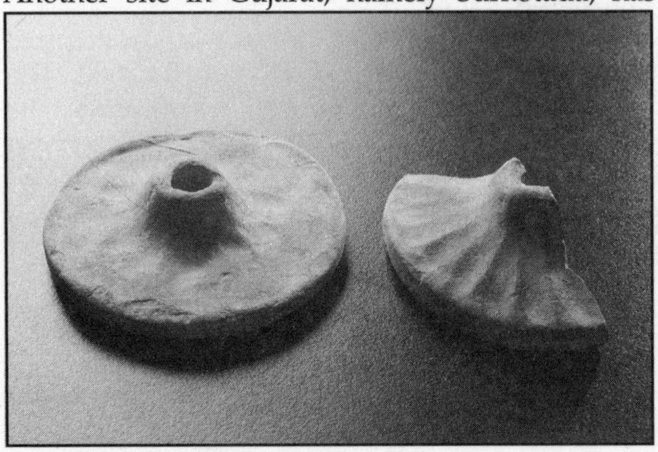

Pl. 1.2 Banawali: Terracotta wheels, showing spokes in low relief. Mature Harappan.

> Through a thorough study of the equid remains of the prehistoric settlement of Surkotada, Kachchha, excavated under the direction of Dr. J.P. Joshi, I can state the following: The occurrence of true horse (*Equus Caballus* L.) was evidenced by the enamel pattern of the upper and lower cheek and teeth and by the size and form of incisors and phalanges (toe bones). Since

no wild horses lived in India in post-Pleistocene times, the domestic nature of the Surkotada horses is undoubtful. This is also supported by an intermaxilla fragment whose incisor tooth shows clear signs of crib-biting, a bad habit only existing among domestic horses which are not extensively used for war.

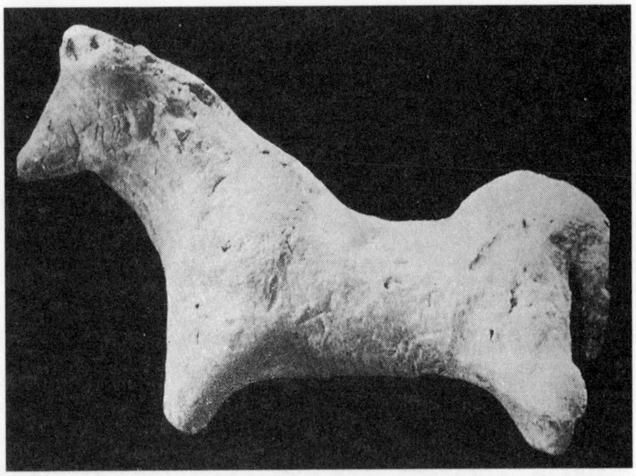

Pl. 1.3 Lothal: Terracotta horse. Mature Harappan.

There are many other sites in the fray, for example, Kalibangan in Rajasthan and Rupnagar (formerly called Rupar) in Punjab. In respect of Pakistan, while the current excavators of Harappa have not yet reported any horse bones, Bhola Nath, a renowned expert of the Zoological Survey of India, examined an earlier faunal collection from this site and categorically affirmed in it the presence of the horse. However, no less important is the occurrence of terracotta figurines of this animal in the Harappan levels at Nausharo, excavated by Jarrige and his colleagues (in press).

Therefore, there is little doubt that the Harappans did domesticate the horse. On the sidelines, much has been made of the absence of this animal from the seals. But may not one put a counter question: 'What about the absence of the camel from these very seals—an animal whose presence in the Harappan levels has also been attested to only by its bones?' Let us be fair enough to accept the horse evidence as it is, and not continue to flog the poor animal.

To take up the last but not the least vital objection relating to a Vedic-Harappan equation, namely the chronological horizon of the Vedas. According to the original 'fatwa' of Max Müller, the Vedas could not have been earlier than 1200 BC, whereas the Harappan Civilization belonged to the third millennium BC. So, prima facie how could the two meet?

However, it may be recalled that later on the clergy himself twice changed his position, first admitting that what he really meant was that 1200 BC was only the minimum date and subsequently adding that no one could really say if the Vedas were datable to 1000, 2000 or 3000 BC. The greatest pity is that in spite of such a clear back-tracking by Max Müller, his ardent followers, as already stated, even today swear by that date.

All this makes it necessary to re-examine the date of the Vedas, using other independent sources. One is the astronomical evidence. For example, the *Aitareya Brāhmaṇa* refers to the shifting of the vernal equinox from the *Nakshatra* Mṛigaśiras to Rohiṇī. According to some astronomers this event is likely to have occurred around 3500 BC. If that be a correct computation, the date of the *Ṛigveda* will have to be much earlier than that. Having practically no knowledge of astronomy, I am in no position to offer any comments. At the same time, I also fail to appreciate the contemptuous attitude of certain scholars towards the astronomical data. The right approach would be to hold an international seminar on this topic, in which all shades of scholars be invited to participate and thrash out the issue.

However, there is another kind of evidence which calls for serious attention. It is based on a combination of data derived from various sources, viz. archaeological, radiocarbon dating, geological, hydrological and literary.

The site of Kalibangan in Rajasthan, which has yielded Early as well as Mature Harappan remains, is located on the bank of the ancient Sarasvatī, now dried up and going in this region by the name of the Ghaggar. Further downstream, in the Cholistan and Sindh regions of Pakistan, it is known as the Hakra and Nara respectively. It is not clear when and how these various names were given to the same stream in different regions. However, upstream, in Haryana, there does exist a river called even today the Sarasvatī which, in junction with the Ghaggar, flows for some considerable length but dries up near Sirsa. A detailed analysis of the course of the Sarasvatī river in ancient times, its origin from the glaciers in the Himalayas and the reasons for its subsequent drying up have been fully dealt with by me in *The Sarasvatī Flows On.*

While we were excavating at Kalibangan, an Indo-Italian team, under the overall guidance of Robert Raikes, carried out several bores in the now-dry bed of the adjacent Ghaggar (ancient Sarasvatī) river and made some important observations which were published in 1968 as 'Kalibangan: Death from Natural Causes'. From these investigations, it became clear that the Mature Harappan settlement at Kalibangan had to be abandoned because of the drying up of the Sarasvatī. According to the radiocarbon dates, the latest strata are assignable to ca. 1900 BC (Lal 1997: 245–46). In other words, the Sarasvatī was flowing around 2000 BC.

Against the backdrop of the foregoing archaeological-cum-geomorphological-cum-radiocarbon-dating evidence, let us cast a glance at what the Vedic literature has to say about the history of the Sarasvatī. To take up just one quotation from the *Ṛigveda* (Verses 7.95.1 and 2):

> *Pra kshodasā dhāyasā sasra eshā Sarasvatī dharuṇamāyasī pūḥ/*
> *prabābadhānā rathyeva yāti viśvā apo mahinā sindhuranyāḥ//1//*
> *ekāchetat Sarasvatī nadī nām śuchir yatī giribhya ā samudrāt /*
> *rāyaśchetantī bhuvanasya bhūrerghṛitam payo duduhe Nāhushāya//2//*

> The Sarasvatī gushes forward with her waters and protects all like a metal fortress; with her might, like a charioteer, she surpasses (lit. obstructs) all other waters (rivers). [1]. Purest among all the rivers and vibrant, the Sarasvatī moves from the mountains to the ocean; manifesting immense riches of the world, she has provided milk and *ghee* (clarified butter) to Nahusha. [2].

From the foregoing verses it is clear that during the days of the *Ṛigveda* the Sarasvatī was a mighty river flowing all the way from the mountains to the sea. As against this, the *Pañchavimśa Brāhmaṇa* (XXV. 10.16) clearly refers to the Sarasvatī having dried up.

The combined evidence from archaeology, geomorphology and radiometry on the one hand, and from the *Ṛigveda* on the other, makes it abundantly clear that the *Ṛigveda* which speaks of the Sarasvatī as a mighty flowing river, cannot be later than ca. 2000 BC. How much earlier, I leave it to others to guess.

We may now pass on to another very significant evidence from the *Ṛigveda.* Verses 5 and 6 of the *Nadī-stuti* hymn (*RV* 10.75) run as follows:

> *imam me Gaṅge Yamune Sarasvatī Śutudri stomam sachatā Parushṇyā*
> *Asiknyā Marudvṛidhe Vitastyā Ārjīkīye śṛiṇuhyā Sushomayā//5//*
> *Tṛishṭāmayā prathamam yātave sajūḥ Susartvā Rasayā Śvetyā tyā/*
> *tvam Sindho Kubhayā Gomatīm Krumum Mehatnvā saratham yābhirī yase //6//*

> O Gaṅgā, Yamunā, Sarasvatī, Śutudrī (Sutlej) and Parushṇī (Ravi), O Marudvṛidhā with Asiknī (Chenab), O Ārjīkīyā with Vitastā (Jhelum) and Suṣomā (Sohan), please listen to and accept this hymn of mine [5].

> O Sindhu (Indus), flowing you first meet the Tṛishṭāmā and (then) the Susartu, the Rasā, and the Śvetā (Swat), and thereafter the Kubhā (Kabul), the Gomatī (Gomal),

the Krumu (Kurram) with the Mehatnu; and (finally) you move on in the same chariot with them (i.e. carry their waters with you) [6].

These verses clearly show that the Ṛigvedic people occupied an area which extended from the upper reaches of the Gaṅgā-Yamunā on the east to the Indus and its western tributaries on the west.

If now we combine the aforesaid evidences about the date of the *Ṛigveda,* viz. pre-2000 BC, and the geographical area covered by it, viz. from the Gaṅgā on the east to the Indus on the west, and ask a very pertinent question, viz. which archaeological culture was there in existence during this period, covering this very area? Howsoever we may try to run away from the issue, we will have to admit that it was none other than the Harappa Culture itself!

In the foregoing pages we have seen that (i) there is little to recommend a Harappan-Dravidian equation, (ii) the often-touted objections against a Harappan-Vedic equation are groundless, and (iii) there is enough circumstantial evidence to suggest that this second equation is the most likely one. However, the issue can be clinched finally when the Harappan inscriptions are satisfactorily deciphered and found to contain Sanskrit/Prākṛit

Postscript

Some Western scholars, and their Indian followers, hold that the Bactria-Margiana Archaeological Complex (BMAC) represents the Āryans and it is these people who entered India from the north-west. But have these learned scholars ever given thought to the fact that from the east of the Indus right up to the upper reaches of the Gaṅgā-Yamunā, which was the main area occupied by the Vedic Āryans, there is *not even a single site* where remains of the BMAC have been found? Why then keep on shooting, to use Mallory's term, a *Kulturkugel* (culture-bullet)?

Bibliography

Dales, G.F., 1964, "The Mythical Massacre at Mohenjo-daro", *Expedition,* 6(3), pp. 36–43.

Elfenbein, Josef, 1987, "A Periplus of the 'Bahui Problem'", *Studia Iranica* 6, pp. 215–233.

Hemphill, B.E., J.R. Lukacs and K.A.R. Kennedy, 1991, "Biological Adaptations and Affinities of Bronze Age Harappans", in R.H. Meadows (ed.), *Harappa Excavations 1986–1990,* pp. 137–82. Madison, Wisconsin: Prehistory Press.

Hock, Hans Henrich, 1975, "Substratum Influence on (Rig-Vedic) Sanskrit"?, *Studies in the Linguistic Sciences* 5, no. 2, pp. 76–125.

Joshi, J.P., 1990, *Excavation at Surkotada 1971–72 and Exploration in Kutch,* New Delhi: Archaeological Survey of India.

Lal, B.B., 1997, *The Earliest Civilization of South Asia,* New Delhi: Aryan Books International.

———, 2002, *The Sarasvatī Flows On: The Continuity of Indian Culture,* New Delhi: Aryan Books International.

Mackay, E.J.H., 1938, *Further Excavations at Mohenjo-daro,* 2 vols., Delhi: Government of India.

Mallory, J.P., 1998, "A European Perspective on Indo-Europeans in Asia", in Mair (ed.) *The Bronze Age and Early Iron Age Peoples of Eastern and Central Asia,* I: 175–201. Washington D.C.: Institute for the Study of Man.

Max Müller, F, 1890 (reprint 1979). *Physical Religion,* New Delhi: Asian Educational Services.

Raikes, Robert, 1968, "Kalibangan: Death from Natural Causes", *Antiquity* XLII, pp. 286–91.

Rao, S.R., 1985, *Lothal Harappan Town (1955–62),* Vol. II., New Delhi, Archaeological Survey of India.

Sergent, Bernard, 1997, *Genes de l'Inde,* Paris: Editions Payot & Rivages.

Wheeler, R.E.M., 1947, "Harappa 1946: The Defences and Cemetery R–37", *Ancient India,* Vol. 3, pp. 58–130.

———, 1968, *The Indus Civilization,* 3rd edn., Cambridge University Press.

2

Two Harappan Motifs and Their Vedic Affinity

P.K. Agrawala

There have been many attempts by scholars to relate the two groups of antiquities with each other, one of Vedic sources and the other of Harappan sites. The seminar gave a fresh opportunity for investigating on those lines as have been set up by competent authorities in this respect so far.

I

A type of pottery is often found at several proto-Harappan, Harappan, or even post-Harappan sites, including historical centres, which shows various type of jar shapes showing perforations on their side walls. Sometime a cylindrical, round-bottom jar has been preserved in its more or less complete form (Fig. 2.1) or in smaller fragments. This pottery containing multiple holes is quiet well known to scholars and indeed stands out from other popular types of Indus earthen as well as metallic ware. It is not quite clear for what usage such pieces were meant although several opinions have been forwarded. They were definately not used to store or contain liquids for any duration; they may have served as sprinklers in ritual context, or for some normal, but now unknown, use in day-to-day requirements. Were they meant to be sievers or strainers of some kind? Maybe, they served as censer, or as night lamps of a kind, as have been sometimes suggested. It is hard to answer such enquiries or queries arising in our mind regarding the perforated pottery and its relevance in wider context of Harappan life. This ware also appears to have links with later Indian pots or vessels and bears obvious proof regarding a Harappan 'tradition' that continued subsequently in the life of the people. The perforated pot was of some specific significance is also attested to by its occurrence even in the burial properties in Harappa.

However, without entering into any discussion regarding the views forwarded by competent authorities on this problem, I wish to draw critical attention to a probable parallelism of it in Vedic ritual life. For example, a vessel containing nine holes or a hundred holes is thus mentioned in the *Śatapatha Brahmaṇa* (5.5.4.27):

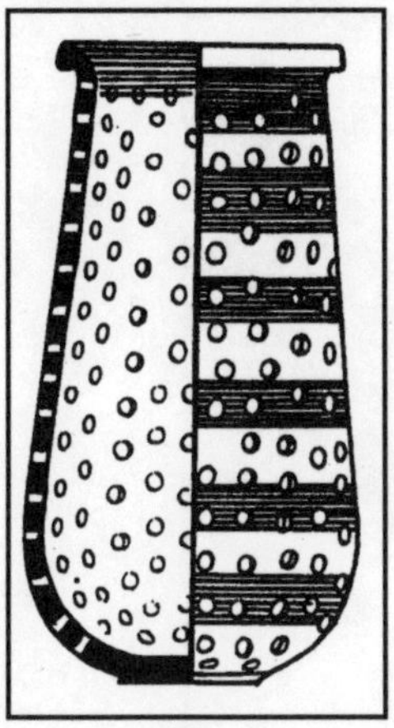
Fig. 2.1

Fig. 2.2

Fig. 2.3

Fig. 2.4

Fig. 2.5

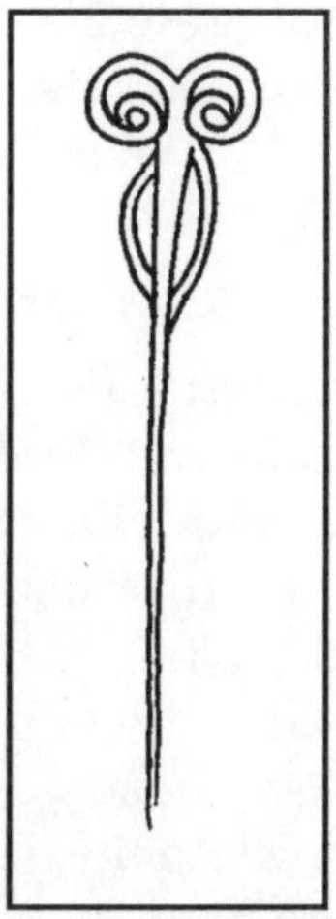
Fig. 2.6

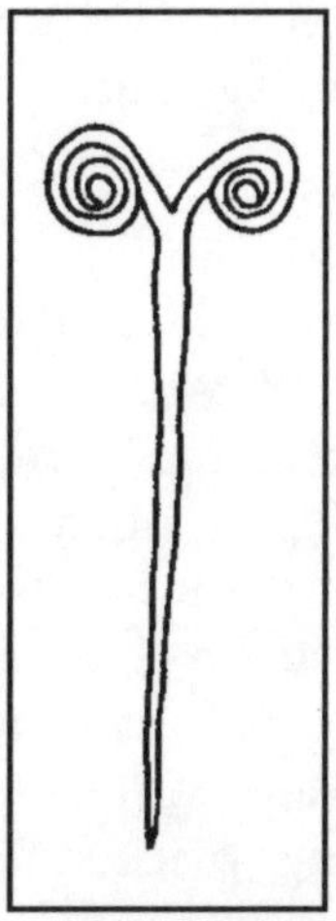
Fig. 2.7

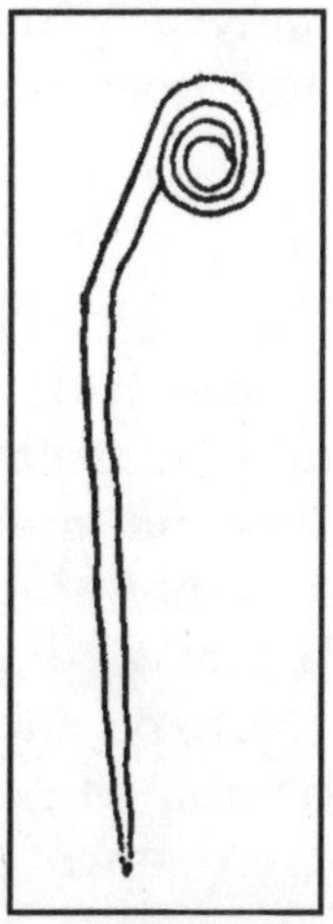
Fig. 2.8

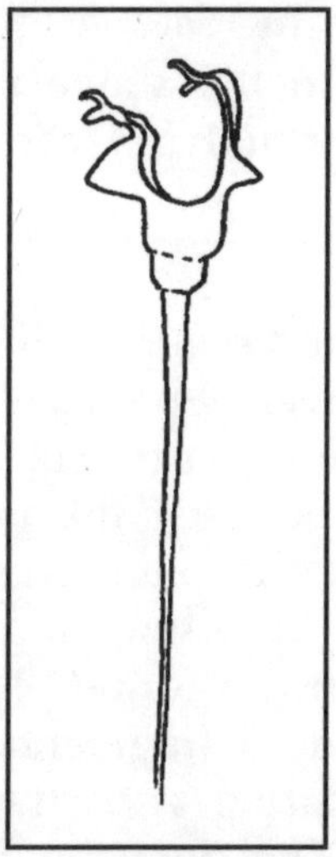
Fig. 2.9

Fig. 2.10

अथ कुम्भः । शतवित ण्णो वा भवति नववित ण्णो वा स यदि शतवित ण्णः शतायुर्वा अयं पुरुषः शततेजाः शतवीर्यस्तस्माच्छत–वित ण्ण .... (वित ण्ण = pierced)

At 12.7.2.13, the same text refers to a *śata-tṛiṇṇā kumbhī*. Its relationship to the *Yajurveda* verse (19.87) manifestly indicates that the purpose and use of such holes or piercings made into a *kumbhī* (jar, pitcher) was to pour liquid in a hundredfold streams for specific ritual requirements. According to the Brāhmaṇa (12.9.1.3), *śatatṛiṇṇā tad yat sā bahudhā vitṛiṇṇā bhavati*. The *Taittirīya Brāhmaṇa* passage (2.4.6.3–4, employing the above Yajush verse) is commented upon by *Sāyaṇā:* बहुच्छिद्रोपेतत्वाच्छतधारः ।

In the above manner, many a Vedic passages can be further corroborated as referring to a ritual pot carrying several holes in its ware, specially produced by potters.

II

We find several allusions to a double-headed animal, avian, or monster, or even a deity concept in diverse passages of the Vedic texts. In this context a unique terracotta figurine from Mohenjo-daro (Fig. 2.10) would be quite interesting and presumably one can find again a link between the two proto-historic cultures under scrutiny, i.e. Vedic and Harappan. The particular piece shows a pair of lion's, or rather tiger's heads opposite each other as issued from the same single neck. It was perhaps made from a double-mould as the entire details are in the round. The object perhaps ended below the neck in a pedestal or was discovered only in a fragmentary preservation as per the underneath details. The two heads are shown as roaring with the mouth wide open and having pricked ears and rolling eyes.

This may be compared to a seal of Mohenjo-daro showing a two-horned bovine-like animal-type with an additional head of "unicorn" joined on its back above but looking in the opposite direction [see pl. 63, Dr. Heinz Mode, *Das Frühe Indien*, Stuttgart, 1959]. Of this same category of imagination is perhaps the delineation on one famous Mohenjo-daro seal (Fig. 2.2) which presents the figure of a two-headed dragon, or *vyāla* as the source of Pipal foliage. The motif indeed has a number of variants in the Harappan repertoire of designs with minor details specifying each of them but invariably conceiving the two dragon-faces as juxtaposed with their long necks meeting in the centre into a circular plaque, topped over a perpendicular feature or post-like depiction (Figs. 2.3–2.5).

Now, it is noteworthy that we have a parallel concept echoed in several Vedic passages. For example, the *Atharvaveda* mentions a two-headed cattle as *dvāyā* (5.19.7). Elsewhere, in the Yajurvedic texts, a *suparṇī*, i.e. female eagle, is stated to have two heads with each one of them as turned to the other side, namely *ubhayataḥ sīrshṇī suparṇī (Vājasaneyi Saṁhitā* 4.19). The *Śatapatha Brāhmaṇa* identified the same creature as a form (or as an epithet) of the great goddess Aditi (3.2.4.16). Still, there is a motif occurring in the *Jaimini Brāhmaṇa* (2.115), which describes an *ubhayatomukhī siṁhi*, i.e. a lioness bearing a pair of heads that feature on either side or face towards opposite directions. This last reference, indeed, appears as if to project a concept more or less identical to one that we find visualized in the above-mentioned terracotta model from Mohenjo-daro. Probably, an allied type of symbolism may be underlined in case of certain proto-historic bronze hair-pins, one showing a pair of stag heads, and others featuring two spirals (Figs. 2.6–2.9).

3

The Ṛigvedic Sarasvatī

O.P. Bharadwaj

The debate over the identification of the Ṛigvedic Sarasvatī is now more than a century old. It was a byproduct of the theory of the so-called Āryan invasion in India, which has lost credence although in some quarters it has only been modified to suggest that groups of Indo-Āryan speakers gradually migrated from the Indo-Āryan borderlands and Afghanistan to northern India.[1]

The controversy, originally restricted to Sanskritists, was soon joined by geographers and archaeologists whose adherence to literary sources was not so firm. With the rise of the ideology-oriented approach to historiography, knowledge of Sanskrit became irrelevant. It was declared that Indology was too important a matter to be left to Indologists. A new concept of history based on "evidence in totality" was invented, which made it easy to submerge the truth under a maze of confusion.[2]

In his General President's address at the Millennium (61st) Session of the Indian History Congress at Kolkata, B.N. Mukherjee declared that "in order to understand the correct implications of his/her data a historian must be well-conversant with the historical objects and must be able to read in original the major texts, documents and epigraphs of his/her period. The demand is valid at least for interpreting those sources which are crucial to his/her period." It is not ironical that the same volume carries an article entitled "Imagining River Sarasvatī—A Defence of Common Sense"[3] from one concerned with the medieval period of Indian history and not known for any knowledge of Sanskrit, not to speak of Vedic language and literature? Is it not reprehensible then that an attempt should be made to trivialize the Ṛigvedic description of the Sarasvatī as a mighty river! Equally unreasonable is the attempt by another section to champion the cause of the insignificant Adbadri-Thanesar rainy season hill torrent, now all but extinct, which is known in literature and even an inscription as Prāchī or Eastern Sarasvatī, clearly pointing to the existence of the original Sarasvatī to its west. A crude attempt is being made to project as Sarasvatī the Somb *nadī* (Aśmanvatī of the *Ṛigveda),* which also rises at Adbadri and joins the Pathrala to become the Ṛigvedic Dṛishadvatī whose bed is now occupied by the Western Jamna Canal.[4]

"Argument" says an adage,[5] "does not always lead to reality". It can, of course, create a multiplicity of theories and a medley of postulates and hypotheses to support them, even on issues which do not admit of any doubt. And, it is as easy to create confusion as it is difficult to dispel it. Let us therefore, ignore the controversy and allow the evidence to speak.

Testimony of the *Ṛigveda*

The *Ṛigveda*[6] describes the Sarasvatī as a mighty river rushing down from the mountains to the ocean with a tempestuous roar, breaking and carrying down ridges of hills like lotus-stems and filling the realms of earth and the wide tract of the firmament. It is superior to her companions, and surpasses all other rivers in her majesty and glory. It is fierce, swiftest of the swift, pure and purifying and fed by many tributaries. As its very name suggests it carries a great volume of waters. It is indeed the mother of rivers and is therefore addressed as the foremost of rivers, *nadītamā.*

Sarasvatī is invoked in the form of a mother cow who is suckling all, whose breast (water-bed) is inexhaustible—a spring of pleasure with which it feeds all best things, which is a giver of wealth, finder of treasures and munificent. It provided milk and *ghee* to Nāhusha. It is prayed to suckle the worshippers for their sustenance. Like a child clinging to its mother the worshipper prays that he may not be removed from it (its valley) to regions which are strange. Hence, it is the best of mothers, *ambitamā.*

Sarasvatī is terrible, *ghorā* (when in flood), therefore prayed not to torment the worshipper with her waters. It is called upon to descend from the sky, from the great mountain to the sacrifice. It is capable of granting desires and bestowing wealth, prosperity and fertility. Being very difficult to ford, it is described as a protecting iron barrier or a fortress and a support as well as the destroyer of enemies like the Pārāvatas and the Paṇis. It is invoked in every deed of might. Made by Prajāpati himself, it is divine among rivers. It is besought to listen to the prayer of her worshippers at their sacrifices, to receive their praises, to shelter and protect them like a tree. It is therefore the 'most divine' or 'the best of goddesses', *devītamā.*

In this account of the Ṛigvedic seers the Sarasvatī appears as the river par excellence. That it joined the ocean is specifically stated. The fact that it flowed in the mountainous region for a long stretch is also clear since it made its way uprooting mountain peaks. Like other big rivers the Sarasvatī must have originated in the highest Himalayas and must have been fed by permanent glaciers. The seers were not able to reach this height; that is why they do not precisely name its source.

The Region Where it Flowed

In verse 5 of *RV.* X. 75,[7] known as the *Nadīstuti* hymn, the Sarasvatī is named between the Yamunā and the Śutudri or Sutlej. This region is known as Kurukshetra in Vedic literature. This is finally confirmed in verse 4 of an earlier hymn *RV.* III. 23, 4, where two Bharata princes Devaśravā and Devavāta invoke the sacrificial fire in the following words.

> नि त्वा दधे वरे आ प थिव्याः इलायास्पदे सुदिनत्वे अह्नाम् ।
> द षद्वत्यां मानुषे आपयायाम् सरस्वत्यां रेवत् अग्ने दिदीहि ।।

> I place thee in the best place of the earth, in the seat of Iḷā on the fairest of days.
> O refulgent Agni! Shine ye at Dṛishadvatī, Mānusha, Āpayā and the Sarasvatī.

The rivers Dṛishadvatī and Āpayā and the lake Mānusha are mentioned here in the third hemistich as one group while in the fourth hemistich Sarasvatī is named alone because it was not close enough to the first group. Mānusha has been identified with the site and lake now called Mānasa, about 8 km to the west of the district town of Kaithal, the Vedic

Kapishṭhala.[8] The river Āpayā, spelled Āpagā in the *Mahābhārata* and the *Vāmana Purāṇa* was only one *krosha* to the east of Mānusha.[9] Not very far to the east of the Āpayā flowed the Dṛishadvatī whose dry bed is now occupied by the Western Jamna Canal, Hansi-Hissar branch.[10] The Āpayā joined the Dṛishadvatī long before the combined stream of the two merged with the Sarasvatī above Vinaśana. These three rivers and one lake were sacred sites for performance of sacrifices and were all in Kurukshetra which was, known as a sacrificial altar of the gods.[11]

Identification with the Ghaggar

If any river of Kurukshetra can claim identification with the Ṛigvedic Sarasvatī, it is the Ghaggar. And, this identification consistently finds support not only in literary tradition but also in archaeological discoveries.

Soon after the Ṛigvedic age, a catastrophic event took place as a result of which the waters of the Sarasvatī were drastically reduced and a process of desiccation started resulting in the loss of its flow in the deserts of Rajasthan. This event has been called in literature as the 'Deluge' or the 'Great Flood'. The course of the Sarasvatī was blocked in its upper reaches and its source shifted from the Himalayan glaciers down to the lower Shiwaliks.

In the description of the Sārasvata, sacrificial sessions on the Sarasvatī, which were performed after *dīkshā* or initiation at its tail end upstream along its course, ending at its source, the Brāhmaṇa and Śrautaśūtra works for the first time describe the site of its vanishing in the sands as Vinaśana and its new source in the Shiwaliks as Plaksha Prāsravaṇa. This description of the reduced Sarasvatī exactly follows the course of the Ghaggar. On the basis of literary evidence and archaeological discovery of fire altars fit for use in congregational rituals, Vinaśana has been identified with the site of Kalibangan[12] and Plaksha Prāsravaṇa with the village and forest division of Lavāsā in Pachhāḍa sub-division of district Nahan in Himachal Pradesh.[13] The river rising at Lavāsā and ending at Kalibangan is now called Ghaggar. Hence the Ṛigvedic Sarasvatī and the Ghaggar both names refer to one and the same river.

Although the Sārasvata sacrificial session was to end at Plaksha Prāsravaṇa or Lavāsā in Pachhāḍa, the source of the reduced Ṛigvedic Sarasvatī, the Brāhmaṇas and the Śrautasūtras and their commentators enjoin it upon the sacrificers to perform the lustral bath at Kārpachava on the Yamunā. Obviously, the water at Lavāsā was not considered fit for the ritual bath. The *Imperial Gazetteer of India*[14] confirms that the water of the Ghaggar in or near the hills, when used for drinking, produced disastrous results causing ailments like fever, enlarged spleen and goiter. So much so that families were said to die in the fourth generation, and the villages along its banks were greatly under-populated. The trait being common to both, the Sarasvatī and the Ghaggar, justifies their identification.

Canto second of Vālmīki's *Rāmāyaṇa* describes the journey of the messengers from Ayodhyā to Rājagṛiha and back to fetch Bharata after the death of Daśaratha. On their way they cross the river Ikshumatī to reach Ajakūlā (the present town of Panchkula) from Bhūliṅgā (present town of Bunga), the capital of the tribe of identical name, occupying the territories of the erstwhile Morni and Ramgarh states. Then they proceed to the capital of the Bodhis which was probably identical with Ropar (present Rupnagar), a town of Harappan antiquity. The Ikshumatī, a river of Kurukshetra, is described as *Pitṛipaitāmahī* and *Devaṛishicharitā,* which are the appropriate adjectives for the Sarasvatī, the daughter of Brahmā and frequented by gods and sages. A variant reading Indumatī for Ikshumatī also applies to the Sarasvatī since it carried Indumat or fire to the ocean. In this situation this Ikshumatī-Sarasvatī is identical with the Ghaggar dividing Ajakūlā from Ramgarh.[15]

The *Padma Purāṇa*[16] describes the Morni hill as the son of the Supārśva or Pachhāḍ signifying that the former was a smaller hill to the lower side, reflecting their correct geographical position. The *Kūrma Purāṇa*[17] places the sacred abode (source) of the Sarasvatī in the northern part of the Supārśva, which again matches the source of the Ghaggar at Lavāsā in the Pachhāḍ confirming its identification with the Sarasvatī. It is pertinent to note that Supārśva means a Plaksha tree also.[18]

The *Yoginītantra* (5, 42),[19] a Tantric work of about 10th century AD says:

> भूलिङ्गेषु भवेत् कोटिज्यामिता च सरस्वती।
> धानुष्को किल कः शम्भुः लक्षः कालिरूदाहृता।।
>
> In the Bhūliṅgas the Sarasvatī resembles the Kotijyā (cosine). It is said that there Śiva of the Mayūra hill (Morni) is the archer and Kālī his target.

This description presents a graphic picture of god Śiva standing on the Morni hill with a strung bow with goddess Kālī (in her temple at the town of Kalka) as his target. Now, the river Ghaggar does skirt the Morni hill making almost a semi-circle and an old temple of god Śiva of about the 10th century AD does stand between the two lakes of Morni. And, from the hill the temple of goddess Kālī at Kalka will make a direct target for an archer with (the "Morni skirting" Ghaggar resembling) his strung bow. The description reflects the personal acquaintance of the writer with local geography. In fact, its striking accuracy makes it certain that the author belonged to this part of the country. The Sarasvatī-Ghaggar equation is obvious.

In the face of all this evidence the identification of the Sarasvatī with Ghaggar, between its source at Lavāsā in Pachhāḍ and its tail end at Kalibangan admits of no doubt. Beyond Kalibangan up to the ocean it has never been questioned. In the words of an archaeologist,[20] "downstream, the course of the Ghaggar-Hakra has been traced up to the Rann of Kutch. When we come to the Indus it becomes clear too that the present Indus flows through the Sukkar-Rori gorge is a late development and that its upper course in Sind was perhaps more to the east and eventually joined the Ghaggar-Hakra course before flowing as a combined river into the Rann of Kutch". And, to quote a noted geographer OHK Spate,[21] "Except for a few streams at each end the drainage of the 100 mile long Shiwalik ridge between Sutlej and Jumna is either dissipated into the fields, or converges into the Ghaggar. The identification of this stream with the Sarasvatī, the lost river of the Vedic hymns, seems secure...."

This fully agrees with the description of *tīrthas* upstream along the Sarasvatī from Prabhāsa through Vinaśana to Plaksha Prāsravaṇa as described by the *Mahābhārata* and the Smṛiti writer Devala. As late as the 11th century AD Alberuni[22] says that "the river Sarasvatī falls into the sea at the distance of a bow-shot east of Somanath". And again, that "the Liṅga of Somanath was originally erected on the coast, a little less than three miles west of the mouth of the river Sarasvatī".

The Upheaval

Why did the source of the Ṛigvedic Sarasvatī shift from the Himalayan glaciers down to Lavāsā in Pachhāḍ and why great volume of waters were so drastically reduced as to be lost in the sands near Kalibangan? What happened? There is ample evidence pointing towards a horrendous catastrophe resulting in a large-scale volcanic-seismic-tectonic upheaval involving the vast region including parts of the Near East, the northern flank of the Arabian Sea, the country along the course of the Sarasvatī and even the Shiwaliks.

There is the story of the Deluge or the Great Flood in the *Śatapatha Brāhmaṇa* which Manu survived. The site on the northern mountain where Manu took shelter has been called Nāvaprabhaṃśana in the *Atharvaveda,* Manoravasrpaṇa in the *Śatapatha Brāhmaṇa* and Naubandhana in the *Mahābhārata* and the Purāṇas. The identification of Naubandhana[23] with Nahan proves the historicity of the event which is further confirmed by the archaeological evidence of an earthquake after the pre-Harappan level at Kalibangan[24] and the geological testimony of the formation of the Shiwaliks with the accumulation of agglomerates and conglomerates with alluvial flood plain deposits.[25] The *prāleyādri* or 'The Mountain of the Deluge' of Kālidāsa[26] is Nahan and his *'Kauñcharundhra'* or 'Break in the Krauñcha Mountain' is the gap in the range from where roads turn to the left for Nahan town and to the right for Paonta and Dehradun. From the east of Ad Badri to the Morni hills the range appears to be covered with red clay, which agrees with its traditional description as *tāmrābha*[27] or of copper hue.

A number of stories, anecdotes and episodes scattered in literary works describe the flow of the Sarasvatī being blocked, the river carrying submarine fire to the ocean, burning the mountain and suffering drastic reduction in the volume of its waters and their partial diversion through other channels.

The *Aitareya Brāhmaṇa*[28] records an incident when the *ṛishis* expelled Kavasha Ailūsha from a Soma sacrifice being performed on the Sarasvatī with the intention that he should die of thirst in the desert. The *Śatapatha Brāhmaṇa*[29] also contains a similar reference of another sacrifice performed by the gods in Kurukshetra. There the gods are said to have declared that the ant who would gnaw the bow-string of Vishṇu would be granted constant enjoyment of food and he would find water even in the desert. A similar story occurs in Śalya Parva[30] of the *Mahābhārata.* While travelling, the three brothers, Ekata, Dvita and Tritia encounter a wolf. Trita runs along the Sarasvatī and falls into a well. Abandoned by his brothers, he performs a mental sacrifice which attracts the attention of Bṛihaspati who brings the gods to the well. The river goddess Sarasvatī shoots forth from the well and Ṭrita is rescued. Evidently, by this time the Sarasvatī had ceased to be a perennial river and people had started digging wells in its bed[31] to tap the underground reserves of water which were replenished by the rainy season floods.

The drying up of the Sarasvatī, named in the Purāṇas as the spouse of Nārāyaṇa,[32] is implied in the story of her quarrel with her co-wife Gaṅgā in which both exchange curses leading to a pledge by the former to end her existence.[33] Ultimately, as decreed by Nārāyaṇa, Sarasvatī is persuaded to stay on and only a small part of herself descends into the holy land of Bhārata as Prāchī-Sarasvatī.[34] This story would be easily seen to conceal a reference to the reduction in the flow of the holy river and the transfer of its name to another small stream on its east.

The Purāṇas[35] describe the conveying of Agni-Vaḍavānala to the western ocean at the instance of god Brahmā by his daughter Sarasvatī who flowed underground and surfaced only when it felt exhausted on account of the unbearable heat.[36] In one case this fire was created by Ṛishi Pippalāda for destruction of gods who had utilized the bones of his father Dadhīchi for manufacturing weapons for killing the demons.[37] Emerging from Plaksha on the Himalayas, Sarasvatī is obstructed on its way by a mountain wanting to marry it forcibly. Under the pretext of taking a bath before the ceremony Sarasvatī entrusts the fire to the mountain which is immediately burnt down by it.[38] This is said to have happened in the Chākshusha Manvantara.[39] Again, in the Vaivasvata Manvantara the same fire is born as Aurvānala to a woman belonging to the tribe of the Bhṛigus who were attacked and plundered by the kshatriyas. The woman was pregnant and escaped concealing the foetus in her thigh *(uru)* which gave the name Aurvānala to the fire that started consuming the earth immediately on its emergence.[40] According to another version the woman gave birth to Ṛishi Aurva who created the fire which was named after him. The fire created for the destruction of Haihaya Kshatriyas who had indulged in large-scale slaughter of the Bhṛigus was, however, confined to the ocean by Sarasvatī.[41] Sarasvatī is said to have conveyed Aurvānala in a golden pitcher and taking its rise at Pippalādāśrama in the Himalayas, it flowed westward reaching Kedara where it pierced the earth's crust to go underground burning with the fire in its hands.[42] It broke forth again at Bhūtīśvara after passing the evil region and then flowed towards Prabhāsa passing through Śrīkaṇṭhadeśa, Kurukshetra, Virāṭanagara, Gopāyanagiri, Kharjūrīvana, Mārkaṇḍāśrama and Arbudāraṇya[43] etc. The *Skanda Purāṇa* predicts the birth of another Vaḍavānala at the end of the current Manavantara[44] and thus implies a connection between Vaḍavānala and the Deluge that is traditionally associated with the end of a Manvantara.

Although the Vaḍavānala episode is related in several versions in different sources,[45] its essential features do not suffer any serious change. Some interesting points deserve special notice here. Firstly, the river Sarasvatī which conveyed the fire to the western ocean flowed through the country of Kurukshetra which is specially mentioned along with Śrīkaṇṭhadeśa which comprised its northern part[46] and Virāṭanagara which lay to its south-west near Jaipur.[47] Secondly, the Bhṛigus with whom the Aurvānala is associated, occupied the lower or western part of Kurukshetra in ancient times as the tradition of construction by Paraśurāma Bhārgava of five pools with the blood of the cruel Kshatriyas at Rāmahrada, present Ram Rai near Jind, suggests.[48] Thirdly, the text mentions the emergence of the burning Aurva after a violent eruption in Kurudeśa[49] which is most befitting because while the concealment of the foetus in or its birth from the thigh *(uru)* is obviously mythical. The emergence of one of the Bhṛigus, after lying low for sometime in Kurudeśa, to avenge the slaughter of his people is most natural. The hoary antiquity and the commonness of the venue of the two events is undoubtedly the only explanation of the introduction of the Bhṛigus in the Vaḍavānala episode. And lastly, the upheaval was volcanic in nature that engulfed Kurudeśa and the mountain range to its north and drastically tampered with the source and course of the Sarasvatī which flowed red with the rubble thrown up and carried down in the process.

All this finds expression in another form in the story of the Sarasvatī carrying bloody water[50] for a complete year[51] as a result of the curse of Viśvāmitra who was annoyed on her failure to deliver Ṛishi Vasishṭha to him. Now significantly it was not the real Sarasvatī that flowed red with blood but her own other self named Aruṇā.

The episode of destruction of the Krauñcha mountain by god Kārttikeya reflects the volcanic aspect of the upheaval. According to the *Mahābhārata*[52] the gods led by Brahmā brought Kārttikeya to the holy Sarasvatī and anointed him as the Commander of their army. There, in the fight against the daityas Kārttikeya with the *śakti* given by Agni, rent asunder the Krauñcha mountain on which sheltered the demon Bāṇa, son of Bali, tormented the gods. The involvement of fire in the destruction of the Krauñcha mountain near the Sarasvatī river clearly points to volcanic eruption in the hilly tract about the upper reaches of the river.

The story of Tripuradāha by god Śiva[53] also appears to rise from the same background. Here, the fiery missile shot by the great god burns down Tripura with all its Asura population and dumps it into the western ocean.[54] It was the Sarasvatī that provided the track for his chariot.[55] The great magnitude of destruction is implied in the suggestion that Tripura actually represented not one but a complex of three prosperous Asura cites.[56]

Yet another episode in the *Mahābhārata*,[57] in which the Great Deluge appears to find an echo, is that of sage Utathya who drinks off the entire water of the ocean on Varuṇa's refusal to return his bride Bhadrā whom the god had forcibly abducted. The country is reduced to desert and Utathya asks the Sarasvatī to go invisible into it so that forsaken by her, it becomes inauspicious.

The *Varāha Purāṇa*[58] specifically describes the existence between Pachhāḍa and Morni hills, of an earthen plateau one hundred *yojanas* on all sides, which is always hot and difficult to touch. In its centre a thirty-*yojana* circle is the zone of fire. And, that world-destroying divine fire burns all the time without any fuel. This spot evidently the site of a volcanic eruption, falls exactly around the source of the Ghaggar/Sarasvatī. This is suggested by another important geological phenomenon. Along the left bank of the river, near Panchakula, can be seen layers of steel-grey volcanic ash in the exposed face of the mountain range. Obviously, these layers are of the matter brought down and deposited by the river.

The *Skanda Purāṇa*[59] states that "the mighty river Sarasvatī tore asunder the earth and going underground turned westward in an invisible course". The scientists at the Central Arid Zone Research Institute, Jodhpur, have confirmed[60] that under the dry bed of the Ghaggar exists a big river which, if properly tapped, can turn Rajasthan into a green state. Results of boring of tube wells in the Ghaggar bed near Chandigarh-Panchkula also tells the same story.[61] There is sufficient evidence to justify the conclusion that according to traditional belief it was Great Deluge that led to disappearance around Kalibangan in the sands of Rajasthan, of the Ṛigvedic Sarasvatī represented by the present Ghaggar river, as a result of diversion of its waters and loss of its catchment area.

The testimony of archaeology substantiates this traditional belief in the occurrence of the Great Deluge. Excavations at the Pre-Harappan/Harappan site of Kalibangan or Vinaśana were carried out by a very competent team consisting of senior officers of the Archaeological Survey of India including J.P. Joshi and led by B.K. Thapar and B.B. Lal.[62] In his remarks on the end of the Pre-Harappan or Period I Kalibangan settlement, Lal[63] says that at several places in the trenches was observed cleavage-cum displacement of the strata and walls, which evidently was the result of some earth movement. He considers it most likely that the site was deserted because of an earthquake. Also in his view occupation of Period II did not come into being immediately after the end of Period I but about 200 years later. Thapar[64] also subscribes to this view and adds that during the time the site remained abandoned a thin layer of sand, largely infertile and wind-blown accumulated over the ruins.

No more observation upon the extent or intensity of the seismic activity that destroyed the Pre-Harappan phase of Kalibangan are available but whatever has been said is enough to justify the conclusion that it came in the form of a catastrophic earthquake probably accompanied by strong volcanic eruptions, that rendered the country uninhabitable for several centuries and must inevitably have involved terrible damage to life and property. Nor is there any reason to believe that its impact was confined to the region of Kalibangan. Lal himself admits elsewhere the possibility of a tectonic movement involving the divide between the Indus and Gaṅgā systems and accounting for the drying up of Ghaggar as a result of the diversion of some of its tributaries to the Yamunā as well as the discovery of the water-laid deposits of Ochre Ware preceding the Painted Grey Ware at the archaeological sites like Hastinapura, Ahichchhatra, Bahadarabad, Nasirpur, Jhinjhina, and Atranjikhera in the Gaṅgā basin. However, instead of identifying this tectonic movement with the seismic activity that hit the Pre-Harappan Kalibangan around 3000 BC as indicated by available evidence, he confines it to the region of the source of these rivers where the Ghaggar and Yamunā basins came close to each other and places it about the first half of the second millennium BC so as to synchronize with the desertion of the site of Harappan Kalibangan as a result of the drying up of the Ghaggar and with the supposed later date of the Gaṅgā basin OCW sites. It looks rather improbable that a tectonic movement involving the expansive divide between the Indus and Gaṅgā systems should have been confined only to the region of their sources. It is also to be remembered that literary evidence supports fierce seismic-tectonic-volcanic activity extensively involving the long course of the river Sarasvatī and its valley and not in the Gaṅgā system which has not revealed any positive proof of widespread seismic upheaval like the one that destroyed Pre-Harappan Kalibangan. Neither are the courses of the Gaṅgā and the Yamunā reported have suffered any major changes at any stage in their known history.

Wheeler's sensational theory of destruction of Harappa and Mohenjo-daro by the savage Āryan hordes of India is no more taken seriously.[65] It was indeed as far back as in 1940 that M.R. Sahni noticed silt deposits perched many feet above the level of the Indus plain near the city of Hyderabad and suggested the destruction of these cities as a result of serious floods caused by major tectonic upheavals.[66] His view gathered support in only 1960 when a field party of the Pennsylvania University Museum undertook an archaeological survey of the Arabian coast of west Pakistan and discovered settlements of the Harappan era that had clearly been seaports but were now located as far as thirty miles inland showing clearly that the coast-line has risen considerably during the past 4,000 years, with the initial rise apparently having occurred during the Harappan periods.[67] It is interesting to note that in his extensive surveys conducted in the same year in southern Baluchistan and the lower Indus, Raikes[68] also reports a marked coastal uplift along the southern flank of the Arabian sea about the Harappan times, which according to him, might have been more extensive so as to cover even the Indus Valley. Raikes[69] asserts that the uplift, accompanied by more or less earthquake shocks, would not only have caused destruction of cities and settlements but would have disrupted the system of river and coast-wise communication on which the commercial life of the culture must have largely depended. And, this event as he pertinently observes[70], may have occurred hundreds of thousands of years ago or merely a few thousand years, and it must be admitted that some of the geologists consulted on the subject tend to think in terms of hundreds of thousands of years which he ascribes to a certain reluctance on their part to consider anything more than 20,000 years old as geology. The view of Raikes is supported by a number of scholars[71] and this makes it quite safe to accept the possibility of the occurrence of this event around 3000 BC.[72]

Although Raikes suspects Sehwan, some 90 miles downstream from Mohenjo-daro to be the most probable area of tectonic disturbance, Lambriok believes[73] that an avulsion and major change of course by the Indus occured considerably upstream of Mohenjo-daro. On the other hand, geological evidence of large-scale rock-faulting in the region[74] justifies the suggestion that these earth movements also embraced the region further north-east to the Shimla foothills across the Thar and the Indo-Gangetic divide[75] and upraised the entire bed of the Sarasvatī and the floor of the sea of its confluence. They might be even more widespread because Sir Leonard Wooley[76] also found at Ur in Mesopotamia indubitable proof of a flood which must have engulfed all the cities in the delta sometime before 3000 BC. The significance of the synchronism and of the identical nature of the event can hardly be over-emphasised and it is no more possible to dismiss the story of the Great Deluge as a myth now as literary evidence finds full support in the concrete testimony of independent archaeological discoveries at different places.

When?

The dating of the event agrees well with literary evidence as well as the testimony of Kalibangan. It is in the *Atharvaveda* that we find the first inklings of the occurrence of the Great Deluge in the mention of the term Nāvaprabhraṃśana which signifies the place of Manu's landing (abandoning the ship) called Manoravasarpaṇa in the *Śatapatha Brāhmaṇa*[77] and Naubandhana in later literature.[78] As already observed the Great Deluge apparently took place at some time between the composition of the nucleus of the *Ṛigveda* and the composition of the *Atharvaveda* and Brāhmaṇas. The generally accepted dating of the *Ṛigveda* to 2500 BC by Winternitz,[79] is not far removed from 3000 BC and one cannot afford to be dogmatic. If a landmark is available the difference of five hundred years becomes meaningless in case of the probable dating of the events of hoary antiquity and for works the composition of which undoubtedly stretched over long periods of time.

At Kalibangan the following dates have been assigned to the two excavated levels of settlements by Lal and Thapar on the basis of C-14 readings:

	Uncorrected	*Corrected after Dales*[80]	*Corrected after Ralph Michael & Han*[81]
		Period I-Pre-Harappan	
B.B. Lal	2400–2250	2950–2800	2930/2960–2700/2820
B.K. Thapar	2450–2300	3000–2850	2970/2990–2850/2870
		Pariod II-Harappan	
B.B. Lal	2200–1700	2700–1900	2630/2670–2060
B.K. Thapar	2300–1750	2850–1950	2850/2870–2110

Keeping in view the fact that the C-14 dating method is not yet considered entirely fool-proof one cannot afford to be too rigid about these date brackets. However, even if they are taken at their face value, one can safely place the end of the Pre-Harappan phase at Kalibangan around 3000 BC at the latest as a result of the Great Deluge that took place in the time of Manu Vaivasvata.

The combined effect of all this evidence makes it appear most probable that the earth movements postulated by Lal and Raikes were caused during the same fierce seismic-tectonic-volcanic upheaval which is known in the literature as the Great Deluge that wrought extensive changes in the topography of the Shiwalik belt between the Yamunā and the Ravi resulting in the diversion of the waters of the Ṛigvedic Sarasvatī or Ghaggar before 3000 BC and leading to its ultimate drying up around Vinaśana in the sands of Bikaner.[82]

Diversion of Waters—Reduction in Flow—Desiccation Sets in

Vājasaneyī Saṃhitā 34, 11 says:

प चनद्यः सरस्वतीमपियन्ति सस्रोतसः ।
सरस्वती तु प चथा सो देशे भवत् सरित् ।।

Griffith translates: "Five rivers flowing on their way speed onward to Sarasvatī. But then became Sarasvatī a fivefold river in the land".

The rendering of this verse is generally on these lines. H.C. Raychaudhuri[83] accepting it, says that "the description of the Sarasvatī as *pañchadhā* (fivefold), or split into five parts, may indicate that in its lower channel, while entering the areas now known as Bahawalpur, Sind and perhaps also Marwar and the littoral of the Rann of Kutch, it had branched off into five distributaries or run into an equal number of distinct channels". This reasoning is fallacious. In the translation the verse speaks of five rivers joining the Sarasvatī which does not warrant its description as fivefold. It can become fivefold only if it is divided into five rivers or channels. Yet, the first line clearly speaks of the five rivers speeding towards the Sarasvatī. Griffith's rendering does not resolve this apparent contradiction. The reason is that his translation does not do justice to the adjective *'sastrotasaḥ'* by interpreting it as 'flowing on their way'. In the Sanskrit word *nadī* for a river movement of water is implied (नदतीति नदी—whose flow creates noise). As an adjective of *'nadyah'* the use of *sastrotasaḥ* would therefore be redundant. The *Amarakośa* (i. 9, 11) defines *strotas* to mean a 'natural, independent flow of water': स्रोतोऽम्बुसरणं स्वतः

The word *srotaḥ* is crucial here and suggests the flow of water from its own independent source. By association, *srotas* should also mean 'source'. The first line then should be translated as 'Five rivers speed towards the Sarasvatī while joining it with their sources also'. In other words they join the Sarasvatī but their source too is the Sarasvatī itself. With this construction the rivers flowing from the Sarasvatī as their source justify its description as fivefold in the plains (*deśe)* even if they rejoin it later. The situation is fully supported by later tradition.

At least four rivers, the Markanda, Aruṇā, Śaradaṇḍā and Prāchī Sarasvatī are connected with the Sarasvatī or its source Plaksha. As already stated when propitiated by the immortal sage Markaṇḍeya the Sarasvatī, rising at Plaksha, followed him wherever he led her. So it was known after him as Markanda which rises at Baraban in the hills of Katasan and passes into Ambala district at Kala Amb below Nahan. The river named Aruṇā in the *Mahābhārata* and Āgneyī in the *Rāmāyaṇa,* identified with the present river Run joins the Markanda a few kilometres below Naraingarh. It has been described as brought into being by the Sarasvatī as her own self. Another tributary joining the Markanda above Kala Amb from the left is named Śaradaṇḍā in the *Rāmāyaṇa,* Sarasvatī in the *Amarakośa* and in a traditional verse and Sarasvatī by Hemādri. This is the present river Sadadeni.[84] Then there is the Ad Badri-Thanesar rainy season torrent, now almost extinct, called Prāchī Sarasvatī in literature and in an inscription of king Bhoja of the imperial Pratihāra dynasty at Pṛithūdaka, present town of Pehowa. It is said to have been born from Plaksha as a result of Vasishṭha's wrath against Viśvāmitra.[85] It ran very close to the town of Thanesar and merged with the combined stream of the Markanda-Aruṇā-Śaradaṇḍā at Urnai before reaching Pṛithūdaka and all ultimately joined the Ghaggar near Akalgarh.

These four rivers are thus known to have been connected with the Sarasvatī-Ghaggar or its source with regard to their origin as well as their end. The situation satisfies the adjective *sastrotasaḥ* for the rivers and the adjective *pañchadhā* for the Ṛigvedic Sarasvatī. As in case of the Ṛigvedic adjectives *saptasvasā* (having seven sisters which makes the Sarasvatī eighth) and *saptathī* (seventh) the description of five rivers reaching the Sarasvatī, which makes it the sixth, and the river becoming fivefold (itself and four above mentioned streams) the poetic account is apparently loose and given without particular care for its accuracy. It does suggest, of course, that all these rivers were born in the Great Upheaval.

Further, it is possible that the Upheaval also resulted in the diversion of Sarasvatī's waters towards the Yamunā through the rivers Giri and Tons which have their sources in the Himalayas very close to where the course of the Ṛigvedic Sarasvatī should have been. It is to be noted that the Tons bring to the Yamunā a major portion of water. With all these rivers as its tributaries and before its main flow went underground, the Sarasvatī would indeed justify its position as the river par excellence in the *Ṛigveda.*

It is safe to conclude that with the partial diversion and drastic reduction in the flow of the Sarasvatī, the process of its desiccation set in and it was complete a couple of centuries before the composition of the Brāhmaṇas and the Śrautasūtras to allow sufficient time for the development of the system of long sacrificial sessions like the Sārasvata *sattras.*

Some Observations

It is neither necessary nor possible to suggest that the Ṛigvedic Sarasvatī received the waters of the Sutlej, the Yamunā and/or Tons.[86] *RV*, iii. 33, 2–3 speaks of the confluence of the Sutlej and the Beas so that even then the former ran in its present course. The Yamunā and the Tons would have to run into or over the Dṛishadvatī, whose bed is now occupied by the Western Jumna Canal, to take a westward course towards the Sarasvatī. In the Brāhmaṇas the Yamunā is clearly mentioned as a river flowing at a distance from the Sarasvatī as well as the Dṛishadvatī. Also the Yamunā, the Sarasvatī and the Śutudri are mentioned as independent rivers even in *RV*. X. 75. In this situation it would be absurd to think of the Helmand river in Afghanistan or its tributary the Arghandab for identification with the Ṛigvedic Sarasvatī.

As for the delineation of the palaeo-channels of the Sarasvatī and its tributaries on the basis of Landsat imagery[87] there is nothing so special about it. It depends on factors like the pattern of drainage scars, distinct tone, texture, surface manifestations like younger alluvium and concentration of vegetation. Similar factors were not unknown in ancient times. Here is what *Mbh.*, Śalya Parva, 35, 84[88] says:

> Owing to the soothing herbs (or scrub), and the loamy soil, the wise recognize (the course of) the Sarasvatī, although not visible (to the common man).

Landsat imagery cannot give the time as to when the channels detected by it were active. Its conclusions are proved to be subjective and erratic view of the possibility of major and minor tectonic changes that might have taken place during the last 5,000 years from the Ṛigvedic age to the present day. Nor can any maps prepared by scholars according to their own perception and in support of their own theories be taken as pieces of evidence.

In their description of the *tīrthas* of Kurukshetra, the *Mahābhārata* and following it the *Vāmana Purāṇa* presents a mix-up of the Ṛigvedic Saravatī-Ghaggar and the Ad Badri Prāchī Saravatī. It follows the *Ṛigveda* in describing the Saravatī as 'the best of rivers', 'the first of all rivers', 'a perennial river', 'tearing asunder thousands of mountains' and 'reaching the ocean'.[89] The adjective *'pañcharūpā'*[90] and the *tīrtha* name *'pañchanada'*[91] are based on the adjective *'pañchadhā'* of the *Vājasaneyī Saṃhitā.* In the inclusion of Vinaśana and Plaksha Prāsravaṇa among its *tīrthas,* enumerated from Prabhāsa to Yamunā,[92] the influence of the Brāhmaṇa-Śrautasūtra accounts is quite apparent. Names of *tīrthas* like Nāgadhanvā, Saptasārasvata, Kapālamochana, Pṛithūdaka and Vasishṭhāpavāha have been included to introduce the Prāchī-Sarasvatī in the picture. The merger of different Sarasvatīs like Suprabhā, Kañchanākshī, Viśālā, Manoramā, Oghavatī and Sureṇu with the Prāchī Sarasvatī as the Saptasārasvata *tīrtha*[93] is intended to enhance the holiness of Kurukshetra which, by now, was perhaps reduced in extent to the Sarasvatī-Drishadvatī doab. Same is the case with the enumeration of the rainy season rivulets Vaitaraṇī, Āpagā, Gaṅgā-Mandākinī, Madhusravā-Amlunadī, Kauśikī, Dṛishadvatī and Hiraṇvatī with the perennial Sarasvatī among the seven rivers of Kurukshetra.[94] These two lists of rivers were introduced with an eye on the adjectives *saptasvasā* and *saptathī* of the Ṛigvedic Sarasvatī.

The *Mahābhārata* and the Purāṇa accounts therefore do not go against the identification of the Ṛigvedic Sarasvatī with the Ghaggar. In fact, the mention of Vinaśana and Plaksha Prāsravaṇa among its *tīrthas* only supports it.

From the earliest times through the ages we come across instances of the change of the sibilants *ś, sh* and *s* to the sonant aspirate *h,* especially when we proceed from the traditional region of Madhyadeśa towards the west. The early change of Vedic *asura* to Avesta *ahura* and Sindhu to Hindu is well known. The list of words for river Yāska[95] gives the form

Harasvatī along with Sarasvatī. The, place-name Taushāyaṇa in Pāṇini[96] has changed to Tohana. And, in dialects of Marwar *sādhu* is pronounced as *hau*, *Śiva* as *Hib*, *Sukhadeva* as *Hukhadeva* and *sāhukāra* as *haukara*.[97] The reverse of this process, i.e. the change from *h* to *ś*, *sh* and *s* cannot be argued since it cannot be explained as to why *daha* should become *daśa* and not *dasha* or *dasa*, why *Tohana* should change to *Taushāyaṇa* and not *Tauśāyaṇa* or *Tausāyaṇa*, *Ahura* to *Asura* and not *Aśura* or *Ashura* and *Hindu* to *Sindhu* and not *Śindhu* or *Shindhu*.

It is likely that the Sarasvatī-Harasvatī on account of its 6–8 km wide bed was called Sāgara-Hāgara in Rajasthan which changed to Hagra—Hakra. The evolution from Hagra to Ghaggar is not too difficult to visualize. Ghaggar came to be re-Sanskritized into Ghargharikā.[98] It makes an onomatopoeic name for the mighty perennial river known for the tempestuous roar of its flood. A *tīrtha* called Ghargharikā Kuṇḍa is named in the *Brahma Purāṇa*[99] among the *tīrthas* of Kurukshetra. It may refer to Plaksha Prāsravaṇa or Lavāsā-Pachhāḍ, the later source of the Ṛigvedic Sarasvatī-Ghaggar or to a sacred pond or well on this river.

Ṛigveda i, 112, 10 and 116, 15 are generally taken to refer to replacement by the Aśvins of the leg of a woman named Viśpalā, broken in the battle of a king or person named Khela with an iron leg. However, Ram Gopal in his annotated English translation of the *Ṛigveda*[100] (to appear in about a dozen volumes) offers a metaphorical construction of the verse where Viśpalā (protectress of people) denotes the river Sarasvatī and Khela means zigzag flow. His translation of the verse runs as follows:[101]

> O Aśvins come here with those aids through which you impelled the wealth-gaining Viśpalā (the protectress of people, the river Sarasvatī) which was blocked in its thousand-prized course, through which you protected the devout *ṛishi*, the son of Aśva.
>
> —*RV*. i, 112, 10

> As a leg (fig. a bank of the river) was broken (fig. breached) like the wing of a bird in the uncertain contest (fig. course) of Khela (fig. of zigzag flow), O Aśvins, you immediately replaced it with an iron leg (fig. a stone embankment) for Viśpalā (fig. the river Sarasvatī) to enable her to walk (fig. to flow) for sure wealth.
>
> —*RV*. i, 116, 15

Ram Gopal's interpretation may suggest the occurrence of probably some minor volcanic-seismic-tectonic upheaval(s) about the source/course of the Sarasvatī even in the Ṛigvedic times. This would explain the presence of more than one layers of ash in the mountain side on the left bank of the river near Panchkula.

Notes and References

1. Thapar, Romila, *Early India—From the Origins to AD 1300*, Allan Lane, Penguin Books, London, 2002, p. 105.
2. Kochhar, Rajesh, *The Vedic People, Their History & Geography*, Orient Longman, 2000.
3. Habib, Irfan, *PIHC*, 61st Session, Kolkata, 2001, pp. 65–92.
4. For identification see Bharadwaj, O.P., *Ancient Kurukshetra—Studies in Historical and Cultural Geography*, Harman Publishing House, New Delhi, 1991, pp. 45–59.
5. तत्त्वावबोधैकरसो न तर्कः।
6. For references see Bharadwaj, 1991, p. 39; Muir, J., *Original Sanskrit Texts*, Vol. V, pp. 337–343.
7. इयं मे गङ्गे यमुने सरस्वति शुतुद्रि स्तोमं सचता परुष्ण्या।....

8. Bharadwaj, O.P., *Studies in the Historical Geography of Ancient India,* Sundeep Prakashan, 1986, pp. 192–200.
9. *Mbh.,* Vana Parvan, 81, 55.
मानुषस्य तु पूर्वेण क्रोशमात्रे महीपते।
आपगा नाम विख्याता नदी सिद्धनिषेविता।।
10. Note 4 supra.
11. *Taittirīya Āraṇyaka,* viii, 1, 1.
12. See Bharadwaj, 1986, pp. 20–43.
13. *Ibid.,* pp. 8–19.
14. Oxford, 1908, Vol. 12, p. 213.
15. See Bharadwaj, 1986, pp. 88–107.
16. Manskha ri Mor ed., Calcutta, Pt. ii, Svargakhaṇḍa, 3, 32(i):
विहङ्गसुमुखो यस्तु सुपार्श्वस्यात्मजः किल।
17. Mor. Ed. Calcutta, Pt. i, 48, 44 (ii):
सुपार्श्वस्योत्तरे भागे सरस्वत्याः पुरोत्तमम्।।
18. *Śabda Kalpadruma,* Vol. V, p. 374 (iii):
सुपार्श्वः पल्क्षव क्षः इति राजनिघण्टुः।
19. Ed. with Hindi tr. Kanhaiya Lal Mishra, Venkateshwar Press, Bombay, V.S.2013, p. 307. Mishra's translation is wrong.
भूलिङ्ग में करोड़ धनुः परिमित सरस्वती है। वहाँ धनुष् कोकिल शंभु और लक्षकालिका स्थित है।
20. Chakrabarti, Dilip K., *India, An Archaeological History,* Oxford University Press, New Delhi, 2001, p. 141.
21. *India and Pakistan,* 1954, p. 485.
22. *Alberuni' India,* Edward C. Sachau, Reprint, S. Chand & Co., Delhi, 1964, Vol. I, p. 261 and Vol. II, p. 105.
23. For identification see Bharadwaj, 1986, pp. 1–7.
24. *Ibid.,* pp. 20–43.
25. *Ambala District Gazetteer,* Chandigarh, 1984, pp. 14–15; *Imperial Gazetteer of India,* Vol. 1, Oxford, 1907, p. 96 f.
26. *Meghadūtam* V. 61 (i).
प्रालेयाद्रेरुपतटमतिक्रम्य तांस्तान् विशेषान्।
हंसद्वारं भ गुपतियशोवर्त्म यत् क्रौ चरन्ध्रम।।.....
27. Eg. *Varāha Purāṇa,* ed. A.S. Gupta, Varanasi, 1983, ch. 81, 11 33–34. ताम्राभे तक्षकस्य पुरशतम्–
28. ii. 19 also *Śāṅkhāyana Brāhmaṇa,* xii. 3.
29. XIV.1.1.8.
30. 35, 7–51.
31. The story specifically places the well in the river bed. *Mbh.,* Śalya, 35,53:
उदपानं च तं द ष्ट्वा प्रशस्य च पुनः पुनः।
नदीगतमदीनात्मा प्राप्तो विनशनं तदा।।
32. See for instance *Brahmavaivarta Purāṇa,* ii, ch. 6.17(i):
लक्ष्मीः सरस्वती गङ्गा तिस्रोभार्या हरेरपि।
33. *Ibid.,* 70–71.
34. *Ibid.,* ii, 7.1:
पुण्यक्षेत्रे ह्याजगाम भारते सा सरस्वती।
गङ्गाशापेन कलया स्वयं तस्यौ हरेः पदम्।।
35. *Skanda Purāṇa,* Prabhāsa Khaṇḍa, 17.53, also *Padma Purāṇa,* Sṛishṭi Khaṇḍa 18. 198.
36. *Skanda Purāṇa,* Prabhāsa Khaṇḍa, 33.44; also cf. Dave, S.K., 'The Sarasvatī Purāṇa', *Purāṇa',* Vol. X, no. 1, Jan., 1968, p. 74.
37. *Skanda Purāṇa,* Prabhāsa Khaṇḍa, ch. 32.
38. *Ibid.,* 33.89.

39. *Ibid.*, 35.34.
40. *Ibid.*, 35.6.
41. *Ibid.*, 34.36.
42. *Ibid.*, 35, 21–26.
43. *Ibid.*, 35, 30–41.
44. *Ibid.*, 35.14.
45. See Chitrav Siddheshvara Shastri, *Prachīna Charitra Kośa,* (Hindi), Poona, 1964, p. 105.
46. Its capital was Bilaspur 33 miles north-west of Saharanpur on the road to Ambala. See Dey, N.L., *The Geographical Dictionary of Ancient & Medieval India,* London, 1927, p. 191.
47. *Ibid.*, p. 38.
48. Bhargava, *op. cit.*, p. 93.
49. *Skanda Purāṇa,* Prabhāsa Khaṇḍa, 35.5:
    कालान्तरे ततो भित्वा कुरूदेशं महाप्रभः।
    निर्गतोत्तंभितशिरा ज्वलदास्यो ति भीषणः।।
50. *Ibid.*, Nāgara Khaṇḍa, 175. 13.
51. *Vāmana Purāṇa, Sm.* 19, 22.
52. Śalya Parva, 43, 50, 51:
    ततः कुमारमादाय देवाः ब्रह्मपुरोगमाः।
    अभिषेकार्थमाजग्मुः शैलेन्द्रं सहितास्ततः।।
    पुण्यां हैमवतीं देवीं सरिच्छेष्टां सरस्वतीम्।
    समन्तप चके या वै त्रिषु लोकेषु विश्रुता।।
    and 45, 71–73
53. *Mbh.*, Karṇa Parva, ch. 24.
54. *Ibid.*, v. 120.
    .... त्रैलोक्यसांर तमिषुं मुमोच त्रिपुरं प्रति।
    तत्सासुरगणं दग्ध्वा प्राक्षिपत्पाश्चिमार्णवे।।
55. *Ibid.*, v. 75.
    कर्म सत्यं तपो र्थश्च विहितास्तत्र रश्मयः।
    अधिष्ठानं मनस्त्वासीत् परिरथ्यं सरस्वती।।
56. *Ibid.*, v. 14.
    ततो मयः स्वतपसा चक्रे धीमान् पुराणि ह।
    त्रीणि का चनमेकं तु रौप्यं कार्ष्णायसं तथा।।
57. Anuśāsana Parva, 139, 22–26.
58. Ch. 80, II. 39–48.
    ... सुपार्श्व शिखिशैलयोर्मध्य समन्तात् योजनशतमेकम् भौमशिलातलं नित्यतप्तं दुःस्पर्शम्। तस्य मध्ये त्रिंशद्योजन विस्तीर्णं मण्डलं वह्निस्थानम् स च सर्वकालमनिन्धनो भगवान् लोकक्षयकारी संवर्त्तको ज्वलते...
59. Venkateshvar Press ed. Prabhāsa, 1, 32, 26:
    भूमिं विदार्य तस्याधः प्रविष्टा गजगामिनी।
    तदन्तर्धान मार्गेण प्रव त्ता पश्चिमामुखी।।
60. *The Indian Express,* Chandigarh, 11 December, 1987, p. 7.
61. Prasher, R.N., "The Subterranean Sarasvati", *Haryana Sahitya Akademi Journal of Indological Studies,* Vol. III, Nos. 1–2, Spring 1988, pp. 301–305.
62. *Indian Archaeology,* 1961–62, p. 39; 1962–63, p. 20 ff; and 1963–64, p. 30 ff.
63. *Kalibangan's Contribution to the Understanding of the Indus Civilization,* IIAS, Shimla, November 2–7, 1977.
64. *South Asian Archaeology,* Ed. Hammond Norman, London, 1973, p. 85 ff and *Ancient Cities of the Indus,* Ed. G. Possehl, Delhi, 1979, pp. 196–203.
65. Cf. Raikes, Robert L, 'The End of the Ancient Cities of the Indus', reproduced in Possehl, *op. cit.*, p. 298.

66. Dales, George F, 'The Decline of the Harappans', reproduced in Possehl, *op. cit.*, p. 309.
67. *Ibid.*
68. *Op. cit.*, p. 302.
69. *Ibid.*, p. 304.
70. *Ibid.*, p. 302.
71. *Ibid.*
72. Dales, *op. cit.*, p. 309.
73. "The Indus Flood Plain and the Indus Civilization", reproduced in Possehl, p. 321.
74. Dales, *op. cit.*
75. Suraj Bhan, *Journal of Haryana Studies,* January 1969, Vol. 1, No. 1, p. 10.
76. *Ur Excavations, The Early Period,* 1958, p. 18.
77. i. 8.1.
78. *Mbh.*, Vana, 185.47 and *Nīlamata Purāṇa,* vv 40–41, pp. 164, 178.
79. "Some Problems of Indian Literature", reprint, Delhi, 1977, p. 20.
80. 1973, p. 162 ff and 1979, p. 332 ff.
81. Ralph, E.K., H.N. Michael & M. Han, in Possehl, pp. 339-342, Table 4.
82. For more references see Bharadwaj, O.P., "The Vedic Sarasvatī", *Haryana Sahitya Akademi Journal of Indological Studies,* Chandigarh, Vol. II, 1987, pp. 38–58.
83. *Studies in Indian Antiquities,* University of Calcutta, Calcutta, 1958, p. 133.
84. N. 15, Supra.
85. *Skanda Purāṇa,* Nāgara Khaṇḍa, 173, 9–10 and 12.
86. Oldham, C.F., "Sarasvati: The Lost River of Haryana", *JRAS,* 1893, Reprint *Journal of Haryana Studies,* Kurukshetra, Vol. XIII, Nos. 1–2, 1981, pp. 1–24. Also Lal, B.B., *The Sarasvatī Flows On,* Aryan Books International, New Delhi, 2002, pp. 11–17.
87. Sahai, Baldev, "Unravelling of the 'Lost' Vedic Sarasvati", in *Vedic Sarasvati,* ed. B.P. Radhakrishna and S.S. Mesh, Memoir 42, Geological Survey of India, Banglore, 1999, pp. 121–142.
88. स्निग्धत्वादोषधीना च भूमेश्च जनमेजय।
    जानन्ति सिद्धा राजेन्द्र नष्टामपि सरस्वतीम्।।
89. *Mbh.*, Vana, 84, 6.
    एषा सरस्वती पुण्या नदीनामुत्तमा नदी।
    प्रथमा सर्वसरितां नदी सागरगामिनी।।
    Vāmana Purāṇa, 32, 3 (i).
    पत्क्षव क्षात्समुद्भूता सरिच्छ्रेष्ठा सनातनी।
    & 4 (i) : सैषा शैलसहस्राणि विदार्य च महानदी।
    & 34, 8 (ii) : वर्षाकालवहा सर्वा वर्जयित्वा सरस्वतीम्।।
90. *Vāmana Purāṇa,* 13, 20: One of the rivers whose water people drink:
    सरस्वती प चरूपा कालिन्दी सहिरण्वती।
91. *Ibid.*, 34, 27.
    प जनदाश्च रूद्रेण कृता दानवभीषणाः।
    तत्र सर्वेषु लोकेषु तीर्थ प चनदं स्म तम्।।
    Also *Mbh,* Vana, 81.8.
92. *Mbh,* Śalya P., 35–53.
93. *Ibid.*, 38, 3–32 and *Vāmana Purāṇa,* 34, 17 and 38.
94. *Vāmana Purāṇa,* 34, 6–8.
95. *Nighaṇṭu,* i, 13.
96. Agrawala, V.S., *India as Known to Pāṇini,* 2nd ed., Varanasi, 1963, p. 74.
97. Bharadwaj, 1986, pp. 176–191.
98. For restoration of geographical names see *ibid.*
99. Mor ed. Calcutta, 25, 64 (ii).
100. Vol. 1, VVRI, Hoshiarpur, 2003, pp. 125, 283.
101. *Ibid.*, pp. 125, 133.

4

Geographical References

The Ocean and Soma

DAVID FRAWLEY

In the following article, I will explore the geographical implications of the *Ṛigveda,* some of which have already been examined in passing. Much of this material is also covered in my book *Gods, Sages and Kings.* Here I will summarize that data and add some new information, particularly related to the geography of Soma. The Vedas reflect a vast knowledge of the earth, mentioning various mountains, rivers, deserts and oceans quite befitting the great subcontinent of India. A hymn of Hiraṇyastūpa Aṅgirasa in the *Ṛigveda* makes this clear:

> Savitar (the Sun God) has revealed eight mountains of the earth, three desert (or shore) regions and seven rivers.
>
> Hiraṇyastūpa Aṅgirasa, *RV* I.35.8[1]

The *Ṛigveda* has a certain geographical horizon. It projects a land of seven great rivers bounded by several oceans and many mountains. It mainly shows the geographical sphere of the Bharatas and their neighbours or the region of north India.

The Ocean

I must emphasize the numerous oceanic and maritime references in the Vedas, as scholars keep ignoring this obvious point while projecting origins for the Vedic culture outside of India. The term ocean (*samudra*) occurs commonly in the *Ṛigveda,* about a hundred times. In fact, the ocean is mentioned many more times than any river or group of rivers by name. Besides the term *samudra,* related terms like *sāgara, arnas* and *sindhu* also mean sea or ocean.

Whole theories of the location of the Vedic people have been built around a few scanty references to rivers like the Kubhā in Afghanistan, while much more common references to the ocean are ignored. Only one river, the Sarasvatī, which is clearly in India, has an extensive mythology about it. Yet, the ocean not only has an extensive mythology about it, there is much oceanic symbolism about all the main Vedic Gods including Indra, Agni, Soma, Sūrya and Varuṇa, just to name a few.

References occur to two oceans, eastern and western (*RV* X. 136.5), to inferior and superior oceans (*RV* VII 6.7; X.98.6), or to two seas called *samudra* and *purisha* (*RV* I.163.1; IV.21.3). There are additional references to four oceans, corresponding to the four directions.[2] These four oceans may relate to the eastern, western and southern seas, and to the lake in Kashmir in the north. An ocean with seven foundations is described (*RV* VIII. 40.5). Sometimes the *Ṛigveda* speaks of many oceans.[3] Given India's proximity to the Arabian Sea, Bay of Bengal and the Persian Gulf, this idea of several oceans is not surprising. The common *Brāhmaṇa* anointing great kings (*AB* viii. 15) is "from one end up to the further side of the earth bounded by the ocean as sole ruler".[4] Similarly, the *purohita* as chief priest guards the king, "as the ocean does the earth (*AB* viii. 25)".[5] Such statements emphatically rule out Central Asia or Afghanistan.

Indra as the Ocean

The main Vedic myth is of Indra slaying the dragon and releasing the seven rivers to flow into the sea.

> All songs give increase to Indra who is as expansive as the sea. *RV* I.11.1
>
> Indra has an extent like the sea. *RV* I.30.3
>
> He slew the dragon lying at the foot of the mountain. The creator fashioned for him his flashing thunderbolt. As milch cows bellowing as they flowed, directly the waters entered the ocean. *RV* I.32.2
>
> Indra, an ocean of wealth. *RV* I.51.1
>
> Indra, extensive as the sea. *RV* I.52.4
>
> Hymns to Indra like the ocean in their convergence. *RV* I.56.2
>
> Indra, not by the seas or mountains is your chariot contained. *RV* II. 16.3
>
> As rivers according to their impulse go forth, the floods as if chariot borne entered into the sea. As rivers uniting to the sea, to Indra they carry the well-pressed Soma. *RV* III.36.6–7
>
> The Soma drops, like rivers into the sea enter into Indra. *RV* III. 46.4
>
> You destroyed the dragon that withheld the waters. Earth in her awareness furthered your thunderbolt. You gave energy to the ocean-going floods. *RV* IV. 16.7
>
> Come to us quickly, Indra, from Heaven or Earth, from the ocean or the heavenly sea *RV* IV.21.3
>
> You slew the serpent that encompassed the floods. You released the waters to the ocean. *RV* VI.30.4
>
> You destroyed the dragon and Heaven approved. You sent forth the flood of the rivers and filled manifold seas. *RV* VI.72.2
>
> As rivers to the ocean strong hymns and songs have entered Indra whose extent is vast. *RV* VI.36.3
>
> By which you released the great floods to the ocean, Indra that power of yours is vigorous. *RV* VIII.3.10
>
> In the slope of the mountains, in the concourse of the rivers, by the power of the hymn the sage Indra was born. Hence, arisen conscious he looks down upon the sea,

from which awakening he stirs. *RV* VIII.6.28–9

To Indra and Agni, like the seer Nābhāka, direct your prayers, who poured out the sea with seven foundations, whose opening is above. *RV* VIII.40.5

Whether you in the east, the south, the north or the west you are called by men, come quickly with your powers; whether you exult yourself on the slope of Heaven, in the Sun-world or in the ocean of Soma. *RV* VIII.65.2–3

Whether you are in the luminous realm of Heaven or in the domain of the sea, whether in the station of the Earth or in the atmosphere, come to us, Indra. *RV* VIII.97.5

The thunderbolt lies within the ocean enclosed by the waters. *RV* VIII. 100.9

Indra is a fourfold ocean, the support of treasures. *RV* X.47.2

To Indra I direct my songs in an unceasing flow, like waters from the bottom of the sea. *RV* X.89.4.

Agni as the Ocean

Agni, the Divine Fire, also has his ocean-going form, which is often a ship. Note the oceanic form or Agni whose vesture is the ocean. Note also the ocean as the support of treasures, suggesting trade by sea.

Who shake the mountains across the wavy ocean. May Agni come with the Maruts. *RV* I.19.7

All delights converge in Agni, as seven mighty streams the ocean. *RV* I.71.7

Agni, you move to the ocean of Heaven ... to the waters which are beyond the luminous heaven of the Sun and to those which stand below it. *RV* III.22.2–3

All the universe rests within your nature, in the ocean, in the heart, in all life. *RV* IV.58. 1,11

From the inferior and superior oceans, he received them, from Heaven and Earth. *RV* VII.6.5–7

Oh Agni, for your firm law our words like cattle are spoken, as rivers to the sea. *RV* VIII.44.25

Agni, whose vesture is the ocean. *RV* VIII. 102.4–6

Agni, the one ocean, the upholder of treasures. *RV* X.5.1

In the ocean, in the Waters, as the God-mind, you are enkindled as the Divine vision, oh Agni, in the udder of Heaven. *RV* X.45.1

Soma as the Ocean

Soma is not simply a mountain god, he is also a water god, often depicted as the ocean. This also reflects that the Soma cult pervaded India from the mountains to the sea. In fact, one could argue that the worship of Soma is also an ocean cult. We will examine this point in more detail later.

Flow on Soma as wealth from four oceans to us, a thousandfold and from every side *RV* IX.33.6

Flow on Soma as peace for us, draw out for our milk an ambrosial juice, and increase the ocean of the hymn. *RV* IX. 61.15

Forming the ray from Heaven, you flow through all forms. Soma, as the ocean you overflow. Soma, beloved enter the ocean. *RV* IX.64.8,17,27

To the ocean the Soma drops, like cows to their home, have come to the source of truth. *RV* IX.66.12

The ocean-going angels have flowed to the wise Soma. *RV* IX.78.3

The Soma libations have extended like the oceans. *RV* IX.80.1

Soma (the Moon) stirs the ocean with the winds. *RV* IX.84.4

The king of the river plunges into the sea, lodged in the rivers, he holds to the wave of the waters. *RV* IX.86.8

Soma flows as the first of the rivers. *RV* IX.86.12

You are the all knowing ocean, oh seer, yours are the five directions in the law, you transcend Heaven and Earth, yours are the constellations, flowing Soma, who are the Sun. *RV* IX.86.29

Thus like rivers down to the sea, the Soma drops have poured into the chalices. *RV* IX.88.6

The king of the rivers has put on the vesture. He has mounted the most righteous ship of truth. *RV* IX.89.2

The ocean roars in the original laws, generating creation as the king of the world. *RV* IX.97.40

Flowing Soma, the Divine King, the vast truth, crosses the ocean by the wave. *RV* IX.107.15

Soma, as the ecstatic, you were the first to extend the ocean for the Gods. *RV* IX. 107.23

Flow on Soma as the great ocean, the Father of the Gods through all the laws. *RV* IX. 109.2.

Varuṇa

Varuṇa is specifically a God of the sea. He is often connected to Soma as a water God but also to Mitra and to Indra.

The Maruts move through Heaven, Agni through the Earth, the Wind moves through the atmosphere. Through the Waters and the oceans, Varuṇa moves. *RV* I.161.14

That is the great magic power of this divine greatest seer, Varuṇa, that no one can challenge, when the diverse flowing streams cannot fill the one ocean with their water. *RV* V.85.6

Varuṇa dug a path for the Sun and led forth the ocean-going floods of the rivers. *RV* VII.87.1

Varuṇa is a secret ocean. *RV* VIII.41.8.

Ships

Vedic references to ships are also numerous like those of the sea. They are not only ships to cross the rivers but to cross the sea.

> Varuṇa knows the station of the birds that fly through the atmosphere. He knows the ocean-going ships. *RV* I.25.7
>
> As a ship across the river (or sea), Agni, take us across to safety. *RV* I.97.8
>
> Agni will deliver us across all difficulties, as a ship across the river (or sea). *RV* I.99.1
>
> When he was lost in the supportless, foundationless, ungraspable ocean, you put forth your strength, oh Aśvins. You bore Bhujyu home, mounted on a ship with a hundred oars. *RV* I.116.5
>
> Aśvins, you bore Bhujyu from the flooding ocean with straight moving bird-horses *RV* I.117.14
>
> Aśvins, you delivered Taugrya (Bhujyu) across the ocean. *RV* I.118.6
>
> Agni, give us a ship for our vehicle and house, with constant oars and quarters, which can take across our heroes and benefactors and our people to safety. *RV* I.140.12
>
> Agni, destroyer of difficulties, deliver us across all danger as a ship across the river (or sea). *RV* V.5.9
>
> The Sun mounted the luminous ocean, having yoked his straight-backed horses. The wise have led him like a ship through the water. *RV* V.45.10
>
> When, oh Aśvins, you cross the ocean, men bring you fruits and delights. *RV* V.73.8
> Pushan, your ships that are within the sea, golden in the atmosphere which travel, by them you go on the embassy of the Sun, made by love, desiring glory. *RV* VI.58.3
>
> You carried Bhujyu, the son of Tugra, from the watery ocean by birds, through the Air. *RV* VI.62.6
>
> Aśvins, Bhujyu cast in the ocean, you bore across the floods with your unfailing horses. *RV* VII.69.7
>
> When Varuṇa and I ascend into the ship, when we go forth to the middle of the sea, then we move with the waves of the waters and swing back and forth as if on a swing for joy. Varuṇa placed Vasishṭha in a ship. Skilful, he made him into a seer by his greatness. A sage, he made him a singer in the brightness of the days, as far as the heavens extended, as far as the dawns. *RV* VII.88.3–4
>
> When the son of Tugra served you, abandoned in the sea, then with wings your vehicle flied. *RV* VIII.5.22
>
> Aśvins, whether you are in a distant habitation, or beyond in the luminous realm of Heaven or in a house built upon the sea come to us. *RV* VIII. 10.1
>
> Oh Divine Varuṇa, guide this hymn of your worshipper with wisdom and skill, by it may we cross over all difficulties; may we mount it as a saving ship. *RV* VIII.42.3
>
> Deliver us across all difficulties, oh Universal Gods, as ships across the waters. *RV* VIII.83.3
>
> Soma, deliver us as a ship across the river (or sea). *RV* IX. 70.10
>
> The ships of truth have delivered the righteous. Varuṇa takes us across the great ocean. *RV* IX. 73.1,3
>
> Those who do not have the power to ascend the sacrificial ship, trembling fall into calamity. *RV* X.44.6

May we ascend the Divine ship with good oars, free of sin, which does not sink, to happiness. *RV* X.63.10

Specific Rivers Flowing to the Sea

Specific rivers are mentioned flowing to the sea, including the Sarasvatī and Sindhu (Indus).

Sarasvatī, pure in her course from the mountains to the sea. *RV* VII.95.2

From the lap of the mountains, happy, smiling, like two running mares, like two bright Mother cows licking their calf, Vipāś and Śutudrī run with fluid. Directed by Indra, seeking power, as chariots they travel to the sea. *RV* III. 33.1–2

Maruts, what medicine of yours is in the Indus and in the Asiknī rivers, what is in the oceans or what is in the mountains. *RV* VII.20.25

The Land of the Seven Rivers

The Vedas describe a land of many rivers flowing to the sea. The number of rivers is specifically mentioned as seven, which occurs many times throughout the entire text.[6] The main term for river is Sindhu, so the land of the seven rivers is Sapta Saindhava. The ancient Persian *Zend Avesta* (Vendidad Fargard I.20) similarly knows of a land of seven rivers (Hapta Hindava). Rivers like Indus and Sarasvatī extended down to a great ocean. These rivers can be identified with the seven goddesses, identified as mothers, streams or voices that give birth to Agni, the fire god (*RV* III. 1.4), or the seven Mothers of Soma (*RV* IX. 102.4). There is also a seal of 'Seven Goddesses' from Harappa. They are said to be the mothers of Indra (*RV* VIII.96.1), the greatest of the Vedic Gods, to whom all hymns flow like rivers to the sea (*RV* I.11.1). The rivers are sacred to the main Vedic Gods, whose worship extends to all of them.

The *Atharvaveda* speaks of seven rivers that extend over a region like heaven and earth (*AV* IV.5.2). Modern scholars have generally identified these with the rivers of the Punjab (five-river region of north-west India) with Sindhu and Sarasvatī. However, in Vedic literature, the Sarasvatī, located in the easternmost section of the Punjab, is the most important of the seven rivers (*RV* VI.52.6). Therefore, the land of the seven rivers cannot be limited to the Punjab, nor can the seven rivers be all made into affluents of the Indus, nor can Sarasvatī be made their easternmost. The land of the seven rivers must have included rivers to the east of the Sarasvatī and outside the Punjab. This is confirmed as eastern rivers like Yamunā, Gaṅgā (also called Jāhñavī) and Sarayu are also mentioned in the Vedas as big rivers.[7] It is not simply the number of times a river is mentioned but how greatly it is extolled.

In fact, it would be absurd to say that the Vedic people could know of Sarasvatī, much less of the ocean, and not of the Gaṅgā. From Sarasvatī to Gaṅgā in their upper regions is only a couple days' journey by horse, while the rivers of Gandhāra are several times farther away, and the ocean yet considerably more distant. The Gaṅgā is a neighbouring river of the Sarasvatī in its upper course, particularly considering the closeness of the Sarasvatī to the Yamunā. Any people on the upper Sarasvatī could not miss the Gaṅgā.

The land of the seven rivers, therefore, included north India from the Indus in the west to the Gaṅgā or Sarayu in the east. I would identify the seven rivers from west to east as the following. These are the most commonly mentioned rivers in the *Ṛigveda* and those described as having the largest stature. 1. Sindhu 2. Asiknī (Chenab) 3. Parushṇī (Ravi) 4. Sarasvatī 5. Yamunā 6. Gaṅgā 7. Sarayu. Probably "seven rivers" was a flexible designation based on the sacred nature of the number seven that we find throughout the Vedas. Each of these rivers could also be described as threefold or sevenfold.

The land of the seven rivers was north India, including rivers east of Sarasvatī. In fact, if we look at a map of the region, it is about an equal distance from Gandhāra (Peshawar) in the west to the Sarayu (Faizabad) in the east and to the coast on the Arabian Sea. As the region was largely flat and had navigable rivers, to have knowledge of the entire region would not have been difficult, given the central location of the Sarasvatī region.

The Sarasvatī River

The main river of the Vedic era is undoubtedly the Sarasvatī, which is described as the largest and most central river, pure in its course from the mountains to the sea (*RV* VII.95.2). It is the great mother of the Āryans. Unique among rivers, it is a great goddess, the subject of three entire hymns[8] as well as numerous references throughout Vedic literature. The Sarasvatī is placed west of Yamunā (Gaṅgā, Yamunā, Sarasvatī; *RV* X.75.5) and is said to flow into the sea (*RV* VII.95.2). It is said to be fed by three, five or seven streams (*RV* VI.61.12).

Sarasvatī is said to be the foremost of the *Nadīs* and the best mother (*RV* II.41.16).[9] She is the best of the seven rivers and the Mother of the rivers, the Mother of Sindhu.[10] Sarasvatī is the best of the seven rivers that are her seven sisters (*RV* VI.61.9–10). She has seven branches (*RV* VI.61.12) and nourishes all the five peoples. She overflows with the rivers or Sindhus (*RV* VI.52.6).[11] This means that Sarasvatī could also be called a Sindhu and that the term Sindhu does not refer merely to the Indus (Sindhu) River. Just as the rivers of north India could all be called Sindhus, they could also be called Sarasvatīs. As a great flood, she is probably connected to the sea.[12] The Sarasvatī or Sarasvat sea is probably another name of the Arabian Sea.

Great *ṛishis* like Vasishṭha and Jamadagni (*RV* VII.96.3), Gṛitsamada (*RV* II.41.16) and Bhāradvāja (*RV* VI.61) are connected to the Sarasvatī as are great kings like Divodāsa (*RV* VI.61) and Bharatas like Devavāta and Devaśravas (*RV* III.23). There is a special prayer not to leave her for other lands.[13]

For Sarasvatī to have been such a great river, there must have been major changes in the river systems of north India, and several rivers now flowing into the Indus or Gaṅgā must have previously flowed into Sarasvatī. The modern Sutlej (Vedic Śutudrī) clearly flowed into the Sarasvatī in ancient times. The Yamunā flowed west into it at an earlier period as well. There is also a possibility that the Beas (Vipāś) and Ravi (Parushṇī) also flowed into Sarasvatī in ancient times. In fact, such modern names are only approximations of rivers that once flowed in their areas. In addition, the region of west India, which is now predominantly desert, was definitely wetter. There are numerous ancient settlements in Cholistan and the Bahawalpur region that are now desert. Otherwise, it is difficult to account for the size of the river as revealed both by land studies and by Vedic literary accounts.

The Land of Ilā, the Main Sarasvatī/ Dṛishadvatī Region

The central land of the Vedas is the place of Ilā, which was mentioned earlier in the book. This land between the Sarasvatī and Dṛishadvatī rivers (*RV* III. 23.4) is also the holy land of the Brahmins, from which the great Vedic teachings originate (*MS* II.17).

Agni, like a father, is first enkindled at the place of Ilā by Manu (or by man; *RV* II.10.1). In the feminine tense, Ilā is identified specifically as the Sarasvatī-Dṛishadvatī region later called Khāṇḍava and Kurukshetra and is a very sacred area. It is said to be the best place on Earth (*RV* III. 23.4), which is also the place of Sudās and the Bharatas (*RV* III. 53. 11). It is said to be the centre of the Earth (*RV* III. 29.4; X.1.6). Most of the references to the place of Ilā are the Viśvamitras. It is also mentioned by a Vītahavya *ṛishi* (*RV* X.91.4), again connecting it to Bharata peoples.

Summary of Ṛigvedic Rivers

The river hymn of the *Ṛigveda* (*RV* X.75), though probably a later addition to the text, has the clearest delineation of the Vedic rivers. It is attributed to a Sindhukshit Praiyamedha. It is probably the same *ṛishi* referred to as Sindhukshit Bharata in the *Jaiminīya Brāhmaṇa* (*JB* III.82) as visiting all the rivers. The Priyamedhas were also connected to the Bharatas. So Sindhukshit was probably a Bharata *ṛishi*. The hymn mentions several rivers verse by verse:

Verse 5 First half—Gaṅgā, Yamunā, Sarasvatī, Śutudrī, Parushṇī
This is the central region of the Puru-Bharatas from the Gaṅgā-Jāhñavī in the East to the Parushṇī in the West. The Dṛishadvatī, Āpayā and Vipāś rivers would go here and the Aṁśumatī, which is identified with the Yamunā.

Verse 5 Second half—Asiknī, Marudvṛidhā, Vitastā, Ārjīkīyā, Sushomā
This is the region of the Anus in Punjab from the Asiknī (Chenab) to Vitastā and Kashmir famous for Soma.

Verse 6 First half—Trishṭāmā, Susartu, Rasā, Śvetā
This is probably the land of Uttara Kuru in Ladakh and Gilgit and perhaps north to western China. The Anitabhā would go here as well.

Verse 6 Second half—Sindhu, Kubhā, Gomatī, Krumu, Mehatnū
This is the land of Gandhāra west of Indus into Afghanistan, the region of the Druhyus.[14]

Marudvṛidhā may be part of the Asiknī (Chenab system) or in the same area. Sushomā is identified by Yāska with the Indus but by others with the Sohan River, a small tributary just to the east of the Indus in Kashmir. In any case, it is by Ārjīkā and the Ārjīkiyā River. Ārjīkiyā is by Vitastā, the river of Kashmir, and so is probably in or by Kashmir as well.

This hymn shows the region of the Purus, Anus and Druhyus but not the Turvaśas and Yadus. It is mainly concerned with the northern rivers, not with the ocean regions that the Vedic people were also well aware of. Probably, northern regions were defined more by rivers, while coastal areas were defined more by the sea. This means that the Ṛigvedic rivers do not necessarily mark all the regions of the Vedic people or Āryans but mainly the Puru-Bharatas and their relatives, the sons of Śarmishṭhā or the northern peoples.

The different books of the *Ṛigveda* all know of the ocean, great mountains, and the seven rivers. They emphasize the Purus and Bharatas who were centred on the Sarasvatī River. This means that the rivers must be interpreted in this larger context. The existence of western rivers cannot be used to reduce the Vedic people to their banks. They appear peripheral to the central Vedic land as border regions. We must also look to see how rivers are mentioned. Some are referred to as great rivers, others occur as tributaries of greater rivers. We cannot make them all equal. Nor, can we use river names to counter the greater importance of the ocean in the Vedic corpus.

River names are rarely mentioned in the hymns, except Sindhu, which has a generic meaning and Sarasvatī, which is also a goddess. Some books of the *Ṛigveda* like books II and IX hardly mention any rivers, though they mention the ocean frequently. That the nineth or Soma Book mentions the ocean commonly but not specific rivers is itself a good statement of the Vedic world view in which the ocean, rather than a single river was the main image. Most of these river references occur in a few hymns like V.53 and X.75 that name a number of rivers. Many are found in the hymns of only one *ṛishi*. For example, nearly all the river references in the Book V of the *Ṛigveda* are in the hymns of Śyāvāva. We should note that river references are even less common in the *Atharva* and *Yajurveda*, than the *Ṛigveda*, which is not to say that the Vedic people left these rivers at a later period. We come to such wrong conclusions if we emphasize a few river references over the greater descriptions of the texts emphasizing the ocean.

A few possible rivers are mentioned whose identity or even status as a river is in doubt. I have not included all of these. In fact, any Mother Goddess in the *Ṛigveda* can possibly be the name of a river. Some river names may refer to more than one river, like the Rasā. On the other hand, one river may have more than one name. For example, Ilā and Bhāratī may also have been names for the Sarasvatī or its tributaries.

Main Rivers Mentioned in the *Ṛigveda*

Book I—Sindhu (126.1), Sarasvatī (3.10–12; 164.49), Jāhñavī (Gaṅgā; 116.18–19), Rasā (112.12)

Book II—Sarasvatī (41.16–18)

Book III—Vipāś (33), Śutudrī (33), Sarasvatī (23.4), Dṛishadvatī (23.4), Āpayā (23.4) Jāhñavī (Gaṅgā; 59.6)

Book IV—Sindhu (43.6), Asiknī (17.15), Vipāś (30.11), Parushṇī (22.2) Sarayu (30.18), Rasā (43.6)

Book V—Rasā (41.15; 53.9), Anitabhā (53.9), Kubhā (53.9), Krumu (V.53.9), Gomatī (61.19), Sindhu (53.9), Parushṇī (52.9), Sarasvatī (43.11), Yamunā (52.17), Sarayu (53.9)

Book VI—Sarasvatī (52.6; 61.1–14), Gaṅgā (45.31)

Book VII—Asiknī (5.3), Parushṇī (18.8), Sarasvatī (36.6, 95.1–6; 96.1–6), Yamunā (18.19)

Book VIII—Gomatī (24.30), Suvastu (19.37), Sindhu (20.24–25; 25.12, 26.18), Sushomā (53.11), Asiknī (20.24), Parushṇī (74.15), Sarasvatī (21.17–18; 54.4), Aṁśumatī (Yamunā 96.14–15)

Book IX—Rasā (41.6), Sarasvatī (67.32)

Book X—Trishṭāmā (75.6), Susartu (75.6), Rasā (75.6: 108; 121.4) Śveta (75.6), Sindhu (64.9; 75.6), Kubhā (75.6), Krumu (75.6), Gomatī (75.6), Mehatnū (75.6), Ārjīkīyā (75.5), Sushomā (75.5), Vitastā (75.5), Marudvṛidhā (75.5), Asiknī (75.5), Parushṇī (75.5), Śutudri (75.5), Sarasvatī (30.12; 64.9; 75.5), Yamunā (75.5), Gaṅgā (75.5), Sarayu (64.9)

The Sarasvatī occurs as the dominant river in Book I, where it is called a great sea (*RV* I.3.12). In Book II, it is called the best goddess, best mother and best river (*RV* II.41.16). In Book III, it is the place of Ilā (*RV* III.23.4) where the Bharatas rule. In Books VI and VII, it has its own special hymns as a great goddess. In Book VIII, it is the great river of kings (*RV* VIII.21.17–18). In Book IX, the Soma book, it grants the fruits of worshipping Soma (*RV* IX.67.32). So the Sarasvatī is the main river of most of the books of the *Ṛigveda*.

Books II, III, VI and VII mainly know of the region of the Sarasvatī extending east to the Gaṅgā and Yamunā and west to the Parushṇī (Ravi) and Asiknī (Chenab). This is the central Ṛigvedic region and their books are the main books of the Divodāsa and Sudās Bharatas. The Asiknī, however, is referred to as a river of enemies. Books IV, V, VIII and X know of western rivers in Gandhāra but also of an eastern Sarayu showing a broader region, the centre of which is marked by the Sarasvatī. The Kaṇvas of Book VIII also speak more favourably of the Turvaśas and Yadus, the southern people, and commonly mention the ocean. These books are dominated by the Trasadasyus, with a later Kuru influence as we have noted, though they do mention Divodāsa and Sudās. They reflect more the peripheral regions and the expansion of the central Bharatas.

Regions in the *Ṛigveda*

Punjab, Kashmir, Afghanistan : Western Rivers

The word Sindhu is prominent in Vedic texts. It can refer to the Indus River or even mean the ocean. The Sindhu is second in importance only to the Sarasvatī. The *Ṛigveda* mentions the main tributaries of the Indus. These include the rivers of the modern Punjab—the Sutlej (Śutudrī), Beas (Vipāś), Ravi (Parushṇī), Chenab (Asiknī), and Jhelum (Vitastā) and smaller western affluents that drain the highlands of Afghanistan (Gandhāra)—the Swat (Suvasru), Kabul (Kubhā), Kuram (Krumu) and Gomal (Gomatī). The Āryans were located in these regions at the time of the *Ṛigveda* as they were later. However, these rivers have changed course even in historical times.

The Punjab region is commonly mentioned in *Ṛigveda,* but did not exist as a Punjab (Pañcha Āpa) or five river region. It was part of a continuous set of rivers from the Gaṅgā in the east to the Sindhu in the west. The Punjab region was well known to the Vedic people, including the Himalayan region above it, Kashmir.

Gandhāra, as a place name, occurs in the *Ṛigveda* (*RV* I.120.1). The *Atharvaveda* (*AV* V.22.14) calls Gandhāra a distant and western land of Śudras, those whose practices are not orthodox, along with Balkh (Bactria). It was regarded as the best region for horses. Camels are also mentioned in the *Ṛigveda*[15] in Book VIII, which would have originated in Bactria and Gandhāra.

Several obscure rivers are mentioned above Kubhā on the Indus. These are probably the rivers of Uttara Kuru. Rasā, Anitabhā are mentioned by Śyāvāśva Ātreya (*RV* V.53.9). Trishṭāmā, Susartu, Rasā and Śvetā occur in the river hymn of Book X (*RV* X.75.6). These could be affluents of the Indus in Gilgit, Ladakh and Leh. Some scholars have equated these rivers with the Amu Daryu (Oxus or Vaksha) or the Syr Darya or some rivers of western China. This is also possible as Uttara Kuru often referred to these regions as well. Vaksha does occur relative to rivers in the *Ṛigveda* (*RV* X.64.9), but does not appear as the name of a specific river.

Sindh and Gujarat: Southern Rivers

The Vedic people had a long familiarity with the ocean, with south-west India as their main coastal region. The Sarasvatī flowed into the Rann of Kachchh, which was then an island, as was the current peninsula of Saurashtra. The Indus reached the Arabian Sea to the north and west of Sarasvatī. This made a large delta of two great rivers that provided a wide access to the sea.

The river Rasā is prominent in the *Ṛigveda* not just as a tributary of the Sindhu but as a great river in itself, connected to the ocean (*RV* X.121.4). I believe that there were two rivers. A northern Rasā was an affluent of the Sindhu in mountain regions or some river yet further north. I would call it Soma Rasā as it was a main river of the Soma lands north of Kashmir. However, there appears to have been a larger Rasā that marked the region of the Āryans from the non-Āryans and was south, by the ocean (*RV* X.108).

In the Purāṇas, the Rasā river divides the gods from the demons and is identified with the Narmadā. In the *Jaiminīya Brāhmaṇa,* the Rasā is mentioned relative to the ocean, as on this side of the ocean as a boundary area.[16] The offspring of the hound Saramā that finds the Paṇis on the Rasā dwell in Vidarbha, which is a southern land below the Vindhyas near the Narmadā River.[17] This suggests that the Rasā was a boundary river like the Narmadā. As the river of the Paṇis or traders, its association with the ocean makes sense. The Narmadā was also sacred to the Bhṛigus, the *gurus* of the Asuras and Rākshasas, and at its joining with the sea was their famous city of Bhṛigukachchha. Revā is another name of the river Narmadā, which means the Rasā became Revā in later ages. It rises in Amarkantak.

The Narmadā is associated with Śaryāta Mānava, whose *ṛishi* is Chyavana Bhārgava, a protege of the Aśvins, mentioned in the Purāṇas to have founded the city of Kuśasthalī (*VP* IV. 1.20) in Gujarat that later became Dvārakā. The Rasā is most often mentioned in the hymns to the Aśvins. The Purāṇas relate the Narmadā with the Vedic kings Purukutsa and Trasadasyu, with Trasadasyu born of Narmadā (*VP* IV.3.7–13). Hence, the Vedic coastal region extended from the delta of the Indus and Sarasvatī to that of the Narmadā. Considering the enormous quantity of water then discharged into the region, it was probably a vast riverine delta like the Gaṅgā-Brahmaputra in the Sunderbans.

Eastern River Regions: Kāśī, Kośala and Videha

While the east of India (east of Sarasvatī) was not the central region of the Purus, it was known to them, and was central at an early period to the Ikshvākus, their main allies. Yamunā is commonly mentioned in the Vedas and the presence of the Vedic people there cannot be doubted. The issue is whether Yamunā was flowing into Sarasvatī or into Gaṅgā in Vedic times. This is still not clear but the shift probably occurred not long after Sudās.

Gaṅgā, east of Yamunā, is mentioned as the first of the rivers in the Vedic hymn to the rivers (*RV* X. 75.5), which indicates that it already had a great importance. It occurs under the name Gaṅgya in the hymns of Bhāradvāja (*RV* VI.45.31), described as having a wide girth. Another name of the river, Jāhñavī, occurs again relative to Bhāradvāja and to porpoises (there is a species of Gangetic porpoise; *RV* I.116.18–19). As the Bhāradvājas were old *ṛishis,* the acquaintance with the Gaṅgā must have been quite old. Jāhñavī (*RV* III.58.6) is also mentioned as an ancient homeland in the hymns of Viśvāmitra, seer of the Book III of the *Ṛigveda* who, according to the Purāṇas, ruled as a king on the Gaṅgā. While Gaṅgā is not the central or foremost of the Vedic rivers, it is still significant, with the Bharata rule extending down probably as far as Kāśī (Benares).

Some modern scholars insist that no rivers east of the Gaṅgā are mentioned in the *Ṛigveda,* but this is not the case. Sarayu (modern Gharghar which flows near Ayodhya) is mentioned several times as a great river. Sarayu occurs along with Indus and Sarasvatī as one of the seven great rivers, suggesting it had seven affluents (*RV* X.64.8–9), which proves that it was a river comparable in size to the other two. It is associated with purīsha (*sarayuḥ purīshaṇi, RV* V.53.9), another name for ocean, particularly the ocean of heaven (the eastern direction) and the origin of the rains. The Maruts specifically are monsoon gods and show how Purīsha is connected to the ocean and the rains.

> Maruts, you raise the water from the ocean (*samudra*) and filled with waters (*purīshiṇaḥ*) you make the rain.
>
> — Śyāvāśva Ātreya, *RV* V.55.5[18]

Purīsha also means marsh or swamp. In the ancient times, east of India was too marshy for cultivation and so was known by this name.

Gomatī, the name of the main river east of Sarayu, occurs in the *Ṛigveda* (*RV* V.61.19), though it appears to be a western river. That it might be an eastern river in some instances cannot be ruled out. Gargarā, as a river name, also given to the Sarayu or a nearby river, first occurs in the *Atharvaveda* (*AV* IV. 15.12). Sadānīrā, a river beyond the Sarayu, is mentioned in the Brāhmaṇas (*SB* I.4.1.14), suggesting an earlier knowledge of the Sarayu and other eastern rivers. The Sarayu marked the region of Kośala, while beyond the Sadānīrā was the land of Videha.

The Purāṇas place early descendants of Manu, like the Sudyumnas, in Utkala, Gaya and Vinata (*VP* IV. 1.12), or regions of south Bihar and Orissa. It is possible that at an early time there were related cultures to the Vedic in east India as far as Orissa, while areas of the Gaṅgā and Brahmaputra rivers in Bengal and Assam were too marshy and largely uninhabitable. Kaliṅga appears as an old kingdom in the *Mahābhārata* as one of the early Purus marries a princess from that region (*Mbh.*, Ādi Parva 95). Such an Orissa kingdom, like the Yādava kingdoms of Gujarat and Maharashtra areas may represent very old civilizations in India.

The Geography of Soma

The geography of the Vedic period can also be understood relative to Soma and its vast symbolism. Soma, like the other Vedic gods, reflects the view of a great land from the mountains to the sea, centred on the Sarasvatī River. Soma is a mountain god and an ocean god as well as the king of the rivers. He represents the forces of water, the plant kingdom and the powers of fertility in the area as a whole. He is connected to lakes. He gives the wealth of four oceans.[19] This suggests the eastern, western and southern oceans with the mountain lakes of the north as the fourth.

The Indra-Vṛitra story similarly reflects the climate and geography of the region, with Vṛitra also signifying a glacier. There were many more glaciers in the Himalayas at that time. They melted and re-formed in winter, gradually feeding the great rivers of north India. This is probably why we have the story of the periodic slaying of Vṛitra by Indra. The rise of temperature that ended the Ice Age gave rise to the monsoon climate. Thus Indra is associated with the clouds—as the rain god. Indra is also the main Soma drinker; so Soma should be found in regions of Indra or regions of the monsoon.

Soma dwells in the waters (*RV* I.23.20). It is contained in various plants (*RV* X.97.7). It grows in the mountains. It is sacred to all the Gods, particularly to Indra, Vāyu, Agni and the Aśvins. The main sacred Soma lands in the *Ṛigveda* are called Sushomā, Ārjīkīyā, Śaryaṇāvat and Pastyāvat.[20] We have noted that Sushomā and Ārjīkyā in the Vedic river hymn (*RV* X.75.5) occur in Kashmir or nearby in the Himalayas not far from the Vitastā River.

Pastyā is identified with Aditi and perhaps the name of the river (*RV* V.55.3). Pastyā is the place of Aditi (*RV* VIII.26.5) in a hymn of Manu. Aditi is mentioned along with the term river (*sindhu*) in the last verse of the hymns of Kutsa.[21] Given Aditi's role as the great Mother Goddess of the Vedic Gods and people, we can identify her as the river Sarasvatī or the nearby Parushṇī, with which Aditi is also identified (*RV* VII.18.8).

Śaryaṇāvat—which is probably the main Soma region—is identified in the *Jaiminīya Brāhmaṇa*[22] with a lake in Kurukshetra district sacred to the Aśvins and the *ṛishi* Dadhyach who taught through the horse's head. The *Ṛigveda* similarly connects Śaryaṇāvat with Dadhyach, the son of Atharva and with the horse's head.

> Indra with the bones of Dadhyach slew ninety-nine resistless Vṛitras. When he was seeking the head of the horse hidden in the mountains, he found it at Śaryaṇāvat.
> —Gotama Rāhūgaṇa, *RV* I.84.13-14[23]

Śaryaṇāvat is associated with the place where Indra defeated Vṛitra (*RV* IX.113.1), symbol of both glacier and cloud. Śaryaṇāvat in the *Ṛigveda* occurs as a great place of mountains.[24]

Reflecting the same information in the Brāhmaṇas, the *Mahābhārata* (*Mbh.*, Vana Parva 83.185-187) mentions a special *tīrtha* or holy place related to Dadhyach in Kurukshetra, where the greatest of the Vedic sages, Aṅgīras, father of the Aṅgīrasa *ṛishis,* was born. It is next to Soma *tīrtha,* a sacred Soma site.

> The Pilgrim, then, O King, bathing in the *tīrtha* of Soma, obtaineth, without doubt, the region of Soma. One should next proceed, O virtuous one, to the most sacred *tīrtha* of the illustrious Dādhīcha, that sanctifying *tīrtha* which is celebrated over the whole world. It is here that Aṅgīras, the ocean of ascetic austerities belonging to the Sārasvata race, was born.[25]

This place of Soma and Dadhyach is in the northern region of Kurukshetra, so not far removed from the mountains. It must refer, therefore, to the upper region of the Sarasvatī and the nearby Himalayas.

Soma is associated with Heaven (*svarga*) as the legendary drink of immorality, the ambrosia (*amṛit)* of the gods who dwell in Heaven. Sarasvatī is connected to Soma (*RV* IX.67.32). In the *Pañchavimśa Brāhmaṇa,* Heaven (*svarga*) was reached by following the Sarasvatī back from its place of disappearance in the desert to its source in a spring where there was a sacred fig tree, a region called Plāksha Prāsravaṇa. This was said to be a forty-four day journey by horse, and was not far from the Yamunā (*PB* XXV.10.16, 23). The journey was equal to the distance between Earth and Heaven (*svarga*). *Jaiminīya Brāhmaṇa* refers to Sarasvatī as speech and Plāksha Prāsravaṇa as Heaven (*JB* II.297-298). It speaks of the sage Uśanas going to *svarga* or heaven on the Yamunā (*JB* III.150). Soma is connected with the Aśvattha or sacred fig (Plāksha) tree that dwells in the third heaven, which is in the region of Manu's ship's descent and is connected to the Ikshavākus (*AV* XIX.39.6-9).

In the *Ṛigveda,* Śaryaṇāvat is associated with heaven[26] and with Vivasvān, father of Manu and Yama. A Soma hymn by the great *ṛishi* Kaśyapa speaks of Śaryaṇāvat (*RV* IX.113.1), King Vaiśvasvata or Yama (IX.113.8) and heaven (IX.113.9). Most importantly, it refers to the Brahmin who recites the language of *Chhandas,* the name of Vedic Sanskrit.[27] This suggests the connection of Śaryaṇāvat, the Himalayan heavenly regions, Sarasvatī and the origins of the Vedic language.

In my earlier book, *Gods, Sages and Kings,* I identified Śaryaṇāvat with Lake Manasarovar in Tibet, which is the source of the Sindhu, Sarasvatī (Sutlej) and Sarayu rivers of Vedic fame. Yet, while Lake Manasarovar was perhaps the ultimate Soma lake and source of the Sarasvatī, the lakes in Kurukshetra and those in Kashmir were important Soma areas as well. Soma referred to plants growing in the lakes of north and perhaps central India. However, it appears that the main Soma lakes were those in the Sarasvatī region, which probably existed even before the river began to dry up.

This may also explain why Soma disappeared. Soma was mainly a plant cult of the Sarasvatī area and the Sarasvatī-based Vedic religion. When the glaciers had largely melted and the Sarasvatī stopped flowing, most of the Soma lakes and the areas of Soma worship also disappeared or shifted.

It cannot be a coincidence that the loss of Soma in the Vedic religion and the demise of the Sarasvatī River went together and occurred about the same time! The loss of the Soma plant and the loss of the Sarasvatī River reflect the same geological, climatic and cultural changes at the end of the Vedic age! Vinaśana Soma and Vinaśana Sarasvatī represent the same phenomenon! That

Sarasvatī and Soma lost their earthy counterparts and became mythological in later texts shows their close connection.

In any case, Soma is pressed (extracted) in the region of the Purus[28] as well as in Śaryaṇāvat, Sushomā and Ārjīkīyā (*RV* VIII. 64, 10-11). It is pressed both in regions beyond as well as in regions nearby (*RV* VIII. 93.6). It is pressed among all the five Vedic peoples,[29] showing that it was widely available throughout the country both in nearby and distant regions, probably not merely as a single plant but as a plant juice mixture and a ritualistic part of the Vedic religion.

Later Soma Mountain Regions

According to Suśruta, the great Āyurvedic teacher, Soma grows in all the mountaineous regions of India. However, the main Soma lands are Kashmir, particularly its lake, and beyond it across on the Indus in the mountains, the regions of Gilgit and Ladakh. These Somas are named after the metres of the Vedic hymns, showing their special importance in the Vedic ritual.

> In the Himalayas, Arbudas, Sahyas, Mahendras, Malayas, Śrīparvatas, Devagiris, Giris, Devasahas, Pāriyātras, Vindhyas, Devasundas and Hladas (lakes) are the inhabitants of the Soma plants.
>
> Somas of the best kind, the Chandramaḥ species, are often found to be floating here and there on the mighty stream of the river Sindhu, which flows down at the foot of five large mountains beyond the north bank of the Vitastā River. The Muñjavat and the Aṁśumat species may also be found in the same region, while those known as the Gāyatri, Traishṭubha, Paṅkta, Jagata, Śaṅkara, and other looking as beautiful as the Moon are found to float on the surface of the divine lake known as the little Mānasa in Kashmir.
>
> —*Suśruta Saṁhitā*, Chikitsā Sthāna XXIX. 28-31[30]

However, we should remember that Suśruta is from the post-Sarasvatī era. That is why he does not mention the Sarasvatī as an important Soma region. This would make sense naming Somas after Vedic metres like Gāyatri. As Soma was named after Vedic metres, Sarasvatī as the Goddess of speech would be the name of the greatest Somas. By Suśruta's time, the Sarasvatī sources of Soma were long a thing of the past, just as the river had long since ceased to flow.

Muñja is a kind of reed, as is probably Aṁśumat. The *Atharvaveda* (*AV* V.22.5,7) relates Mujavat with Balkh, the region of Bactria in northern Afghanistan, where even today there is a Muñjan region in the Hindu Kush. It also (*AV* V.22.14) relates Mujavat with Gandhāra, or eastern Afghanistan. Mujavat is named in the *Ṛigveda* as a place of the Soma (Maujavata; *RV* X. 34.1) in the hymns of Kavasha Ailūsha. Kavasha is the *purohit* of Kuruśravas, the Kuru who took refuge in the mountain region of the Indus, and a late figure in the text. His era was one in which the Sarasvatī was already flowing through a desert, Probably as the Sarasvatī region dried up, more exotic and distant forms of Soma came to be sought as substitutes.

Therefore, the main Soma mountain land of the Vedic people is the Himalayas, which is the mountaineous region of Manu. While centred on the Sarasvatī, it also extended to regions north, west and east. Soma is both a Himalayan as well as an oceanic symbolism, reflecting the great subcontinent of India.

Southern Lands of Soma

Soma was not simply a plant of the northern mountains but part of a great symbology of the mountains to the sea that reflects the geography of north India as a whole. Ilā was the daughter of Manu, a flood figure from the south. The Bhṛigus, who are prominent in *Manu Smṛiti*, are *ṛishis* of the south. They are connected to Soma and their family, particularly famous ancient Bhṛigu seers like Kavi and Uśanas. They have many hymns in Book IX, the Soma book of the *Ṛigveda*. Specifically, the Bhṛigus are sons of Varuṇa, but Varuṇa and Soma are closely connected as deities of water. Soma also crosses the ocean as the Vast Truth (*ṛitam bṛihat*) of Vedic thinking,[31] suggesting that the Soma cult went beyond India, perhaps reaching Babylonia and Egypt.

In Purāṇic stories, Śukra of the Bhṛigus had the knowledge of immortality or rejuvenation—which is the knowledge of Soma—that Kacha, the son of Bṛihaspati seeks from him.[32] So the southern *ṛishis* are also connected to Soma. This suggests that both Vedic king and *ṛishi* traditions from the north and the south were intertwined from a very early period. Even Rāvaṇa went to the Himalayas to perform his austerities! This is not surprising. It is simply tracing the rivers of India from their entrance into the ocean back to their source in the mountains. The rivers were regarded as forms of Soma, carrying the Soma *rasa* of the Himalayas. Tracing the course of rivers was a great Vedic pilgrimage. Just as today we find south Indians having *āśramas* in the Himalayas and going there for pilgrimage, this was probably also the case in Vedic times, reflecting the sacred geography of the region. Similarly, the northern mountain and river people probably maintained trading communities along the coast in ancient times as they did later.

Besides the northern Soma lands were southern Soma regions by the sea like the famous site of Somnath in Gujarat. These were not as important for the Soma plant, which was mainly a mountain and lake herb, but were important for the Soma religion of which the plant was only one part.

Varuṇa, the God of the sea, is connected with Soma and regarded as the king of the Gods. Varuṇa is the father of the Bhṛigu *ṛishis*, a great Vedic family, who are called Varuṇas (*VP* II.4.39). Soma was the first one to perform the Rājasūya sacrifice for anointing kings and represents the first king. It is in oceanic form that Soma becomes king. The *Ṛigveda* states, "The Ocean roared in the original law, generating creatures as the king of the world (*RV* IX. 97.40)".[33]

When Manu and Ilā came north along with the Agni cult, a Soma cult and the Soma king tradition came with them.[34] In fact, Manu's daughter Ilā has lunar characteristics and is herself connected to Soma. Ilā means nourishing food, like Soma. As Manu is the sun, his counterpart is Soma or the moon. As Manu or the sun is the *ṛishi* or ascetic-seer, Soma or the moon is the king or king-seer. The whole concept of the lunar dynasty (*Chandra* or *Soma Vaṁśa*) may be dated back to Soma as Soma is also the moon. The Vedic tradition had moon kings of the south and west and sun kings of the north and east.

This is what convinces me that the Vedic Āryans moved from south-to-north in the pre-Ṛigvedic period. Otherwise, there is no way there could be so much oceanic symbolism throughout the *Ṛigveda*. If the Vedic people were from Afghanistan or other northern and western regions as some claim, they would not have acquired such familiarity and facility with maritime life. Vedic people perhaps took refuge in the Himalayas during a flood period, which explains their Himalayan connection, but they maintained a connection with the south. In addition, the Himalayas were always the sacred mountains of the entire Indian subcontinent.

Indra and Varuṇa

We should remember that in the *Ṛigveda*, Indra is the *svarat* or self-ruler and Varuṇa is the *samrat* or emperor.[35] Indra's seat of power was more the Sarasvatī in the north. Varuṇa's seat of power was more the ocean in the south. The union of Indra and Varuṇa as the hymns of Vasishṭha (*RV* VII. 82-85) showed the union of the northern and southern kingdoms, or mountain and ocean regions. Varuṇa as the emperor symbolized the Vedic empire by the sea and perhaps across the sea. Indra as the self-ruler symbolized the spiritual seat of power in the north. Just as Varuṇa is connected to the Bhṛigus, Indra is connected with the Aṅgirasas who are his main companions in Ṛigvedic mythology. We see here again the north-south division and its integration. Indra's combination with Varuṇa is the unification of the northern Bharata region with the southern region of the Turvaśas and Yadus.

We find a similar symbolism in the *Mahābhārata* with the great cities of Indraprastha on the Yamunā to the north and Dvārakā on the ocean to the south. Indra and Varuṇa are reflected in Śiva and Vishṇu of later thought as fire and water deities. Kṛishṇa, from the land of the Yadus, reflects the Vishṇu-water symbolism. Arjuna was also regarded as an incarnation of Indra.

The Ārya Religion as the Soma Cult

The Soma cult pervades all the Vedic books. The Soma cult is a cult of all the Vedic people, like the fire ritual. Like Agni, all the thirty-three Vedic Gods dwell in Soma (*RV* IX. 92.4). All the Vedic Gods drink the Soma, which gives them power, particularly Indra who is the greatest of the Gods. The Vedic fathers, Pitara, or ancestors are connected to Soma.[36] That is why Book IX is considered to be the most important and best of all the books of the *Ṛigveda*. Soma is the king not only of the Kshatriyas but also of the Brahmins. He is the original Brahmin priest, the guide of the poets and the *ṛishi* among the sages (*RV* IX. 96.6).[37] He is the great maker of the *ṛishis* (*RV* IX. 96.18). He is the great world father (*RV* IX. 96.5).

The Soma Book IX contains some of the oldest hymns of the *Ṛigveda*, like those of the Rāhūgaṇa, father of Gotama and Uchathya, father of Dīrghatamas, as well as Kavi and Kaśyapa.[38] Therefore, we cannot make the Soma cult a peripheral or Iranian cult borrowed by the Vedic people, as Talageri has suggested.[39] It is one of the great pillars of Vedic culture from the very beginning. *Soma is an all-India cult that reflects the traditions and geography of the entire subcontinent, including not only the Himalayas to the north but also the ocean to the south. In fact, the Soma cult contains the worship of the ocean as well.*

The Soma cult connected the Vedic religion not only with the Himalayas but also with the ocean, with the entire course of the Himalayan rivers from the mountains to the sea. In the main Ṛigvedic myth, Indra slays the dragon Vṛitra and releases the seven rivers to flow into the sea. What Vṛitra holds is also Soma. Indra in slaying Vṛitra releases the Soma. In this regard, India or Āryavarta is the greater land of the Soma from the mountains to the sea.

The Agni-Indra cult was more a northern cult with its seat of power at the place of Ilā on the Sarasvatī. The Soma-Varuṇa cult was more a southern cult with its seat of power at Somnath or Dvārakā along the coast. But the two cults were intertwined, as were the two peoples. Soma also had its northern mountain forms and Agni also had his southern ocean forms.

The Soma Plant

As for the identity of the Soma plant—which is a subject of wide speculation—it was not simply one plant, though there may have been one primary Soma plant, but a plant mixture or simply the sacred use of plants. That is why Soma is mentioned relative to all the plants (*RV* X. 97.7) and why so many different types of Soma are mentioned. Water itself, particularly that of the Himalayan rivers, is a kind of Soma (*RV* VII. 49.4).

Some scholars emphasize *ephedra* as the main Soma and connect it with Afghanistan and Iran where *ephedra* is common. They note that *ephedra* was the main Soma plant of the Persians. First, we must note that *ephedra* also commonly grows in different places in India. Second, *ephedra,* which today is still called Somalatā, is a type of Soma but not the only type, nor does it resemble the characteristics of the Soma plant as described in the *Ṛigveda*. Nor can Soma, if it were an Iranian plant, explain the oceanic symbolism of Soma in the *Ṛigveda*. The *Ṛigveda* describes Soma as a watery plant, growing near water (*RV* VIII. 91.1) and as flowing with a milky juice gained by crushing the plant. *Ephedra*, on the other hand, is a dry plant that has almost no juice at all.

Nor is Soma the Amanita mushroom, as other scholars have claimed, though this also may have been another type of Soma. It is usually described with leaves, which mushrooms do not have. Śaryaṇāvat, the main Ṛigvedic Soma land, means 'abounding with reeds', with śara (*Śaccharum sara*) being a type of reed related to sugarcane. It was mainly used to make arrows and was also sacred to Agni. The later great Soma land of Muñjavat also means 'abounding with reeds' with muñja being a type of reed often regarded as the same plant as śara. This again shows Soma growing in marshy or aquatic areas and being some sort of reed.

The *Atharvaveda* (*AV* XI. 6.15) mentions five great plants of which Soma is the best, including marijuana, barley and darbha (kuśa or durva), showing that many plants had Soma-like qualities.[40] Here, Soma is again connected with another type of reed (darbha, *Saccharum cylindricum*), which could have easily been pressed to get their juice, much like sugarcane. Some is also connected with kushṭa (*Saussurea lappa*) and with the Aśvattha tree and grows in the Himalayas in the *Atharvaveda* (*AV* XIX. 39.5,6). It came in three forms, as cooked with grain or barley (*yava*), milk (*go*) or curds (*dadhi*).[41] It was often used with *ghee* and honey (*madhu*) as well.

The Somas were mainly special plants growing in mountain lakes and riverine regions. With the shifting of the rivers, this cult changed, but reverence for Himalayan plants and rivers remained a characteristic feature of the Hindu religion.

Uttara Kuru and Kashmir

Uttara Kuru is later a mythical land of the Gods. In the *Aitareya Brāhmaṇa* (*AB* viii. 14) it is the northern region of the Vedic people beyond the Himalayas. I would identify it as a mountain land of the Soma on the upper Indus and Himalayan regions. It extended from where the Indus flows out of the mountains in the west to Mount Kailāśa and Lake Manasarovar in the east, where the great Vedic rivers of Sindhu, Sarasvatī (Sutlej branch) and Sarayu originated, to the regions beyond. It perhaps included the Tarim Basin in China which was on the down slope of the trans-Himalayan range in which Kailāśa is located, which had ancient Āryan populations like the Tokharians.

Uttara Kuru appears as a general name for the mountain regions of the Himalayas and Tibet. The Tarim Basin of western China was where the Buddhists placed their ancient mythic holy land of Śamballa and where the Theosophists place the cradle of humanity. So, in the broadest sense, Uttara Kuru stands for the trans-Himalayan lands of Kashmir, western Tibet and western China. Some scholars would include Balkh (Bactria) and the Fergana valley above Samarkand into Uttara Kuru. These areas were part of this greater mountain region as well.

Kaśyapa *ṛishi* is associated with Kashmir, Kaśyapa Mīra or Kaśyapa's lake. He is also connected with the sun, as the eight or central Āditya that does not leave Mount Meru (*TA* I.7.20). This would connect him to Meru or Mount Kailāśa and with Manu or his father Vivasvan. The Buddha is said to have existed five thousand years before Śākyamuni was called Kaśyapa, suggesting Buddha as a Sun God, and associated with Śāmballa. Therefore, I would make Uttara Kuru as the greater Himalayan region, the mountain refuge land of Manu (symbolizing not a person but a culture) and also the original Ārya land of the Iranians (who forgot the earlier oceanic basis of Ārya culture).

Uttara Kuru was a holy land, a land of the Gods, not to be conquered. One Vedic king, Atyarāti Jānaṁtapi, tried to conquer it even against the wishes of his *purohit*, Satyahavya Vasishṭha, and because of that was defeated (*AB* viii. 24). Perhaps, he was a Pāñchāla and his defeat there aided in the return of the Kurus.

The Realms Beyond, Pārāvata

The *Ṛigveda* speaks of mysterious lands beyond, Pārāvata, not to be confused with Parvata, which means mountain. These are said to be three (*RV* VIII. 32.22), which are beyond the lands of the five Vedic peoples. There is even a Pārāvata Samudra or ocean beyond (*RV* VIII. 12.17). There are two oceans as Arvavat and Pārāvata (*RV* VIII.13.15) or two regions of that nature (*RV* VIII.82.1; VIII.97.4). In another verse, Pārāvata is contrasted with Sindhu, the Indus River or the ocean (*RV* X. 137.2) Soma is pressed in the regions of Arvavat, Pārāvata or Śaryaṇāvat (*RV* IX.65.22), meaning in nearby regions, far away regions or the region of Śaryaṇāvat. Agni shines across the supreme Pārāvata and its shore (*RV* X.187.2). While Pārāvata perhaps at times means the realm beyond or heaven, it appears to also mean earthly realms beyond, perhaps beyond the Himalayas, the mountains of heaven. It could refer to the sea or a large lake like the Aral Sea or Lake Baikal, or even the Caspian.

The Maruts appear in strange attire like people from the realms beyond, Pārāvatas (*RV* V.52.11). Sarasvatī is the destroyer of the Pārāvatas (*RV* VI.61.2). Elsewhere, the Pārāvatas are givers of gifts (*RV* VIII.34.18). They could be ancestors of the Scythians who had frequent contacts with Indians.

The Vedic Land and People: The *Ṛigveda*

The main *Ṛigveda* land was between the Sindhu in the west and the Sarayu in the east, with the Sarasvatī in the centre. These are the three times seven rivers of the *Ṛigveda* (X.64.8-9). It was marked by the Vindhya Mountains or Narmadā River to the south and to spread from the Arabian Sea (*Samudra*) in the west to the Bay of Bengal (*Purisha*) in the east. However, most of the Gaṅgā-Brahmaputra delta region, and much of the Gaṅgā valley east of Sarayu was a swamp or jungle (*Purisha*), which was not tamed until later in the Vedic period as in the stories of Sagara and Bhagīratha.

This is also the land of the Seven Rivers. Its boundary kingdoms were Gandhāra with the western affluents of the Sindhu to the north-west. Uttara Kuru or Kashmir and Ladakh into western Tibet and Kailāśa along with the northern branches of the Sindhu marked the north. Aṅga and Videha with the lower reaches of the Gaṅgā marked the east. Vidarbha across the Narmadā in Maharashtra marked the south, perhaps extending as afar as Kaliṅga (Orissa).

The Later *Vedas*

The *Atharvaveda* (*AV* IV. 16.3) speaks of two oceans as the flanks of Varuṇa, the ocean god. It also speaks of the rain (Māruts) that bring the rains from the ocean (*AV* IV.15.5) and the rain god, Parjanya, who brings the rain from the ocean (*AV* IV.15.12). Such ideas show knowledge of both the Arabian Sea and the Bay of Bengal.

The *Atharvaveda* has few geographical or river references. Yet, we can find mention of an area from Balkh (Afghanistan) to Bihar (Aṅga and Magadha) (*AV* V.22.7,14) and from the western to the eastern seas. This is similar to the land of the *Ṛigveda* but perhaps slightly larger. Again, it is quite an extensive area. The *Atharvaveda* does mention the Sarasvatī River (*AV* VI.30.1), as does the *Yajurveda*, which states that it is joined by five streams as a fivefold Sarasvatī (*SYB* 34.11). But the river does not have the same prominence in the later Vedas that it has in the *Ṛigveda*.

The Brāhmaṇas speak of kingdoms from Gandhāra in the west to Aṅga and Videha in the east, with Vidarbha in the south (*AB* vii.34). They refer to various peoples, particularly of the south and east, as fallen or disqualified Āryas, including those of Bengal (Puṇḍras), south India (Āndhra, Draviḍa) and Nepal (Kirāta) (*AB* vii. 18). The Brāhmaṇas mention the Sarasvatī but in several instances describe it flowing through the desert. This occurs relative to the story of Kavasha Ailūsha (*AB* ii. 19, *KB* xii, 3) which refers to his hymn to the Waters in the *Ṛigveda* (*RV* X.30). Kavasha is also connected with King Kuruśravas (*RV* X. 33.4).

The *Mahābhārata* knows the entire Indian subcontinent including Laṅkā, the Draviḍian Kingdoms (Cholas, Pāṇḍyas, Cheras), Prāgjyotish (Assam) and Balkh (Bactria), and various foreign people like Chīnas, Śakas, Hūṇas, and Yavanas. The *Rāmāyaṇa* knows a similar region. Bharata's sons Pushkala and Takshaka found Pushkalāvatī and Takshaśilā in the north-west. Rāma himself conquers south India and Laṅkā. The Purāṇas know these regions.

The Empire of Sudās and the Later Bharatas

Probably the land spoken of in the river hymn of Book X (*RV* X. 75) and in the hymns of Śyāvāśva Ātreya (*RV* V.52, V.53) is similar to that of the empire of Sudās. It extended from Gandhāra or eastern Afghanistan in the west, to Kashmir and Ladakh in the north. To the east it extended down the Gaṅgā as far as the Sarayu, if not to Videha and Aṅga. To the south-west it extended down the Indus and Sarasvatī rivers to the Arbian Sea in Sindh and Kachchh.

The Bharata land per se was marked by the Parushṇī (Ravi) in the west and the Gaṅgā in the east (extending perhaps as far as Kaśī). It extended down the Sarasvatī to the sea, which gave the Bharatas a strong sense of the ocean and a familiarity with ships and trade.

The Empire of Janamejaya and the Early Kurus

This is the region described in the *Aitareya Brāhmaṇa* (*AB* viii. 14). It is of Janamejaya long before the Mahābhārata War. Its central region is that of the Kurus, Pañchālas, Vaśas and Uśīnaras or a region from the Gaṅgā in the east to Vitastā (Jhelum) in the west. The central region is somewhat west of that of Sudās. Its western area probably extended not only to Gandhāra but also to additional parts of Afghanistan like Balkh, the Helmand or Harirud regions. Its northern area is that of the Uttara Kurus and Uttara Madras, presumably Kashmir, Baltistan, Gilgit and Ladakh and probably beyond into western China. Its eastern areas extended into Videha and Aṅga or into Bihar, while regions of Andhra Pradesh and Bengal were regarded as beyond its borders (*AB* vii. 18). Its southern or south-western area, related to the Satvats or the northern Yadus, would probably extend to Kachchh and Gujarat or all the Yadu regions, probably including Vidarbha (Maharashtra), which is known in the text.

This covers quite a large territory. It is a region similar to that of Sudās but extends further west and has knowledge of more eastern regions as well. This was the situation at the beginning of the Kuru dynasty many generations before the Mahābhārata War. The Sarasvatī was already in decline at this time. We are also not certain if the Bharatas still occupied the Sarasvatī all the way down to the sea because the Sarasvatī was already flowing into the desert.

Āryavarta in the *Manu Smṛiti*

Manu Smṛiti (*MS* II.17) describes the land of Brahmāvarta as that between the two divine rivers Sarasvatī and Dṛishadvatī, the Kurukshetra region. Next comes the land of the Brahmaṛishis, which includes the regions of the Kurus, Matsyas, Pañchālas and Śurasenakas (*MS* II. 18). This would include the regions south to Mathura, the city of the Śurasenas, and east to the upper Gaṅgā, the region of the Pañchālas at that time.

Then it describes the Middle Region or Madhya Deśa as between the Vinaśana or place of disappearance of the Sarasvatī on the west and Prayaga (modern Allahabad) on the confluence of the Gaṅgā and Yamunā to the east and between the Himalayas and the Vindhya Mountains (*MS* II.21). This middle region was probably the land dominated by the Puru-Bharatas. It extended from Allahabad (Prayāga) in the east to region around Anupgarh to the west. It shows the gradual relocation from the Sarasvatī to the Gaṅgā.

Lastly, it describes Āryavarta as the region between the eastern and western oceans and also between the Himalayas and the Vindhya Mountains (*MS* II. 22). This would include Punjab and Sindh to the west and such regions as Kaśi, Kośala, Videha, Aṅga, Magadha and Vaṅga to the east.

Such a statement reflects a movement of the middle region to the east. Though the old sacred land of Sarasvatī-Dṛishadvati is mentioned, it marked the west of Madhya Deśa, not the centre as was earlier the case. This is probably the situation at the time of the Mahābhārata War, by which time there was already a shifting east from the drying up Sarasvatī. The Bharatas were no longer on the lower regions of the Sarasvatī. Their main sites of habitation were on the Gaṅgā and Yamunā.

Later in the Purāṇas the middle region was between the Gaṅgā and Yanunā or even Gaṅgā and Gandhak, with the Sarasvatī being a peripheral western region.

Other Regions

Ancient India and its surrounding regions had other kingdoms besides the Vedic Bharatas, though generally related to it. An Iranian kingdom began in Balkh, as well as other Āryan cultures in the regions of West and Central Asia. Kingdoms of Śakas, Persians, Medes, Parthians, Armenians and Greeks occurred in this area for many centuries, some extending back into Vedic times.

Central India had a culture of the Yādavas centred on the Narmadā that was at the fringes of the Vedic world. While there are many stories of Ikshvākus defeating the Yadus, it is clear that the Yadus continued and dominated a large region of central India, an area larger than the Bharata-Ikshvāku people to the north. In fact, one could argue that although the Bharata-Ikshvāku people were the dominant people of India in terms of culture, the Yadus were the dominant people militarily. They were connected to Rākśasa kingdoms to the south.

East India had a culture in Bihar and Orissa, Gaya and Kaliṅga, that was quite old, probably older than the Vedic Aṅga and Videha kingdoms to the north, and older than any

Bengal culture. This was the Sudyumna culture of the Purāṇas (*VP* IV. 1.11-12), related back to Manu. Later, the Anus were said to have come to this region and formed their own kingdoms (*VP* IV. 18.1-2). A Vedic type of culture began in Andhra Pradesh to the south by the time of the *Aitareya Brāhmaṇa* (*AB* vii. 18), if not earlier credited to the descendants of Viśvamitra.

We should not forget that such groups had their own seers, kings and cultures that were only similar to the Vedic but also different. The Vedic Bharata rule did not cover all of India, though it had a wide influence on the subcontinent. It was mainly involved with the region from the Sarayu to the Sindhu in the north and the great Sarasvatī River in the centre. Naturally, such a large subcontinent would have many local variations of cultures as did ancient Europe or the Middle East.

Such different groups may have had their own Vedas with a similar division of *Ṛig, Yajur, Sāma* and *Atharva,* Brāhmaṇas and Upanishads, or variations on these, just as the Celtic Druids had similar traditions. The Vyāsa-Bharata Vedas that have been preserved may be more typical of such ancient texts than unique or exhaustive of them. The Vyāsa Veda is only one such compilation of similar ancient teachings, which had many variations among them. However, we should recognize that the Vedic deities, the Vedic ritual, and the Vedic yoga and *ṛishi* culture were much older than the *Ṛigveda* and accepted by many other groups other than the Purus.

The Śānti Parva of the *Mahābhārata* mentions numerous versions and branches of the Vedas. One of Vyāsa's goals was to put a stop to this uncontrolled proliferation by producing a 'standard' version. That he was not entirely successful is clear from the fact that Tittīri and Yājñavalkya came out with two competing versions of the *Yajurveda*. Only the *Ṛigveda* has escaped this fate with only two recensions that vary hardly at all (Baśkalya and Śakalya), probably because the text was already quite old and had already been formalized long before Vyāsa.

Among Indo-European groups like the Hindus, Persians, Greeks and Celts, we find similar tradition of religion, philosophy, ritual, astronomy and medicine. They had similar Upanishadic type philosophies, similar temple and fire worship, similar calendars and astronomical observations, and similar bardic, poetic and mythic tradition. Perhaps, they all had originally their own Veda or some portion of the eternal Veda. Their cultures are all probably quite older than we think. Ārya type kingdoms may have occurred from Europe to Central Asia by the time of the Ṛigvedic Bharatas. Related cultures also spread south and east to Indonesia.

Notes and References

1. *RV* I.35.8, *ashṭo vyākhyat kakubhaḥ pṛithivyās trī dhanva yojanā sapta sindhūn*
2. *RV* I.164.42; IX.33.6; X.47.20
3. *RV* I.161.14: VI.50.13; VI.72.3; VII.70.2; VIII.20.25; IX.80.1
4. *ā antād a parārdhāt pṛithvyai samudraparyantāyā ekarāḷiti*
5. *samudra iva bhūmim*
6. *RV* I.32.12; I.34.8; I.35.8; I.71.7; I.102.2; I.141.2; I.164.3; I.191.14; II.12.3; III.1.4; IV.28.1; V.43.1; VI.61.10; VII.7.6; VII.18.24; VII.67.8; VIII.24.27; VIII.41.2.9; VIII.54.4; VIII.69.12; VIII.96.1; IX.54.2; IX.66.6; IX.86.21.36; IX.92.4; X.13.5; X.43.3; X.49.9; X.64.8; X.67.12; X.104.8
7. *RV* VI.45.31; V.53.9; X.61.9
8. *RV* VI.61; VII.95; VII.96
9. *RV* II.41.16, *ambitame nadītame devītame sarasvatī*

10. *RV* VII.36.6, *sarasvatī saptathī sindhumātā*
11. *RV* VI.52.6, *sarasvatī sindhubhiḥ pinvamānā*
12. *RV* I.3.12, *maho arṇaḥ sarasvatī*
13. *RV* VI.61.14, *mā tvat kshetrāṇyaraṇāni ganma*
14. *RV* X. 75-5-6, *imam me gaṅge yamne sarasvatī śutudri stomam sachatā parushṇyā; asiknyā marudvṛidhe vitastayā ārjīkīye sṛiṇuhyā sushomayā; trishṭāmayā prathamam yātave sajūḥ susartvā rasayā śvetyā tyā; tvam sindho kubhayā gomatīm krumum mehatnvā saratham yābhirīyase.*
15. *RV* VIII.5.37; VIII.6.48; VIII.46.22.
16. *JB* II.441, *eshā ha vai sā rasā yaishārvak samudrasya vāpāyatī.*
17. *JB* II.442, *te haite vidarbheshu sārameyā.*
18. *RV* V.55.5, *udīrayathā marutaḥ samudrato yūyam vṛishṭim varshayathā purīshiṇaḥ.*
19. *RV* IX.33.4, *rāyaḥ samudrāṁśchaturo asmabhyam soma viśvataḥ.*
20. *RV* I.84.14; VIII.6.39; VIII.7.29; VIII.64.11; IX.65.22-23; IX.113.1-2; X.35.2; X.75.5.
21. *RV* I.94-98; 100-106; 108-112.
22. *JB* III.64 *śaryaṇāvad dha nāmaitat kurukshetrasya jaghanārdhe saraskam.*
23. *RV* I.84.13-14. *Indro dadhīcho asthabhir vṛitrāṇyapatishkutaḥ jaghāna navatīrnava; ichchhannaśvasya yachchhiraḥ parvateshvapaśritam tad vidachchharyaṇāvati.*
24. *RV* X.35.1; *RV* I.84. 12-14.
25. *Mahābhārata*, Ganguli translation, Vana Parva, p. 182.
26. *RV* VIII.6.39, *mandasvā su svarṇara utendra śaryaṇāvati matsvā vivasvato maṭī.*
27. *RV*. IX.113.6, *yatra brahmā pavamāna chandasyām vācham vadat.*
28. *RV* VIII.64.10, *ayam te mānushe jane somaḥ pūrushu sūyate*
29. *RV* IX. 65.22-23, *ye somāsaḥ parāvati ye arvāvati sunvire ye vādaḥ śaryaṇāvati; ya ārjīkeshu kṛitvasu ye madhye pastyānām ye vā janeshu pañchasu*
30. Bhishagratna, K., *The Sushruta Saṁhitā*, Vol. II, pp. 537-538.
31. *RV* IX. 107.15, *tarat samudram pavamāna ūrmiṇā rājā deva ṛitam bṛihat; arshan mitrasya varuṇasya dharmaṇā pra hinvāna ṛitam bṛihat*
32. *Mbh.* Ādi Parva 76-77. It is perhaps this knowledge of immortality and rejuvenation that the Bhṛigus also gave to the ancient Egyptians and was the basis of their mummification techniques that used many tropical herbs and spices. Egypt like Bhṛigu India followed a Venusian calendar and approach. Venus was also the planet of rejuvenation.
33. *RV* IX. 97.40, *akrānt samudraḥ prathame vidharman janayan prajā bhuvanasya rājā.*
34. Note that there is also an ocean or *samudra* form of Agni as in *RV* VIII. 102.4, suggesting that the Agni cult had maritime connections as well. Elsewhere Agni is compared to a ship as in *RV* I.99.1.
35. *RV* VIII. 82.2. *samrāḷ anyaḥ svarāḷ anya uchyate vām mahāntāvindrāvaruṇā mahāvasū.*
36. *RV* X. 15.5, *upahūtāḥ pitāraḥ somyāso*
37. *RV* IX. 96.6, *brahmā devānām padavīḥ kavīnām ṛishir viprānām.*
38. Note our subsequent discussion of the seers of the *Ṛigveda*.
39. S.G. Talageri, *The Rig Veda: A Historical Analysis.*
40. *AV* XI, 6.15 *pañcha rājyāni vīrudhām somaśreshṭāni brūmaḥ; darbho bhaṅgo yavaḥ sahas te no muñchantvaṁhasaḥ*. The five great plants, of which Soma is the best, appear to be Soma, *darbha* (a kind of grass), *bhaṅga* (marijuana), *yava* (barley) and *sahas* (identity unknown).
41. *RV* II. 42,7, *gavāśiram yavāśiram; RV* IX. 63.15 *dadhyāśiraḥ*

5

वैदिक-हड़प्पा संस्कृति

धार्मिक वृक्ष अश्वत्थ

वेद कुमारी घई

हड़प्पा एवं मोहेंजोदड़ो से प्राप्त कई मुद्राओं पर एक देवमूर्ति दो फांग अश्वत्थ व.क्ष के भीतर खड़ी दिखाई गई है। मोहेंजोदड़ो की मुद्रा संख्या 430 में मुद्रा के उपरिभाग में दायें ओर एक पीपल का पेड़ व.क्षाकार आलवाल से उभर रहा है। इसके अन्दर बायीं ओर मुंह किये एक देवमूर्ति है। देवता के सिर पर त्रिशूलाकार श्र ङ्गमुकुट है जिसके नीचे सिर के पीछे क त्रिम चोटी लटक रही है। तीन पत्ते व.क्ष के दो फांग तने के बाहर की ओर निकले हुए हैं। लगता है कि व क्ष दो भागों में फट गया है और उसके भीतर से देवता प्रकट हो गया है। देवता के सामने एक भक्त या देवपुरोहित त्रिशूलाकार मुकुट और नकली चोटी धारण किये हाथ जोड़कर प्रार्थना कर रहा है। उसके घुटने के पास एक काष्ठपीठ है जिस पर कुछ बलि रखी है। उस देवपुरोहित के पीछे एक बकरा खड़ा है। मुद्रा के निचले भाग में सात मनुष्य बायीं ओर मुंह किये खड़े हैं। जान मार्शल तथा मेके, दोनों विद्वान् व क्ष के अन्दर की देवमूर्ति को तथा सात देवमूर्तियों को देवियां मानते हैं। जान मार्शल के मतानुसार तो मात देवी ही सिन्धुसभ्यता की परम देवता थी पर कुछ अन्य विद्वानों के अनुसार, जिनमें पुरातत्त्ववेता केदारनाथ शास्त्री सम्मिलित हैं, सिन्धु संस्क ति के देवगण में नर अंश प्रधान था। अश्वत्थ निवासी पुल्लिंग देवता परमदेवता था

इस 430 संख्या मुद्रा पर टिप्पणी करते हुए जान मार्शल लिखते हैं

> पीपल की शाखाओं में खड़ा देवता बहुत छोटा और बेढब बना हुआ है। परन्तु पुल्लिंग लक्षणों से हीन होने के कारण और इसलिये कि भारत में व क्षदेवता प्रायः स्त्रीलिंग हैं और देवदूतों की पंक्तिबद्ध सात मूर्तियां भी स्त्रीलिंग प्रतीत होती हैं, यही मान लेना ठीक है कि पीपल के अन्दर खड़ा देवता देव नहीं किन्तु देवी है। पंक्तिबद्ध नीचे खड़ी सात मूर्तियां भी स्त्रीलिंग प्रतीत होती हैं। नीचे खड़ी सात मूर्त्तियां भी मेरे विचार में प्रधान देवी की दासियां अथवा निम्न कोटि की सहायक देवियां हैं। उनके सिरों पर पंख के समान वस्तुएं शायद व क्ष की शाखायें हैं जैसा कि देवदार की पूजा के सम्बन्ध में काफिरीस्तान के लोग आज भी ऐसी शाखाओं को अपने सिरों पर पहनते हैं[1]

इसी विषय में मेके लिखते हैं "इसमें सन्देह नहीं कि यद्यपि व क्षाधिष्ठात देवता एक देवी है। उसके सामने प्रार्थना करने वाली मनुष्याक ति भी देवी ही प्रतीत होती है क्योंकि उसने प्रधान देवी के समान ही शिरोवेष्ठन पहना है। नीचे के

रिक्त स्थान में अंकित सात मानुषी मूर्त्तियां भी निम्नकोटि की देवियां ही हैं। सम्भवतः वे प्रधान देवी की पुत्रियां हैं''[2]

इस प्रकार इन दोनों विद्वानों के विचार में मुख्याधिष्ठात देवता, उपासक और सात मानुषीमूर्त्तियां सभी स्त्रियां हैं। केदारनाथ शास्त्री के मतानुसार वे सब पुरूष हैं। मार्शल ने इन्हें स्त्रीरूप मानने में दो कारण दिये हैं – प्रथम यह कि मूत्तियों के सिरों के पीछे लम्बी चोटियां हैं और दूसरा यह कि शरीर के अर्ध्वभाग में उन्होंने कोटनुमा वस्त्र पहना है। ये दोनों कारण समुचित नहीं। सिन्धु संस्क ति के देवगण और देवपुरोहित चोटी धारण करते थे। जिसे तिरछा कटा कोर माना जा रहा है वह तो पार्श्व शरीर का अधोभाग है। सिन्धुकालीन देवताओं के शरीर पर कहीं भी कोटनुमा कपड़ा नहीं मिलता। पुल्लिंग देव या तो नग्न होते हैं या केवल लंगोटधारी। देवी-मूर्त्तियां छोटा सा घाघरा पहने दिखाई देती हैं। सिन्धु संस्क ति के बहुत से देव अंशः नररूप और अंशतः पाक्षरूप दिखाई देते हैं। मोहेंजोदड़ो की मुद्रा संख्या 347 पर अंकित संकीर्ण देवता का उपरी भाग मानुषी, नीचे का विहंगाकार और पीठ मुंडहीन बाघ की है।

अश्वत्थ सिन्धु-सरस्वती निवासियों के परमोत्क ष्ट देवता का आयतन होने के कारण अति पवित्र पूज्य व क्ष था। *अथर्ववेद* उन्नीसवें काण्ड के उनतालीसवें मन्त्र में अश्वत्थ को देवसदन कहा है ''अश्वत्थो देवसदनः''। *ऋग्वेद* 10.97.5 में तथा *यजुर्वेद* 12.79 में भी इसी प्रकार कहा हैः–

अश्वत्थे वो निषदनं पर्णे वोक्सविष्क ता
गोभाज इत किलासथ यत् सनवथ पुरूषम्

अश्वत्थ में तुम्हारा बैठने का स्थान है और पत्ते पर तुम्हारा निवास है।

अथर्ववेद के त तीय काण्ड द्वितीय अनुवाक का छटा सूक्त अश्वत्थ का ही वर्णन तथा स्तुति प्रस्तुत करता है। इस सूक्त के आठों मन्त्रों का देवता अश्वत्थ है। अश्वत्थ व क्ष की शाखा से शत्रुओं को हटाने की बात आठवें मन्त्र में कही गई है।

प्रैणान्व क्षस्य शारवयाश्वत्थस्य नुदामें[3] अश्वत्थ से प्रार्थना की गई है कि वह व क्ष का नाश करने वाले इन्द्र, मित्र और वरूण से मित्रता करे तथा उन सब शत्रुओं का नाश करे जो प्रार्थक से द्वेष करता है।

प्रमान् प्रंसः परिजातो श्वत्थः रवदिरादधि।
स हन्तु शत्रून्मामकान् यानहं द्वेष्मि ये च माम
तानश्वत्थ निः श्र णीहि शत्रून्वैबाधदोधतः।
इन्द्रेण व त्रध्ना मेदी मित्रेण वरूणेन च।।[4]

अश्वत्थ के बारे में कहा है कि यह खादिर आदि दूसरे व क्षों में अपनी जड़े जमाकर प्रोहण करता है। यद्यापि प्रदीप्त करते समय जिन दो अरणियों का प्रयोग किया जाता है उनमें से ऊपर की अरणि अश्वत्थ की लकड़ी की होती है और नीचे की अरणि शमी की लकड़ी की होती है।

अश्वत्थ देवता को अंकित करने वाली मुद्रा (430 संख्यांक) के निचले भाग से सात मनुष्याक तियों को सात मरूत् माना जा सकता है। *ऋग्वेद* के आठवें मण्डल के छियानवें सूक्त में आठवें मन्त्र में 63 मरूतों का उल्लेख है। सायण इस मन्त्र पर भाष्य करते हुए लिखते हैं – षष्टि त्र्युत्तरसंख्याका मरूतः ते च तैत्तिरीयके ईद ङ् चान्याद ङ च इत्यादिना नवसु गणेषु सप्त सप्त प्रातिपार्दताः। अर्थात् सात सात मरूत् नौ गणों में कुल मिला कर 63 होते हैं। *अग्निपुराण* में सात गणों में सात सात कर के 49 मरूतों की चर्चा की गई है – शुक्रज्योतिश्च चित्रज्योतिश्च सप्तसप्तका देवगणा मारूतेषु गणेषु सप्त कपालेषु अग्नौ पुराणे च एत एव प्रसिद्धाः। सात शिरोगत प्राणों से युक्त आत्मा को वेद में मरूत्वान् शिशु कहा है।

सप्त क्षरन्ति शिशवे मरूत्वते

(*ऋग्वेद* 10.13.5. *अथर्ववेद* 7.57.2)

मरूत् इन्द्र के सैनिक हैं अतः इन्द्र को भी मरूत्वान् कहा है। *ऋग्वेद* के तीसरे मण्डल के सैंतालीसवें सूक्त में इन्द्र के सहायकों के रूप में मरूतों का वर्णन है जिन्होंने व त्रहनन में तथा शम्बर वध में इन्द्र की सहायता की। प्रथम मण्डल

के एकसौ चौदहवें सूक्त में रूद्र कों मरूतों का पिता बताया गया है।

इदं पित्रे मरूतामुच्यते वचः स्वादोः स्वादीयो रूद्राय वर्धनाम्

(ऋ.1.114.6)

मुद्रा संख्यांक 387 से प्रतीत होता है कि अश्वत्थ और एकश्र ंग दोनों अश्वत्थ निवासी प्रधान देवता के प्रतीक थे। अश्वत्थ देवता का आयतन था और एकश्र ंग उसके आयतन का संरक्षक था। मुद्रा संख्याक 387 पर उपरिभाग में अश्वत्थ व क्ष है तथा निम्नभाग में दो एकश्र ंग हैं। मुद्रा संख्यांक 430 पर अंकित महिषमुण्ड का मुकुट अश्वत्थ निवासी महादेव के दोनों चित्रों का समन्वय है। मेके को चन्हुदड़ो से पक्की मिटट्ी की मुद्राछाप मिली थी। इस मुद्रा पर दो देवपुरोहित आमने सामने खड़े होकर एक हाथ से श्र ंगमय अश्वत्थ को थामे हुए हैं जबकि दूसरा हाथ कटि पर रखे हुए हैं।[5] मेके को न तो इस अभिप्राय का पता लगा और न ही उन्होंने पीपल की टहनियों के नीचे भैंसे के सींगों को पहचाना। यह सींग और पीपल का अभिप्राय महिषमुण्ड देवता के मुकुट से भी काफी साम्य रखता है। केदारनाथ शास्त्री का मत है कि अश्वत्थ निवासी देवता सिन्धुकालीन देवगन में सर्वोच्च देवता था और महिषमुण्ड देवता जिसका मुकुट अश्वत्थ और एकश्र ंग दोनों चिन्हों का समन्वय है उस सर्वोच्च देव से निम्नकोटि का देवता था।[6] उनके विचार से सिन्धु संस्क ति काल में अश्वत्थ देवता का वैसा ही स्थान रहा होगा जैसा कि वैदिक और पौराणिक काल में प्रजापति अथवा ब्रहमा का था। श्री क ष्ण ने *भगवद्गीता* में अपनी विभूतियों के प्रसंग में कहा है कि व क्षों में मैं अश्वत्थ व क्ष हूँ "अश्वत्थः सर्वव क्षाणाम्"[7]। आज भी भारत में पीपल या अश्वत्थ व क्ष को पूजनीय माना जाता है। कोई भी जानबूझ कर इस अश्वत्थ व क्ष को नहीं काटता। हिन्दु इस व क्ष को जल से सींचने में प्रण्य मानते हैं इसकी परिक्रमा करते हैं तथा धागे से इसके तने को लपेटते हैं। इस पर सिन्दूर का लेप करते हैं। स्त्रियां पुत्र प्राप्ति के लिए इस व क्ष का पूजन करती हैं। पीपल की शाखाओं से जलपात्र भी बांधा जाता है ताकि पितरों को त प्त किया जा सके। किसी की म त्यु होने पर उसका पुत्र या निकट सम्बन्धी कई दिनों तक इस व क्ष पर जल चढ़ाते हैं। पीपल के व क्ष के नीचे खड़े होकर लोग असत्य नहीं बोलते। इस प्रकार भारतीय संस्क ति में अश्वत्थ या पीपल का महत्त्वपूर्ण स्थान रहा है और यह परम्परा सिन्धुकाल से चली आ रही है। ब्रहमतरू होने के कारण अश्वत्थ को जानतरू और स ष्टितरू माना जाता है और सिन्धु निवासी भी इसे जानतरू स ष्टितरू मानते थे। उनका विश्वास था कि पीपल के शिखण्डधारी को अपने सिर पर धारण करने से शिखण्डधारी व्यक्ति यथार्थ ज्ञान का अधिकारी बन जाता है परन्तु यह अधिकार देवताओं को ही प्राप्त था। प्राचीन सुमेरियन देवताओं के मुकुटों में वमक षम के सींगों के बीच देवता द्रुभ की मंगलमय शाखा दिखाई देती है। सम्भवतः देवद्रभ शाखा शिखण्ड का यह अभिप्राय सुमेरियन लोगों ने सिन्धु लोगों से लिया था। मेसोपोटेमिया में यह शाखा शिखण्ड कुछ समय के लिए प्रकट होता है फिर उत्तर काल में लुप्त हो जाता है। सिन्धु सभ्यता में यह विशेषता इसके दीर्ध जीवन काल में निरन्तर दिखाई देती है। इसलिए लगता है कि यह कल्पना सर्वप्रथम भारत में उत्पन्न हुई।

पूर्ण विकसित सिन्धु सरस्वती सभ्यता जो हड़प्पा मोहेंजोदड़ो के अवशेषों में मिलती है, उसके विकास की विभिन्न अवस्थाओं के अवशेष बोलान दर्रे के मेहरगढ़, नौशारो, पेशावर के पास लेवन, कोट दिज़ी और हिसार के निकट कुनाल से प्राप्त हुए हैं। इन स्थानों की खुदाइयों के अवशेषों में लाल मिटट्ी के पात्रों पर पीपल के पत्तों तथा सींग का अभिप्राय अंकित है जिससे यह प्रतीत होता है कि अश्वत्थ पूजा अत्यन्त प्राचीन संस्क ति का अवेशष है। बी अलचिन तथा आर अलचिन ने 1977–78 में लेवन की खुदाई में प्राप्त इस अभिप्राय क विषय में लिखा था –

यह स्पष्ट रूप से प्रकट होता है कि यह स्थान प्रारम्भिक समय से विशाल सिन्धु सभ्यता का भाग था जिसमें ये प्रतीक विद्यमान थे जो बाद में पूर्ण विकसित सिन्धु सभ्यता के सभी भागों में प्रचलित रहे। इस प्रकार सींग और पीपल के पत्तों का अभिप्राय लेवन में भी उन्हीं धार्मिक विश्वासों को सूचित करता है जो कोट दिजी में और बाद में मोंहजोदड़ो में मिलते हैं।"[8]

Notes and References

1. मार्शल, जान, *मोंहेंजोदड़ो एण्ड द इण्डस सिविलाइज़ेशन*, पष्ठ 64-65.
2. मेके, *फर्दर एक्सकेवेशन्स एट मोंहेंजोदड़ो*, ग्रन्थ 1. पष्ठ 338 श्री के.ना.क त. "सिन्धु सभ्यता का आदि केन्द्र हड़प्पा से उद्धत", पष्ठ 87.
3. *अथर्व* 3.2.6.8;
4. 3.2.6.1-2.
5. मेके, *चन्हुदडो एक्सकेवेशन्स*, ग्र. 2. फलक 52 मुद्रा 36.
6. केदारनाथ शास्त्री, "सिन्धुसभ्यता का आदिकेन्द्र हड़प्पा", प. 89
7. *भगवद्‌गीता*, 10.26
8. एस पी गुप्त, *इण्डस–सरस्वती सिविलाइज़ेशन* प. 34 पर बी अलचिन और आर अलचिन, लिखित लेख लेवन–ए स्टोन टूल फैक्टरी ऑफ फोर्थ टू थर्ड मिलेनियम बी.सी'' हडप्पन सिविलाइज़ेशन पष्ट 521–554 से उद्धत।
   एस खत्री तथा आचार्य द्वारा कुनाल (हिसार के निकट) से प्राप्त तथा बी बी लाल और बी के थापर द्वारा कालीबंगन (उत्तरी राजस्थान) से प्राप्त लाल मिटट्टी के पात्रों पर भी यही अभिप्राय प्राप्त हुए हैं। एस पी गुप्त वही पष्ट 64 तथा पष्ट 72.

6

The Sarasvatī and the Homeland of Early Ṛigvedic *Rishis*

In the Light of Recent Scientific Researches

S.P. Gupta

In Indian historical writings, unfortunately, it was taken for granted that those who composed the Ṛigvedic hymns belonged to a definitive group of people forming a single ethnic entity bound by kinship and language and that the region where the early hymns of the *Ṛigveda* were composed had covered an area from eastern Iran to Afghanistan; it was only in the later times that these people moved into the Land of Seven Rivers, i.e. mainly Punjab.[1]

The *Ṛigveda*: A New Religious Order

To me, the Ṛigvedic hymns represent only a new and growing religious and philosophical system, adding to and enlarging its base to cover many beliefs in supernatural, godheads, rituals, etc., and not a particular group of people. Similarly, the early hymns of the *Ṛigveda* were composed in *Brahmāvarta,* the land between Sarasvatī and Dṛishadvatī and not in eastern Iran or Afghanistan.

To begin with, the hymns were not the compositions of a single person but a group of ten priestly families and several individuals, all called *ṛishis.* They shared a common approach to human life in relation to the universe. The hymns, devoted to Agni, Soma, Indra and others, kept on growing in number, over a long period of time, covering several generations of these *ṛishis,* such as those of the Kaṇvas, Viśvamitras, Aṅgīrasas, Bhṛigus, Kaśyapas, and others, as well as their sons and the pupils. Each *ṛishi* composed the hymns or *sūktas* separately. Some of these hymns, 1,028 of them, were then collected at one place and called *Ṛik Saṁhitā,* which was divided in ten books or *maṇḍalas.* Each hymn had several verses or *mantras,* the total number of which comes to 10,552. This is also called *Ṛigveda.*

The composers of the early hymns of the *Ṛigveda* seem to have belonged to different ethnic groups, speaking, perhaps, different dialects. For example, in *maṇḍalas* II, III, V, VI and VIII it is repeatedly mentioned that there were at least five major groups of people *(Pañcha Janas* III. 37.9) besides many others who lived in the Sarasvatī valley, polished the dialects and turned them into a language, called 'Vedic Sanskrit'. It is in this language that the hymns were composed but this language has several words of the old dialects also.

The *Ṛigveda,* according to one analysis, belongs to four different periods—the oldest is Maṇḍala VI followed chronologically by Maṇḍalas III, VII and a part of I. To the third phase belong the Maṇḍalas IV, II and a part of I. To the fourth phase belong V, VIII, IX and a part of I. Maṇḍala X is the latest edition with several old and new hymns. However, broadly speaking, according to another analysis, Maṇḍalas II, III, IV, V, VI and VII belong to Early Period while Maṇḍalas I, VIII, IX and X belong to Later Period.[2]

The Sarasvatī

As far as the river Sarasvatī, is concerned, medievalists like Irfan Habib[3] have recently questioned the very existence of this Ṛigvedic river. According to Habib it has always been, as it is this day, a small and 'petty' stream, locally called 'Sarsuti'. It has always been a rain-fed river which covered a very short distance in the north-east Haryana in the Yamuna Nagar District and a little beyond it, towards the south, but certainly not beyond Sirsa. According to him there is absolutely no truth in the claim that at one point of time it reached the sea and that it was a perennial river. According to him Ghaggar, an important river of Haryana, never joined the Sarasvatī. For him the Satluj had also nothing to do with the Sarasvatī System. He says that the identification of the Dṛishadvatī with the Chautang is a myth. One has to appreciate his zeal to negate everything which has been said during the last one hundred and more years even by explorers, excavators, geologists, climatologists and Remote-Sensing scientists, leave aside archaeologists, all of whom have joined Hindu forces, according to him.

The impression that he is trying to create in the minds of the people is that the theory of the Sarasvatī-Ghaggar-Hakra identity is the recent creation of the pro-Hindu forces in the academics. This, to say the least, is malicious propaganda simply because for more than a hundred years this equation has been established on very cogent grounds—historically, geologically, linguistically, hydrologically and archaeologically. C.F. Oldham (1874 and 1893), Aurel Stein (1942) and many others worked it out even before the country was divided or the RSS and VHP were born, and by those who were neither Hindus nor Muslims.[4]

In any case, the fundamental issue is whether literature and tradition can be verified by archaeological methods supported by methods of pure sciences? Habib says 'no' while I say 'yes'. I have examples from many parts of the world. The classic example is that of the Holy Land Archaeology in which the traditions of the Bible have been verified by archaeology and other sciences at sites like Jericho.

Scientific Investigations

I would like here to give an overview of the scientific investigations conducted in India on the Sarasvatī in order to show that negation of facts of history, literature, archaeology, geology, palaeo-climatology and the results of Landsat Imagery produced by Yashpal *et al.* is intentional. Otherwise, it is now a proven fact that the Sarasvatī emerged from the glaciers and ended up into the sea (Figs. 6.1 and 6.2).

In fact, it was the first use of images taken by the US Satellite Landsat and analyzed, by the most competent Indian space scientists to throw light on a long-standing historical problem connected with the Ṛigvedic rivers. These images clearly showed the signatures of several palaeo-channels to determine the truth of history. The attached map clearly shows these signatures (Fig. 6.3).

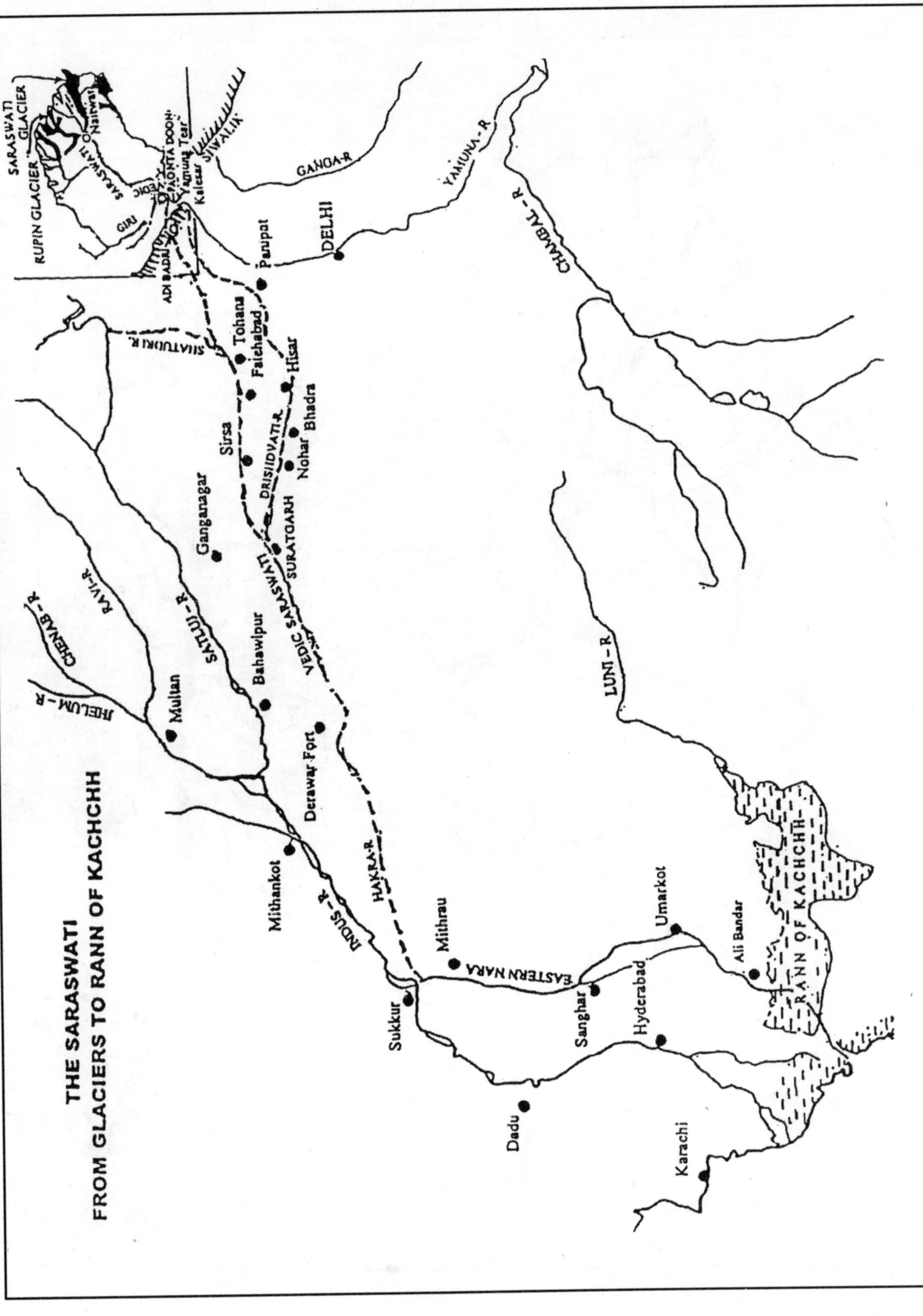

Fig. 6.1 The Course of the Vedic Sarasvatī from the Mountains to Sea.

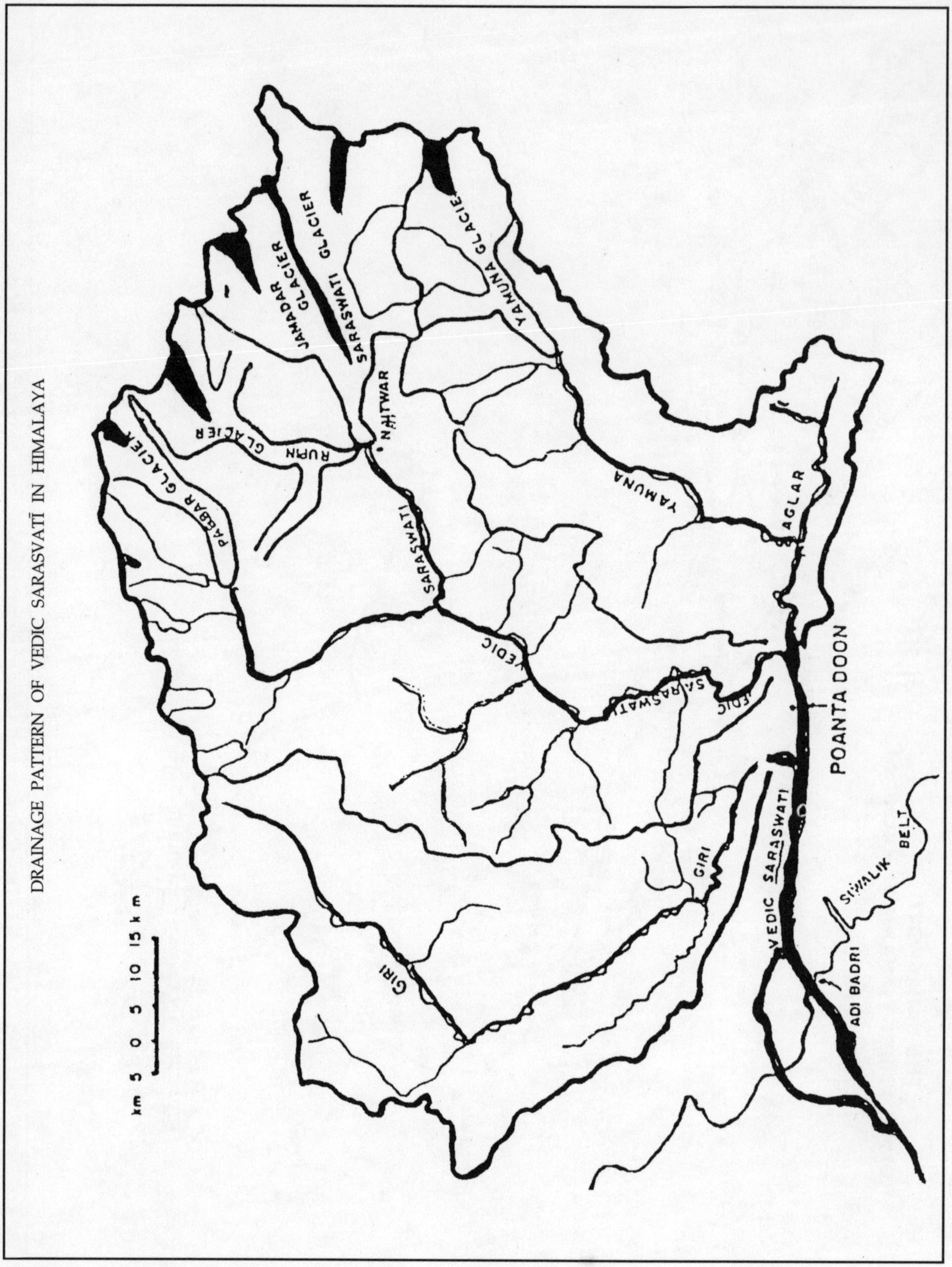

Fig. 6.2 The Source of the Sarasvatī – the Glacier of Garhwal (after Puri and Verma).

"There is overwhelming evidence from satellite imagery as well as hundreds of archaeological finds made during the last 7-8 decades that the Vedic Saravatī flowed from the Himalayas through the present Ghaggar-Hakra bed in Punjab, Haryana, Rajasthan, Bahawalpur (Pakistan) and then through the Nara bed in Sind (Pakistan), finally to debouch itself into the present Rann of Kachchh (Kutch). During the proto-historic period, the Sutlej flowed into the Ghaggar-Hakra bed in Punjab at one time, abandoning it in response to tectonic movements in the region and joining it again at other points in time in Bahawalpur State. The high concentration of Early Harappan, Harappan and Late Harappan sites along the Hakra palaeo-channels in Bahawalpur region confirms observations made by Stein (1942) that the Sutlej joined the Hakra at different times. It is highly probable that the Yamuna also was a tributary at the same time as the Sutluj or continued to be so even when vagaries of Sutlej led to abandonment of this bed. The Sarasvatī was finally abandoned by both the Sutlej and the Yamuna, the main perennial sources and literally left 'high and dry'." Observes Baldev Sahai, a leading member of Prof. Yashpal's team.[5]

The Ṛigvedic Rivers, the Nature of the Sarasvatī and Early Hymns of the *Ṛigveda*

In all there are around 25 rivers mentioned in the *Ṛigveda*. Of these the Sarasvatī has been mentioned 68 times (41 times in the early *maṇḍalas* and 27 times in the later *maṇḍalas*). The maximum number of times that the river has been mentioned is in Maṇḍala VI, the oldest *maṇḍala*.[6] It means that the early Ṛigvedic *ṛishis* lived on the Sarasvatī and composed the first ever hymns. It also means that the Sarasvatī was alive and not lost till then.

However, to begin with, the *Ṛigveda* as a whole presents a fairly good idea about the rivers of the region with which the Ṛigvedic people were familiar. In this context what is important to note is the sequence in which the rivers are mentioned in the *Ṛigveda*. In Maṇḍala X (X.75.5) these are mentioned in a sequence which runs from the east to the west. The names of the rivers start from the Gaṅgā in the east and end in the Indus in the west. The Sarasvatī has been placed between Yamunā and Satluj which are the living rivers in India even today. But, those like Kochhar (1997) and Sharma (1999) have been blinded by their Leftist ideology[7] and place the Sarasvatī in Afghanistan. B.B. Lal vehementally criticizing this theory observes that "in Afghanistan there are no rivers by the name of Yamunā and Sutlej, nor are there Dṛishadvatī and Āpayā. For this argument there is no reply whatsoever. Further, there is no sea in Afghanistan. So how can the Ṛigvedic Sarasvatī be placed there".[8]

Sarasvatī, it may be mentioned, has been described in the *Ṛigveda* as a mighty and huge river descending from the mountains with tempestuous roar (VII. 95.2). Midway it was breaking and carrying down ridges of hills like lotus stems (VI. 61.2). It is far superior to her companions (VII. 95.4) and surpasses all other streams by her sheer majesty (VII. 95.1) and glory (VI. 61.13). This river is fierce (VI. 61.13) and swiftest of the swifts (VI. 61.13). Which was it? The present-day 'Sarsuti' or the Old Sarsuti called 'Sarasvatī' in the Vedas? (See Appendix for the actual verses written in Devanāgarī script).

The Tributaries of the Sarasvatī

It may also be noted that in the *Ṛigveda*. (III.23.4) Dṛishadvatī was a major tributary of the Sarasvatī along with Āpayā which once flowed between the Sarasvatī and Dṛishadvatī. Geological and geomorphological studies show quite clearly that the Satluj was also once upon a time one of the most important tributaries of the Sarasvatī, bringing water from the Tibetan glaciers on perennial basis (the Satuj emerges from the Mansarovar lakes) though not acceptable to medievalist Habib. In other words, the Sarasvatī of the Vedas was indeed a large river with several tributaries which at one point of time brought a lot of water to the main stream round the year. One wonders as to why the medievalists are trying to impose the present and the medieval past on the ancient past if not for reasons of politics of history.

As mentioned above, the *Ṛigveda* says that the Sarasvatī was a mighty river emerging from the mountains and going to the seas (VII.95.2). All kinds of evidences put together shows that the Sarasvatī had originally emerged from the glaciers in the Garhwal region, north-east of the Paonta Doon area, as has been worked by V.K.M. Puri, former Director, Glaciology Division, in the Geological Survey of India, (G.S.I.) and B.C. Verma, another former Geologist in the G.S.I, working on the terraces of the Markanda-Sarasvatī Divide.[9] These glaciers are in the north-east Garhwal (Fig. 6.2).

The Glaciers of Garhwal and the Ultimate Source of the Sarasvatī

The main glaciers in the Garhwal region are Yamunā Glacier, Jamadar Glacier, Rupin Glacier and Pabbar Glacier and the so-called 'Sarasvatī' Glacier. Of these, the Rupin Glacier and the 'Sarasvatī' Glacier are important since it is out of their waters that the Ṛigvedic Sarasvatī may have emerged. At the place called Naitwar, the glaciers formed the snowline, i.e. at this place the snow melted and became water. This water channel flowed towards south-west. The place where it touched the Shivaliks and made its way into the plains is called 'Adi Badri'. At a later date, due to the neo-tectonic movements, a huge land mass between Bata and Markanda river got uplifted due to which the water in the channel ran backwards till it reached the Yamunā Tear (Fig. 6.1) and made a new entry.

From the same Yamunā Tear, which is a natural gap in the Shivaliks caused by the tectonic movement, emerged another water-channel, called Dṛishadvatī (mod. Chitang or Chautang), which joined the combined channel of the Ghaggar, a rain-fed river (and not at all perennial as Habib would like us to believe), which emerged from the hills near Kalka, (Sirmur region 30° 04' N: 77° 12' E), and Sarsuti below Sirsa. In this context it may also be noted that this water channel was once upon a time joined by the great perennial river Satluj, slightly south of Ropar at Shatrana (25 km south-west of Patiala) in District Ambala although from around 2000 BC it started shifting towards the south-west, and presently it joins the Chenab. (Fig. 6.2). But Greek and Arab sources clearly state that up to AD 1200 it had not joined the Chenab. Before that the Satluj had joined the Hakra, same as Sarasvatī, between Sirsa and Patiala, but later at Kudawala (29° 33' N: 73° 52' E) through three Naiwals, all now in Pakistan, as M.R. Mughal[10] and Yashpal, Baldev Sahai *et al.* have shown (Figs. 6.3 and 6.4).

The Course of the Sarasvatī

Explorations conducted for more than a hundred years show that this Sarasvatī-Ghaggar channel (the *Saṅgam* or confluence took place near Rasula) passed through the deserts of Suratgarh and Hanumangarh in India and Marot and Derawar Fort in Bahawalpur region of Pakistan where it is generally called Hakra, Wahind, etc. Beyond that, for more than 150 km, this channel is presently completely covered under the shifting sands of Cholistan, a part of the Thar Desert. After this it is again found, through which now the Eastern Nara Canal, made by the Britishers, passes, almost parallel to the Indus. Finally, it fell into the sea near the Rann of Kachchh (Fig. 6.1). It may be noted that at one point of time the Sarasvatī near Rang Mahal (Suratgarh) had more than 8 km of width as has been demonstrated by Hanna Rydh of Sweden[11] whose scientists made several borings in the dry bed of the Sarasvatī and published sub-surface data (Figs. 6.5, 6.6 and 6.7). It may be pointed out that this reconstruction of the available remains of the course of the Sarasvatī (combined channel of the present-day 'Sarsuti', Ghaggar, Chitang, Hakra, Eastern Nara) from the Shivaliks through

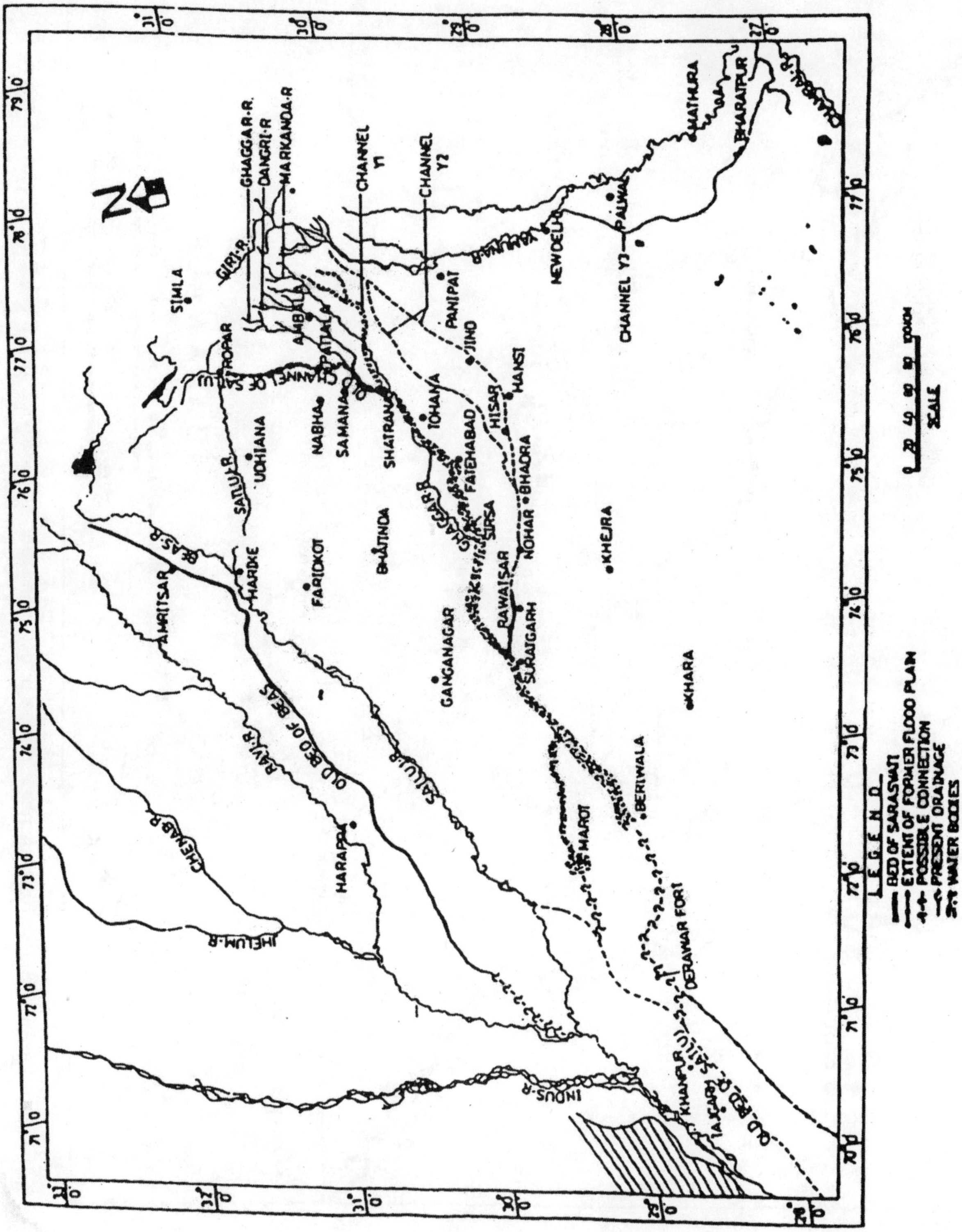

Fig. 6.3 The Map of the New and Old Channels of rivers from Yamuna to the Indus recorded by Landsat Imagery (after Yashpal *et al.*).

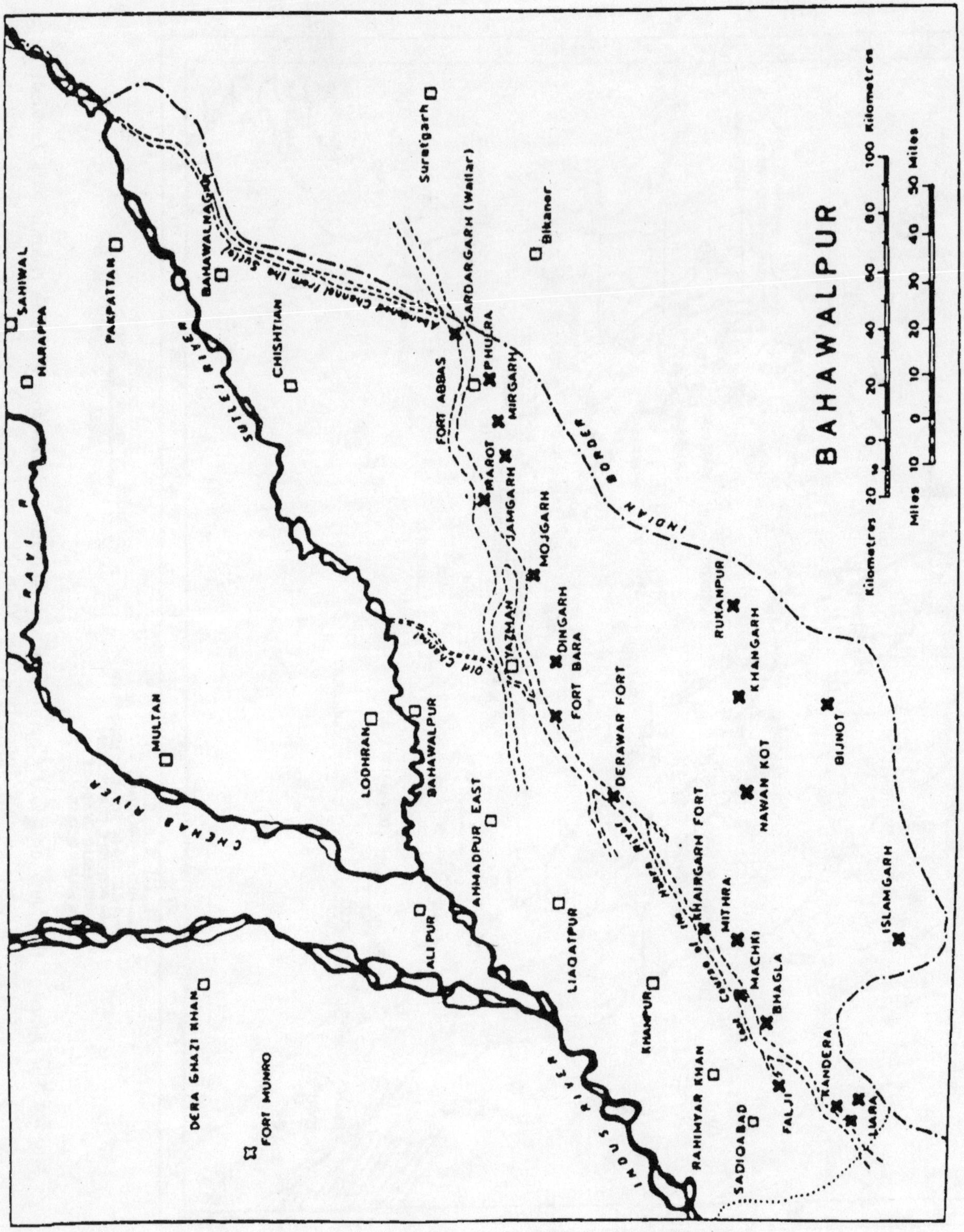

Fig. 6.4 The shifting channels of the Sutlej in relation to Sarasvatī and the Indus System of rivers (after M.R. Mughal).

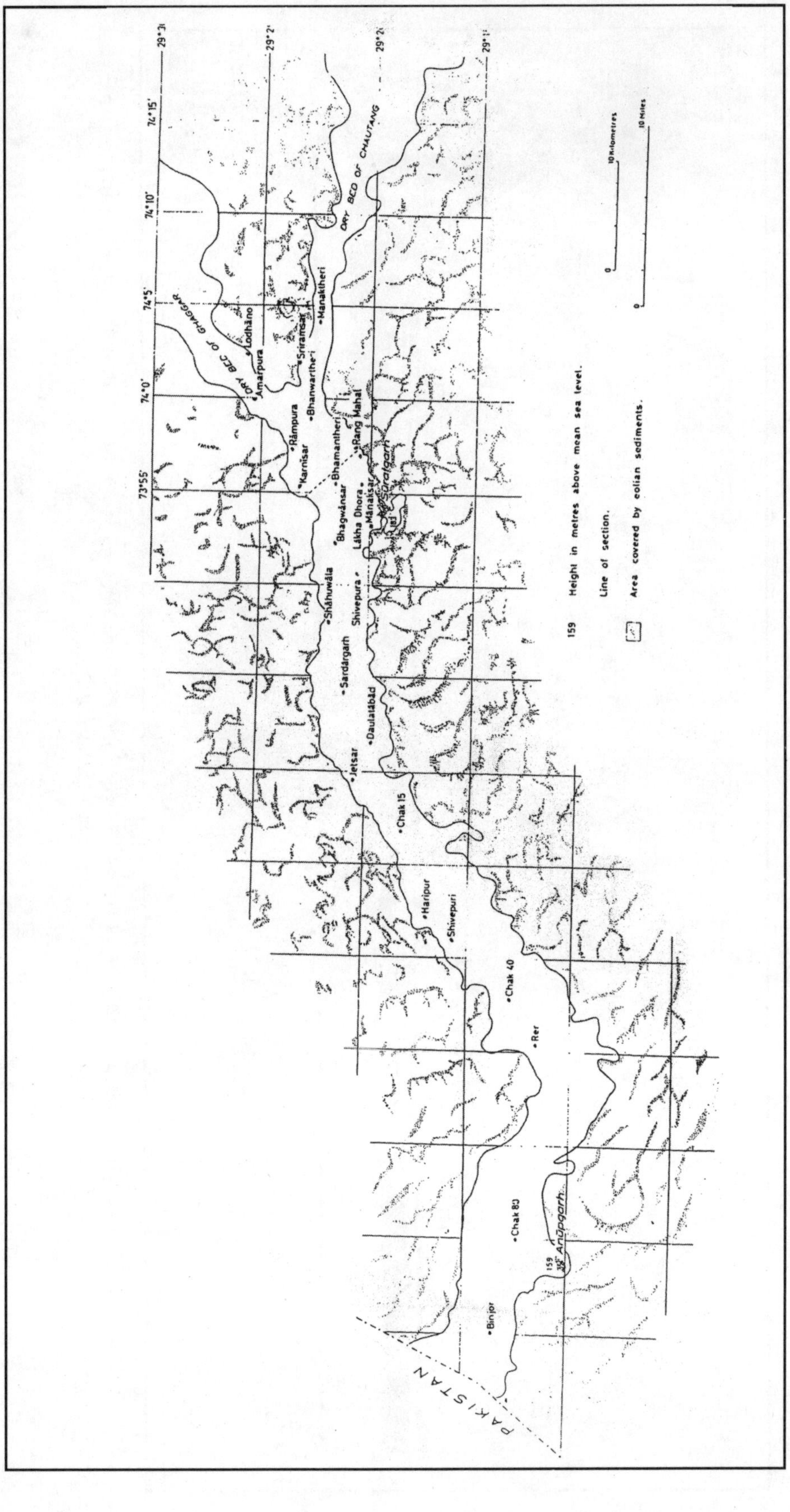

Fig. 6.5 The dry bed of the Ghaggar-Sarasvatī near Rangmahal (after Hanna Rydh).

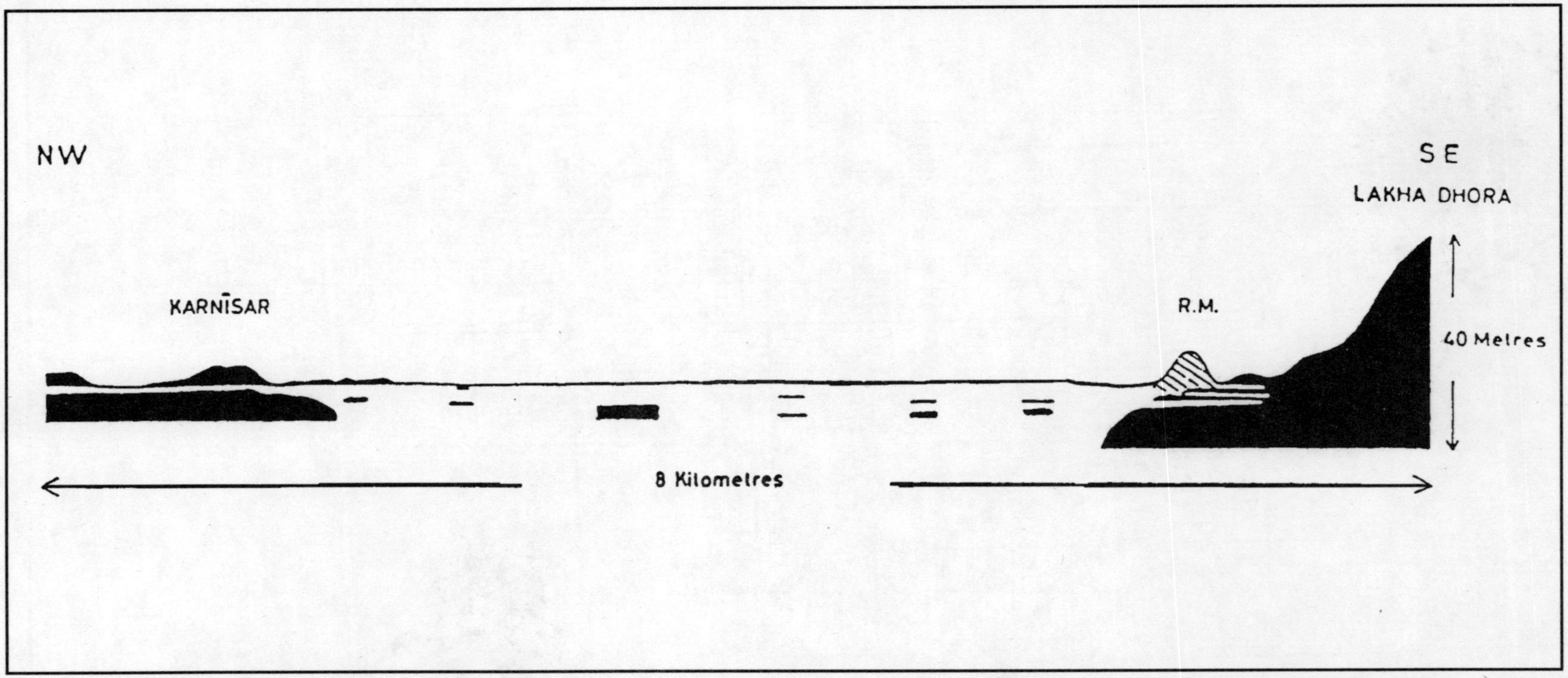

Fig. 6.6 Cross-Section through the dry bed of the river Sarasvatī-Ghaggar-Hakra near Suratgarh in Rajasthan (after Hanna Rydh).

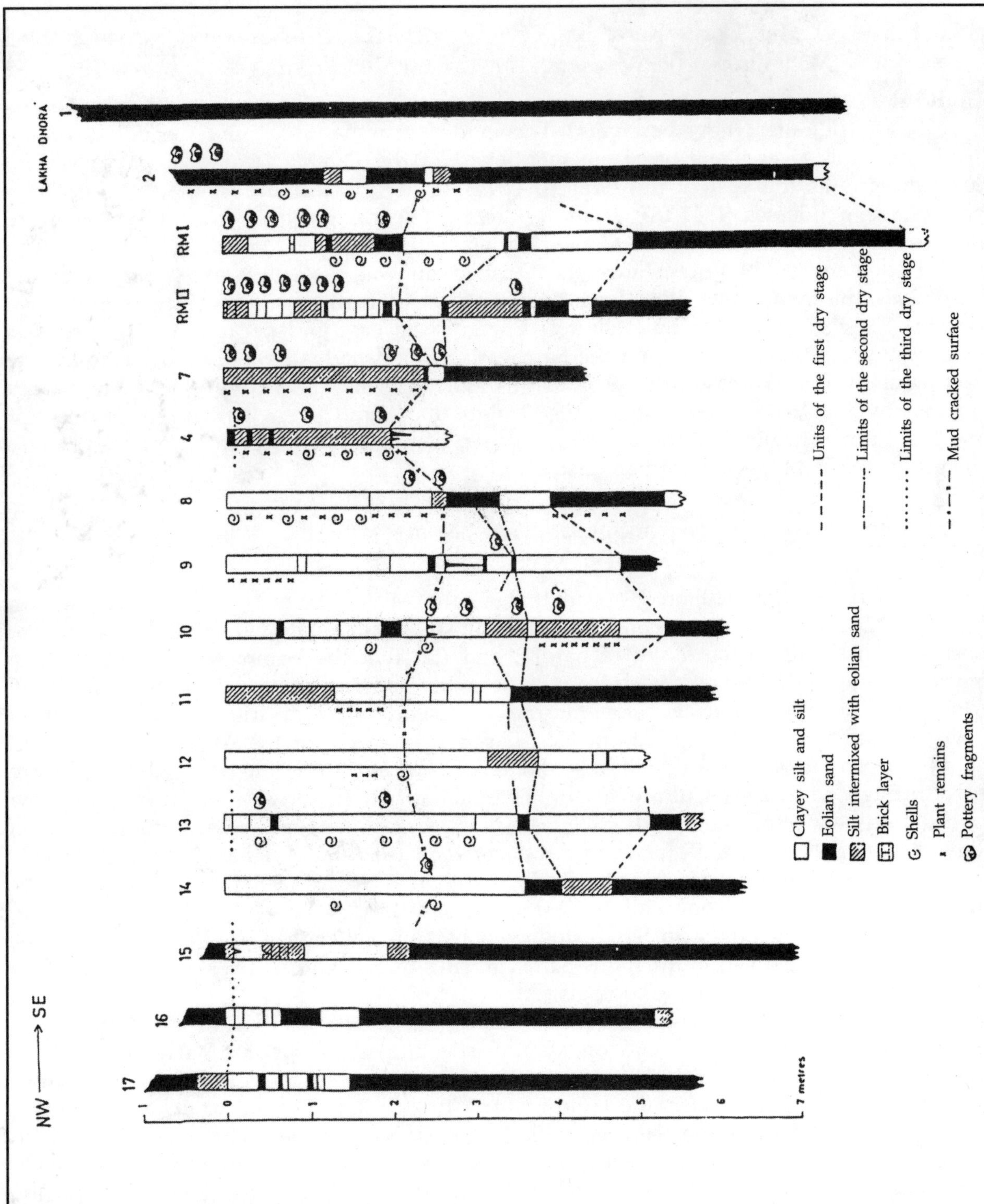

Fig. 6.7 The sediments of the dug and drilled pits in the dry bed of Sarasvatī-Ghaggar – Hakra near Suratgarh.

the Bahawalpur region is based upon the Landsat Imagery (Yashpal, *et al.)* as noted earlier, and also the archaeological explorations conducted by Mughal.[12]

Original Home of the Early Ṛigvedic *Ṛishis*: *Brahmāvarā*—Between Sarasvatī and Dṛishadvatī-Yamunā in Eastern Haryana

Where did the early Ṛigvedic *ṛishis* compose their hymns? In the Sarasvatī basin or the Indus basin or basins of other Ṛigvedic rivers? The evidence at hand favours the banks of the Sarasvatī since this river alone has been mentioned in the *Ṛigveda* around 50 times and in various contexts—as the best of the river (II.41.16), as the best of the mothers (II.41,16), as the best of the goddesses (II.41.16), as the goddess of learning, etc., while other rivers are mentioned only a couple of times. As noted earlier, in the earliest Maṇḍala (VI) it has been mentioned as many as 14 times. Since the Dṛishadvatī was also very much sacred to the Ṛigvedic *ṛishis*, the hymns may have been composed on its banks also. As Yashpal *et al.* have shown, this river in course of time, shifted towards the east and became Yamunā. In the post-Ṛigvedic times the land between the Sarasvatī and Dṛishadvatī was called Brahmāvarta, perhaps precisely for the reason that it is in this land that the knowledge of ultimate reality was gained by the Vedic seers. Medievalist Habib finds fault even in these references for reasons best known to him but the distribution map of the Early Indus-Sarasvatī sites clearly establishes this fact of ancient Indian history. (Fig. 6.8).

The Collapse of the Theory and Model of 'Nomadic Vedic Aryans' Propounded by Max Müller

It now brings us to Max Müller. He said that (i) the earliest layer of the *Ṛigveda*, at best belonged to 1200 BC, and (ii) it contained the 'most primitive' thoughts of the 'child-like responses' of the *ṛishis* to the forces of nature, and (iii) that the hymns were composed 'in the north-west' by those 'who came from outside' with 'some memory' of the homeland still lingering. He dubbed the *ṛishis* as belonging to the 'nomadic pastoral tribe.[13] Thus, right from 1951, when B.B. Lal excavated the site of Hastinapur, the search for the Āryans was confined to the non-urban archaeological cultures and sites, starting from the Painted Grey Ware Culture, through the Banas Culture to the Late Harappan cultures.[14] The trend has now changed due to new archaeological discoveries and geological studies. The dichotomy between the Ṛigvedic complex and Indus-Sarasvatī has narrowed down. B.B. Lal has changed his views propounded till 1998 and now in 2002 he strongly feels that the Indus-Sarasvatī and the Vedic Civilization may have been one and the same.[15] The reason behind this change is the re-study of the *Ṛigveda* by Bhagwan Singh, followed by Shivaji Singh, G.C. Pande and others, and also the frequent analysis of the Indus-Sarasvatī sites by S.P. Gupta. Lal's views are gaining acceptance amongst most of the Indologists.

What has now clearly emerged from the writings of Bharti[16] is that the real culprit was Max Müller who played a big fraud on an unsuspecting nation because like many of his predecessors and contemporaries, he too was motivated to help the Christian missionaries in India in their efforts to convert the Hindus into Christianity. He tried to do it till the end of his life—the leading Brahmo Samajis of Bengal were written personal letters by him to this effect although he clearly failed and died a very sad man. He, it may be noted, never came to India simply because he never liked India; his praise of India was his naked duplicity. Thus, on the one hand, he told to the world that the Vedic Āryans were 'primitive' and 'nomadic' and on the other, on the basis of commonality of Latin and Greek with Sanskrit, the British and the Hindus are cousins, implying thereby that 'do not protest against the British

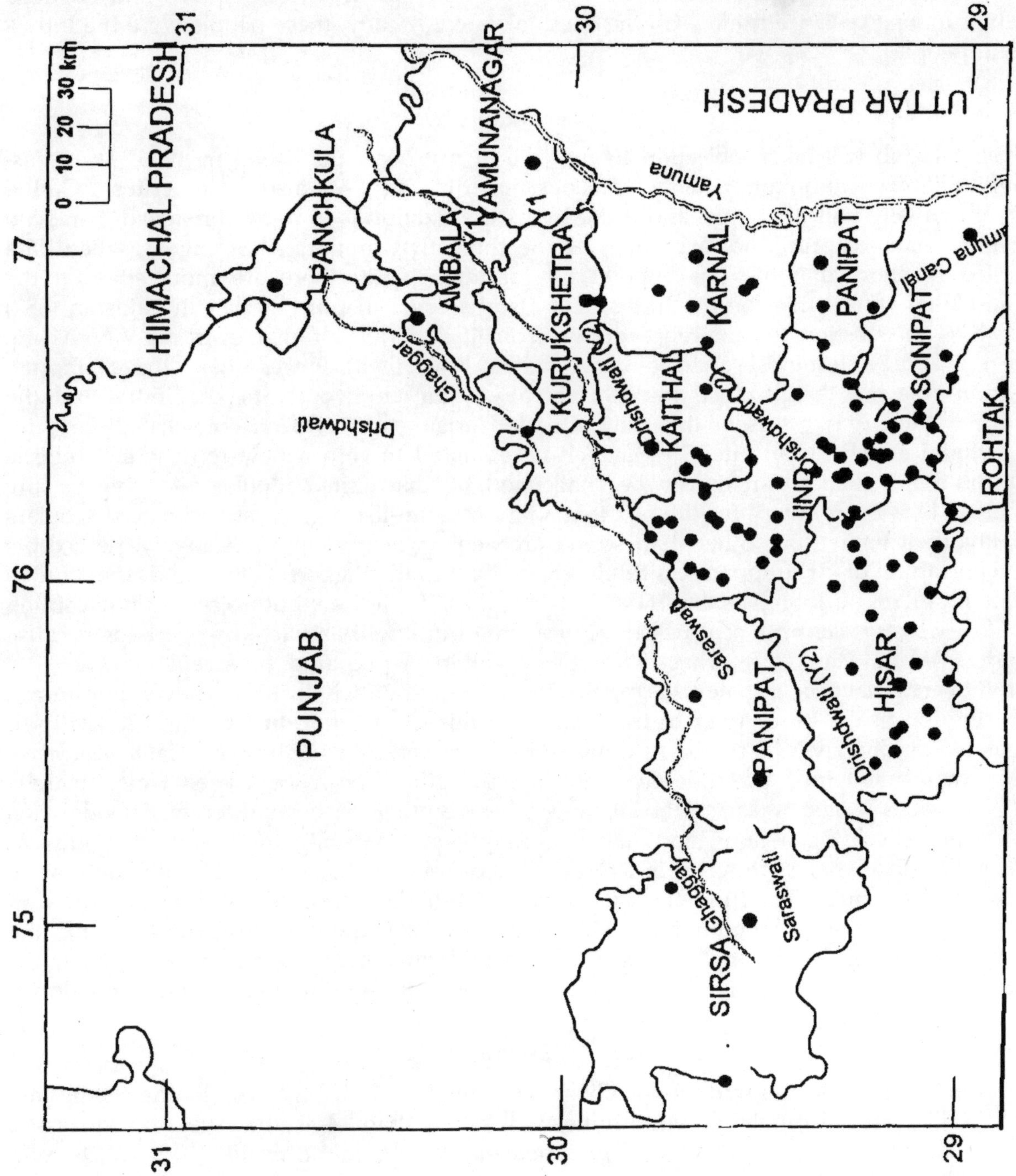

Fig. 6.8 Concentration of Early Indus – Sarasvatī sites between Sarasvatī and Yamuna, the Original Home of the Early Vedic Ṛishis.

Govt. because the British are your brothers'. In doing so he befooled everyone inside and outside India because stealthly he was serving the cause of British Imperialism in India. The fact of the matter is, as Bhagwan Singh (1996) has shown, that the Ṛigvedic *ṛishis* were fully aware of their contemporaries who were living in luxury in urban settlements and engaged themselves in long-distance trade with the West, archaeologically, these people were the Indus-Sarasvatī people.

The Nomenclature

Medievalist Habib has taken objection to the title of my book published in 1996, *The Indus-Sarasvati Civilization* although I had said the same thing in 1991 also.[17] He writes, "Giving a name amounts to half the battle, and if the Indus Civilization is to be re-christened 'Sarasvatī Civilization', name capture, not argument, is the thing that matters".[18] Strangely, when data are quoted to show that there is a powerful argument since there are more sites on the Sarasvatī-Hakra (1,074) than on the Indus, and also beyond, all put together in Pakistan (682) then he tries to question the inference drawn from it and raises finger even on V.N. Misra, one of the India's foremost archaeologists, when he (Misra) writes that "the Harappan Civilization was not the product of one river alone, but of two rivers, the Indus and the Sarasvatī".[19] And, it is precisely this new situation arising out of archaeological discoveries made in India and Pakistan after 1947 which necessitated to coin a new term which reflects the ground-reality which can hardly be challenged by discredited ideologues. Give us any good reason to reject it except for the fact that a few Muslim-fearing, racist and biased scholars do not favour it for reasons other than sound archaeological principles. Strangely, he accepts the nomenclature of "Harappan Culture" given by Stuart Piggott (1950) and the "Indus Civilization" given by John Marshall (1931), as he himself admits,[20] but objects to our coining a new term which is cent per cent based on new data from field-archaeology, perhaps because I am not a White Man, only whose superiority Habib is prepared to accept.

Moreover, I have in my new term, the 'Indus-Sarasvatī Civilization', never minimized the contribution of the Indus river in the making of this civilization. In fact, the *Ṛigveda* itself mentions the Sindhu river 83 times (18 times in early *maṇḍalas* and 65 times in later *maṇḍalas*). I have always maintained that this civilization is the gift of both the rivers. Unfortunately, R.S. Sharma goes a step ahead of Habib and takes recourse to even utter falsehood when he says that by coining a new term like this S.P. Gupta is trying to project the Indus as Muslim river, since after partition it is largely in Pakistan, and Sarasvatī as Hindu river since it is in India. He writes, "The fundamentalists want to establish the superiority of the Sarasvatī over the Indus because of communal considerations. In the Harappan context they think that after partition, the Indus belongs to the Muslims and only the Sarasvatī remains with the Hindus."[21] Lal (1996) has dealt with this utter falsehood in some details to nail him down.

Vedic Urbanism

Of late, primarily due to the writings of Bhagwan Singh,[22] R.S. Bisht,[23] G.C. Pande,[24] B.B. Lal[25] and others like Shivaji Singh[26] besides mine, it is more than clear that the Ṛigvedic *ṛishis* were fully aware of the 'Urban' way of life: *Samrata, Rājana, Sabhā, Samiti* (*RV*. VI.278; VIII. 21.8); Lal, like many others has also drawn our attention to the *Śatapatha Brāhmaṇa* (V.1. 1.12-13) which says "By offering the Rājasūya he becomes Rājā and by Vājapeya he becomes Samrāṭa". It clearly reflects the political hierarchy in the society and not nomadism of the people.

Warfare, such as the War of Ten Kings mentioned in the *Ṛigveda*, as well as long-distance trade through sea, rivers and land, coupled with piracy, metals and metallurgy, roads and lanes, multi-storey houses, fortifications, writing, etc., are also mentioned in the Vedic literature which clearly prove, according to Bhagwan Singh (1996), that the Ṛigvedic *ṛishis* were far from being 'nomadic'. Obviously, even though the Ṛigvedic *ṛishis* were living a frugal life, some as *'munis'* and *'tapasvis'*, most of them knew that beyond their hutments and villages there lay a host of cities in which the people were engaged in activities connected with the 'city economy'.[27]

In other words, Max Müller cleverly imposed the lifestyle of the Vedic *ṛishis*, whose motto was 'simple living and high thinking', over the entire population of their contemporaries and called them not only 'primitive' but also 'nomadic'. But we all know that though even now India is predominantly rural, some modern most cities also exist side by side. Hence, even during the Indus-Sarasvatī times if the two kinds of settlements existed side by side, it is not surprising. As a matter of fact, archaeology supports it. There were more villages than the cities, hardly two dozens, during the period of the Indus-Sarasvatī Civilization, broadly in the 3rd millennium.[28]

Looking at all these kinds of evidence, there is no choice left except to find out an urban culture of which the Ṛigvedic people were the witnesses. And, this could be none else but the Indus-Sarasvatī.

The Story of Two Urbanizations in India

It is common knowledge that in Indian history there are two major periods of urbanization, the Proto-Historic, the 'Indus-Sarasvatī' of the 3rd millennium BC and the Early Historic from the 6th century BC or so. Since enough is known about the second urbanization which belonged to the Early Historical Period, only the first urbanization is left to date the *Ṛigveda* which cannot be later than 2000 BC because, first, this was the end of the Mature Indus-Sarasvatī Civilization, a conclusion based upon the radiocarbon dates, now accepted all over the world, and second, this was also the time of the drying up of the Sarasvatī. Radiocarbon dates of the latest levels of Kalibangan, etc., provide proof for one fact that almost all the urban settlements were deserted during this time.[29] How far further back in time, from 2000 it goes is anybody's guess. However, since in 3000 BC Anatolia and West Asia also saw the Indo-European words appearing there, as has been shown by Mallory,[30] it will not be surprising if this was the date in India too, if not earlier. Europe also seems to have acquired the 'Indo-European Culture', marked, as scholars feel, by horse and chariots. It happened in the Bronze Age of the 3rd millennium, if not earlier. As one can see, so far I have confined myself to Sarasvatī, *Ṛigveda* and the Homeland of the Early Ṛigvedic *ṛishis* and their culture and the culture of their contemporaries, the Mature Indus-Sarasvatī Civilization, since this is the real issue in the present-day controversy.

Some Significant Dates of Early Indian History

It is now common knowledge (Gupta 1996) that the sites of the Mature Indus-Sarasvatī Civilization were not confined to the Sarasvatī basin; it had spread over a very vast area covering Gujarat, Sindh, parts of eastern Baluchistan, Punjab, Haryana and northern Rajasthan. (Fig. 6.8). This was also the region of what we call the Early Indus-Sarasvatī Civilization, the date of which is now placed in the early to mid-4th millennium BC, for example, the Hakra-Ravi Phase as found at Harappa is dated to 3500-3300 BC while Amri and Balakotian cultures are dated to 3800 BC. These are also generically connected with the Mature phase of the Indus-Sarasvatī Civilization dated between 2600 BC and 2000 BC.[31] In other words, there is a history of 2000 to 1500 years of the pre-Ṛigvedic Civilization in India, in case we agree to the correlation of the Mature Phase of the Indus-Sarasvatī Civilization and the Ṛigvedic period.

Shivaji Singh[32] has rightly shown that the region of Sindh or the lower Indus plains and delta became the most likeable area for habitation and sea-trade of the *Ṛigveda*, followers of the later times. Sindhu has been mentioned as many as 85 times in Maṇḍalas VIII, IX, I and X. This shows that during the later Ṛigvedic times the people moved from Haryana to Sindh and the *ṛishis* composed their hymns there also.

Ṛigveda and the Early Indus-Sarasvatī Civilization

How do I look at the *Ṛigveda* vis-á-vis the Indus-Sarasvatī Civilization? The more I read the *Ṛigveda*, the more I see it as representing a 'Developed Stage' of human civilization, since it has a great amount of *abstract thoughts* which is the hallmark of high level of intellectualism. Similarly, the *language* in which the hymns were composed is also quite developed. An undeveloped or underdeveloped culture does not develop these two faculties in the people. Max Müller was thus not honest enough when he called the Vedic Civilization 'primitive'. He was totally biased, perhaps he was paid for it by the East India Company which hired him to translate the Vedas at the instance of Macaulay.[33]

There was, however, a Pre-Ṛigvedic phase of the Vedic Civilization. If archaeologically I have to understand it and fix its date, then undoubtedly it is the Early Indus-Sarasvatī Civilization, broadly dated between 3500 BC and 2500 BC for the present.

The Significant Convergence

It may be pointed out that at the peak, the Indus-Sarasvatī Civilization covers the region of north-eastern Baluchistan, Punjab, northern Rajasthan and central Haryana with sites like Rehman Dheri, Harappa, Kalibangan and Kunal[34] (Fig. 6.8). Elsewhere[35] I have shown that although presently there is no linguistic proof of the Pre-Ṛigvedic and Early Indus-Sarasvatī Civilization, at least archaeologically speaking, yet hundreds of graffiti marks appearing on the Early Indus-Sarasvatī pot-sherds, several of them entering into the Mature Indus-Sarasvatī script, do suggest the existence of Pre-Ṛigvedic language and script in the western sector of the Vedic and the Indus-Sarasvatī Zone. B.B. Lal has also pointed out that the region of the Early Vedic Civilization and the region of the Indus-Sarasvatī Civilization were practically the same[36] (Fig. 6.9).

Conclusion

To conclude, the Sarasvatī was undoubtedly a major water-flow with waters from various rivers joining it at various points of its length during the Ṛigvedic period. It was perennial in nature without which neither it could run over 1,500 km and reach the coasts of the Arabian Sea nor it could support more than a thousand Indus-Sarasvatī settlements on its banks. The *Ṛigveda* would also not have described it so very eloquently as we have shown above. Those who try to impose the 'present' on the 'past', like Irfan Habib and R.S. Sharma, are doing it uncharitably and with Left Fundamentalist bias since we know that climatic and hydrological causes coupled with neo-tectonic movements caused the decay in the supply of water in the Sarasvatī around 2000 BC before that, during the Mature Indus-Sarasvatī period, there was more rainfall.[37] It was the 'moist' period as Gurdip Singh has pointed out on the basis of his studies on the pollens collected in the Sambhar Lake near Jaipur in Rajasthan. Slowly

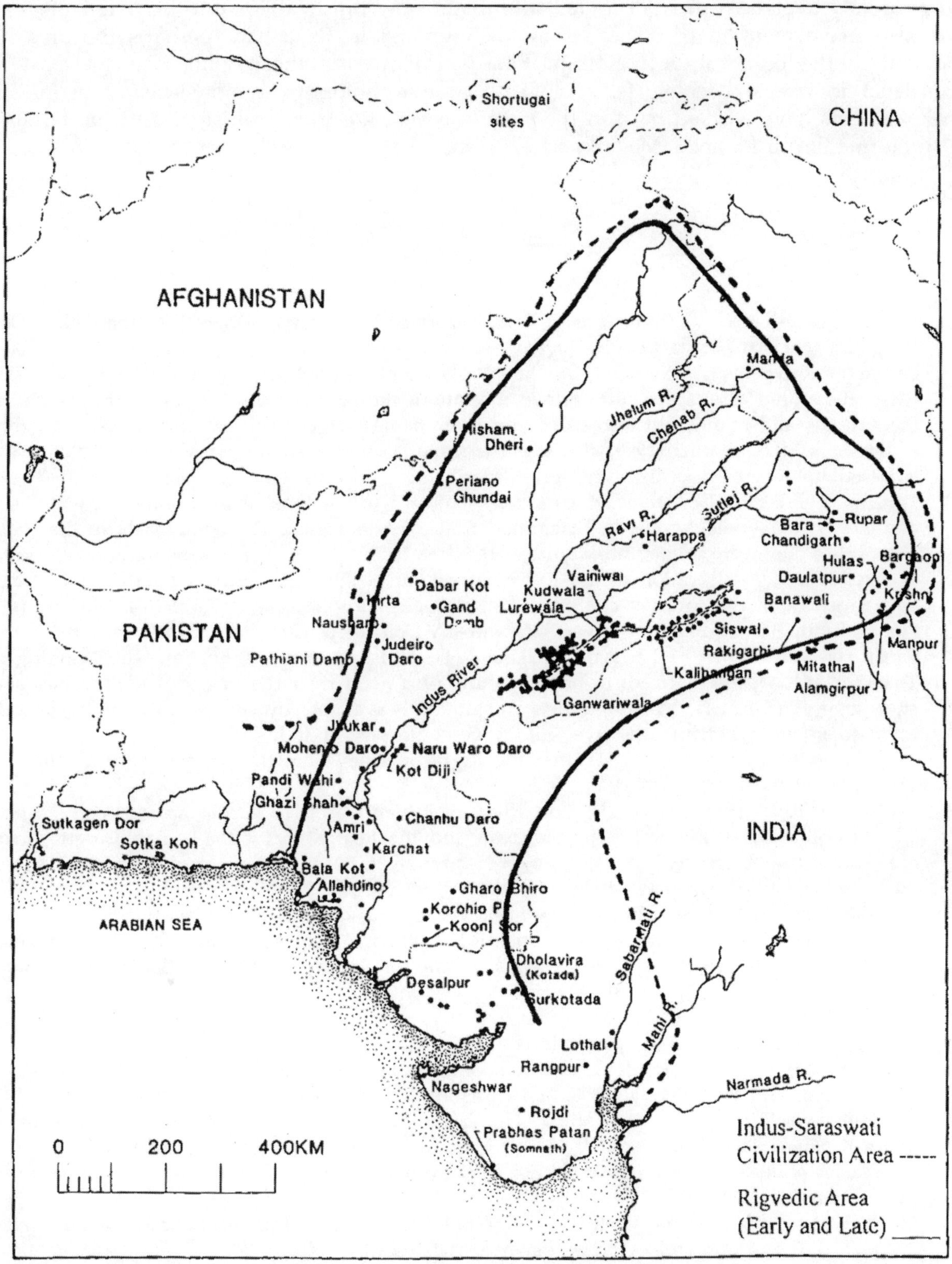

Fig. 6.9 Area covered by Indus – Sarasvatī Civilization and its overlap with the area covered by Early Vedic Civilization.

and gradually the Sarasvatī went underground and now practically lost to us. The Later Vedic texts also make mention of it.[38] It is lost at Vinaśana in Rajasthan, perhaps the area near Kudawal in the Bahawalpur region of Pakistan. However, those who 'dig' the past and reconstruct it, like archaeologists, geologists, geomorphologists, remote-sensing people and other scientists have worked hard in the field to reveal the truth of history and the falsehood of some medievalists and 'Majority-haters': the Sarasvatī was a great river in the 3rd millennium.

Notes and References

1. Kochhar, Rajesh 1997, *The Vedic People: Their History and Geography*, (Orient Longman, New Delhi) "Arguing that a major part of the *Ṛgveda* was composed in south Afghanistan (after *c.* 1700 BC) before the Ṛgvedic people entered the Punjab plain and well before they moved east of the Gaṅgā River, the author asserts that during their migrations the Indo-Āryans not only carried with them their rituals and hymns but also place and river names which they selectively re-used", (blurb of the book). R.S. Sharma (1999) also says the same because it suits their Marxist ideology which is based upon anti-Majoritism and pro-Minoritism.
2. Talagiri, S.G. 2000, *The Rigveda, A Historical Analysis* (Aditya Prakashan, Delhi), p. xvii, "As per our theory, the Vedic Āryans had migrated from east to west.... The actual data in the *Ṛgveda* shows that they were in fact inhabitants of the area to the east of the Punjab traditionally known as Āryāvarta". (Stratification of the Ṛgvedic text on p. 78). Also, Shivaji Singh, 1998, "Sindhu and Sarasvatī in the *Ṛgveda* and their Archaeological Implications", *Puratattva*, No. 28, p. 2.
3. Habib, Irfan, 2001, "Imagining River Sarasvatī—A Defence of Common Sense", *Proceedings of the Indian History Congress*, 61st Session, Kolkata (2000-2001), pp. 67-92. "The 'Sarasvatī' running past Thanesar is too petty a stream to fit the picture of a great river that the Ṛgveda's verses above cited suggest". Furthers, "A straightforward solution is available, by which we are no longer called upon to inflate a petty plains river into a veritable second Indus".

   Here, the author tries to say that the Ṛgvedic seers were the greatest liars on the earth. They played the biggest fraud in history.
4. Oldham, C.F. 1874, "Notes on the Lost River of Indian Desert", *Calcutta Review*, Vol. 59, pp. 1-27. Also, Oldham, C.F., 1893, "The Sarasvatī and the Lost River of the Indian Desert", *Journal of the Royal Asiatic Society*, Vol. 25, pp. 49-76. Aurel Stein, 1942, "A Survey of Ancient Sites Along the Lost Sarasvatī", *Geographical Journal*, Vol. V, 99 (4) pp. 179-82.
5. Sahai, Baldev 1999, "Unraveling of the 'Lost' Vedic Sarasvatī", *Memoir, Geological Society of India*, No. 42, p. 138. Also, Yashpal, Baldev Sahai, R.K. Sood and D.P. Agrawal, 1980, "Remote Sensing of the 'Lost' Sarasvatī River", *Proceedings of the Indian Academy of Sciences* (Earth and Planetary Sciences), Vol. V, 89 (3) pp. 317-31.
6. Shivaji Singh, *op. cit.*, pp. 26-27.
7. Kochhar, *op. cit.*, pp. 118-31, particularly p. 131.
8. Lal, B.B., 2002, *Why Perpetuate Myths*, A booklet published by NCERT, New Delhi, p. 4.
9. Puri, V.K.M. and B.C. Verma, 1998, "Glaciological and Geological Source of Vedic Sarasvatī in the Himalayas", *Itihas Darpan*, Vol. IV, No. 2, pp. 7-20. Also, Puri, V.K.M., Deepak Srivastava and R.K. Singh, 1996, "Status of Glaciological Studies in Satluj Catchment, Kinnaur District, H.P.", *Proceedings of the Symposium on North-West Himalaya and Foredeep*, Geological Survey of India, Spl. Publication 21 (2) pp. 321-25.
10. Mughal, M.R., 1997, *Ancient Cholistan*, (Ferozsons (Pvt.) Ltd. Rawalpindi-Lahore-Karachi), pp. 40-59. Figs. 1,2. and Appendix-A (List of Ancient Sites in Cholistan).
11. Rydh, Hanna, 1959, *Rang Mahal:* Papers of the Lund Universitests Historiska Museum, Series 4, No. 3, Lund (Sweden) Gleerup, C.W.K.
12. Mughal, *op. cit.*

13. Max Müller, 1859, *Ancient Sanskrit Literature* (London).
14. Lal, B.B., 1951, "Excavations at Hastinapur and Other Explorations in Upper Ganga and Sutlej Basins", *Ancient India*, Nos. 10-11. Also, *Purātattva*, No. 8 in which there are several articles by different authors on this topic.
15. Lal, B.B., 2002, *op.cit.*, (NCERT, New Delhi) p. 9. Also, *The Sarasvatī Flows On*, 2002(a), (Aryan Books International, New Delhi).
16. Bharti, B.D., 1992, *Max Müller—A Lifelong Masquerade* (Erabooks, New Delhi).
17. Gupta, S.P., 1993, "Palaeo-Anthropology and Archaeology of the Vedic Aryans", in (S.B. Deo eds. and S. Kamath) *Aryan Problem* (Proceedings of a Seminar held in 1991 at Bangalore), Mythic Society, Bangalore.
18. Habib, Irfan, *op. cit.*, p.68.
19. Misra, V.N. 1996 *Purātattva*, No. 26, p. 138.
20. Habib, *op. cit.*, p. 68, "Both terms are valid, the first referring to the geographical region of the Indus basin, and the other to the type site". But to him it appears that the Distribution Pattern of Sites is not at all valid in archaeology. This is the level of understanding of archaeology of a medievalist.
21. Sharma, R.S., 1999, *Advent of the Aryans in India* (Manohar Publishers, New Delhi).
22. Bhagwan Singh, 1996, *The Vedic Harappans*, (Aditya Prakashan, New Delhi).
23. Bisht, R.S., 1999, "Harappan and Rigveda: Points of Convergence", in *The Dawn of Indian Civilization up to 600 B.C.* (ed. G.C. Pande), PHISPC, New Delhi, pp. 393-442.
24. Pande, G.C., 2001, *Vedic Sanskriti*, (Hindi) Lokabharati, Allahabad.
25. Lal, B.B., 1998, *India 1947-1997: New Light on the Indus Civilization* (Aryan Books International, New Delhi).
26. Shivaji Singh, 1998, *op. cit.* pp. 26-38.
27. Lal, B.B., 2002, *op. cit.*, also, Bhagwan Singh, *op. cit.*, also, Shivaji Singh, *op. cit.*
28. Mughal, *op. cit.*, also, G.L. Possehl, 1999, *Indus Age: The Beginnings* (Oxford & IBH Publishing Co. Pvt. Ltd., New Delhi).
29. Possehl, G.L., *op. cit.*
30. Mellory, J.P., 1989, *In Search of the Indo-Europeans Language, Archaeology and Myth* (Thames and Hudson, London).
31. Gupta, 1996, *op. cit.*, Appendix-B, Radiocarbon Dates.
32. Shivaji Singh, *op. cit.*, p. 27.
33. Bharti, B.D., *op. cit.*, pp. 13, 20, 26.
34. Lal, B.B., 2002, *op. cit.*
35. Gupta, S.P., 1996, *op. cit.*, p. 35.
36. Lal, B.B., 2002, *op. cit.*
37. Gurdip Singh, *et al.*, 1974, "Late Quaternary History of Vegetation and Climate of the Rajasthan Desert, India", *Philosophical Transactions of the Royal Society of London*, Vol. 267 (389) pp. 467-501.
38. *Pañchaviṁśa Brāhmaṇa* (XV. 106). *Jaiminīya Upanishad Brāhmaṇa* (4.26).

Appendix

The original references taken from the *Ṛigveda* which occur in the text:

नि त्वा दधे वर आ प थिव्या इलयास्पदे सुदिनत्वे अह्नाम्।
द षद्वत्यां मानुष आपयायां सरस्वत्यां खेदग्ने दिदीहि।।

— (III.24.4)

अम्बितमे नदीतमे देवितमे सरस्वति।
अप्रशस्ता इव स्मसि प्रशस्तिमम्ब नस्क धि।।

— (II.41.16)

आपप्रुषी पार्थिवान्युरू रजो अन्तरिक्षम्।
सरस्वती निदस्पातु।।

— (V.61.11)

प्र या महिम्ना महिनासु चेकिते द्युम्नेभिरन्या अपसामपरतमा।
रथ इव ब हती विश्वने क तोपस्तुत्या चिकितुषा सरस्वती।।

— (VI.61.13)

इयं शुप्मेभिर्विसखा इवारूजत्सानु गिरीणां तविषेभिरूर्मिभिः।
पारादतघ्नीमवसे सुव क्तिभिः सरस्वतीमा विवासेम धीतिभिः।

— (VI.61.2)

यस्या अनन्तो अह्वतस्त्वेष श्चरिष्णुरर्णवः।
अमश्चरति रोरूवत्।।

— (VI.61.8)

इमं मे गङ्गे यमुने सरस्वति शुतुद्रि स्तोमं सचता परूष्ण्या।
असिकन्या मरूद धे वितस्तयार्जीकीये श्रणुह्या सुषोमया।।

— (X.75.5)

उत स्या नः सरस्वती जुषाणोय श्रवत्सुभगा यज्ञे अस्मिन्।
मितज्ञुभिर्नमस्यैरियाना राया युजा चिदुत्तरा सखिभ्यः।।

— (VII.95.4)

व हदु गायिषे वचो सुर्या नदीनाम्।
सरस्वतीमिन्महया सुव क्तिभिः स्तोमैर्वसिष्ठ रोदसी।।

— (VII.96.1)

7

Vedic vis-à-vis Harappan Culture

Some Thoughts

Devendra Handa

The *Ṛigveda* is generally and rightly believed to be the earliest literary document not only of India but also of the entire world. The language used for this and the other Vedic compositions is commonly designated as the Vedic Sanskrit (called *Chhāndas* by Pāṇini in about sixth–fifth century BC), which is a precursor of the classical Sanskrit. In his famous address to the Asiatic Society of Bengal in 1786, Sir William Jones (1788; Bhargava: 1971) observed that

> The Sanskrit language, whatever be its antiquity, is a wonderful structure; more perfect than the Greek, more copious than the Latin, and more exquisitely refined than either: yet bearing to both of them a stronger affinity, both in roots of verbs, and in the forms of grammar, than could possibly have been produced by accident; so strong indeed, that no philologer could examine them all without believing them to have sprung from some common source, which perhaps no longer exists. There is a similar reason, though not quite so forcible, for supposing that both the Gothic and the Celtic, though blended with a different idiom, had the same origin with the Sanskrit; and the old Persian might be added to the same family.

This wonderful observation later gave rise to various questions and theories regarding the name, locale and spread of the original people who used that common source, the lost original language, which was given the name of the Original Indo-European (OIE) later. The people using the Vedic Sanskrit are postulated by most of the scholars as belonging to that original stock which moved eastward from its original home and settled in the north-west part of the Indian subcontinent. The theories of the original home of these people in different areas have been propounded and a general belief is that they moved eastward from the West. This is in consonance with the idea of the superiority of the West over the East, which perhaps lay embedded in the Western psyche when these theories were propounded. Many of the indigenous scholars, however, believe that it was the other way round. The date of the *Ṛigveda* is also indeterminate. The religious devout believe it to have been divine revelation and very old whereas Max Müller first believed it to be a work of ca. 1200 BC but when his own contemporaries like Goldstucker, Whitney and Wilson raised objections against his ad-hocism he modified his view and confessed that it was very difficult to determine whether the Vedic hymns were composed in 1000 or 1500 or 2000 or 3000 BC (Max Müller: 1890). A careful study of the *Ṛigveda,* however, reveals that the Vedic people who called themselves Āryans (a term often misinterpreted and grossly misused) at the time of the composition of the hymns were settled in the Sapta-Sindhu, the Land of the Seven Rivers, covering roughly the region from Gandhāra (Afghanistan) to the western Uttar Pradesh, i.e. the valleys of the seven rivers between the Indus and the Gaṅgā. The Sarasvatī, breaking and carrying down ridges of hills like lotus stems, fierce, swiftest of the swift, mightiest of her class, superior to her companions, vibrant and purest amongst all the rivers, moving from the mountains to the ocean *(Ekāchetat Sarasvatī nadīnāṃ śuchiryāti giribhya ā samudrāt / Ṛigveda* VII.95, 2a) with a tempestuous roar, was regarded as the best of mothers *(ambitame),* the best of the goddesses (*devītame)* and the best of the rivers *(nadītame)* in the period of the *Ṛigveda* (II.41, 16). Dṛishadvatī (identified with modern Chautang in Haryana) and Āpayā were its tributaries (*Ṛigveda* III.23, 4). According to the *Mahābhārata* (Vana Parva 83.68) the Dṛishadvatī formed the southern boundary of Kurukshetra while the Sarasvatī flowed to its north. There are numerous references to the Sarasvatī in the *Ṛigveda* but the *Nadī-stuti* mentions almost all the important rivers, along with their tributaries, in two of its famous verses (X. 75, 5–6) –

> *Imaṃ me Gaṅge Yamune Sarasvatī Śutudri stomaṃ sachatā Purushṇyā/*
> *Asiknyā Marudvṛidhe Vitastyā Ārjikīye śṛiṇuhyā Sushomayā//*
> *Tṛishṭāmayā prathamaṃ yātave sajūḥ Susartvā Rasayā Śvetyā tyā/*
> *Tvaṃ Sindho Kubhayā Gomatīṃ Kramuṃ Mehatnvā sarathaṃ yābhirīyase//*

> O Gaṅgā, Yamunā, Sarasvatī, Śutudrī (Satluj) and Parushṇī (Ravi), O Marudvṛidhā with Asiknī (Chenab), O Ārjikīyā with Vitastā (Jhelum) and Sushomā (Sohan)! Please listen to and accept this hymn of mine.
>
> O Sindhu (Indus), flowing, you must meet first the Tṛishṭāmā (and then) the Susartu, the Rasā, and the Śvetā (Swat), and thereafter the Kubhā (Kabul), the Gomatī (Gomal), the Krumu (Kurram) along with Mehatnu; and (then) you move on with them in the same chariot (i.e. carrying their waters with you).

These two verses give the names of nineteen rivers though the first verse of the hymn refers to *sapta-sapta-tredhā*, i.e. twenty-one rivers. Of the missing two, one may be presumed to have been the Vipāś (Beas).

The *Nadī-sūkta,* which forms part of the Tenth Book (Maṇḍala) of the *Ṛigveda,* regarded as the latest portion of the work, gives the geographical horizon of the Ṛigvedic people very clearly. The Gaṅgā has been mentioned only once in the entire *Ṛigveda* indicating that it was only vaguely known to a few people on the eastern fringe of the vast area occupied by the Vedic people. It is notable that the distribution of the Harappan sites also does not extend beyond the Gaṅgā; only a few sites are known between the Yamunā and the Hindon, its tributary, and the Gaṅgā. Interestingly, these sites also represent the late phase of the Harappan culture. It should be remembered that later Gaṅgā became the river par excellence, the holiest of all the rivers.

Yamunā has been mentioned thrice in the *Ṛigveda* whereas the Sarasvatī is lauded quite often. There are three independent hymns devoted to Sarasvatī and many stray verses referring to her. She is praised as the mother of the rivers *(Ṛigveda* I.134, 4). The river is identified with a small stream rising from the Shivalik hills and entering the plains at Ad Badri in district Yamuna Nagar (Haryana) and flowing past the cities and towns of Kapāla-Mochana,

Pipli, Kurukshetra, Pehowa, etc. It is joined by the Ghaggar and the Chautang (Vedic Dṛishadvatī) downstream from Pehowa and enters Pakistan where it ultimately falls into the Rann of Kachchha, known successively as Ghaggar in India and Hakra, Raini, Wahind and Nara in Pakistan. A large number of archaeological sites are located on its dry bed all through yielding remains associated with the Harappan and later culture.

The poets of the Vedic hymns sometimes talk of their earlier sages *(pūrvebhiḥ ṛishibhiḥ)* but do not know of any other land or people. It is well known that migrating races remember the land of their origin for centuries. Had the Ṛigvedic people come to settle in the above-mentioned region from elsewhere in the West, they could not have failed to give indication of that. To accuse them of an organized conspiracy to deliberately omit the name of the people or country from a record containing hymns composed during the course of a long time and by hundreds of authors belonging to different families, some of which may have been inimical to each other, will be a travesty of facts. And, to say that the Sarasvatī, the river par excellence *(nadītamā)* in the *Ṛigveda*, described as rising from the mountains and flowing to the sea, located between the Yamunā and the Śutudrī and having Dṛishadvatī as its tributary, was named after the original river of this name identified with Helmand in Afghanistan and mentioned as Harakhvatī in the *Āvestā* (Habibs: 1991–92; Sharma: 1999), will be putting the cart before the horse. Harakhvatī does not debouch in any ocean (Afghanistan is far away from the sea), it is not located in the east between the Yamunā and the Śutudrī and nor does it have Dṛishadvatī as its tributary forming the boundary of Kurukshetra with it. The posterity of the *Āvestā* to the *Ṛigveda* is well established to need any further elucidation. It is equally inappropriate to identify it with the Sindhu which has been mentioned along with its tributaries in a sequential order in the *nadī-sūkta* (Lal: 2002). Even from the archaeological viewpoint, the identification of the Harakhvatī with original Sarasvatī cannot be upheld. The people settled on the Harakhvatī should have represented the earliest phase of the settlements and yielded archaeological relics akin to those as found spread over the vast region to its east towards the Yamunā. Their cultural and material remains should have been the precursors of those obtained from numerous sites between the Harakhvatī and the Yamunā. But the reality is far from it. The Harakhvatī valley has yielded archaeological remains, which cannot be regarded as earlier than those found at Mehrgarh in Pakistan and Kunal in India. On the other hand, archaeological remains found there represent rather a late phase. So we have to look for the archaeological remains of the Vedic people elsewhere in the geographical horizon detailed by the *nadī-sūkta*.

When a grandiose civilization was exposed as a result of the excavations at Harappa in 1921, and later at Mohenjo-daro and various other sites, there arose a controversy to culturally affiliate the archaeological relics. The research journals of the third and fourth decade of the last century contain numerous articles on the issue. When Harappa was re-excavated by Mortimer Wheeler who discovered the fortification there, he accused 'Indra' ('Purandara' i.e. the destroyer of *'puras'*, fortified towns), figuratively the Āryans, of destroying the city (*pura*), without mentioning the name of Dr. Vasudev Sharan Agrawala who delivered an invited lecture at Harappa at that time and made references to it quoting from the Vedic hymns. Corroborative evidence to this theory was sought in thirty-seven skeletons found during nine years of excavations at Mohenjo-daro, some complete and others fragmentary, thought to have resulted from an alien attack. A large number of scholars following Wheeler started taking it as the gospel truth, though soon his own pupil, B.B. Lal (1954 and 1955), brought forth the evidence showing that it was untenable archaeologically. The theory of the mythical massacre at Mohenjo-daro (Dales: 1964) has been proved to be wrong as the skeletons found there came from different stratified horizons and also some skeletons bore cut-marks that had healed. The entire area occupied by the Harappans shows continuity and transformation rather than any abrupt break.

Another major obstacle in identifying the Indus Valley and the Vedic civilizations was the absence of the remains of horse and the spoked-wheels in the former in contradistinction to numerous references to the animal and chariots with such wheels in the Vedic literature. The excavations at Surkotada in Kachchh by Jagat Pati Joshi (1990) have yielded the bones of domestic horse, a fact corroborated even by a western palaeontologist, and spoked wheels have been witnessed in the excavated remains of Banawali, Kalibangan and Rakhigarhi (Lal 2002).

Buddha Prakash (1964), and of course, many other scholars, believed that the Harappa culture or the Indus Valley Civilization represents the Vedic Civilization. The view has been reinforced by D.N. Tripathi (1988), K.D. Sethna (1992), S.R. Rao (1993), Bhagwan Singh (1995), George Feuerstein, Subhash Kak and David Frawley (1995), S.P. Gupta (1996), etc., who believe the Vedic Civilization to be an indigenous phenomenon and the Indus Valley Civilization as representing the cultural remains of the Vedic people. Some scholars refer to the Vedic people as belonging to the Āryan race but it may be pointed out that the latest researches in the field of genetics have thoroughly demonstrated the hollowness of the racial theory. There has been a complete biological continuity during the period of 4500–800 BC (Hemphill: 1991), which should cover the whole span of the Indus Civilization, rightly renamed as Indus-Sarasvatī Civilization (Gupta: 1996) as the number of archaeological sites of this culture on the Sarasvatī far outnumber those existing in the Indus valley.

Traditions die very hard. Lal (2002) has shown the continuity of various cultural traits from the Harappan period to the present day. Ornamentation, make-up and toiletry, particularly the practice of applying vermilion (*sindūra*) to the *māṅga* (line of partition of the hair on the head) and wearing of bangles in the left arm by married Hindu women goes back to the early Harappan times. Ornaments like the multiple and spiralled bangles, gold or silver cones on the head, necklaces with transverse holes in the discular beads, combs with teeth on both sides, three-in-one toiletry gadgets, hopskotches, gamesmen in chess, dice with a definite system of markings, toys for the kids, bird-cages, under and over-ground cooking ovens, three-legged *chaklās* or *pāṭās* for rolling the bread before being baked, various types of utensils including the frying pans and feeding bottles, similar shapes and decorations, use of *kamaṇḍalus,* cots and bedspreads, ploughs and the method of double-cropping, use of wedge-shaped bricks in the construction of wells, wheel-carts with similar width between the wheels, boats and ships with cabins and masts, purifying the house-floors with cow-dung, worshipping *Śiva-liṅga* placed in the *yoni-pīṭha,* sacrificial altars, the use of apsidal shape in religious structures (altars and later Indian temples and *vihāras*), method of construction laying the bricks in double-bond, use of plumb-bobs in construction, the proportions of weights and measures, using weighing scales with pans, worshipping trees and plants, *svastika* as an auspicious symbol, use of writing tablets, method of teaching, practising yoga in various *yogāsanas* and meditation, etiquette of saluting with folded hands (as in *namaste*), etc., are some of the numerous examples which have come down to us from the Harappan times. Various scholars have tried to explain many other similarities—flora, fauna, customs and rituals, cultural objects, etc., occurring in the Harappan remains and mentioned in the *Ṛigveda* and continuing later, even to the present in certain cases.

It thus becomes clear that if the Ṛigvedic Āryans were living in the Sapta-Sindhu region, their archaeological remains should also be found there. And, the relics left for posterity by the people of the Indus-Sarasvatī Civilization are the only ones found from this entire region. The pattern of the distribution of the earlier, mature and late phases may be chalked out but that does not indicate the movement of the people from the Harakhvatī or Helmand towards the east, not to speak of their eastward movement from further west at an early stage of their settlement in the region.

The corelation of literary and archaeological data shows another consonance. The Sarasvatī which was a mighty river flowing from the Himalayas to the western sea and is known from numerous references from the family books of the *Ṛigveda* (Maṇḍalas II–VII) which are regarded as earlier than others, is described in the *Pañchavimśa Brāhmana* (XXV. 10, 16) to have been lost (dried up) in the sands of the desert at Vinaśana/Parīṇaḥ, generally identified with Sirsa in Haryana or Kalibangan in Rajasthan (Bharadwaj: 1986). Radiocarbon dates reveal that the mature Harappan settlement of Kalibangan located on the bank of the ancient Sarasvatī (Ghaggar) was abandoned around 1900 BC because of the drying up of the river which was its life-giver, consequential of some tectonic upheaval near the source of the river (Lal: 1997). The evidence is of crucial importance for not only corroborating the literary statement but also providing a clue to the date of the *Ṛigveda,* which should be anterior to this date. It was probably because of this calamity that people now searched new pastures and moved towards the Gaṅgā basin.

In the age of the Brāhmaṇas the Sarasvatī recedes into the background and the rivers of the Gaṅgā plain come into prominence (Basu: 1969). The *Śatapatha Brāhmaṇa* (I.4, 1, 17) mentions the river Sadānīrā forming the boundary between the Kosalas and the Videhas (*Saiṣā apyetahi Kosala- videhānāṃ maryādā*). The name Sadānīrā indicates that it was a perennial river and is generally identified with the Gandak. The *Śatapatha Brāhmaṇa* (I.4, 1, 10) describes king Videgha Māthava of Videha along with his priest Rāhūgaṇa as carrying the sacred sacrificial fire from the banks of the Sarasvatī over Kosala across the river Sadānīrā. This is a clear indication of the shift of the civilization from the Sarasvatī to the Sadānīrā. The five principal Ṛigvedic tribes, viz. the Anus, Druhyus, Purus, Turvaśas and the Yadus pale into insignificance and are not heard of again. The Bharatas of the early Vedic period also lost their prominence, some others also disappeared while many new tribes like the Kurus and Pañchālas emerged and came into prominence. New divisions sprang up and different types of sovereignty emerged. The archaeological remains from the Gaṅgā valley bear witness to this changed scenario and are datable only to the second millennium BC onwards. With newer geographical setting, there was the need for newer material equipment and archaeology bears it out. The religious-cultural traditions may have continued and their presence even to this day is the sure evidence of the continuity of beliefs and customs.

We thus see that there is a marked consonance in the inferences, which can be drawn from literary and archaeological data. The differences, if any, may be explained because of the limitations of archaeological diggings and as a result of imagination and hyperbole in the literary compositions. I am sure persistent work would enable us even to identify and distinguish the archaeological remains associated with different tribes and states in ancient India.

Bibliography

Basu, Jogiraj, 1969, *India of the Age of the Brāhmaṇas,* Calcutta.
Bhagwan Singh, 1995, *Vedic Harappans,* New Delhi.
Bharadwaj, O.P., 1986, *Studies in the Historical Geography of Ancient India,* Delhi.
Bhargava, P.L., 1971, *India in the Vedic Age,* 2nd ed., Lucknow.
Buddha Prakash, 1964, *Ṛigveda and the Indus Valley Civilization,* Hoshiarpur.

Dales, G.F., 1964, "The Mythical Massacre at Mohenjo-daro", *Expedition,* 6(3), pp. 36-43.

Gupta, S.P., 1996, *The Indus-Sarasvatī Civilization: Origins, Problems and Issues,* Delhi.

Habib, Irfan and Faiz Habib, 1991–92, "The Historical Geography of India, 1800–800 BC", *Proceedings of Indian History Congress,* 52nd Session, pp. 72–97.

Hemphill, B.E., J.R. Lukacs and K.A.R. Kennedy, 1991, "Biological Adaptations and Affinities of Bronze Age Harappans", in R.H. Meadow (ed.), *Harappan Excavations 1986–90,* Madison, Wisconsin, pp. 137–82.

Jones, Williams, 1788, "The Third Anniversary Discourse", *Asiatic Researches,* Vol. I, pp. 415–31.

Joshi, J.P., 1990, *Excavations at Surkotada 1971–72 and Explorations in Kutch,* New Delhi.

Lal, B.B., 1954–55, "Excavation at Hastināpura and Other Explorations in the Upper Gaṅgā and Sutlej Basins 1950–52", *Ancient India,* New Delhi, Nos. 10 & 11, pp. 4–151.

——, 1997, *The Earliest Civilization of South Asia,* New Delhi.

——, 2002, *The Sarasvatī Flows On : The Continuity of Indian Culture,* New Delhi.

Max Müller, F., 1890, *Physical Religion.* Reprint, New Delhi, 1979.

Rao, S.R., 1993, *The Aryan Invasion Theory: A Reappraisal,* New Delhi.

Sethna, K.D., 1992, *The Problem of Aryan Origin: From an Indian Point of View,* New Delhi.

Sharma, R.S., 1999, *Advent of the Aryans in India,* New Delhi.

8
The *Mahābhārata* and the Sindhu-Sarasvatī Tradition

SUBHASH KAK

Introduction

The *Mahābhārata* as an encyclopaedia of early Indian culture and history may be expected to shed light on the Sindhu-Sarasvatī (SS) or Indus Tradition. For example, the *Mahābhārata* and the Purāṇas call Vishṇu and Śiva by the name *Ekaśṛīṅga,* the "one-horned one", or the unicorn, which is one of the most striking images from the mature phase of the SS Tradition.

The Śānti Parva (chapter 343) of the *Mahābhārata* speaks of the single-tusked boar (*varāha*) who saves the earth as Vishṇu's incarnation. Here, Varāha is described as being triple-humped, a figure that we see in the Harappan iconography. There is other continuity of motifs and styles between the SS Tradition and the classical Indian culture.

Geologists believe that the river Śutudrī braided into several channels after its course changed from being a tributary of the Sarasvatī to that of the Sindhu. The Epic remembers this in the legend that sage Vasishṭha wanted to kill himself by jumping into the Haimavatī, but the river saved him by breaking up into a hundred shallow channels, hence its ancient name *Śatadru* (Chaitraratha Parva, chapter 179). This is example of an event in the Epic that occurred in the 4th or the 3rd millennium BC.

The change in the focus of the civilization from the Sarasvatī river to the Gaṅgā is not only implicit in the Purāṇic story of the descent of Gaṅgā but also from the statement in the *Mahābhārata* (Vana Parva, chapter 85) that in the Tretā Pushkara was the holiest *tīrtha,* in Dvāpara it was Kurukshetra, and in the Kaliyuga it is Prayāga.

The *Mahābhārata* telescopes early genealogical history. The Purāṇic king-lists provide useful clues to the sequence of events. Some of the main events are: Generation 45, Bhagīratha, Gaṅgā changes course; Generation 65, Rāma Dāśarathī, Dvāpara begins; Generation 94, Mahābhārata War. Given that the Mahābhārata War took place several centuries before the Buddha, it is clear that even if we allocate only twenty years to each generation, the Purāṇic king-lists reach back into the early phases of the SS Tradition.

The astronomical references in the Vedic texts date back to the 4th and 5th millennia BC.[1] The *Mahābhārata* in turn describes events that belong to the earliest layers of the Vedic lore. For example, there is much material in the Ādi Parva on Yayāti, one of the earliest kings in the Purāṇic lists. There is also description of the westward emigration of Āryan tribes through the device of Yayāti expelling his sons. Such emigration stories are part of the Ṛigvedic narrative.[2]

The Greek historians inform us that the Indians during the time of the Mauryas remembered more than 150 generations of kings spanning over 6,000 years. (We assume that these lists remember the prominent kings only). The earliest calendar in India was centennial, with a cycle of 2,700 years. Called the *Saptaṛishi* calendar, it is still in use in several parts of India. Its current beginning is taken to be 3076 BC. Notices by the Greek historians Pliny and Arrian suggest that during the Mauryan times, the calendar used in India began in 6676 BC. It is very likely that this was the *Saptaṛishi* calendar with a beginning of 6676 BC.

The SS Tradition has been traced to about 7000 or 8000 BC in Mehrgarh in north-west India. It is seen to have evolved in four distinct stages as follows:[3]

Table 8.1 Phases of the SS Tradition

1.	**Early Agriculture Economy Era** **8000 BC – 5500 BC**	Mehrgarh, Period I Aceramic, Neolithic, 8000–5500 BC
2.	**Regional Growth Era** **5500 BC – 2600 BC**	Mehrgarh, Period II, 5500–4800 BC Mehrgarh, Period III, 4800–3500 BC Harappa, Period I, 3500–2800 BC Harappa, Period II, 2800–2600 BC
3.	**Integration Era** **2600 BC – 1900 BC**	Harappan Phase Harappan Period, 3C, Final, 2200–1900 BC
4.	**Localization Era** **1900 BC – 1300 BC**	Late Harappan Period, 1900–1300 BC Harappa, Periods 4 and 5, 1900–1700 BC Beginnings of the Gaṅgā Phase

The Early Agricultural Economy Era (ca. 8000–5500 BC) witnessed the beginning and maturation of the agricultural economy. In the Regional Growth Era, (5500–2600 BC) we see regional styles and different phases of evolution. Although uniformity begins to emerge in 2800 BC (or a couple of centuries earlier), the Harappan state with numerous cities and towns emerges in the Integration Era (2600–1900 BC). The uniformity is seen in the writing, system of weights and styles of pottery. The uniformity across a very wide area emphasizes social classes and considerable trade.

In the Localization Era (1900–1300 BC) we witness unbroken continuity in several cultural expressions but we do not see writing and the use of standardized weights. Evidently, this was a consequence of a breakdown of long distance trade. By the end of this Era, a new integration is seen in a geographical area across the entire north Indian plains.

If one juxtaposes these phases with the events of the *Mahābhārata*, it appears that at the end of the War the region changed from a period of several isolated, independent kingdoms to that of a larger state. The unification created at the end might have provided the climate in which epic poetry was patronized by the king. This idea supports the view that the growth of the Epic from its original form took place during the transition to the Integration Era or perhaps at the end of the Localization Era. In this article I will explore several issues related to the date of the Mahābhārata events and the text and their relationship to the SS Tradition and the Indic people in West Asia.

The Date of the Mahābhārata War

Let us consider the epoch for the Mahābhārata War. By popular tradition, the Kali age started with the death of Kṛishṇa, 35 years after the War. The Kali calendar has a beginning of 3102 BC, therefore, it is believed that the Mahābhārata War took place in 3137 BC. The Kali age is supposed to have begun with a grand planetary conjunction.

The first mention of the Kali calendar is by the astronomer Āryabhaṭa in his treatise on astronomy with an internal date of AD 500. The earliest epigraphical reference is in the 5th century inscription of King Devasena where it is alluded to indirectly and in the Aihole inscription of 3735 Kali (AD 634). Because of these late references, some scholars have suggested that the Kali calendar was started at a later period with an assumed conjunction at the beginning of the era for convenience of calculations and therefore, the Aihole inscription cannot be taken as a proof of the date of the War.

Modern studies using powerful software that can reconstruct the ancient skies indicates that there was actually an approximate conjunction of the planets on 17 February, 3102 BC as mentioned by Āryabhaṭa. This may only be a coincidence. Even if the Kali calendar is as old as its starting date, its connections with the Mahābhāta War do not appear to be equally ancient. There are also other traditions related to the War. Some of them are old, some new. The most prominent competing theories may be gathered into the following four classes:

1. *The date of around 1000* BC. This is the date popularized by western Indologists as being most "reasonable" based on archaeological data. Repeated in numerous school texts, it has achieved a certain kind of canonicity. This date was first proposed within the framework of the Āryan invasion theory. Although this theory has been discredited, the date has taken an independent life of its own.
2. *The date of 1924* BC. Based on Purāṇic genealogies that see a gap of 1,000 years or so between the War and the rule of the Nandas (424 BC) we get the date of 1424 BC. But Pargiter, while editing these accounts from the various Purāṇas,[4] suggested that the original number was 1500 which was wrongly copied in various texts as 1000, 1015, or 1050. I accept the arguments of Pargiter and, therefore, consider the Purāṇic tradition to support the date of 1924 BC. Furthermore, the date of 1424 BC sits in the middle of an obscure period, and it is hard to see how the events of that age would not have left markers in the archaeological record.
3. *The date of 2449* BC. This is based on a statement by Varāhamihira in AD 505 in chapter 13 of the *Bṛihat Saṁhitā*, where it is claimed that the commencement of the Śaka era took place 2,526 years after the rule of the king Yudhishṭhira. If the Śaka era meant here is the Sālivāhana era (AD 78), then the date follows. Some scholars have suggested that this Śaka era refers to the one started by an earlier Śaka king in Central Asia and that this date is not at variance with the Kali date of Āryabhaṭa.
4. *The date of 3137* BC. The traditional value, mentioned by Āryabhaṭa and in the Aihole inscription of AD 634.

I shall examine these three different dates while considering the evidence from the *Mahābhārata*, the Purāṇas, archaeology and astronomy.

The *Mahābhārata* and Archaeology

Is the *Mahābhārata*—the text of 100,000 verses—which is a source for the events of the War to be taken as history? The epic itself claims to have been originally just 8,800 verses composed by Kṛishṇa Dvaipāyana Vyāsa and called the *Jaya.* Later, it became 24,000 verses, called the *Bhārata,* when it was recited by Vaiśampāyana. Finally, it was recited as the 100,000 versed epic (the *Mahābhārata)* by Ugraśravas, the son of Lomaharshaṇa.

Thus, the tradition acknowledges that the *Mahābhārata* grew in stages. The core of the story is very ancient and there is astronomical evidence in it related to the Aśvamedha rite that indicates a period before the 3rd millennium BC.[5] The details of the final version may very well include episodes that are poetic exaggerations. We see such poetic imagination at work by comparing the *Rāmāyaṇas* of Vālmīki and Tulasīdāsa. We may also compare the story of Rādhā, which does not appear in the *Mahābhārata* or the *Bhāgavata Purāṇa,* but has become a part of the Kṛishṇa legend due to later texts.

Many of the characters of the *Mahābhārata* are mentioned in the Vedic texts that, on account of being considered sacred, have not suffered interpolations and should thus represent historical persons. Kṛishṇa for example, is mentioned in the *Chhāndogya Upanishad.* Other names occurring elsewhere include Vichitravīrya, Śāntanu, Dhṛitarāshṭra, Janamejaya, and Parīkshit.[6]

Due to its expansion over several centuries, the Epic includes late material. This means that dating the events of the Epic based on archaeological finds could be misleading. Some scholars have correlated the Painted Grey Ware (PGW) pottery of the period of 1100–900 BC found in Hastinapur (modern Hathipur) to the Kauravas. But there is no basis for such correlation. The Kurukshetra site itself has structures that go back to about 3000 BC.

Pāṇini's grammar (ca. 400 BC) knows the *Mahābhārata*. In the sūtra 6.2.38, it mentions both the *Bhārata* and the *Mahābhārata.* Also, the Epic in its long descriptions of the religions of the day, describes the Vedic, Sāṅkhya, Yoga, Pāśupāta, and the Bhāgavata traditions. There is no mention of Buddhism, so we can be certain that it was substantially complete prior to 400 or 500 BC. The language of the Epic does not always follow Pāṇinian constructions which also indicates that it is prior to 500 BC.

Even the political life described in the *Mahābhārata* does not correspond to the imperial ages of 400 BC—AD 400 that has sometimes been assigned to it in the West. Cattle raids occur prominently in it, not imperial conquest. There is no reference to the Śiśunāga kings, the Nandas, the Mauryas, or the Śuṅgas. On the other hand, the Buddhist Jātakas, were written during the time of these dynasties, are aware of the characters of the Epic. One Jātaka, for example, speaks disparagingly of Draupadī for having four husbands.

Dion Chrysostom, Greek Sophist (AD 40–105) mentions that the Indians possess an *Iliad* of 100,000 verses. Together with its appendix, the *Harivaṁśa,* the Epic does add up to this total.

Recent archaeological discoveries indicate that the Sarasvatī river dried up around 1900 BC, leading to the collapse of the Harappan Civilization that was principally located in the Sarasvatī region (accounting for about 70 per cent of all the Harappan sites). The *Ṛigveda* celebrates the Sarasvatī as the greatest river of its day, going from the mountains to the sea *(giribhya asamudrāt* in *RV* 7.95.2).

There are two schools of thought related to the drying up of the Sarasvatī river. According to the first one, the Sarasvatī ceased to be a seagoing river in about 3000 BC, explaining why the 3rd millennium settlements on the banks of the Sarasvatī river end in the Bahawalpur region of the Punjab and do not extend to the sea; there was a further shrinking of the river in about 1900 BC due to an earthquake when its two principal tributaries were captured by the Sindhu and the Gaṅgā river systems. According to the second view, the Sarasvatī flowed to the sea until 1900 BC when it dried up. The first view explains the geographical situation related to the Harappan sites more convincingly.[7]

Given the understanding of the drying up of Sarasvatī, with its pre-eminent status during the Ṛigvedic times, it follows that the Ṛigvedic hymns are generally anterior to 1900 BC. If one accepts the theory that the Sarasvatī stopped reaching the sea in 3000 BC, then the Ṛigvedic hymns are prior to 3000 BC. If the tradition that Vyāsa was the arranger of the Vedas is correct, the latter explanation would mean that the Mahābhārata War could indeed have occurred in 3137 BC.

The Purāṇic Tradition

The Purāṇic lists come down to the 4th or the 5th century AD and they are quite accurate in their details of the post-Mauryan period for which independent inscriptional evidence is available. One would expect that they would be accurate for the period prior to the Mauryas also. The regnal years are given in the Purāṇas only for the post-War kings.

The king-list for Magadha has the following dynasties in the post-Bharata War period:[8]

1. Bṛihadrathas (32 kings)	967 years
2. Pradyotas of Avanti (5 kings)	173 years
3. Śiśunāgas (10 kings)	360 years
4. Nandas (Mahāpadma + sons)	100 years
5. Mauryas (9 kings)	137 years
6. Śuṅgas (10 kings)	112 years
7. Kaṇvas (4 kings)	45 years
8. Āndhras (30 kings)	460 years

One may question the reliability of the earlier parts of this list since the average span of reign for the pre-Nanda kings is more than twice as much for the post-Nanda ones. The explanation appears to be that it was during the Mauryan age that comprehensive king-lists were made and consequently, only the better-known names of the earlier period were included. The centennial counting system, named after the *nakshatras*, made certain that the count of the dynastic totals was accurate. The length of the Bṛihadratha dynasty may also be questioned. But, it may represent the cumulative sum of several early dynasties.

During the pre-Nanda period, the lists also provide for 24 Aikshavākus, 27 Pañchālas, 24 kings of Kāśī, 28 Haihayas, 32 Kaliṅgas, 25 Aśmakas, 36 Kurus, 28 Maithilas, and 23 Śūrasenas.

We know that Chandragupta Maurya started his reign in 324 BC. Therefore, if we were to accept these periods, the dynastic eras for the post-Bhārata age will be:

1. Bṛihadrathas	1924–957 BC
2. Pradyotas	957–784 BC
3. Śiśunāgas	784–424 BC
4. Nandas	424–324 BC
5. Mauryas	324–187 BC

It is most significant that the Purāṇic king-lists imply 1924 BC as the epoch of the Mahābhārata War. Since this epoch is virtually identical to the rough date of 1900 BC for the catastrophic drying up of the Sarasvatī river, it suggests that the two might be linked if they are not the same. The disruption due to the earthquake may have been a contributing factor to the Mahābhārata War, or the War could have served as a metaphor for the geological catastrophe.

Around AD 500, a major review of the Indian calendar was attempted. The astronomers Āryabhaṭa, Varāhamihira and others used the *nakshatra* references that the *Saptaṛishi* were in Maghā at the time of the Mahābhārata War to determine its epoch. Āryabhaṭa declared the war to have occurred in 3137 BC, and Varāhamihira assigned it to 2449 BC. This discrepancy arose perhaps from the different assumptions regarding the *nakshatras* (27 or 28) in the calculations of the two astronomers.

It is likely that the fame of the Kaliyuga with its beginning assigned to 3102 BC prompted a change in the beginning of the *Saptaṛishi* era to about the same time, that is to 3076 BC.

The Purāṇic memory of the Mahābhārata War having occurred in 1924 BC may represent the transference of a much earlier event to the cataclysmic event at the end of the Harappan period. The memory of the War in popular imagination may represent the conflation of two different actual events.

The date of 1000 BC or so is just not possible because it is at variance with the astronomical facts related to the period. Furthermore, it is at variance with the Purāṇic genealogies which, we know, are quite accurate in the post-Mauryan period and are likely to have been accurate earlier as well. Then there are various remembered lines of teachers that show up in various texts. Specifically, the *Bṛihadāranyaka Upanishad* remembers a line of 60 teachers. We do not know how many years should be assigned to each teacher but this line could span substantially more than a thousand years. Considering that this Upanishad was written in about 800–600 BC in the most conservative reckoning, this long list makes it impossible for the Ṛigvedic period to end in 1000 BC, as required by the War in that epoch.

Recently, astronomical evidence related to the mention of eclipses and the placement of planets in the narrative of the *Mahābhārata* has been examined by several scholars.[9] The date of 3067 BC (35 years after 3102 BC rather than 35 years before it) has provided a nice fit for a large number of data points. But such analysis depends on subjective interpretation of the stray astronomical references. Neither can we be sure if the passages used are from the core text or from the much later accretions. Therefore, such an approach will remain highly controversial.

This leaves us with the dates of 1924 BC and 3137 BC. I do not think we have evidence at this time to pick one of these two as the more likely one. If one gives credence to the Purāṇic genealogies, then 1924 BC would be the time for the War; if, on the other hand, we go by the astronomical evidence related to the Vedas and the subsequent literature, then 3137 BC remains a plausible date. If the pre-Nanda Purāṇic lists are not accurate for the regnal periods, then the War probably occurred a few centuries later than 1924 BC.

The Indic Kings of the West

We mentioned in the Introduction that the *Mahābhārata* mentions the five descendents of Yayāti, two became Yavanas and the Mlechchhas. This seems to remember a westward emigration. This particular migration may have occurred in a very early period in the Vedic world that spanned Jambudvīpa and the trans-Himalayan region of Uttara Kuru. We have a later evidence for another westward movement to the lands ranging from Babylonia to Turkey.

The Mitanni, who worshiped Vedic gods, were an Indic kingdom that had bonds of marriage across several generations with the Egyptian 18th dynasty to which Akhenaten belonged. The Mitannis were known to the Egyptians as the Naharins, connected to the river *(nahar),* very probably referring to the Euphrates. At its peak, the Mitanni empire stretched from Kirkuk (ancient Arrapkha) and the Zagros mountains in western Iran in the east, through Assyria to the Mediterranean Sea in the west. Its centre was in the region of the Khabur River, where its capital, Wassukkani (Vasukhani, "a mine of wealth") was probably located.[10]

The first Mitanni king was Sutarna I (good sun). He was followed by Baratarna I (Paratarna, great sun), Parasuksatra (ruler with axe), Saustatar (Saukshatra, son of Sukshatra, the good ruler), Paratarna II, Artadama (Ṛitadhaman, abiding in cosmic law), Sutarna II, Tushratta (Daśaratha), and finally Matiwazza (Mativaja, whose wealth is thought) during whose lifetime the Mitanni state appears to have become a vassal to Assyria.

The early years of the Mitanni empire were occupied in the struggle with Egypt for control of Syria. The greatest Mitanni king was Saukshatra who reigned during the time of Tuthmose III. He was said to have looted the Assyrian palace at Ashur. Under the reign of Tuthmose IV, more friendly relations were established between the Egyptians and the Mitannis.

The daughter of King Artadama was married to Tuthmose IV, Akhenaten's grandfather, and the daughter of Sutarna II (Gilukhipa) was married to his father, Amenhotep III, the great builder of temples who ruled during 1390–1352 BC ("khipa" of these names is the Sanskrit *kshipa,* night). In his old age, Amenhotep wrote to Tushratta many times wishing to marry his daughter, Tadukhipa. It appears that by the time she arrived Amenhotep III was dead. Tadukhipa was now married to the new king Akhenaten, becoming famous as the queen Kiya (short for Khipa).

The Egyptian kings had other wives as well. Akhenaten's mother, Tiye, was the daughter of Yuya, who was a Mitanni married to a Nubian. It appears that Nefertiti was the daughter of Tiye's brother Ay, who was to become king himself. The 18th dynasty had a liberal dose of Indic blood.

But how could an Indic kingdom be so far from India, near Egypt? A plausible scenario is that after catastrophic earthquakes dried up the Sarasvatī river around 1900 BC, many groups of Indic people started moving West. We see Kassites, a somewhat shadowy aristocracy with Indic names and worshiping Sūrya and the Maruts, in western Iran about 1800 BC. They captured power in Babylon in 1600 BC, which they were to rule for over 500 years. The Mitanni ruled northern Mesopotamia (including Syria) for about 300 years, starting 1600 BC, out of their capital of Vasukhani. Their warriors were called *marya,* which is the proper Sanskrit term for it.

In a treaty between the Hittites and the Mitanni, Indic deities Mitra, Varuṇa, Indra, and Nasatya (Aśvins) are invoked. A text by a Mitannian named Kikkuli uses words such as *aika* (*eka,* one), *tera* (*tri,* three), *panza* (*pañcha,* five), *satta* (*sapta,* seven), *na* (*nava,* nine), *vartana* (*vartana,* round). Another text has *babru* (*babhru,* brown), *parita* (*palita,* grey), and *pinkara* (*piṅgala,* red). Their chief festival was the celebration of visuva (solstice) very much like in India. It is not only the kings who had Sanskrit names; a large number of other Sanskrit names have been unearthed in the records from the area.

Documents and contract agreements in Syria mention a warrior caste that constituted the elite in the cities. The ownership of land appears to have been inalienable. Consequently, no documents on the selling of landed property are to be found in the great archives of Akkadian documents and letters discovered in Nuzi. The prohibition against selling landed property was dodged with the stratagem of "adopting" a willing buyer against an appropriate sum of money.

Information of the mythology of the Hurrians of the Mitanni is known from related Hittite and Ugaritic myths. The king of the gods was the weather god Teshub who had violently deposed Kumarbi paralleling the killing of Vṛitra by Indra. Major sanctuaries of Teshub were located at Arrapkha (modern Kirkuk) and at Halab (modern Aleppo) in Syria. Like Indra, Teshub also had a solar aspect. In the east his consort was the goddess of love and war Shaushka (Venus), and in the west the goddess Hebat (Hepat). In addition, a considerable importance was attributed to impersonal gods such as heaven and earth as well as to deities of mountains and rivers. Temple monuments of modest dimensions have been unearthed.

The general Indic influence in the area may also be seen in the comprehensiveness of the god lists. The most "official" god list, in two Ugaritic copies and one Akkadian translation, consists of 33 items, exactly as is true of the count of Vedic gods. These gods are categorized into three classes, somewhat like the three classes of the Vedic gods, although there are differences in details.

The main Semitic gods are Yahvah and El or (Il or al-Il, as Allah). The *Ṛigveda* mentions Yahvaḥ in 21 different hymns. Ilā is the deity for the Ṛigvedic Apri hymns and it represents Agni in *Yajurveda* (VS) 2.3, whereas Ilā represents Earth, speech, and flow. The Vedic Yahvaḥ is, as an epithet, associated with movement, activity, heaven and earth; it means the sacrificer and Agni, the chief terrestrial god. It is associated with energy like the Yahvaḥ of the Semites. It may be compared to Śivaḥ, an epithet for auspiciousness in the *Ṛigveda*, that later is applied regularly to Rudra. It is plausible that the Vedic Ilā and Yahvaḥ were adopted by the Semites through the mediating agency of the Mitanni.

Greek accounts tell us that the Ugaritic believed in a cosmic egg out of which the earth emerged which is reminiscent of *brahmāṇḍa* of the Vedic view. How do we know that the Mitannis were Indic and not Iranian? There are several reasons, but to be brief, I shall only give three: 1. the deities Indra, Mitra, Varuṇa, and Nasatya are Indian deities and not Iranian ones, because in Iran Varuṇa is unknown and Indra and Nasatya appear as demons; 2. the name Vasukhani makes sense in Sanskrit as a "mine of wealth" whereas in Iranian it means "good mine" which is much less likely; 3. *satta*, or *sapta*, for seven, rather than the Iranian word *hapta*, where the initial *'s'* has been changed to *'h'*.

Why could not the Mitannis be the descendents of a pre-Vedic people as in the Gimbutas model of the spread of the Indo-Iranian people from the Kurgan culture of the steppes of Central Asia? They would then have had no particular affinity for Indic deities. If the pre-Vedic people in Central Asia already had Indian deities, how would these small bands of people impose their culture and language over what was perhaps the most densely populated region of the ancient world? Furthermore, that view does not square with our knowledge of the astronomical tradition within India. The Vedic Saṁhitās have very early astronomical data and its geography is squarely within India. The *Vedāṅga Jyotisha*, a late Vedic text, already belongs to the middle of the second millennium BC. The earlier texts remember events within the Indic geographical area going back to the third and the fourth millennia BC. The theory of a proto-Indoāryan people in Iran from whom the Āryans of India descended in the second millennium BC does not work for the same reasons.

The idea of invasion or large-scale immigration of outsiders into India displacing the original population in the middle of the second millennium BC has been rejected since it is not in accord with archaeological facts, skeletal records, and the continuity of the cultural tradition.

The Indian textual tradition also does not permit us to accept the Gimbutas model because of the length of time required for the rise of the voluminous Indian literature.

Over fifty years ago, Roger T. O'Callaghan and W.F. Albright published in *Analecta Orientalia* of Rome a list of 81 names (13 from the Mitanni, 23 from the Nuzi, and 45 from the Syrian documents) with Indic etymologies. Out of this list, Dumont has provided the etymology of 45 names.[11] Analyzing the names, Dumont concludes that the names are clearly

Indic and not Iranian. The initial *s* is maintained and the group *śv* is represented by the similar sounding *sw* and not the Avestan *aspo.* Also, most of the names are *bahuvṛihi* or *tatpurusha* compounds.

Considering the language, it is clearly an Indic dialect because the initial *v* is replaced by *b,* while medial *v* becomes the semivowel *w*. Like Middle Indic (Prākrit) dialects, the medial *pt* transforms into *tt,* as in *sapta* becoming *satta.*

Dumont stresses its relationship to Sanskrit in the characteristic patronymic names with the vṛiddhi—strengthening of the first syllable, like in Saumati (the son of Sumati) or Sausapti (the son of Susapti). The worship of the Vedic gods like Indra, Vāyu, Svar, Soma, Ṛia, Vasus has already been noted. The fact that the Mitanni names suggest a Middle Indic dialect is supportive of the thesis that the emigration of the various groups from India took place after the early Vedic period had come to an end.

Our argument actually goes beyond the presence of people in West Asia whose languages were Indic, as was the case with the Mitanni. There is evidence that Indic religion and culture had adherents even outside of groups with Indic speech.

The *Avestā* speaks of the struggle between the worshippers of Ahura Mazda and the *daevas*. Zarathustra nowhere names the *daevas* and it is only in the later texts that Indra and the Nasatyas are so labelled. Many of the Vedic *devas* (such as Mitra, Bhaga, Agni, Vāyu, and Indra as Vṛitraghna) continue to be counted amongst the good *ahuras.* It appears that the triple division of *deva/asura/rākśasa* corresponding to *sattva/rājas/tamas* was divided into the dichotomy *deva* versus *asura/rākśasa* in India and that of *deva/asura* versus *daeva (rākśasa)* in Iran. The term *daeva* as synonym with *rākśasa* and distinct from *deva* survives in Kashmir.

The *ahura-daeva* opposition in the Zoroastrian texts is expressed as one between the Mazdayasnas and the Daevayasnas. It is a conflict in which Zoroaster wished to defeat and convert the worshippers of the *daeva* religion. The Yasts speak of legendary heroes and kings who participated in this struggle. The wars against the Daevayasnas by Vistaspa (Yt. 5.109, 113; 9.30–31), Jamaspa (Yt. 5.68–70), and Vistaru of the Naotara family (Yt. 5.76–77) represent this ongoing conflict in the historical period.

In Vendidad, the Zoroastrians are encouraged to take possession of the lands, waters, and harvests of the *daeva,* worshippers (Vd. 19.26). Elsewhere (Vd. 7.36-40), it is recommended that the art of medicine should be first tried on the *daeva*-worshippers and if they survive then it should be attempted on the Mazdayasnians.

Although the Zoroastrian heresy triumphed in Iran and the great Persian kings of the middle of first millennium BC followed the religion of Ahura Mazda, the *daeva* worshippers survived, especially in the West, in the Mesopotamian religion.

The *devas* as well as *daevas* survived for a pretty long time in corners of Iran. The evidence of the survival of the *devas* comes from the *daiva*-inscription of Xerxes (ruled 486–465 BC). The revolt by the *daeva* worshippers in West Iran is directly referred to:

Proclaims Xerxes the King: When I became king, there is among these countries one which was in rebellion. Afterwards, Ahuramazda bore me aid. By the favour of Ahuramazda I smote that country and put it down in its place.

And, among these countries there was a place where previously daiva were worshipped. Afterwards, by the favor of Ahuramazda I destroyed that sanctuary of daiva, and I made proclamation: 'The daiva shall not be worshiped!' Where previously the daiva were worshipped, there I worshiped Ahuramazda at the proper time and in the proper manner. And, there was other business that had been done ill. That I made good. That which I did, all did by the favor of Ahuramazda. Ahuramazda bore me aid until I completed the work.

The analysis of early Persian history has shown that the Mazandaran, the region south of the Caspian Sea and the Alburz mountain range, remained for long a centre of *daeva* worship. There were also the successors to the *deva* worshippers of the Mitanni kingdom. It has been suggested that the Xerxes inscription refers to the suppression of these people.

Burrow takes the *daeva* worshipping people to be proto-Indoāryans and sees them as the remnants of a population that stretched from West Asia to India. The Iranians coming down from the north-east drove a wedge between this belt, leading to the eventual assimilation of the western *daeva* worshippers in the course of centuries.

Irrespective of what the original movement of the Indoāryans was before the fourth or fifth millennium BC, it is clear that since their Indian branch recognizes the geography of only their region, it is either necessary to push back the proto-Indoāryan phase to the fourth or the fifth millennium BC or to postulate their movement out of India as is suggested in the Purāṇas.

Concluding Remarks

The material from the *Mahābhārata* and the Purāṇas provides us many tangled hints. Given the extensive nature of the king-lists and the teacher-lists, it is impossible that the origin of the *Mahābhārata*-Purāṇa tradition could be brought down to the beginning of the second millennium BC as espoused by the proponents of the theories of Āryan invasion and migration. The Mahābhārata War occurs at the 94th generation in these lists, and even if one were to assign just 20 years for each generation and assume that the lists were exhaustive, one would have to account for nearly 2,000 years before the War which, even in the most conservative dating for the War, takes us square into the beginnings of the Integration Era of the SS Tradition.

The Epic and Purāṇic evidence on the geographical situation supports the notion of the shifting of the centre of the Vedic world from the Sarasvatī to the Gaṅgā region in early second millennium BC. O.P. Bharadwaj's excellent study of the Vedic Sarasvatī using textual evidence[12] supports the theory that the *Ṛigveda* is to be dated about 3000 BC and the Mahābhārata War must have occurred about that time.

The *Mahābhārata* clearly belongs to a heroic age, prior to the rise of the complexity of urban life. The weapons used are mythical or clubs. The narrative of chariots could be a later gloss added in the first millennium BC. The pre-urban core events of the Epic would fit the 3137 BC date much better than the 1924 BC. But this would suggest that the Purāṇic tradition at a later time conflated earlier events with the destructive earthquakes of 1924 BC and remembered the later event accurately using the centennial *Saptaṛishi* calendar. The Indic kings of West Asia are descendents of Vedic people who moved West after the catastrophe of 1924 BC.

Notes and References

1. Kak, S., 2000, *The Astronomical Code of the Ṛgveda*, Munshiram Manoharlal, New Delhi.
2. Talageri, S.G., 2000, *The Rigveda: A Historical Analysis,* Aditya Prakashan, New Delhi.
   Frawley, D., 2001, *The Rig Veda and the History of India,* Aditya Prakashan, New Delhi.
3. Gupta, S.P., 1996, *The Indus-Sarasvati Civilization,* Pratibha Prakashan, Delhi.
   Lal, B.B. 1997, *The Earliest Civilization of South Asia,* Aryan Books International, New Delhi.
   Kenoyer, J. M., 1998, *Ancient Cities of the Indus Valley Civilization,* Oxford University Press, Karachi.
4. Pargiter, F.E., 1975 (reprint), *The Purana Text of the Dynasties of the Kali Age,* Deep Publications, New Delhi.

5. Kak, S., 2002, *The Asvamedha: The Rite and its Logic,* Motilal Banarsidass, Delhi.
6. Agarwala, G.C. (ed.), 1979, *Age of Bharata War,* Motilal Banarsidass, Delhi.
7. See Note 1. See also, Kak, S., 2001, *The Wishing Tree: The Presence and Promise of India,* Munshiram Manoharlal, New Delhi.
8. See Pargiter, *op cit.*
9. See Agarwala, *op cit.,* for summary of early attempts. Recently, the historian of astronomy Narahari Achar has in unpublished work argued for the date of 3067 BC with an error of a few decades. Achar's work does not depend on the classical Siddhantic ideas which increases its persuasiveness.
10. Kak, S., 2003, *Akhenaten, Surya, and the Ṛgveda.* Louisiana State University, Baton Rouge.
11. Dumont, P.E., 1947, "Indo-Aryan Names from Mitanni, Nuzi, and Syrian documents", *Journal of the American Oriental Society,* Vol. 67, pp. 251–253.
12. Bharadwaj, O.P., 1984, "Identification of Vinasana and Some Consequential Observations", in *Svasti Sri* (ed. K.V. Ramesh), Agam Kala Prakashan, Delhi.
Bharadwaj, O.P., 1987, "The Vedic Sarasvati", *Haryana Sahitya Akademi Journal of Indological Studies,* Vol. II, Nos., 1–2, pp. 38–58.

9

The *Ṛigveda* and Harappa

N. Kazanas

The Argument

The Vedic culture or tradition spans many millennia from the composition of the *Ṛigveda* and the subsequent Vedic Saṃhitās to modern times. This unfolded in Saptasindhu, the land of the seven rivers in north-west India and Pakistan and adjacent regions reaching to the east and to the southernmost tip of the subcontinent. The Harappan culture or the Indus-Sarasvatī Civilization (ISC) is, as others and I have argued in many studies (Kazanas 1999, etc; Frawley 1997, 2001; etc.), one of the expressions of this tradition whose beginnings are lost in the mists of pre-history. Some have argued that the (Ṛig-)Vedic and the Harappan cultures converge (Bisht 1999–2000; Singh 1995; etc.). This is true of the later Vedic or post-Ṛigvedic culture but not of the Ṛigvedic one. In this article I present the main evidence showing that the *Ṛigveda* (*RV*) is much older than the early ISC and that, therefore, the Vedic Tradition is indeed, much older than mainstream academics hold.

Levitt's Study

In a recent publication S.H. Levitt examines the development of the "early Indic tradition" and the development of religion in ancient Meṣopotamia. After comparing several elements in the two religions, he concludes:

> We can date the early Indic tradition on the basis of comparable points in ancient Mesopotamia. By this, the Ṛigveda would date back to the beginning of the the 3rd millennium BC, with some of the earliest hymns perhaps even dating to the end of the fourth millennium BC (2003: 356).

Indeed, since the *RV* is the earliest text of the Indo-Āryans, its date of composition would help establish the beginnings of "the early Indic tradition". Having at this time made a comparative study of Vedic, Mesopotamian and Egyptian religion (Kazanas Forthcoming) I concur with Levitt's view. But I would like to draw the discussion farther taking into account much evidence (more Vedic and less Mesopotamian) which somehow escaped Levitt's attention. This evidence from comparisons between the *RV* and the ISC and between the Vedic and Mesopotamian traditions indicates that the bulk of the *RV* was composed before 3000 and probably before 3200[1], and is therefore older than the most ancient Mesopotamian religious texts. Any date prior to 3200 antedates the very early phases of the ISC, which matures in *c.* 2600–2200, declines thereafter and seems to collapse in large part and/or move eastward after *c.* 1900. The mature Harappan phase would seem to converge with post-Vedic texts, late Brāhmaṇas and Upanishads, perhaps, and certainly the sūtra literature. This dating differs from that of the AIT (Āryan Invasion/Immigration Theory) which has been the mainstream view and which assigns the *RV* to *c.* 1200-1000, the other Saṃhitās *c.* 1000-800 and the Brāhmaṇas *c.* 800–600.

Before proceeding, let me first clarify an important point. Levitt states that "Indic religion is in large part a religion of ancient Mesopotamian type" (p. 356). This is not true and Levitt's subsequent statement that he has pointed out "a few similarities which are more germane to later Indic civilization than Vedic civilization, though their Vedic precursors can at times be seen" does not improve matters. Neither, later Indic nor Vedic religion is of the Mesopotamian type although some similarities, e.g. polytheism, reverence towards the bull (of heaven) and the cow (of plenty), obviously do exist. And this for two very important reasons, i.e. two constituents in the Veda that are absent from Mesopotamia. First, in the Veda (as in the later Hindu religion) people go to heaven or hell (or reincarnate) according to merit gained in this life whereas in Mesopotamia all humans irrespecive of merit go to the Netherworld which is below the *Apzu,* the underworld waters (Bottero 2001). Second, even the early *maṇḍalas* of the *RV* have statements about the One Power of which all gods are expressions, e.g. *RV* I, 164, 6; III, 55, etc. The simultaneous presence of monism and polytheism in the *RV* was extensively explored by K. Werner (1989; see also Kazanas 2001: 289). At a very early stage in Mesopotamia there probably was a single Primal Cause or Source for all the divinities (Bottero 2001: 74) but what unfolds from the start of historical times is mere polytheism. Consequently one can hardly claim that the two religious traditions are of the same type.

However, there is another aspect that will help towards dating the *RV* and this is a comparison between parallel themes or motifs in the two religions/mythologies. Indeed, I have discussed more than twenty affinities such as the Seven Sages, the Flood, the Sun-boat, the eagle flying to heaven, and so on (Kazanas Forthcoming 68ff). Of these I shall examine here only two themes—the horse-sacrifice and the dismemberment of a divine being to create the world(s). I shall demonstrate that in both cases the Vedic material is not borrowed and evidently anterior.

Vedic and Mesopotamian Religion

It is generally believed that the Mesopotamian culture is older than the Indic and that the Indus-Sarasvatī culture borrowed from the former—material artefacts, modes of building, astronomy, alphabet, mythological material, etc. (McEvilley 2002; Bottero 2000; Dalley 1998; Pingree 1998; *et al.*). Although this belief is widespread and well-established, based of course on the AIT which has the Indo-Āryans enter into their historical habitat *c.* 1500, I shall show that if there was any borrowing the borrowers would be the Mesopotamians.

Apart from any other adventitious evidence, a good criterion is the IE (= Indo-European) nature of particular religious themes. Obviously, if a certain theme or element in the Vedic religion is found in other IE traditions then it is more likely that it is Proto-Indo-European and therefore inherited rather than a loan from Mesopotamia. This element then should be assigned to a date before the dispersal of the IEs in the 5th millennium or much earlier.[2] It is, of course, possible that the element was inherited from a much earlier common culture now lost, or that it was developed independently by the Indo-Āryans and the Mesopotamians, but if there was influence then this ran from east westward. Let us now see what the horse-sacrifice tells us.

In Mesopotamia a horse-sacrifice is documented in a liturgical text repeatedly mentioning god Marduk and belonging to the Babylonian ritual related to gods Shamash and Adad (Albright and Dupont 1934). One interesting detail of this ritual is that the priest whispers an incantation "into the left ear of the horse" before its immolation. The lowest terminus for this text is *c.* 800 and the upper *c.* 2000 (*ibid.*, 117–18). Indeed, the horse came to Mesopotamia from Iran a little before 2000 but was put to common use *c.* 1600 (Saggs 1989: 213–14). Before this, the Mesopotamians used asses for their carts and the text mentions the ass as well.[3]

The corresponding Vedic ritual *aśvamedha* is abundantly documented and much commented upon by ancient scholiasts and modern scholars. C. Watkins wrote "We may legitimately look upon the *Aśvamedha* as the principal Indo-European kingship ritual" (2001: 265). One of the minor features in the Vedic horse-sacrifice is the whispering by the priest to the horse's right ear. Full if varied descriptions of this lengthy and complex rite are found in the *Śatapatha Br* Book XIII, in the *Vājasaneyī Saṃhitā* Bks XXII–XXV, in the *Taittirīya Saṃhitā* spread through Bks IV to VII, and in other texts. Evidence for a simpler, perhaps, ritual is found in *RV* I 162 and 163, two hymns praising the horse, and in III 53, 11 in which king Sudās's horses are to be let loose to wander and thus win wealth for him. (Part of this ritual was to let a royal stallion wander freely for a year in neighbouring countries; the king and a band of 400 warriors followed it, claimed the regions through which the horse passed, and if challenged gave battle.)

Unlike the NE cultures, a rich horse mythology is attested in almost all the IE traditions (except the Hittites) and some form of horse-sacrifice was performed among the Greek, Roman, Celtic and Nordic peoples (Anderson 1999). One frequent myth, among others, is that of a god taking on the form of a horse for various reasons. For example, in Vedic mythology Saraṇyū, the daughter of god Tvashṭri marries Vivasvant, the Sungod, then disappears and takes the form of a mare; her husband becomes a stallion, mates with her and as a result the Aśvins are born (*RV* X, 17, 1–2; *Bṛihaddevatā* VI, 162 ff). We find a similar tale in Greece when goddess Demeter became a mare to avoid the harassment of Poseidon, god of the sea, but he became a stallion and mated with her on the plains of Arcadia; as a result were born Areion, a noble horse with black mane, and a girl, and Demeter came to be worshipped in Arcadia as Demeter *'Epiῦς Erinus (= saranyū.* The story is in Pausanias VIII 25, 5). A slightly different myth appears among the Scandinavians when Loki, the god of tricks and transformations, becomes a mare to attract from work the giant-mason's stallion Svadilfari; as a result is born Sleipnir, a horse with eight legs, the swiftest animal in the world, which is given to Odin, king of the gods *(Edda* p. 35–36; Crossley-Holland 1993: 11–14). Surely, it would be absurd to claim that the horse-sacrifice spread from Mesopotamia to all these IE-speaking regions and that, then, each one of them developed almost identical horse-mythologems.

In India, the wild horse is present from *c.* 17000 and there is evidence for its domestication in the Ganges basin *c.* 5000 and in the ISC *c.* 2400 (Kazanas 2003; Chakrabarti 1999; Sharma 1980). Here, we have additional corroboration from the sun-chariot and the sun-boat. The sun-chariot, drawn by horses, is a common IE motif found in the Vedic religion, Iranian, Greek, etc. It is absent in Mesopotamia, where the boat is the vehicle of the sungod (as in Egypt). The boat as a vehicle for the sun and other deities is found also in the Vedic tradition: in *RV* VII 88, 3–4 Vasishṭha sails with god Varuṇa in the latter's boat; in VI, 58, 3 Pūshan, the glowing figure of the sun, sails in the aerial ocean with his fleet of golden ships; and in *Atharvaveda* XVII 1, 25–26 the sun *(āditya* and *sūrya)* is on a boat of 100 oars. This too is found in the Greek lore having thus an IE pedigree. But the horse-drawn chariot is a very common IE image and therefore very old. Consequently, there is no question of the Veda being indebted to Babylon. Nor, can it be claimed that this rite descended from a remote common cultural background since the horse did not come to Mesopotamia much before 2000. All that can be said is that it was instituted in Babylon *c.* 2000–1600 after the importation of the horse and Marduk's rise to pre-eminence *c.* 1800–1600; the Babylonians decided to add this noble creature to the animals they had been using for sacrifice and so enhance the nobility of their own (new) chief god(s). Albright and Dupont mention several Indo-Mesopotamian affinities but, above all, the whispering to the horse's ear is a detail strongly suggestive of borrowing by the Mesopotamians.

An additional detail is the presence of seven spots, like the Pleiades, on the forefront of the sacrificial animal. This is a rare image, but it is found in both Vedic texts *(Śatapatha Brāhmaṇa* XIII, 4, 2, 1–4) and Mesopotamian ones (Albright and Dumont, 119–23).

A very similar image is found in the Finnish epic *Kalevala.* In this epic the cosmic cow rose upward out of superhuman Ilmarinen's smithy "With her horns all golden-shining/ With the Bear-stars on her forehead.../ [and] on the ground her milk she wasted" (de Santillana and Dechend, p. 101). The Bear-stars are not exactly the Pleiades but they too are seven. Moreover, we find two more affinities with Ṛigvedic lore: the image of the sky-cow shedding her milk down to earth is common in the *RV*(I, 164, 27–8; III, 55, 1; VI, 66, 1; etc.); then Ilmarinen erects his smithy complete with bellows and out of it fashions the world-mill Sampo while the Ṛigvedic lord of prayer and holy-power *brahman,* Bṛihaspati, creates the generation of gods as a smith with blasting and smelting. (*RV* X, 72, 1–2; the Greek divine smith Hephaistos is in no way cosmo- or theo-gonic.)

The Finno-Ugrians may not have borrowed from the Indo-Āryans this particular image of the cosmic cow and the 7 stars but the name 'Sampo' is said to come from Vedic *skambha* 'support' and in their universal aspect both *skambha* and *sampo* are constituted of sky, earth and other cosmic elements (Santillana and Dechend, pp. 26, 111, 233). Furthermore, apart from the cosmic egg on the lap of Ilmatar, virgin daughter of the Air (Onians 2000: 177) which might be another loan from the Indo-Āryans, there are definite lexical borrowings by the Finno-Ugrians: e.g., Sanskrit *śata*'100', *ūdhar* 'udder', svasṛi 'sister', *vajra* 'Indra's weapon' appear in Finnish as *sata, utar, sisar, vasara.* (For many more examples and appearances in other Finno-Ugric dialects see T. Burrow 1973: 24ff.)[4]

Thus, if the image is not independent in the two traditions, it is more probable that the Finno-Ugrians were the borrowers. In any event, with regard to the Vedic and Mesopotamian horse-sacrifice, all this indicates that probably it is the latter who borrow.

Just as significant is the theme of creating the worlds out of the dismemberment of a divine being. The *Purusha sūkta* (*RV* X 90) deals at length with this theme. It seems to divide into two parts: the first part (stanzas 1–5) resembles the *Nāsadīya* hymn X 129 in that an unknown Being is said to manifest with its one-fourth as the cosmos and be immanent in it, yet, at the same time, with its other three parts, the Being remains beyond or transcends the cosmos. Then, part two (stanzas 6–16) describes the sacrificial dismemberment of manifest (anthropomorphic) Purusha, born of Virāḷ, who was born of the first Purusha (st 5) and the creation of different worlds and creatures from his members: from his mind the moon; from his eye the sun; from his mouth Indra and Agni; from his breath the wind Vāyu; his mouth became the caste of brahmin-priests; his arms the warriors; his thighs the mercantile caste and his feet the servile caste of men.

In the *Enūma Elish* Marduk fights, defeats and kills Tiamat, the mother of the older generation of gods, a kind of Vedic Aditi. Here, she has a gigantic, monstrous form with four eyes, a horn and a tail but she is not necessarily a dragon-serpent, as some have claimed (for details see Heidel 1969: 83–88). She has spawned serpents and during the fight as well as during the final deadly blows of Marduk and her dismemberment, she reminds one of a repulsive demonness: Marduk sliced her in two, making the sky and earth; with her liver he made the zenith and from her eyes the rivers Tigris and Euphrates and so on *(MM 255–7).* This epic is a glorification of Marduk who slays a demonic monster then creates the world and its hub, the country between and along the two rivers, and thus becomes the new king of the gods. However, beneath this version lurks a different story where Tiamat was a primal Mothergoddess, consort of Apsu: she gave birth to the good gods (those that now fought against her), cared for her offspring and probably willingly offered herself originally to the cosmic sacrifice that generated the worlds (Heidel, *ibid.,* Jacobsen, 187). So, I think here too the Mesopotamians may have borrowed from the Vedic tradition.

The Indo-Āryans would not have borrowed because the divine dismemberment must go back to the PIE era, since the Scandinavians preserved the similar myth of the dismemberment of the first giant-being Ymir (=V *Yama)* by which the gods made the world *(Edda* 10ff; Kazanas 2001: 280). In Greek mythology Hesiod gives the castration of Ouranos from whose blood and organs spring up different divine beings (*Theogony* 176ff; White 1935): this seems to be an amalgam of the IE myth (Vedic Purusha, like Scandinavian Ymir, and perhaps Indra hacking up Vṛitra to release the waters and bring out the sun in *RV* I 32) and of various NE versions like Kumarbi castrating Anu. The IE theme is very old. So in this case, again, the Mesopotamian presentation is very crude but, as was said, contains hints of an earlier finer version, which has subtler affinities with the Vedic culture. (Of course, both traditions may derive from an older culture, now lost.)

As was said earlier, many more themes, like the seven Sages and the Flood (both again of Proto-Indo-European origin), could be examined to show not only close affinities in the Vedic and Mesopotamian religious thought but also probable influence running from India westward and therefore the anteriority of Vedic formulations. (For an extensive survey see Kazanas Forthcoming.) However, enough has been said to demonstrate that the Indo-Āryans were in Saptasindhu, that is the land of the Seven Rivers as the *RV* calls it, at the very latest from before 2000. Both *Enūma Elish* and the horse sacrifice in Mesopotamia are connected with the rise of Marduk as supreme god—which accompanies the rise of Babylon *c.* 1800. Consequently, the *Śatapatha Brāhmaṇa,* which fully describes the horse sacrifice, must be assigned to an earlier date, say 1900, and the *RV* to a date well before 2000, given the generally accepted differences between the two texts.

But why stop here? Can we not find other evidence that will help pinpoint the dates of the Vedic texts with greater exactitude? Yes, there is good evidence—apart from the parallel developments that Levitt adduces.

Memories of Migration

To begin with, the *RV* has no memory of an invasion/immigration. Considering that, according to the AIT, the hymns were composed soon after the arrival of the Indo-Āryans, I find it strange that there is no reference to any trekking or (possible) dangers encountered during the journey. In view of this total lack of references to a recent migration, it is even stranger that some writers claim that the *RV* was composed wholly or in part before the Indo-Āryans arrived in Saptasindhu (Kochhar 2000). Other IE peoples (Celts, Scandinavians, Greeks, *et al.*) do have memories of their migration even if these are not very accurate. The Iranians most interestingly recall having lived in a place called *Haptahandu* (=Saptasindhu) before settling in Iran. (For a full discussion, Kazanas 2002: 281–7). There are peoples who did migrate and retained no memory of this like the Hittites and Slavs but the records of these people appeared many centuries after their settlement whereas the *RV* follows more or less immediately upon the alleged invasion/immigration. The later Indic texts also mention no migration. On the contrary, they have many references to migrations out of Saptasindhu. However, the important point is that there is *no indication whatever* of an Indo-Āryan entry in *c.* 1500. Consequently, much of the *RV* could be very old, going back even to the 5th millennium, when the domestication of the horse and full copper metallurgy (both in the *RV)* became fairly widespread. Until now the only sure indication of an entry into Saptasindhu occurs in *c.* 6000–4500 when there is a definite change in the skeletal record of the region—though, of course, it is not known whether this change is due to new people immigrating, captives in war, bands of marauders, caravans of merchants, etc. Otherwise, as all expert archaeologists of that region aver, there is an unbroken cultural continuity from *c.* 6500 to *c.* 600 (Shaffer & Lichtenstein 1998: 258).

Archaeoastronomy

With regard to the *ŚB (Śatapatha Br.)* we see that the old mainstream dating *c.* 800–600 is way wrong. On the basis of our discussion so far we need a date of 1900 at the very latest. Archaeoastronomy provides a much much earlier date.

B.N. Achar, astronomer at Memphis University (USA), used modern "Planetarium Software" and reconstructed with his computer programmes and monitor the star positions over north India for several millennia past. The *ŚB* has a reference (II, 1, 2, 2–3) to the effect that the *Kṛittikās* (Pleiades) are fixed in and do not swerve from the east. This astronomical event according to Achar could have been observed only *c.* 3000 (1999). A few years earlier S. Kak arrived at a similar date, *c.* 2950, (1994); Achar cites also S.B. Dikshit who had propounded the same idea 100 years earlier but later Western scholars rejected it so as not to upset mainstream orthodoxy.[5] This is the only near-secure evidence we have and it places the *ŚB c.* 3000–2900.

Achar published another paper (2000) in which he shows that the *Vedāṅga Jyotisha* is not of 400 as western scholars think nor of 1300 as some Indians claim but of *c.* 1800. (For a detailed discussion, Kazanas 2002). Now, since *Vedāṅga Jyotisha is* certainly a younger text, the *ŚB* must be at least several centuries older.

The *Ṛigveda* and Harappa

Placing the *ŚB* in the 3rd millennium, whether early (2900) or late (say, 2200), we meet the ISC in its very early or late phase. This now gives us a good criterion for dating the *RV.*

The ISC has many characteristics which are found in various post-Ṛigvedic texts but not in the *RV* itself. This was noted by some scholars back in the 1980s (e.g. Allchins 1982). The first and obvious feature is literacy of which the *RV* knows nothing yet from early Harappan times (*c.* 3100) many sherds and seals with undeciphered writing have come to the surface. A second conspicuous characteristic of the mature Harappan culture is urbanization (regular blocks, large buildings, domestic and urban water-supply: McIntosh 2001: 100–01); this too is wholly unknown to the *RV.* To be brief, here are other ISC elements absent in the *RV:* ruins of towns; fixed fire-hearths/altars; bricks *ishṭakās,* the common building material of ISC (as opposed to Ṛigvedic stone, wood and mud); silver (distinct from Ṛigvedic copper and gold); rice *vṛīhi,* which is cultivated in the ISC and is common as food and as offering in the later ritual, is not found in the *RV* unlike wheat/barley (*yava*); cotton (*karpāsa*) is also extensively cultivated in the ISC but has not a single mention in the *RV* (unlike *ajina* 'skin', *avi* 'wool' and *sāmūla* 'woollen shirt' and *tārpya* perhaps 'silken garment').

Arguments *e silentio* are not convincing when they refer to one or two features. This would apply here if the *RV* did not mention only one or two or three of the items listed. One could understand that any text could well fail to refer to some elements of the culture in which it is produced. But here we have far too many and important items: moreover, they are essential characteristics of the ISC distinguishing it from other cultures. The only reasonable explanation for the absence of all these ISC elements in the *RV* is that the *RV* antecedes the ISC—despite some Indian writers, like R.S. Bisht (1999–2000) and B. Singh (1995), who see the *RV* converging with the ISC[6]. (It is like claiming that a lengthy novel is of the 1990s yet it does not mention the collapse of the communist regimes, globalization, "reality" shows on TV, mobile telephones and the like.) The *RV* could be regarded as contemporaneous with or subsequent to the ISC only if it mentioned some of the features listed above, particularly urban structures, bricks, cotton and rice, which give to the ISC its uniqueness. All such elements appear gradually in post-Ṛigvedic texts and fully in the sūtra literature.

Thus, the *RV* (the bulk of it) is earlier than 3000, when the ISC begins to emerge in Saptasindhu. The native tradition of the Purāṇas and astronomers (from 1st to 6th centuries AD) say that its present arrangement was made on the eve of the great civil war of the Bhāratas (whence the epic *Mahābhārata*) which occurred at 3137, that is 35 years before the death of Kṛishṇa at 3102 which ushered in the Kaliyuga, the Dark Age of ignorance and greed. One may doubt this tradition thinking it too late and unsubstantial. On the other hand, we have the classical reports of Arrian, Pliny and Solinus, all deriving from Megasthenes who was the Greek ambassador to Pāṭaliputra in *c.* 300 and all agreeing that the kings of India go back more than 6000 years. Thus, the Purāṇic tradition is not as young as it first appears but must go back to at least the 4th century BC, if the Megasthenes report is to be taken as seriously as the ancients took it.

There is, however, additional corroborative evidence for the date of the composition of the *RV* before 3000.

Archaeoastronomy and the *Mahābhārata*

Achar, the Memphis astronomer, presented a third paper in Montreal in 2001. In this he examined several astronomical references in Books III, V, and XIII of the *Mahābhārata.* His simulated sky-map showed that of all calculations by Westerners and Indians only that of K. Raghavan (in 1969) was correct. The exact year on the basis of all the data examined was 3067. For instance Kṛishṇa leaves for Hastināpura on the day of the Revatī *nakshatra* in the month *Kaumuda (=Kārtika,* i.e. mid-Oct. to mid-Nov.) and arrives there on the day of *Bharaṇī (Mbh.* V, 81, 6ff); on the day of *Pushya* Duryodhana rejects all offers of peace; Kṛishṇa departs on the day of *Uttara Phalgunī and* tells Karṇa that the *amāvasyā* (=day of the New Moon) will come after 7 days; Karṇa then describes the positions of some planets at that time (V, 141, 7–10). All these data converge in agreement with Achar's sky formation only in the year 3067.

At first 3067 would seem to be the date of the great war being 70 years later than that of the native tradition. However, if we bear in mind that an oral (or perhaps written) tradition of poems and songs about a heroic event would start about three generations after the event, then 3067 is not the date of the war but *that of the basic, initial core of the epic.* The bards retained the star formations of the year in which they began to sing of the events of the war. In any case, the war would not be later than 3067. Thereafter, the initial songs were embellished in the re-telling and accretions were piled on increasingly as is evident by the many tales included on the epic that are irrelevant to the main plot. Accretions continued even in the early centuries AD. However, all this secondary material and the new style of language do not affect the date 3067 indicated by the astronomical references. If the epic had been composed, as is often claimed, after 1500 BC and even AD 300, the bards or the compilers would have no means of knowing the star dispositions in the sky of 3000—and the references are far too many to ascribe them to coincidence.

The *RV* knows nothing of the great Bhārata war and is unreservedly and universally thought to be earlier. Linguistically and stylistically also the hymns are much earlier than any portions of the *Mbh.* Thus, the *RV* must be many centuries older than even the earliest core of the *Mbh.*

The River Sarasvatī

This river is lauded in the *RV* as a great one in late and early hymns (except Book IV). In II, 41, 16 Sarasvatī is called *naditamā ambitamā devitamā:* best river, best mother, best goddess. In VI, 52, 6 it is said to be *pinvamānā sindhubhiḥ:* 'swollen by three or more rivers'; in VI 61, 8–13 it is endless, swift-moving, roaring, most dear among her sister currents and, together with her divine aspect, nourishing the five Indo-Āryan tribes. In VIII, 21, 17–18, says that King Chitra bestows gifts only like Indra and Sarasvatī and that Chitra and many lesser kings dwell along the river's banks. In VII, 96, 2 and X, 177 pray to the rivergoddess for sustenance and good fortune while X, 64, 9 calls the river "great" and "nourishing". All these passages describe the river in the present and cannot be refering (as some scholars falsely claim, like Witzel 2001: 66) to a river known in the past or in some other region, or a river now considerably shrunk. Then there is the significant passage VII, 95, 2 saying that the mighty river flows pure in her course 'from the mountains to the ocean' *giribhyaḥ ā samudrāt.*

Some scholars again claim that here *samudra* does not mean 'ocean/sea' but 'confluence' and especially the point where tributaries flow into the Indus. But there is no hint anywhere that Sarasvatī ever flowed into the Indus. The meaning 'terminal lake(s)', adopted by Witzel, is entirely fanciful. M. Mayrhofer gives for *samudra* only 'confluence' and 'sea' *(EWA).* And certainly the Ṛgvedic poet could and would have used (not *ā samudrāt* but*) ā sarobhyaḥ* 'to the terminal lakes' with the same cadence. The use of the word *saras* in the plural would also have indicated the alleged etymological connection of the name *Saras-vatī* she -who-has (terminal) lakes'. So we must take it that the river flowed indeed from the mountains to the ocean.[7]

The river is thought to have dried up almost completely by 1900 (Allchins 1997: 117; Rao 1991: 77–79). In previous years it had lost tributaries to the Indus in the west and the Ganges in the east. Is there any evidence that it flowed down to the Indian (or Arabian) ocean at any earlier period? G. Possehl examined (1998) all the palaeoenvironmental and geological data relevant to the Sarasvatī river and concluded that the river could have flowed down to the ocean only before 3200 at the very latest and, more probably, before 3800! He re-stated his finds in his study of 2003 (pp. 8-9). P.H. Franceford has been just as certain of a date 3600–3800 in his survey of 1992. All this helps us place the passages describing the grandeur of river Sarasvatī at a date before 3200 at least. And, this comes into harmony with all the other indications and especially the absence of the ISC elements in the *RV*discussed in ξ10, above, and the archaeoastronomical identifications in the *ŚB* and the *MBh* (ξ9).

Conclusion

In concluding this overview we can confidently say that while there is no evidence of any kind of an invasion/immigration into Saptasindhu *c.* 1700–1500, all kinds of evidence declare that the Indo-Āryans had been residing there from the early 5th millennium and that the *RV* or the bulk of it had been composed before 3200.[8] Even Levitt, with far scantier evidence and argumentation dated some of the earliest *RV* hymns "to the end of the 4th millennium BC". I have supplied here more substantial evidence for such an early date. Consequently, the Indic/Vedic tradition can be said to begin long before 3200 and the *RV* antedates the early Harappan phase. No historical event, no actual linguistic data (as distinct from conjectures and speculations) and no arguments used by the proponents of invasionist/ immigrationist scenarios can be accommodated within this new scheme of dates.

Notes and References

1. All ancient dates in the text will be BC. Dates and numbers with or without authors' names in brackets indicate modern publications to be found in the Bibliography.
2. Some Indo-Europeanists would argue for a dispersal in the 4th and others even in the 3rd millennium (Drews 1993). Others again have pushed the date back in the 6th or 7th millennium (Misra 1992).
3. Albright and Dupont (116–17). They cite also Sir Flinders Petrie who found horses buried with humans in Giza, Egypt, from the 16th century (pp. 113–14). The horse came to Egypt in the 17th century. The Egyptians had no horse mythology of any kind. Thus, obviously, such finds can hardly count as horse-sacrifices in the sense discussed here.
4. It has been often claimed that the Indo-Āryans also borrowed from the Finno-Ugrians lexical items on their way from the Urals to Saptasindhu just as they borrowed from the Dravidian and Muṇḍā languages in Saptasindhu. There is some controversy about all this. But even if such loans are demonstrated to be true, they constitute no proof of an entry in *c.* 1700–1500 as the AIT holds; the entry could have occurred very much earlier, in the early 5th millennium.
5. M. Witzel writes an introduction to Achar's paper and another paper (published in the same issue of the Harvard *EJVS*, supervised by himself), advising us against accepting Achar's finds. His main objection is that the *ŚB* mentions "iron" when, in fact, the Iron Age does not begin in India much before 1300. Witzel is quite wrong and loads the dice somewhat unprofessionally. The *Brāhmaṇa* does not mention "iron" anywhere. Only in V, 4, 1, 2 it has *ayas* 'copper, bronze' and *lohāyasa* 'red copper'. For a detailed discussion of this issue see Kazanas 2002: 293–95. So this *Brāhmaṇa* could not, on this count, be assigned to after 1300. There is nothing else in the *Brāhmaṇa* that could help date it with greater accuracy.
6. Bisht, for example, cites numerous occurrences of *pur* as evidence that the *RV* knew of towns and fortifications (p. 410ff). So does D. Frawley (2002: 13). This is wrong, of course: *pur* in the *RV* never means 'fort' or 'town' but a magical, esoteric defence. Merely citing verses in the *RV* but not analyzing and exploring their meaning is not very sound scholarship. Here are some examples merely cited by both writers. In II, 35 the Offspring-of-Waters *Apāṃ Napāt is* protected in *āmāsu pūrshu* (usually translated as 'forts of unbaked bricks' even though bricks are nowhere mentioned!); the phrase means 'non-artificial natural defences' (in this case obviously 'divine'). In I, 166, 8 Agastya prays to the Maruts to protect *(raksh-)* from evil *agha* and injury *abhihruti* the man they favour *(av-)* with 'hundredfold defences' *śatabhujibhipūrbhiḥ* no such many-walled structure existed (allowing for the hyperbole) and, moreover, it is difficult to see how people can be protected from evil by hundredfold forts/towns! VI, 48, 8 is a similar prayer to Agni to protect *(pā-)* from anxiety *aṃhas* the fire-kindler with '100 *purs*': clearly one cannot be protected from anxiety with 100 forts/cities (again allowing for a hyperbole) but only with internal occult

defences. A final example: X, 101, 8 is a prayer to Viśvedevās "to fashion inviolable metal *purs*" to protect the rite of Soma-pouring; obviously no forts or towns are meant to be built around the sacrificial locus but magical, other-wordly defences against demons. Not one *pur* is built and not one is destroyed by human beings! See Kazanas 2003: 224–5 and n. 12; also <www.omilosmeleton.gr/english/(en_index.html> *'Rgvedic pur).*

7. Some scholars persist in presenting Sarasvatī as a memory of (Indo-)Iranian *Haraxvaiti* the river the Indo-Āryans allegedly left behind them when they allegedly came to Saptasindhu (Witzel 2003). This proposition collapses not only by the application of common sense, but also on linguistic grounds. The word for 'lake' in Iranian is *vaiti-*; the **Harah* is found only in the compound name of the river and has no other cognates in the language. The Vedic *sarasvatī* 'she-who-has-*saras* (=lakes, swirls)' has as cognates the *√sṛi/sar-; sara, sarit,* etc.; it has also cognates in Gk *hallo-mai* and *helos,* in Latin *salire* and Tocharian B *salāte.* Surely, it would be absurd to suppose that the Indo-Āryans came to Saptasindhu and out of Indo-Iranian **harah* developed such exact cognates with other IE languages. Surely, it would be more reasonable to say in this case that the Iranians moved out of Saptasindhu (as their tradition remembers) and gave the name Haraxvaiti to a river that reminded them of Sarasvatī having meanwhile turned the IE *s* to *h* and having lost the cognates with *√sṛi* and *saras*!
8. Until the turn of our millennium, one "argument" or piece of "evidence" frequently used by adherents of the AIT was the increasing appearance of remains of the true horse after 1700 and their virtual absence in mature Harappan sites—which was taken as "proof" that the Indo-Āryans brought the horse into Saptasindhu at about this time. This is used frequently in many publications (Witzel 2001: ξ 21 par excellence, Sharma 1995) and as a decisive factor (Hock 1999: 13). R. Meadow also expresses doubts about the presence of the true horse in the ISC (2002). However, all such writings are, unfortunately, a misrepresentation of the facts, as I demonstrated (2003: 196–97). Meadow's doubts spring from an unfounded suspicion (should I say 'prejudice'?) he entertains against Indian archaeologists. Here, I shall give the references which can be pursued in Kazanas 2003. For evidence of true horse before 1800 see: Kochhar 2000: 186,192; Chakrabarti 1999: 49ff; Lal 1997: 285–86; Allchin and Joshi 1995:95; Dhavalikar 1995: 116–17; Thomas *et al.* 1995: passim; Sharma 1980. The presence of the true horse in mature and early Harappan sites is now well established.

   The absence of spoked wheels in the ISC has also been used to support the AIT. This too is false. The spoked wheel was known in the ISC no less than the *RV*. Apart from their representation on seals, terracotta figurine wheels, painted and incised, have been found in several mature Harappan sites (Lal 2002: 74 and Figs 3, 28ff; there are also figurines of horses!). R.S. Bisht also mentions depictions of spoked wheels from early Harappan levels (1997: 252; also Kazanas 2003: 226–27).

Bibliography

Achar, B.N.N., 1999, "On Exploring the Vedic Sky with Modern Computer Software", *EJVS* 5a2.

——, 2000 "A Case for Revising the Date of Vedanga Jyotisa", in *Indian Journal of History of Sciences,* 35a3, pp. 173-83.

——, 2001 "Planetarium Software and the Date of the Mahabharata War", paper given in Montreal and sent privately to ND Kazanas.

Albright, W. & P. Dumont, 1934, "A Parallel Between Indic and Babylonian Sacrificial Ritual", in *Journal of American Oriental Society* 54, pp. 107-28.

Allchin, B. & R., 1982, *The Rise of Civilization in India & Pakistan,* Cambridge University Press, Cambridge.

——, 1997, *Origins of a Civilization,* Viking Penguin, India.

Allchin, F.R. and J.P. Johsi (eds.), 1995, *Excavations at Malvan* (with contributions from A.K. Sharma, K.R. Alur, K.T.M. Hedge *et al.*), Delhi, Archaeological Survey of India (Memoir No. 92).

Anderson, E.R., 1999, "Horse-sacrifice and Kingship...", *Journal of Indo-European Studies*, Vol. 27, pp. 379-93.

Bisht R.S., 1997, "Excavations at Banawali...", in V. Misra & J. Pal, eds., *Indian Prehistory... Proceedings on Indian Prehistory and Protohistory*, Allahabad, Allahabad University, pp. 249-62.

——, 1999-2000, "Harappan and the Ṛgveda: Points of Convergence", in *History of Science, Philosophy and Culture in Indian Civilization*, gen ed. D.P. Chattopadhyaya, Vol. 1, pt. 1, *The Dawn of Indian Civilization up to 600 BC*, ed. G.C. Pande, *PHISPC*, Centre for Studies in Civilization, New Delhi/ Shimla.

Bottero, J., 2001, *Religion in Ancient Mesopotamia* (1998) trans T.L. Pagan, Chicago/London, Univ. Chicago Press.

Burrow, T., 1973, *The Sanskrit Language*, London, Faber & Faber.

Chakrabarti, D.K., 1999, *India: An Archaeological History...*, New Delhi, Oxford University Press.

Crossley-Holland, K., 1993, *Norse Myths* (1980), London & NY, Penguin.

Dalley, S. (ed.), 1998, *The Legacy of Mesopotamia*, Oxford, Oxford University Press.

——, 1998 *Occasions and Opportunities I and II*, in Dalley S., (ed.), 1998, pp. 9-55.

de Santillana, G. & H. von Dechend, 1977, *Hamlet's Mill* (1969), Boston, D.R. Godine.

Dhavalikar, M.K., 1995, *Cultural Imperialism...*, New Delhi, Books & Books.

Drews, R., 1993, *The End of the Bronze Age...*, Princeton NJ, Princeton University Press.

Edda, 1996 Snori Sturluson, Everyman (1987), London.

Francefort, P.H., 1992, "Evidence for Harappan Irrigation...", in *Eastern Anthropologist*, Vol. 45, 9, pp. 87-103.

Frawley, D., 2001, *The Rigveda and the History of India*, Delhi, Aditya Prakashan.

——, 2002 'Witzel's Vanishing Ocean...' http://www.bharatvani.org/davidfrawley/ 'ReplytoWitzel.doc'.

Frawley, D. & N. Rajaram, 1997, *Vedic Aryans and the Origins of Civilization*, New Delhi, Voice of India.

Heidel A., 1969 *The Babylonian Genesis*, Chicago/London, Chicago University Press.

Hock, H.H., 1999, "Out of India? The Linguistic Evidence", in J. Bronkhorst & M. Deshpande (eds.), *Aryan & Non-Aryan in South Asia...*, HOS, Cambridge, Massacheusetts.

Jacobsen, K.T., 1976, *Treasures of Darkness*, New Haven, Yale University Press.

Kak, S., 1994, *The Astronomical Code of the Ṛgveda* (new ed. 2000) Delhi, Munshiram Manoharlal.

Kazanas N., 1999, "The *Ṛgveda* and Indo-Europeans", *ABORI*, Vol. 80, pp. 15-42.

——, 2001, "Indo-European Deities and the *Ṛgveda*", *JIES*, Vol. 29, pp. 257-93.

——, 2002, "Indigenous Indoaryans and the *Ṛigveda*", *JIES*, Vol. 30, pp. 69-128.

——, 2003, "Final Reply" in *JIES*, Vol. 31, 1-2, pp. 187-240.

——, "Vedic, Mesopotamian, Egyptian Religiophilosophical Thought", in *Golden Civilizations*, *PHISPC*, Centre for Studies in Civilization (in press).

——, 2004, "Ṛigvedic *Pur*", <www.omilosmeleton.gr/english/en_index.html>

Kochhar, R., 2000, *The Vedic People*, Orient Longman, Hyderabad, (1997).

Lal, B.B., 1997, *The Earliest Civilization of South Asia*, New Delhi, Aryan Books International.

——, 2002, *The Sarasvati Flows On*, New Delhi, Aryan Books International.

Levitt, S.H., 2003, "The Dating of the Indian Tradition", *Anthropos*, Vol. 98, pp. 341-59.

Mayrhofer, M., 1956-1996, *KEWA & EWA, Etymologisches Wörterbuch des Altindischen*, Heidelberg, Carl Winter.

McEvilley, Th., 2002, *The Shape of Ancient Thought*, New York, Allworth Press.

Mc Intosh, J.R., 2002, *A Peaceful Realm...* Boulder (Col), Westview Press.

Meadow, R.H., 2002, "A note on the Horse..." *JIES*, Vol. 30, pp. 183-87.

Misra S.S., 1992, *The Aryan Problem...*, New Delhi, Munshiram Manoharlal.

MM = Dalley S., 1991, *Myths from Mesopotamia*, Oxford, Oxford University Press.

Onians, R.B., 2000, *The Origins of European Thought...*, Cambridge, Cambridge University Press.

Pingree, D., 1998, "Legacies in Astronomy and Celestial Omens", in S. Dalley (ed.), 1998, pp. 125-38.

Possehl, G.L., 1998, "Did the Sarasvati Ever Flow to the Sea?", G.S. Phillips *et al.*, eds., *Arabia and its Neighbours..., (in Honour of Beatrice de Card/)*, Turnhout, Brepols, pp. 339-54.

——, 2003, *The Indus Civilization: A Contemporary Perspective*, Roman & Littlefield (Non-NBN).

Rao, S.R., 1991, *Dawn and Devolution of the Indus Civilization,* New Delhi, Aditya Prakashan.
Saggs, H.W.F., 1989, *Civilization Before Greece and Rome,* New Haven/London, Yale University Press.
Shaffer, J. & D. Lichtenstein, 1999. "Migration, Philology & South Asian Archaeology", in J. Bronkhorst & M. Deshpande (eds.), *Aryan & Non-Aryan in South Asia,* Cambridge Massacheusetts, HOS (239-260).
Sharma, G.R., 1980, *History to Prehistory: Archaeology of the Vindhyas and the Ganga Valley,* Allahabad University, India.
Sharma, R.S., 1995, *Looking for the Aryans,* Orient Longman, Hyderabad.
Singh, Bh, 1995, *The Vedic Harappans,* Delhi, Aditya Prakashan.
Thomas, P.K. *et al.*, 1995, "Harappan Subsistence Patterns with Special Reference to Shikarpur, a Harappan Site in Gujarat", in *Man & Environment,* India, Vol. XX, No. 2, pp. 33-41.
Watkins, C., 2001, *How to Kill a Dragon: Aspects of IE Poetics,* Oxford, Oxford University Press, (1995).
Werner, K., 1989, "From Polytheism to Monism.", *Cosmos,* Vol. 5, *Polytheistic Systems,* (ed.) G. Davies, Edinburg University Press, pp. 12-27.
White, H.E., 1935, *Hesiod...* Loeb Ed., Cambridge Massacheusetts, HUP & London, Heinemann.
Witzel, M., 2001, "Autochthonous Aryans?", *EJVS* 7-3, pp. 1-93.
——, 2003 "Ein Fremdling im Rgveda", *JIES,* Vol. 31, Spring-Summer.

10

Kunal Excavations

New Light on the Origin of Harappan Civilization

J.S. KHATRI & M. ACHARYA

Introduction

The dazzling discoveries at Harappa and Mohanjo-daro in the early 1920s changed the the notion prevalent amongst almost all the Western historians that no civilization was in existence in Indian subcontinent prior to the Buddha and/or invasion of Alexander in 326 BC.

The most unfortunate political partition of the subcontinent in 1947 between India and Pakistan resulted in the removal of vast area consisting of a large number of sites belonging to the Indus Valley Civilization from the proud control of the Government of India. But within five years of partition, the Archaeological Survey of India, universities and State Department of Archaeology engaged themselves in systematic explorations in the nuclear zone of Indus Valley and Sarasvatī Valley (presently Ghaggar Valley) in Rajasthan, Punjab, Haryana and Gujarat. It resulted in the discovery of a large number of sites of pre-Harappan and Harappan culture.

Before the discovery of Mehrgarh, Baluchistan was considered a secondary zone for cultures and all the classical ware, i.e. wheel turned biochrome, polychrome and grey ware found in Baluchistan were considered as diffusionistic traits coming from Mesopotamia and Iran. Now we know these views were superfluous. These wares were much earlier produced in Baluchistan than the West Asia. Many types of this ware were found together which establishes the fact that it was basically a matter of coexistence of various fashions in pottery.

Fortunately, the excavations at the port city at Lothal in 1954, Ropar (Punjab) in 1955, Kalibangan (Rajasthan) in 1960 and Banawali (Haryana) in 1974 revealed the exuberance, decay and metamorphosis of the Indus Civilization in the second millennium BC. These excavations have also enlarged the horizon of our knowledge about the village culture known as pre-Harappan culture or Sothi culture immediately preceding the urban settlements of Indian Civilization in Indus-Sarasvatī Valley. Although we did not know till the discoveries made

Fig. 10.1 General view of the excavations.

at Kunal, District Fatehabad (Haryana) about the ancestry of the Indus Valley Civilization, we only formed an idea of the matrix of the pre-Harappan Culture and of the successors of the Harappans.

The Site

Kunal (29° 30′N Lat. and 75° 41′E Long.) a sleepy village in Tehsil Ratia, District Fatehabad (earlier in Hissar) can be approached from Bhuna, a town 12 km east from the sites. The site of Kunal is being excavated by the Department of Archaeology & Museums, Government of Haryana. Excavations at this site have provided extremely significant evidence, which is crucial to an understanding of the early Indian culture. It has left archaeological records of the process change which led to the formation of the Harappan culture. At the same time, the discovery at Kunal of the unique items of Early Harappan culture, what is generally termed as Pre-Harappan culture, has also added a new dimension to the Indian history and archaeology of this region in particular.

The site (Fig. 10.1) is spread over an approximate area of nine acres but the nucleus is not more than four acres in extent, the hub is only half of it. The total occupational deposit is only around 4.10 m. The site lies on the dry bed of ancient river Sarasvatī, which finds an important place in the early Vedic literature. This river starts from Ādibadri (district Yamuna Nagar, Haryana) and flows past Kurukshetra-Thanesar, Arnai (*Aruṇā-Sarasvatī Saṅgama*), Pehowa (ancient Pṛithūdaka), Bohar (ancient Bahiryalesha), Sirsa (ancient Śairīshika), etc. Several proto-historic and historic cities are located on the bank of this river. Near Tohana, it was captured by the Joia-Nalah of Rangoi; on the left bank of this Joia-Nalah is located Kunal.

Excavations

The archaeological excavations revealed three successive phases of Early Harappan culture which records the process of change that led to the formation of the Harappan culture.

Period-IA

Initially the land was undulated and low, hence the first settlers brought from nearby region a huge quantity of red *kaṅkarī* soil and dumped here to make the land even as well as to raise the

Fig. 10.2 Close view of circular and rectangular structures.

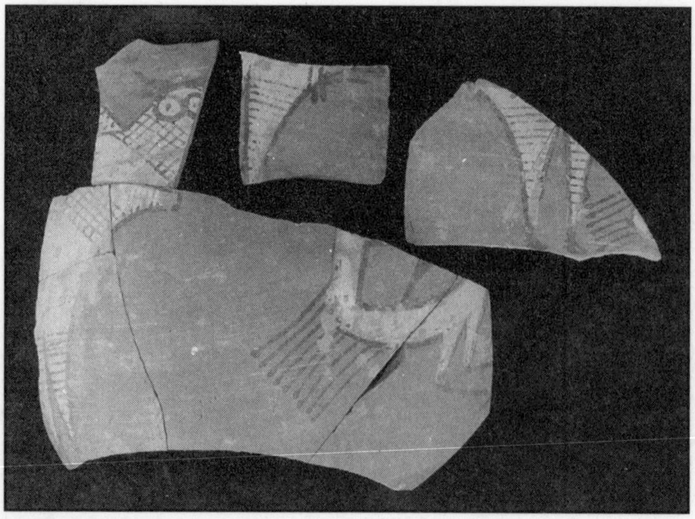

Fig. 10.3 Pottery.

ground level by about 0.70 m. The people started living on this artificially raised ground and constructed their dwelling pits. A dwelling at the site has been found consisting of two units—one round hut and adjacent to it one refuse pit. These dwellings were semi-subterranean which are generally called 'pit dwellings'.

A living pit is approximately 2 m in diameter and 1.10 m in depth with rammed floor and smoothened walls over which were raised some kind of conical super structure of wood and grass. The discovery of a few post-holes around one of the living pits dug on the ground level plus the rather shallowness of the pit proves beyond doubt that a hut, at least 2 m high wattle-and-daub structure, was raised above the ground. The presence of hearth in each pit further confirms their use as dwellings. These pits are found cut through not only the artificially raised red *kaṅkari* soil but also the natural soil. Adjoining each dwelling pit was a refuse pit. At least four dwelling pits along with the refuse pits have been unearthed so far.

During this phase domestication of animals and agriculture was started. The pottery repertoire is also very significant. It is dominated by the so-called Hakra Ware found in the lowest levels of Jalilpur and devoid of several Kalibangan-I fabrics. It was also noticed, while pottery was mainly wheel-made, some hand-made pottery was also prepared.

It also has a handmade near black-and red ware. There is also a dull-chocolate coloured burnished ware with paring marks, the like of which has not been reported from many sites. A dull-red ware with wavy incised decorations on the outer surface found at several Early Harappan sites was a major component of the pottery repertoire. However, the most characteristic pottery of this period is the dull-red (or red washed) pottery with painted decorations in two colours—black outline and white filling. It is in profusion, quantitatively found elsewhere. Some designs are also monochrome, criss-cross diamond-shaped geometric patterns done in black or sepia. The faunal and floral motifs are most noteworthy. Horned-deity type painted motifs which include a bull type animal head with highly curved and decorated horns in monochrome and/or bichrome was very common. A large variety of *pīpal* leaf designs are also in the pottery repertoire.

Fig. 10.4 Pottery.

The cultural complex includes, besides a very rich and almost exclusive pottery repertoire,

Fig. 10.5 Pottery.

a large number of bone-tools and micro-blades of chalcedony and copper implement such as arrowheads and fish-hooks. Although the presence of copper is scarce, it may be noted that the arrowheads of this period are basically of two types—in the first, two sides show marked curvature at the base and other type is the usual inverted 'V' shaped, with side absolutely straight. This cultural phase is altogether new in this part of India as those were not found at any of the sites like Kalibangan, Banawali, Mitathal and several other cognate ones.

Period-IB

This phase represents the expansion of the settlement and elaboration of the semi-subterranean houses of round pits. First, the size increased from half to one metre. These pits were now lined with finely moulded mud bricks. At least three such pits (Circular structure I, II and III) having 2.92 m, 2.75 m and 2.64 m outer diameter respectively were unearthed (Fig. 10.2).

Circular structure-I had five mud brick (11 × 23 × 39 cm) courses and had an average depth of 1.18 m with a mud brick paved floor.

The circular structure-II had cut into six working levels and had five courses of mud bricks of varying size (11 × 24 × 39, 10 × 22 × 37, 11 × 23 × 39 cm). The maximum depth of this structure was 1.12 m with mud floor.

In circular structure-III only two brick courses (11 × 24 × 39 cm) were extant. Two well-designed as well-constructed fine brick lined hearths were also found inside this structure. The bricks used in these three structures do not conform to the ratio of bricks used in so-called Pre-Harappan and Harappan structures.

This phase of Kunal is more advanced from the earlier one. The pottery repertoire of Period-IA continues to occur in large numbers, mainly the bichrome red ware using black and white colours for painting geometrical patterns and also of faunal and floral designs, including the animal head, with highly curved horns marked with three parallel lines of white and black colours alternating in a rhythmic fashion. The *pīpal* leaf, beautifully hatched, or solidly filled, or else leaf-within-leaf pattern, using black, sepia and white colours, presents the most popular, and perhaps the most sacred motif (Figs. 10.3-10.5).

More significantly, now we get particularly all the six Kalibagan-I fabrics in pottery, including the grey ware, internally incised red ware, pots with roughened surface at the bottom achieved by splashing wet clay, etc. These are also the potteries found in the

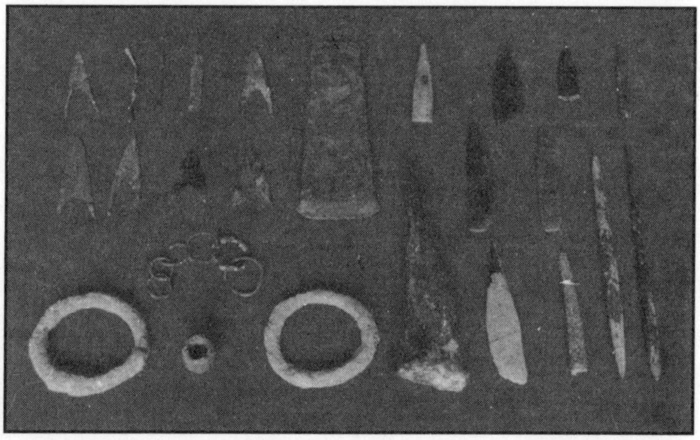

Fig. 10.6 Copper arrow heads, celts, bangles, rings and bone tools.

lowest level of Banawali, Siswal and other sites in Sarasvatī and Dṛishadvatī river valleys. The black- and red ware also continues to occur in small quantities and so also the plain dull chocolate burnished ware with parting mark on thick fabric.

The occurrence of red sturdy ware, nearer to classical Harappan forms, shapes and fabrics and also terracotta cakes for the first time from this level confirms the beginning of Harappan culture. This group of pottery is in dull red, grey and chocolate colours.

Period-IC

This phase marks the climax and represents the real transitional phase between the Early Harappan and Mature Harappan culture-complexes. The dwelling changed from the semi-subterranean huts to regular square and rectangular houses including rooms meant as kitchen and bathroom built of standardized mud bricks on the ground level which was further raised at various points to provide height and stability to living quarters. Interestingly, the brick size was found to be standardized in two ratios of 1:2:3 and 1:2:4 measuring 13 × 25 × 39, 11 × 22 × 33 cm and 9 × 18 × 36, 11 × 22 × 44 cm, etc. Both were used simultaneously while it is generally believed that former ratio was adopted by the Sothi-Kot Diji people of Early Harappan time while the latter was adopted by the Harappans. It is a common knowledge that 1:2:3 ratio bricks cannot always produce the so-called 'English Bond', a feature that produces greatest strength to the structure and saves it from falling apart in blocks. It further establishes the fact that the Mature Harappan technologies started appearing in the Early Harappan times in the field of architecture also. Further, the houses are extremely modest in dimension and elaboration when compared to those of the Mature Harappan period. The developed drainage system is also comparable to at least one of the most popular types used at Harappa, Mohenjo-daro, Kalibangan, Banawali and Lothal—soakage jars fixed in the street-pits were made to do the same job. Both the devices were adopted to keep the streets neat and clean. The refuse pits further helped the people not to choke the streets with household garbage.

The Period has been divided into two sub-phases IC(i) and IC(ii). It is significant that these sub-phases also exhibit features which clearly demonstrate developing stages of culture. Each one is marked, it may be noted with the feature generally labelled 'Change with Continuity'. The houses, the drainage system, the street, etc., did not change much except for the fact that as time passed, the dwelling became slightly larger and better built. And this is not too surprising because the site remained throughout its existence only a village.

Period IC (i)

Agriculture and domestication of animals was already practised. It is sometimes believed that the Early Harappans did not develop devices to store grain but at Kunal, during this period we do find round silos or pits plastered with lime and clay mixture.

No evidence of the disposal of the human dead have so far been found. But disposal of dead animals by the Early Harappans of Kunal is very interesting. A large number of pits containing charred animal bones with ash and charcoal have been found. Most of the bone tools show marks of burning. These may have been the sacrificial pits of sort.

It is also important to note that approximately 6 × 8 m furnace for copper smelting and making tools was also found in this phase. This furnace with brick edging was plastered with a mixture of husk, clay and potsherds. The floor of the furnace had become red and hard by constant firing. From here, a classical example of terracotta crucible with molten metal still sticking to the inner surface has come to light. Incidentally, this area also yielded a few

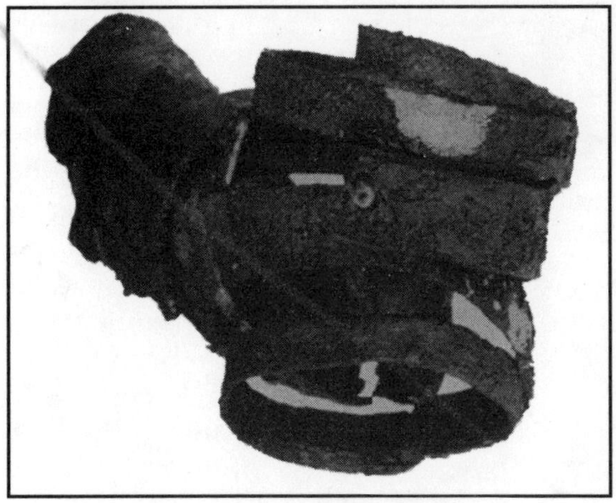

Fig. 10.7 Silver Crown I.

Fig. 10.8 Silver Crown II.

Fig. 10.9 Silver tiara.

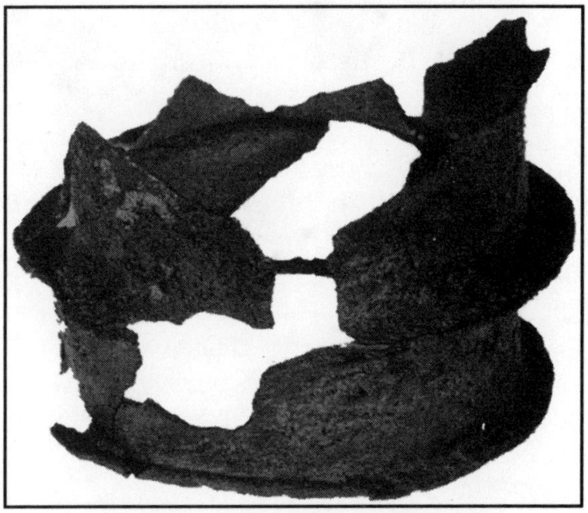

Fig. 10.10 Silver armlet.

copper objects, viz., three chisels, a ring and an antimony rod. Thus, it is beyond doubt that the copper ingots came from other site but the objects were manufactured here itself. Significantly the copper objects of this phase like coiled finger ring, coiled cone, inverted V-shaped arrow-heads, flat axe, fish-hooks and spear-heads etc. (Fig. 10.6) are also of the so-called Mature Harappan type.

Pride of this place of course goes to the items of regalia. In one of the rectangular mud-brick houses, a virtual treasure of ornaments was buried in a simple dull-red globular pot of Early Harappan fabric. In this treasure of gold are included six disc-shaped beads with two holes at the top of each for stringing into a necklace, three tubular beads and two trefoils weighing about 35 gm. The silver objects include two crowns or tiaras (Figs. 10.7 & 10.8), one heavier than the other, each with a large fully bloomed flower having petal topped with a decoration like the Greek letter *alpha* (Fig. 10.9). Along with these two silver objects, one large silver armlet (Fig. 10.10) with horizontal mouldings, one necklace made of eleven round sheet beads with thread channel and two terminals placed in silver sheet in the shape of a container, and a few bangle pieces were also found. Due to heavy corrosion the silver objects

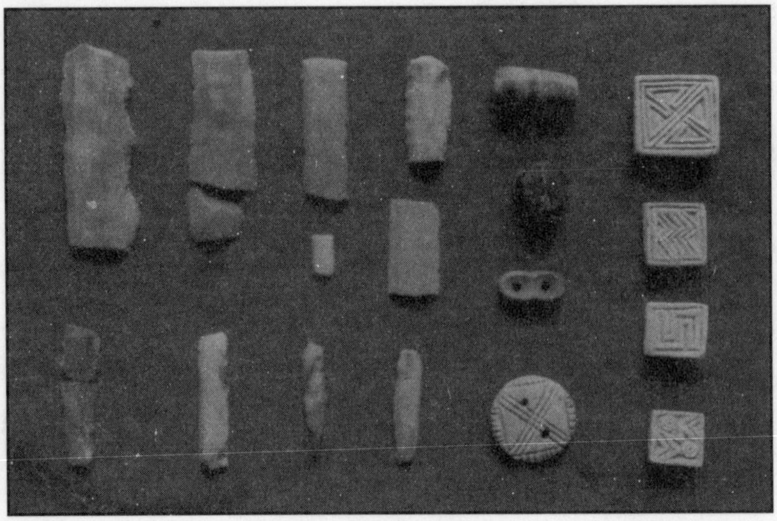

Fig. 10.11 Chert blades, beads spacer and steatite seals (with knob).

have become fragile. All these together, it seems quite likely, belonged to some king or a socially distinguished elite because not only the forms of the objects but also because silver is foreign to this region. The objects themselves are exotic but since at no other place such ornaments of royal association have been found, it is difficult to make conjecture about the place of their origin. A large hoard of the 12,445 semi-precious stone beads includes—3,370 carnelian, 2,806 steatite, 5,690 lapis lazuli, 487 shell and 92 of agate has also been found. These are indeed, the first discovery of its kind from the Early Harappan levels. Never before such magnificent objects were found at any Harappan or Indus-Sarasvatī site.

This makes the whole gamut of luxury item as 'richest' when seen in the context of the rural nature of this settlement and Sothi Culture-complex. Most of the shapes of the beads are similar to those found at Harappa and Mohenjo-daro. This too proves beyond doubt that Mature Harappan types of stone and metal beads were manufactured centuries before the emergence of Harappan cities. And this includes classical faience and carnelian beads, too. Small chert blades are also not wanting (Fig. 10.11).

One of the most important contributions of this site is the discovery of 8 steatite (Fig. 10.11), 2 terracotta and 2 shell seals (Fig. 10.12). Out of 8 seals of steatite, one seal is circular with a hole in centre and carved on both sides. The shapes and sizes of shell and terracotta seals are different from those of steatite seals. These are earliest examples of seal manufacturing in India so far. The steatite seals are different from the known Harappan seals albeit their shapes and style are quite similar. The discovery of steatite seals makes it absolutely clear that typical Mature Harappan square seals with hole in the knobbed back along with a hole were made centuries before the emergence of the urban centres in the Sarasvatī and the Indus basins. All the seals, however, bear only geometrical designs. Thus neither writing, nor human and animal pictures of the Mature Harappan types have been found here. A part of this lacuna was filled up, at another Early Harappan site, Dholavira in Kutch, where stage III, also the transitional phase, has yielded four steatite square seals with pictures of typical Harappan human, animal and floral motifs though still without association of a Mature Harappan writing.

Fig. 10.12 Terracotta seal & steatite seals (without knob).

The birth of Harappan writing can be traced from the graffiti marks found on the pottery from all the periods. These marks are mainly post-firing except a few examples of pre-firing. Some of the popular graffiti marks are also found painted on the pots. These are classified into four groups:

(i). 36 different signs that were adopted by the Mature Harappans in their writing script. (Table 10.1)
(ii). 8 groups of two or three Mature Harappan writing characters. (Table 10.2)
(iii). 23 signs in the form of geometrical patterns. (Table 10.3)
(iv). 26 other designs and signs which do not fall in any of above groups. (Table 10.4)

The pottery of Kunal is notable for its variety of shapes and designs. During this phase pottery was in greater use and variety of shapes and forms, e.g. vase of different sizes, jars, bowls, basins and troughs, dishes, dish-on-stand, etc. have been found. The paintings are monochrome and bichrome using white most frequently with the most popular bucrannian motif and *pīpal* leaf. Decorative motifs are mainly geometrical, however, a few sherds with animal and bird motifs like bull, deer, horse, peacock, crane, etc. and *pīpal* and other floral motifs were also found. Most interesting and baffling is the presence of a black-and -red ware, a distinct and different red ware, grey ware painted with tan red and cream white (different from fabric of Kalibangan), black-painted red ware (pot is painted in black from inside the rim to more than half portion of outer body), and four types of incised on the outer surface of the pottery (including Hakra ware type) are present at Kunal throughout. But what is most significant from our point of view is the first occurrence of red ware pots of well-levigated clay. Some of these pots have forms closer to the classical Harappan forms, such as jars and dish-on-stand. We have clearly observed the beginning of Mature Harappan shapes, fabrics, thickness, etc., but in dull red ware, grey ware and dull chocolate ware.

Quite a few sherds of jars with clear impression of fine cloth in the inner surface were extremely significant. These are the sufficient evidences of the cotton cloth used by the people centuries before the civilization reached the mature urban phase. A few shapes of terracotta cakes including one triangular have also been found from this level.

Period IC (ii)

At present, this period represents the last phase of human settlement at the site. The upper deposit of the site was removed by the villagers for cultivation purposes. Presence of Painted Grey Ware pottery on the site also reveals this. Therefore the levels of this phase have been highly disturbed. The upper surface of the mound shows the traces of recent tillage of the land. There are stratigraphical reasons to believe that 30 to 40 cm of deposit on the top of the mound was removed by ploughing the surface. Hence the structural remains of this phase are very limited. Available habitational deposit revealed typical black-on-red ware with bright red strip over a thick surface of well-levigated clay. The painted designs are also of the mature urban phase of the Indus-Sarasvatī Civilization as found elsewhere. However, the potteries of earlier phase continue to occur in sufficiently large numbers and varieties to warrant the conclusion that here neither the culture nor the people changed. It remained a village throughout but it did feed the city-dwellers with agricultural produce, cattle base and other products and also the luxury goods.

TABLE 10.1 : KUNAL GRAFFITI

Harappan Characters (Found adopted by the Mature Harappans in their repertoire of characters)

Sr.No.	Kunal Graffiti	Quantity	Harappan Character*	Sr.No.	Kunal Graffiti	Quantity	Harappan Character*
1		2	3	19		2	212
2		1	18	20		10	214†
3		6	86†	21		1	216†
4		9	87†	22		2	225
5		9	89†	23		3	4823
6		3	95	24		1	231
7		1	117	25		2	233
8		3	132†	26		1	9832
9		2	134	27		4	261†
10		1	135	28		2	281†
11		14	137†	29		1	309
12		1	146†	30		1	299
13		1	148	31		1	313
14		3	153	32		1	324†
15		1	155†	33		4	4497
16		3	162†	34		1	1904
17		2	167†	35		2	9102
18		1	168	36		2	410

Total = 104 Sherds

* Iravatham Mahadevan, 1977, 'The Indus Script-Texts, Concordance and Tables'

TABLE 10.2 : KUNAL GRAFFITI
Harappan Characters (in a group)

Sr.No.	Kunal Graffiti	Quantity	Harappan Character*
1		1	 365† 4808
2	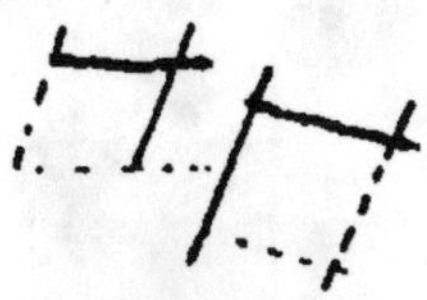	2	 4006 5090
3		2	 1179
4	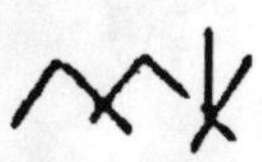	1	
5		1	 4037
6		1	 225 2120
7	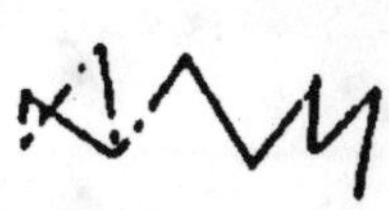	1	 1253
8	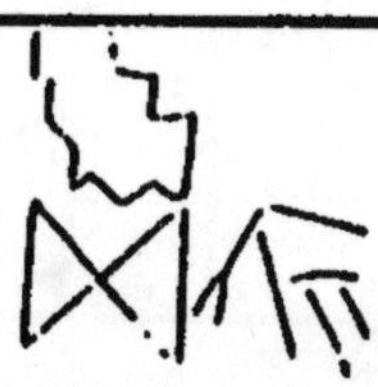	1	 3118

Total = 10 Sherds
* Iravatham Mahadevan, 1977, 'The Indus Script-Texts, Concordance and Tables'

TABLE 10.3 : KUNAL GRAFFITI
Geometrical Patterns

Sr.No.	Kunal Graffiti	Quantity
1		1
2		1
3		1
4		4
5	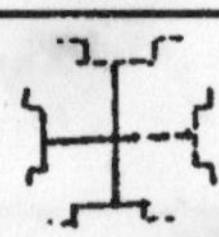	1
6	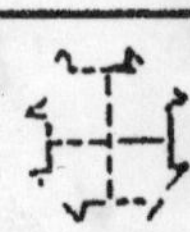	1
7		2
8		2
9		1
10		1
11	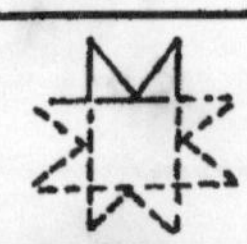	1
12		1
13		1
14	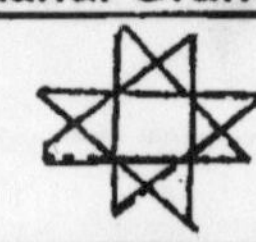	1
15		1
16		18
17		1
18		1
19		1
20	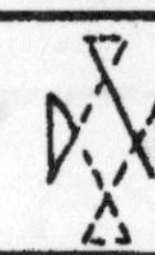	1
21	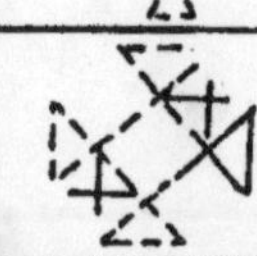	1
22		1
23		1
24	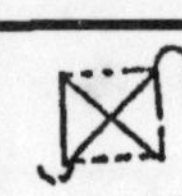	1
25		3

Total = 49 Sherds

TABLE 10.4 : KUNAL GRAFFITI

Other Signs (not found favour with the Mature Harappans for their writing system)

Sr.No.	Kunal Graffiti	Quantity
1		6
2		1
3		1
4		1
5		1
6	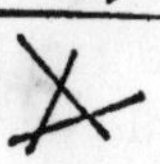	1
7		1
8		1
9		1
10	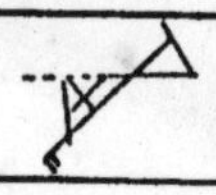	1
11		1
12		1
13		1
14		1
15		1
16		1
17	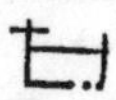	1
18	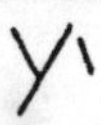	1
19		1
20		1
21	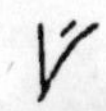	1
22		1
23	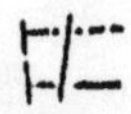	1
24		1
25		1
26		1

Total = 31 Sherds

Chronology

Radiocarbon Dates

BETA 77727	3016 BC	(Period IB)
BETA 77726	2837 BC	(Period IB)
BETA 77728	2577 BC	(Period IC)

The chronological bracket may be between 3500-2500 BC, the period of Early Indus-Sarasvatī or Harappan Civilization.

Period II

The deposits of this period are almost removed from the site. But one of the remains particularly interesting is the construction of a water channel. This 'V' shaped-water channel was constructed around the habitational area. The depth and width of the channel varies from place to place. Its maximum depth and width is 3.45 m and 4.15 m from the top respectively. Moreover, the water channel was not continuous but it seems to have been blocked at four places. It means the four passages were made for the movement of public. Thus, the habitational area of the village was now divided into two parts—one inside and other outside the area of the water channel. This settlement pattern is somewhat the continuation of the concept of citadel and the lower city of the Harappan settlement.

A few Painted Grey Ware sherds along with Early Harappan pottery were also found in the deposit of water channel. Thus, it is clearly evident that this channel served the purpose of a moat for the protection of the settlement of Painted Grey Ware people.

Scientific Investigation

1. X-Ray Micro Analysis of Silver Object:

(i) Metallic Composition Silver (round-sheet beads):

Silver	71.54%
Aluminium	6.31%
Chloride	22.15%

(ii) Metallic Composition Silver Container:

Silver	37.27%
Aluminium	12.72%
Silica	18.76%
Chloride	12.02%
Potassium	5.47%
Calcium	4.73%
Iron	9.02%

XRF study of the soil samples deposited over the silver bead indicates the presence of gold traces in the soil.

2. Energy Dispersive X-Ray (EDAX) Micro Analysis:

Gold Objects

(i) Metallic Composition Micro Tubular Beads:

Gold	77.71%
Aluminium	12.09%
Silver	6.26%
Iron	3.94%

(ii) Metallic Composition Micro Bowl-Shaped Terminals:

Gold	83.55%
Alluminium	8.64%
Silver	4.43%
Iron	3.58%

(iii) Metallic Composition Disc Shaped Beads:

Gold	69.50%
Alluminium	16.45%
Silver	8.86%
Iron	5.19%

Copper Objects

(i) Metallic Composition

Three Arrow-Heads	Copper 30.32%, 30.66%, 42.80%
Coiled Bangle	Copper 37.91%
Thin Wire Ring	Copper 50.22%

Other components in all these copper objects were alluminium, silica, potassium, calcium and iron. Among these the highest percentage from 31.32% to 42.17% was that of silica. It was probably due to superficial deposit of the soil over the objects.

It is a well-known fact that smelting technology of alluminium and iron was known to the people of Early Indus -Sarasvatī or Harappan Civilization. Therefore, it is obvious that the presence of alluminium and iron might be as a byproduct from smelting flux during the extraction of silver, gold and copper from the ore.

11

The Peoples of India and the Dawn of Civilization in the Indian Subcontinent

Y. KRISHAN

On the basis of linguistic classification of the population, India is the home of four speech-family groups : (i) Āryan, also called Indo-European; (ii) Dravidian; (iii) Muṇḍā or Kol; and (iv) Sino-Tibetan.

The Āryan speech family originally consisted of Sanskrit, Pāli (the language used by Hīnayāna Buddhists), Ardhamāgadhi (the language used by the Jainas), which are not spoken now and modern day Prakṛits, the vernacular language of the different states of northern India, viz., Hindi, Gujarati, Rajasthani, Marathi, Bengali, Oriya, Assamese, Punjabi and Pahari. These vernaculars being derived from Sanskrit, belong to the Āryan speech family. They are the languages of over 70 per cent of India's population.

The Dravidian speech family is represented by Tamil, Telugu, Kannada and Malayalam, all in the southern states of India. They are called Austric languages by linguists. The Dravidian speaking people constitute nearly 20 per cent of India's population.

The third speech family, Muṇḍā or Kol, is the language of tribal groups, Muṇḍā, Bhils, Sentals, etc. in eastern and central India. They constitute nearly 2 per cent of the population. In linguistic classification, there are Austric languages which also include Khasi, Mundari, etc.

The fourth and the last speech family, viz., Sino-Tibetan speaking population is found on the borders of northern and north-eastern Himalayas. They are less than 1 per cent of the population.

Anthropologists consider these speech family groups also as racial groups, though this may not be true of the Dravidian speech family people.

From the physical parameters of skin pigmentation (black, yellow, fair), the shape of the head (broad or long-headed), stature, form of the nose and face, etc., the Muṇḍā speech family and Sino-Tibetan speech family groups represent distinct racial or ethnic elements in India's population.

As regards the Dravidian speaking people, Dravidian is a non-Āryan language. But on the basis of their language they cannot be held to be a non-Āryan group.

Anthropologists[1] have classified Dravidians as Australoid—Negritos—who are dark-skinned, short statured or pygmies. The Dravidian speaking people of south India are not short statured and their skin colour is dark rather than black. Racially there is no significant difference between the Dravidians of south India and the Āryans of north India. Some anthropologists consider that the Dravidian speaking people of south India are a people of east Mediterranean stock, which is a branch of the Caucasoid, the other branch being the Āryan. Again the fact that Dravidian is a non-Āryan language does not mean that the speakers of the language are also non-Āryans.

The Āryans or rather the Indo-Āryans of north India, are classified as Āryans on the grounds of their speech and are classified as Caucasoid[2] by anthropologists on the basis of their physical features. According to the dominant body of indologists, archaeologists, linguists and historians, the original home of the Vedic Āryans, who composed the *Ṛigveda*, was Central Asia, preferably the Caucasus.

On the basis of comparative linguistics, Vedic Sanskrit of India, Avestan of Iran, and a host of European languages, Greek, Latin, Germanic, etc., are akin, that is, they all belong to a common speech family.[3] Indo-European languages became cognates, being issues of linguistic monogenesis.

The speakers of the different languages belonging to a common speech family must have originally naturally lived at one place wherein they must have used a common spoken language, conveniently identified as proto-Āryan. Linguistic monogenesis gave rise to common habitat and racial monogenesis: proto-Āryans fathered Indo-Europeans. ".... the new theory of Language... produced a new theory of Race...."

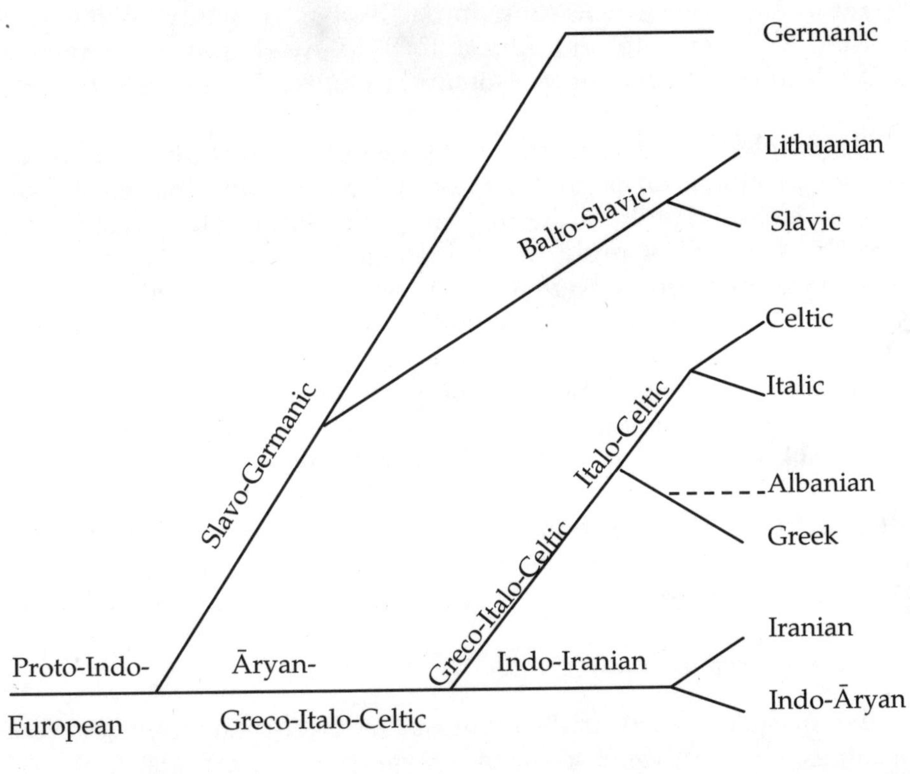

Fig. 11.1 Schleicher's family tree of Indo-European languages.

The construction of a proto Indo-European race, based on a common speech, was further sought to be supported by similarities and parallels between Vedic (Indo-Āryan) and Indo-European mythologies (e.g. Varuṇa of the *Ṛigveda* is Ouranos of the Greeks, Dyaus of the *Ṛigveda* is Zeus of the Greeks, Parjanya, rain-god of the *Ṛigveda,* is Parkunas of Lithuanian, Ushas (Dawn) of *Ṛigveda* is Eos of the Greeks and Aurora of the Romans) and common features in the functional role of the deities of nature.

Further support for a Central Asiatic home of the Indo-Europeans was found in the proposition that India and Iran formed one linguistic and cultural unit[4]—common religious beliefs and practices—aniconic character of the religion of the Ṛigvedic people and early Iranians (Medes and Persians), worship of the forces of nature and performance of animal sacrifices and fire-cult. There is linguistic affinity between Avestan Iranian and Vedic Sanskrit: *soma* (Vedic); *haoma* (Iranian); *atharvan* (Vedic), *atharavan* (Iranian); *asura* (Vedic); *ahura* (Iranian); *deva* (Vedic), *daeva* (Iranian), *mantra* (Vedic), *Manthra* (Iranian), are a few illustrative examples. Likewise there is considerable similarity in the names of gods of the Vedic Āryans and of the Avestan Iranians: illustrative examples being Mitra (Vedic); Mithra (Iranian); Varuṇa (Vedic), Arun (Iranian); Vāyu (Vedic); Vayu (Iranian); Yama (Vedic), Yima (Iranian); Vāta (Vedic), Vata (Iranian); Aśvina (Vedic); Aspina (Iranian).

On grounds of linguistic affinity and of identity in religious beliefs and cults, scholars have postulated a group or community named Āryan, 'whose speech can be regarded as the ancestor of the speeches of India and Iran, and who had a common homeland somewhere in Central Asia from where they migrated, one branch of migrants (Iranians) settled in Iran and the other in the north-west India (Vedic Āryans).

This is further sought to be supported by the proposition that after this 'split', the *Ṛigveda* was composed by the Vedic Āryans in an area, now known as Afghanistan en route their movement from Central Asia to north-western India. Names of many of the rivers in the present-day Afghanistan are similar to and appear to be derived from the names of various rivers in the *Ṛigveda* : Kubhā is Kabul river, Gomatī is Gomal, Krumu is Kurram, Sarasvatī is Haraqaiti.

Thus, there are a number of basic assumptions in determining the race of the Āryans of India and their original home: (a) a proto-Āryan speech was the mother of the different members of the Āryan speech family including, in particular, Vedic Sanskrit and Iranian Avestan. (b) a priori, the speakers of proto-Āryan belonged to a proto-Āryan race of Central Asia of which Indo-European peoples were the off-springs, (c) the Central Asiatic Āryans were the ancestors, inter alia of Vedic Āryans and Iranians, both being branches of Indo-Europeans. (d) Similarities and parallels between Vedic and European mythologies are deemed to corroborate the linguistic evidence, and (e) Composition of the *Ṛigveda* in Afghanistan.

According to the current chronology, it was the Āryan branch which migrated to India in about 1500 BC and established the Ṛigvedic civilization in the north-western India by about 1200 BC.

These postulate about the original home of Āryans, and the development of Sanskrit are purely speculative historical reconstructions.

First and foremost, the term Āryan has a social as well as geographical, nay domiciliary, connotation rather than racial.

In Sanskrit[5] the term Ārya (Āryan) means:

(i) A respectable, honourable person. It distinguishes Vedic Āryan from non-Vedic *dāsa* or *dasyu*. In later times, the term came to mean a *dvija* (twice born), that is the three upper castes—Brāhmaṇa, Kshatriya and Vaiśya—were deemed to be *Āryas,* as distinct from śūdras. It defined social status rather than racial character.

(ii) In Sanskrit literature, the term *ārya* means an inhabitant of Āryavarta, who could be of any caste, high or low. It is indicative of a person's 'domicile' instead of his 'race'.

(iii) The term *āryan*, as a rule, has no linguistic connotation. Pre-Paṇinian Vedic Sanskrit was not the spoken language of the mass of Āryans. It was the language of the Brāhmaṇas who were specialists in reciting *mantras* while performing Vedic *yajñas*—public sacrifices and domestic fire worship, *agnihotra.* Again the Prākṛits, the languages of the people or spoken vernaculars also developed from proto-Āryan (more precisely proto-Vedic Sanskrit) and, as such, are as much members of the Āryan speech family as Vedic Sanskrit. Māgadhi, later known as Pāli, was the prime vehicle of communication of the Buddhists and Ardhamāgadhi of the Jainas. In fact the Buddha[6] directed his followers not to put his words into Vedic Sanskrit; he warned: who does so would commit sin; a monk must learn the Buddha's words in his own dialect. So Aśoka's inscriptions are all in Prākṛit. And both the Buddha and Mahāvīra were addressed as *Ārya* (*Pāli ariya ayya*); the Buddhist monastic community were called *ārya saṁgha* and the noble truths of Buddhism as *ariya satyāni.*

(iv) Comparative linguistics does strongly suggest the existence of an Āryan speech family consisting of various Indo-European languages—Sanskrit, Avestan, Greek, Latin, etc. But linguistic monogenesis does not establish racial identity. It is very relevant to recall the strong warning of Grierson "against basing ethnological theories on linguistic facts", especially in India. Grierson[7] had observed:

> There are many instances of tribes which have in historic times abandoned one language and taken to another. A striking example is afforded by the tribe of Nahals in the central provinces. These people appear to have originally spoken a Muṇḍā language akin to Kurku. It came under Dravidian influence, and has become a mixed form of speech, half Muṇḍā and half Dravidian. This, in turn, has fallen under the spell of Āryan tongues, and is now in a fair way to becoming an Āryan language. If we were to judge by language, a hundred years ago we should have called the tribe Muṇḍā. Ten years ago it was quite possible to claim it as a Dravidian, a fifty years hence it would probably be described as an Āryan race.

Further there is no anthropological material evidence in the form of skeletal remains of an Āryan race who were the speakers of the proto-Āryan or Āryan speech family language : their skulls do not have racial similarity. It is not established that the speakers of the different languages, belonging to the Āryan, speech family, were descendants of one parent Āryan race. In other words, linguistic familial kinship does not mean racial kinship among the speakers. However, biological anthropologists remain unable to lend support to any of the theories concerning an Āryan biological or demographic entity within the contexts of linguistics and archaeology.

(v) Mythological parallels and similarities are, at best, suggestive but not definitive. According to scholars it may not be wholly correct to assume that the various mythological elements of Indo-European mythologies are of Indian origin or treating the Indo-European period as the very starting point of all mythological notions.[8]

There is also no corpus of literature in proto-Āryan corresponding to the corpus of Vedic or Avestan literature.

Thus, the first postulate that the original home of Āryans was in Central Asia is based on the proposition that the ancestors of the people speaking Indo-European or Āryan speech family languages must have once lived at one place, whose common spoken language, "an unknown and nameless parent", was christened "proto-Āryan". In other words, the sister language-streams have been traced back to one original spring"—the proto-Āryan language—spoken by one racial group—proto-Āryan—and whose habitat was conjectured to be Central Asia. As we have shown, this proposition itself is hypothetical, nay imaginative, conjectural, and at best a working hypothesis, rather than a factum of history. In fact, the theory of Central Asiatic home of Āryans suffers from the vice of multiple presumptions, unproved inferences, rather conjectures, which remain uncorroborated by evidence. In consequence it is highly improbable that the Vedic Āryans were immigrant proto-Āryans or their descendants from Central Asia.

Regarding the composition of the *Ṛigveda* in Afghanistan, the evidence is presented in a twisted manner.

The names of the various rivers falling in the Sindhu (Indus) are given in the *Ṛigveda*[9] (X.75.5 and 6). The *Ṛigveda* first cites in hymn (X.75.5) the names of rivers of India falling into the Sindhu; the names of the rivers of Afghanistan are given in the next hymn (X.75.6). If the movement of the Indo-Āryans was from west to the east, the rivers of Afghanistan in *Ṛigveda* (X.75.6)[10] would have been cited first. Again Gaṅgā is named first and Vitastā (Jhelum) last in the names of the Indian rivers. If the Indo-Āryans had moved from west to the east, Vitastā would have been first river they would have met after the Indus.

It must also be noted that the *Ṛigveda* has no memory of the Āryans having migrated to India from Central Asia or from any area outside the Indian subcontinent.

However, the linguistic and religious identity of the Vedic Āryans and Iranians only has been established beyond doubt. Only their common home and the time when they split, one branch going to Iran and the other settling in India are still to be determined.

Prior to the discovery of the Harappan or Indus Civilization in 1922, it was presumed by historians that Dravidians were the inhabitants of north-western India. This assumption was based on the existence of a small colony of Brahui[11] speaking people in Baluchistan as Brahui belongs to the Dravidian speech family or group of languages. No other material evidence—archaeological or even anthropological—of Dravidian settlements in this region has been found.

The excavations at Mohenjo-daro and Harappa revealed a highly developed urban civilization. It is unique in many respects : territorially[12] it is the most extensive—more extensive than the ancient civilizations of the Nile, the Tigris and Euphrates (Babylonia) and of Assyria. It is also the earliest urban civilization which had towns and practised non-agricultural trades and crafts. Cattle was the principal farm animal of the Harappans whereas in the ancient civilizations of West Asia, the principal domesticated animals were goats and sheep. The cities or towns were also well-planned whose civic amenities excite admiration: brick houses with bathrooms, elaborate and covered drainage system, wide roads aligned to the direction of the winds. Artisans were skilled as they used technology in their crafts such as the potter's wheel and wheeled carts. Trade, including import and export, was a major activity. This civilization has been dated to 3100 to 1900 BC. The Indus Valley people were farmers and traders, who appear to be very much different from nomads, horsemen and cattle breeders. However, the script of the Indus Valley people still remains to be deciphered conclusively.

The race of these Harappans has been determined again on the basis of a tenuous piece of evidence, earlier referred to, of the existence of an isolated island of the people of the Dravidian speech family, viz., Brahui in Baluchistan: Harappan Civilization was a highly developed civilization of the Dravidians.

The skeletal remains, particularly the skulls, human figures depicted on the seals and statuette figurines tell a different story about the race of the peoples of Harappan settlements: biologically the Harappans were a plural community consisting of Negrito, proto-Australoid, Mongoloid, Sumerian, and Alpinoid. Of these, the Alpinoid alone are a Caucasoid people, racially akin to Indo-Europeans[13] or Indo-Āryans.

On the other hand, the Āryan invaders were believed to be a nomadic, pastoral people who used horse-driven chariots, which gave them mobility and iron with which they acquired more destructive weaponry. It has been suggested that the Āryans, because of superior weaponry and mobility, were able to overwhelm the Harappans and drive them to south India.

We consider it patently naive to think that a people who had created the apparatus of civilization and who were proficient in multiple technologies, were defenceless against nomadic hordes. Again factually, iron is mentioned only in the *Yajurveda* and the *Atharvaveda,* that is, only the Āryans of the post-Ṛigvedic period used iron. Further, iron is used for the first time in India by the peoples of Malwa, of the middle and lower Gaṅgā valley and of Karnataka. Iron is found in the north-western region of the Indian subcontinent much later. It is, therefore, an anachronism that the Ṛigvedic Āryans possessed weapons made of iron in their alleged wars against the Harappans.

Again, further excavations in the states of the Punjab, Haryana, Rajasthan, Gujarat, Punjab, etc., have exposed a very large number of ancient settlements. Some of the more important settlements are Ropar in Punjab, Banawali and Rakhigarhi in Haryana, Kalibangan in Rajasthan, Rangpur, Dholavira and Lothal in Gujarat, Alamgir in the U.P., etc., to name a few of the numerous sites. They bear no evidence of destruction by invaders. The skeletons have no cut marks that are caused by violence. The skeletal remains belong to different levels. If there had been a massacre, the skeletons would have been in one level only.

The findings of an American archaeologist J. Shaffer[14] are conclusive:

> Current archaeological data do not support the existence of an Indo-Āryan or European invasion into South Asia at any time in the pre-or proto-historic periods.
>
> The Indo-Āryan invasion as an academic concept in eighteenth and nineteenth century Europe reflected the cultural milieu of that period. Linguistic data were used to validate the concept that in turn was used to interpret archaeological and anthropological data.

Further, satellite surveys have revealed the reduced bed of a mighty river flowing from the western Himalayas to the Arabian Sea across the present-day Haryana and Rajasthan desert. This river was fed by the Yamunā (which now flows towards the east into the Gaṅgā) and by the Sutlej[15] (which later joined the Indus in the west). Scholars believe that this was the great Sarasvatī river of the *Ṛigveda*

The Sarasvatī of the *Ṛigveda* is the mother of rivers and is more generally celebrated than any other river in that Veda. It surpasses all other waters in greatness. The Gaṅgā is inconspicuous. The waters of Sarasvatī were considered pure, as of the Gaṅgā in later times. It was this river which was the spine, the axis of the great civilization which has now been named as the Sarasvatī Civilization. Other Harappan settlements which had been excavated first, viz., Mohenjo-daro and Harappa and the river Indus around which they developed, are now on the periphery of the Harappan Civilization which developed along the Sarasvatī (see Map 11.1). Maximum number of Harappan sites have been found in the basin of the dried up Sarasvatī. The number of Harappan sites excavated in the basin of the Indus are about 100 whereas the number of sites along the Sarasvatī over 600. It is therefore understandable

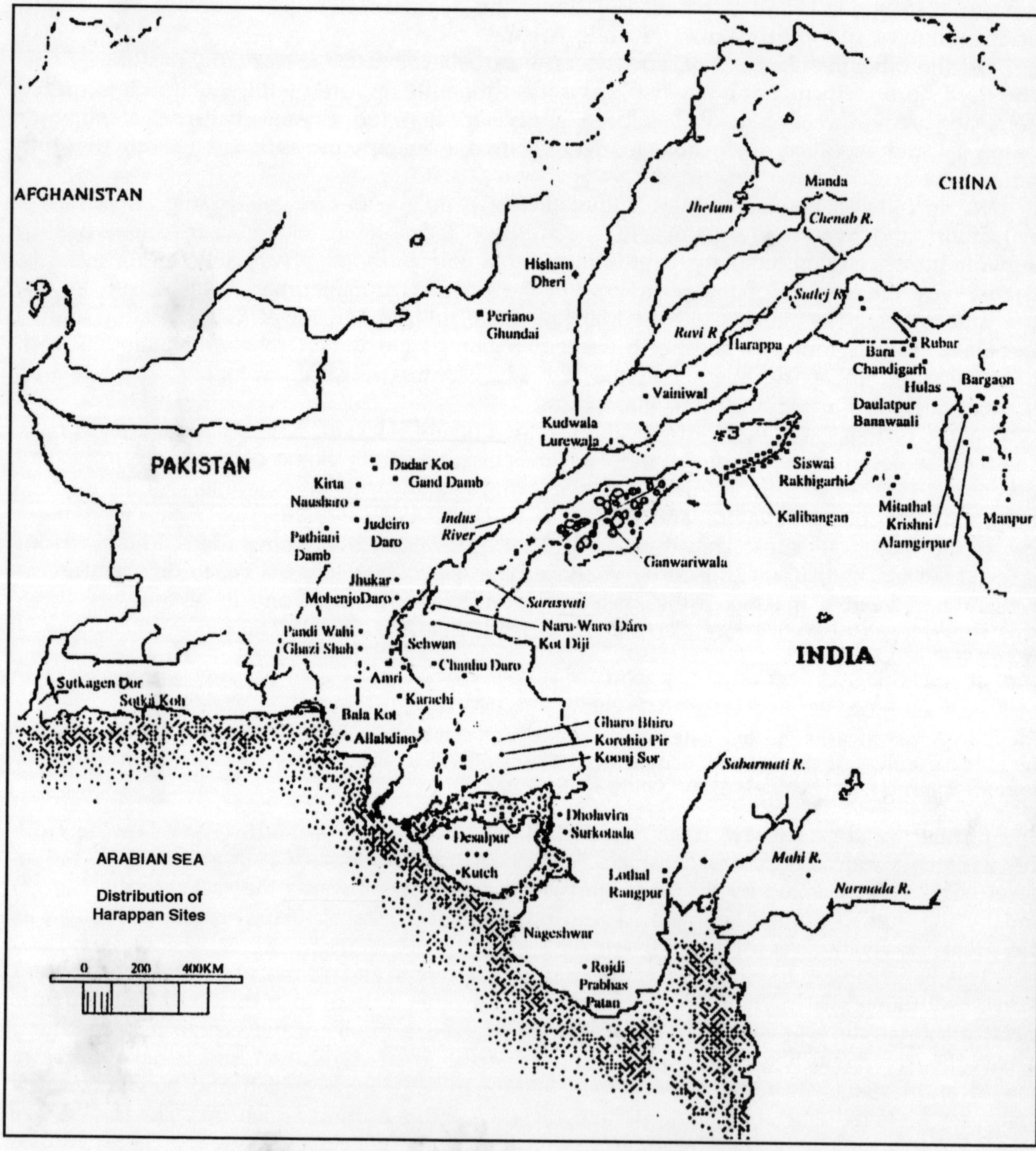

Fig. 11.1 Archaeolgical Map of Harappan Sites.

that what was hitherto known as the Harappan (Indus) Civilization is now named more appropriately as the Harappan or Sarasvatī Civilization.

This civilization died out due to ecological and geological changes. From satellite and field surveys it appears that this region suffered from severe prolonged drought lasting over three centuries from about 2200 BC. During the same period the Yamunā and the Sutlej changed their courses. Instead of flowing into the Sarasvatī, the Yamunā started flowing towards the east into the Gaṅgā. The Sutlej also altered its course somewhat and now flowed into the Indus. The Sarasvatī thus dried up. Drought and drying up of the Sarasvatī turned the area into a vast desert. The Indus or Harappan Civilization also now named as the Sarasvatī Civilization, was not destroyed by hordes of invading Āryans. In fact, "Archaeologically it cannot be proved that Āryans came to India from outside either peacefully or as invaders".[16]

Dales[17] an eminent archaeologist, has described this hypothesis of destruction of Indus Valley settlement by invading Āryans as "mythical massacre". In fact, a historical fabrication.

There is evidence to show that there was a radical shift in the centre of civilization in northern India. The Vedic civilization of the Sarasvatī Valley in Haryana and Rajasthan, shifted to the Gaṅgā Valley in east India, the U.P., Bihar and Bengal, which was the region of the Epic and Puraṇic civilization as distinct from the Vedic.

In brief, archaeological findings establish that the Harappan Civilization was not liquidated by invaders. It died due to natural causes.

Historically, this story of Āryan-Harappan conflict is a product of imagination.

First and foremost, it suffers from conflict of chronology. The *terminus ad quem* of the Harappan Civilization is at the latest 1900 BC and must have attained maturity sometimes between 3000-2000 BC.[18] On the other hand Max Müller, who had formulated the theory of Āryan invasion of India by Central Asiatic Āryans, had arbitrarily assigned the date of migration of Central Asiatic Āryans to India at 1500 BC and composition of the *Ṛigveda* in 1200 BC though Max Müller had himself conceded, "Whether the Vedic hymns were written in 1000, 1500 or 2000 or 3000 BC, no power on earth will ever determine." Nonetheless, he assigned to 1200, BC the compilation of the *Ṛigveda*. If this chronology is maintained, then the invasion of India by Central Asiatic Āryans would have taken place 400 years after the Harappan Civilization disappeared.[19]

Further, the *Aitareya Brāhmaṇa* mentions that the vernal equinox shifted from one lunar asterism (*Mārgaśīrasha*) to another (*Rohiṇī*). Astronomically this event occurred about 3500 BC. The date of the composition—rather compilation—of the *Ṛigveda* therefore, would be still earlier. On the basis of this chronology, the Vedic Āryans did not destroy the Harappan Civilization.

The Boghas Kuei Inscription in Anatolia (Asia Minor) refers to Nasatya (Aśvins), Indra and Varuṇa. The Kassite and Mittani inscriptions in north Syria refer to Sūrya and gods of Vedic mythology—Daksha and Dīti. These inscriptions have been dated to second millennium BC. This makes the *Ṛigveda* contemporaneous with and not posterior to the Harappan Civilization.

Again as already noticed, there is no material evidence of the destruction like mass of skeletons on extensive scale and demolition of the towns and buildings. They were abandoned rather than demolished.

The theory of Dravidian Harappans having been driven out en-masse to south India by Āryan invaders is also incredible. It would have been natural for the migrant Dravidian Harappans to replicate the significant features of their civilization in their new home—brick-built houses and planned townships. They also used iron, a metal absent from Harappan sites. Further, the Harappans had a script which, however, remains undeciphered so far. The so-called emigrant Harappan Dravidians of south India used stone, not brick, for construction, did not create planned townships with admirable civic facilities—wide roads aligned with the wind direction, elaborate drainage system, segregation of workplace and residential areas—as we find in the Indus Valley. They also adopted scripts derived from Brāhmī of the Āryans. It would have been most unnatural for the Dravidians to discard the Harappan scripts if they had been refugees from the Indus civilization.

Thus, the theories of historians that Dravidians were the original or pre-Āryan inhabitants of north-western India and of Āryan invaders destroying the Dravidians/Harappan Civilization are a figment of imagination.

The prehistoric Dravidian settlements of south India have been classified by archaeologists as Neolithic (New Stone Age). The Harappan Civilization, in terms of material culture, belongs to the Bronze Age, which is post-Neolithic. It is historically absurd that bronze age Harappans migrated to south India where they reverted to the more premature Stone Age.

A.R. Kennedy's masterly summing up of the evidence regarding absence of different racial elements in India's population deserves to be quoted.

> The presence of Indo-European languages in South Asia is a fact. Vedic texts are indisputable sources of Indian culture history. What is not certain is that: (1) specific prehistoric cultures and their geographical regions are identifiable as Aryan; and (2) that the human skeletal remains discovered from reputed Aryan burial deposits are distinctive in their possession of a unique phenotypic pattern making them apart from non-Aryan skeletal series. What the biological data demonstrate is that no exotic races are apparent from laboratory studies of human remains excavated from any archaeological site, including those accorded Aryan status. All prehistoric human remains recovered thus far from the Indian subcontinent are phenotypically identifiable as ancient South Asians. Furthermore, their biological continuity with living peoples of India, Pakistan, Sri Lanka and the border regions is well established across time and space.[20]

The demise of the Harappan Civilization was brought about by ecological suffocation: cataclysmic climatic changes and tectonic movements disrupting the hydrology of the area. In consequence the region suffered from prolonged dry weather extending over 200–300 years. This was aggravated by changes in the course of rivers which drastically reduced the surface water and underground water levels. There was perhaps disruption of trade through the Gulf in the Middle East. The result was desertification of the vast agricultural plains of south-west Punjab, Haryana, Rajasthan, north Gujarat and Sindh, food scarcity, degradation and decimation of urban settlements resulting in the doom of a great civilization.

To Conclude

(i) Vedic Sanskrit is one of the Indo-European group of languages. Its speakers, however, did not descend from an Indo-European race. In fact, there is no evidence that such a race ever existed.

(ii) There is no definitive evidence that the Āryans of India were immigrants into India.

(iii) There is no definitive evidence that the river of the Harappan sites area was the Sarasvatī river of the *Rigveda* around which the Vedic Civilization grew.

(iv) The identification of Vedic Āryans with Harappans is problematic: no nexus has been established so far between the two civilizations.

(v) There is, at present, no evidence that the Harappans were Dravidians who were driven out to south India by invaders who are supposed to have destroyed, rather extinguished, the Harappan Civilization.

(vi) There is no evidence that the Vedic Āryans destroyed the Harappan Civilization.

(vii) The original home of the Indo-Āryan and Iranians the time when they split and migrated therefrom to the areas where they are settled at present still remains to be determined.

Decipherment of the Harappan script is perhaps the key to resolving the first six issues. We will have to wait till we are able to read that script to see the dawn of civilization in India.

Notes and References

1. Aborigines of Australia, Melanesia, Phillipines, Malay Peninsula and Andaman Islands etc.
2. A recent study about the genetic composition of the Western Euroasian and Indian population has revealed that a key mitochondrial DNA of the Western Eurasian strain is to be found in 70% of the population of Europe whereas this is limited to slightly over 5% of the population in India. Thus, there is only a small fraction of the caucasoid-specific mitochondrial lineage in the Indian population. This strain is also distributed more or less evenly between north India and south India.
3. Speech-Family Tree Proto-Vedic Sanskrit or Proto-Indo European

European Speech Families	*Sub-Speech Families*	*Asiatic Speech Families*
Celtic, Greek, Italic, Germanic, Baltic or Lithuanian, Slavonic		Iranian, Vedic Sanskrit, Classical Sanskrit, Prakrit, modern north Indian vernacular.

See also Schleicher's family tree of Indo European languages Fig. 11.1.

4. Chatterjee, Suniti Kumar, *Iranianism,* The Asiatic Society, Calcutta, 1972, 1993 (reprint) p. 8.
5. Trenckner, V., *A Critical Pali Dictionary,* Copenhagen, 1924-48 gives the meaning of *ariya (Skt. ārya)* : (a) belonging to the Āryan race or speaking Āryan language; (b) of noble birth (and education), high caste, eminent; mostly (c), said of the Buddha's law, his disciples, their discipline and practices.
6. Edgerton, Franklin, *Buddhist Hybrid Sanskrit: Language and Literature,* Banaras, 1954, p. 5.
7. Grierson, G.A., *Linguistic Survey of India,* pp. 28-30 reproduced in Siddheshwar Varma, *Linguistic Survey of India : A Summary,* Hoshiarpur, 1972, p. 1, 105-06.
8. Macdonell, A.A., *Vedic Mythology,* Delhi, 1971-2, pp. 3-4, 7. Macdonell has also stressed "Many equations of name once made in the first enthusiasm of discovery and generally accepted, have since been rejected and very few of those that remain rest on a firm foundation." *op. cit.,* p. 8.
9. *Ṛigveda* (X.75.5). Gaṅgā, Yamunā, Sarasvatī, Śutudru (Sutlej), Parushṇī (Ravi), Marudvṛidhā (unidentified) with Asikinī (Chandrabhāgā) and Vitastā (Jhelum), Ārjīkīyā (Vipāśa) with Sushomā (they hasten towards the Sindhu).
10. *Ṛigveda* (X.75.6). "You, Sindhu, in order to reach the swift moving Gomatī, have united yourself first with Trishṭāmā, the Śvetyā, the Kubhā (Kabul), Gomatī (Gomal), Krumu (Kurram) and the Mehatnū in conjunction with which streams you do advance."
11. Some scholars have explained that the Brahui-speaking people in Baluchistan migrated to this area during medieval period. Further, as Gilbert Slater in *The Dravidian Element in Indian Culture,* New Delhi, 1976, p. 16 has pointed out "for the fact that Sanscritic languages have pushed the Dravidian languages, with the exception of Brahui, into the extreme south of India is no reason for supposing that the 'Āryan' conquerors who spoke Sanscrit exterminated or expelled the Dravidians in or from the rest of India, any more than the fact that French is a romance language is evidence to show that Caesar's legions exterminated the Celtic-speaking inhabitants of Gaul."

Thomas R. Trautmann in *Āryans and British India,* New Delhi, 1997, p. 3 observes regarding the theory of Indian Civilization—that it was produced by the clash and subsequent mixture of high-skinned civilizing invaders (the Āryans) and the dark-skinned barbarian aborigines (often identified as Dravidian). "It is the crab-grass of Indian history and I should like to uproot it."

12. Sarasvatī Harappan Civilization is four times in extent of the other contemporary civilizations.
13. Wheeler has noted the discovery of long-headed skulls (Indo-Europeans) in the excavations at Harappa.
14. Shaffer, J., "The Indo-Āryan Invasions : Cultural Myth and Archaeological Reality", J. Lukacs (ed.) *The People of South Asia,* New York, 1984, p. 88.
15. Under the Indus Water Treaty of 1959 between India and Pakistan, the waters *inter alia*, of the Sutlej have been entirely allocated to India. Water from the river could be entirely diverted to India and it would cease to flow into the Indus.
16. Thapar, B.K., *The Āryans—A Reappraisal.*
17. Dales, G.P., 'The Mythical Massacre at Mohenjo-daro' in *Expedition* No. 6, *Journal of the Pennsylvania University,* 1964, pp. 36-43.
18. Harappan chronology has been undergoing revision with progress of excavations. One of the recent studies places this civilization between 2700-1300 BC. On the basis of carbon dating, the Mature Harappan Civilization is placed between 2600-2000 BC.
19. Harappan chronology has been undergoing revision with progress of excavations. One of the recent studies places this civilization between 2700-1300 BC.
20. Kennedy, Kenneth A.R., *ibid.*, p. 112.

12

Were the Āryans Barbarians?

N.K. OJHA

The protagonists of the Āryan invasion theory draw a sharp line between the Harappan and the Ṛgvedic people, focusing largely on their urban and rural characteristics respectively. In the process they did not hesitate even in terming the Āryans as nomadic, unurban, uncivilized and barbarian people, completely ignoring some of their excellent and significant traits as mentioned in the *Ṛgveda,* which is the basis for their hypothesis. Scholars like Leonard Woolley,[1] Stuart Piggot,[2] R. Mortimer Wheeler[3] and others believe that the war escapades of Indra, as mentioned in the *Ṛgveda,* resulted in the collapse of the fortified cities of Harappa and Mohenjo-daro, and that the Āryans were alien to city life, they could destroy, but not rebuild the cities. Sir Woolley observes that the Harappan Civilization was non-Āryan and was destroyed by the Āryans (there is indeed no other explanation of its destruction) who were non-urbanized and semi-barbarians. He further writes that the Harappan element in the Hindu civilization is due to the survival of Harappans as slaves or serfs of the Āryan conquerors. R.C. Majumdar objected to this view of Woolley and sent a rejoinder holding that the *Ṛgveda* is the earliest manifestation in a permanent and intelligent form, of the ideas and beliefs of mankind and their gradual evolution. He further pointed out that Maurice Winternitz in his *History of Indian Literature* did not support the idea that the Āryans were barbarous or semi-barbarous people.[4]

Correlating the destruction of Harappa and Mohenjo-daro with the material culture of the Ṛgvedic people lacks prudence, for we all know that even the civilized people have many a time shown no reluctance in destroying and suppressing the rival people and committing crime against humanity in the furtherance of their vested interests. The era of imperialism and colonialism in the history of the mankind amply highlights these vested interests (and people) falsifying the notion of some scholars that the barbarous, uncivilized and unurbanized people ought to cause destruction and wage wars. In fact, wars have very often been fought amongst equals, developed, undeveloped, friends and foes. We find numerous hymns in the *Ṛgveda* seeking the blessings of Indra, the lord of war, for victory in such encounters. Indra was invoked everytime the Ṛgvedic people went to war, whether the enemies were aliens or co-brothers. The 'Battle of Ten Kings' is an apt example of this.

Perhaps these frequent references to Indra have prompted some scholars to over-emphasize the war-like passion of the Āryans and segregate them from the Harappans. But this segregation is not acceptable to many scholars like B.B. Lal,[5] G.C. Pande,[6] S.P. Gupta,[7] O.P. Bharadwaj,[8] R.S. Bisht.[9] They believe that the Harappans and Ṛigvedic people belonged to the same stock as there are many points where the two cultures converge. O.P. Bharadwaj[10] has identified Harappa with Hariyūpiya, the battle-scene in the 'Battle of Ten Kings'—as mentioned in the *Ṛigveda.* Hariyūpiya was ruled by an Āryan king named Abhyavartin Chāyamāna. At one time even Wheeler[11] had conjectured to identify these two with each other. In the 'Battle of Ten Kings'—both Āryan and non-Āryan kings participated. This identification, if accepted, can lead to some logical inferences, i.e. the people of Harappa at a given point of time had an efficient and strong army which could maintain peace and enforce law and order for the smooth functioning of administrative authority.

The Harappan and Ṛigvedic people followed distinct religious practices which were totally Indian. Unlike other contemporary civilizations, community worship was not performed by the people of Harappa. No wonder, Stuart Piggot[12] could not find any temple remains in the Indus basin. Rather they believed in the individual worship as was the case with the Ṛigvedic people. We find references to the performance of sacrifices in the open. In the later Vedic period sacrifices were performed at a larger scale, always in the open, in which hosts of priests participated. The fire altars at Kalibangan, Dholavira, Banawali, etc., point to the same practices.

The archaeological evidence runs counter to the notion of Wheeler[13] and Woolley[14] that the idea of town life and planning, which reached a fully developed stage at Harappa and Mohenjo-daro, was borrowed from Mesopotamia. R.S. Bisht,[15] who excavated Dholavira and Banawali believes that the pre-Harappan culture was fairly advanced and some of the elements were adopted and refined by the succeeding Harappans. All these cultures had strong, comparable socio-economic infrastructures and there was a regular interaction and exchange among them. Kunal is another example. Throughout it remained a rural site but having urban amenities of life. It maintained a regular interaction and exchange with the cities of the Harappans. Many preceding cultures evince the existence of fortification system and inner planning.

R.S. Bisht[16] substantiates his claim with references to words and sentences from the *Ṛigveda.* After the perusal of the hymns of the *Ṛigveda,* he enumerates 27 adjectives on the basis of etymology used for all kinds of *puras*—Āryan and non-Āryan. Out of these 15 belonged to the Āryans and 11 or 12 to the non-Āryans and amongst that too *dṛiḷhā* meaning firm and strong, is used commonly for settlement of both. The term used for non-Āryan *puras* and forts are *dṛiḷhā, dṛiṇhitā, aśmanmayī, jarimā, charishṇu pur, āmā pur, śāradī pur* and *śarman* or *śārardīpur, dāsī, dāsapatnī, kṛishṇayonī adevī* and *dehī.* The adjectives used for the Āryan *puras* are *dṛiḷhā, adhṛishṭā, āyasī, patṛi, śatabhuji, pṛithvī, mahī, urvī, bahulā, saubhagā, isha, gomatī, nārmiṇī, śubhrā* and *bhadrā.*

The superlative used to classify the Āryan *puras* on account of size, form, strength and use prove beyond doubt the existence of *puras* in the Ṛigvedic period. The Āryans were great builders of cities. Indra is not only the destroyer of *puras* but also the protector and keeper of the *puras.* He has been called *purandara*[17] and *puronah.*[18] Indra is called *Purpati,* the lord of cities who possessed all the cities as a husband does his wives.[19] Agni, Viśvedevaḥ, Māruts and other gods are invoked to protect the Āryan *pura.*[20] Soma has been called a *paura. Paura* is the term used for townsmen.[21] In view of the number, size, form, strength and use of these cities it is highly unjustified to consider the Ṛigvedic people as nomads, who could only destroy and not build cities. Even the descriptions of *grāmas* and *mahāgrāmas* in the *Ṛigveda* portray the life of settled people, having well-established social, religious, economic and political institutions.

Conformity to social norms by the people at large posits the fact that the relationships in the Ṛigvedic society were well-defined. Patriarchal in nature, strict discipline was enforced in the family by its head. The father had the right to inflict even severe punishment on his sons is quite evident from the examples of Śunaḥśepa and Rijraśva.[22] An insolvent gambler is disowned by his parents.[23] The wedding hymn describes beautifully the position of the newly married wife in the house of her in-laws. She commanded respect, wielding authority over the husband's father, brother and unmarried sisters.[24] The participation of the wife in the household sacrifices was regular. Prayers were offered for a long, happy, prosperous and harmonious marital life surrounded by sons and grandsons.[25] Desire for daughters is not expressed in the *Ṛigveda* as the son alone could secure salvation for his parents and continue the line. The adoption of male child had the recognition of the society, though generally not favoured.[26]

The institution of marriage was the foundation of the family life. The Ṛigvedic people followed the set procedures and practices, which have now become rituals in the Hindu marriages. The wedding hymn[27] delineates the oldest marriage ceremony. The bridegroom and party goes to the bride's house in a procession where they are warmly received and entertained. The bride also takes part in the marriage-feast.[28] After the festivities the ceremony commences with the bridegroom grasping the hand of the bride and leads her round the fire.[29] After this the bridegroom and bride become husband and wife. The groom takes his bride home in a car.[30] Then follows the consummation and the beginning of the conjugal life. Adherence to these practices in continuty for millennia shows their sanctity and efficacy in the Hindu society. Similarly, there are certain hymns and verses in the *Ṛigveda,* which outline the ceremonial procedures at birth, death, ancestor-worship and other occasions of daily life. It may not be possible to discuss all of them here but it is clear that the early Vedic society was well organized. Of course, it was not free from sins and evils and the evil-doers were punished by the society.

The *Ṛigveda* enshrines the principles and goals of an ideal life that must have been adopted by the majority of people in their lives. These principles are relevant to all the stages in the evolution of human civilization and can be a matter of pride for the people of any age, area and culture. The Āryans believed that it was the divine knowledge that purified them and the one who followed the path of truth remained protected.[31] Only the virtuous tread the path of truth.[32] The worshippers have been called upon to be pure and pious; firm and unshaken.[33] In hymn I.168.3 of the *Ṛigveda* the sage pronounces the holding of right and duty in his hand envisaging that the two go together and are inseparable. Life is made of action, i.e. duty. Rights without duties are not appreciated and duties without rights cause frustration. It has been enjoined on man to leave lethargy and laziness and perform noble deeds. The gods bless the one who toils and moils but punish the lazy and lethargic.[34] Idle, wicked, inhuman and doers of ignoble actions were called non-Āryans, possessing demonic nature.[35] The idea of brotherhood was also very dear to the people, for we find many references to the guests being entertained by the householders. They knew that the riches have wings and revolve from one man to another. Sharing of food was very common and he who ate alone was considered a sinner.[36] The wealth free from debt was regarded as a noble possession.[37] The bounteous enjoyed the immortal bliss.[38] Blessed were the hands that supported the destitute.[39] The learned men have been advised to uplift the fallen and forlorn.[40] Hymn IX. 63. 5 lays stress to ennoble all men of the universe; and verse VI. 10. 7 to give up hatred. There are scores of other verses that exhibit the sublimity and wisdom of the Ṛigvedic people. Still some learned scholars have callously called them nomadic barbarians.

Education is another yardstick to measure the progress of the people at a given point of time because it segregates the civilized from the savages. The Āryans attached great significance to the acquisition of knowledge. The monumental *Ṛigveda* is the outcome of their quest for knowledge. Knowledge is manifested through the purity of language. Sanskrit, the language of the Vedic people, has been recognized as the purest of the pure. Linguistically fully developed, it is both complicated and sophisticated because of the multiplicity of the meanings of the words and their derivatives. The people who developed and conversed in such a rich language could not be primitives. Only the genius and scholars speak pure language is rightly mentioned in the *Ṛigveda*.[41] To achieve this objective due emphasis was laid upon acquiring education. Education was imparted to the people at large, though orally. First, the teacher recites some verse and then the students repeat his words in a chorus.[42] This tradition was continued by the Brahmins almost to the present. The relationship between the teacher and pupil was of respect and affection. The teacher made his pupils efficient, non-violent, fearless and contented. The students revered and respected the teacher.[43] When the knowledge learnt by heart was put to writing, volumes of Sanskrit literature were produced. Women were also included in the ambit of education. Some of them attained perfection and composed hymns of the *Ṛigveda*. The names of Apālā, Ghoshā, Nivāvarī, Viśvavarā are just a few to be mentioned in this connection.

Faith and reverence, purity and charity, tolerance and brotherhood, duty and right, education and knowledge are undoubtedly the most essential traits of any civilized world. All these traits are interspersed in hundreds of verses in the *Ṛigveda* implying that the people must have been following them. It could never mean that they were unaware of these virtues and were not following them by any stretch of imagination. Though the people were aware of these virtues and were striving for a pious life yet have been called barbarians. It seems intriguingly subjective as it served the interests of the imperialists in India. By minimizing the Indian heritage, they could prolong their rule. The Western imperialists adopted the same tactics in Africa and America. They committed most heinous crimes against humanity in the continents, enslaving and trading the Africans is just one example out of hundreds. The Western scholars never called their co-brothers brutes or uncultured people. Rather they have been eulogized as harbingers of civilization and adventurous people. The word barbarian with its derivatives and meanings is reserved only for the original inhabitants of America, Africa and Asia, no matter what stage of development has been attained by them. The Ṛigvedic people are the victims of this biased approach.

The expressions attached with the word barbarian are self-explanatory of the racial bias. The meaning of the word in the English dictionaries has generally been explained as, an uncultured or brutish person; a tout; a member of a primitive community or tribe. As an adjective it means rough and uncultured, uncivilized. However, in some dictionaries the word has been explained more elaborately giving its origin as well. According to *The Webster New Twentieth Century Dictionary of the English Language*[44] the meaning of barbarian is, "barbarian n. [L. barborus; Gr. barbaros, foreign; so called by the Greeks because the talk of the foreigner sounded like bar-bar]:

1. A member of a people or group with a civilization regarded as primitive, savage etc.
2. An insensitive, coarse or unmannerly person; boor.
3. A cruel; savage, brutal person.
4. A foreigner. The Greeks and Romans called other peoples barbarians."

The Concise Oxford Dictionary[45] explains this word as:

barbarian n. l. (in ancient time) a member of a people not belonging to one of the great civilizations (Greek, Roman, Christian) 2. an uncultured or brutish person. adj. 1. of or relating to ancient barbarians. 2. uncultured; brutish. -ORIGIN ME: from Ofr. barbarien, from barbare, or from L.barbarus, from GK. barbaros 'foreign'.

Thus, self-declared superiority of the Western civilization lay at the origin and use of the word barbarian. The imposition of this so-called superiority on the interpretation of the facts of Indian history is nothing but an attempt to kill objectivity—the essence of true history. Objective and unbiased study clearly establishes the continuity of Indian culture, civilization and heritage of a single people through the early Vedic and Harappan ages, without the remotest reference to uncivilized or barbarian conflict of two imaginary divergent people.

Notes and References

1. Woolley, Leonard, 1963, *History of Mankind-Cultural and Scientific Development*, Vol. I, George Allan and Unwin Limited, London, UNESCO, pp. 406-58.
2. Piggot, Stuart, 1950, *Prehistoric India*, Penguin, p. 144.
3. Wheeler, R. Mortimer, 1968, *Early India and Pakistan*, Thomas and Hudson, London, p. 113.
4. Winternitz, Maurice, 1927, *History of Indian Literature*, Vol. I, Calcutta, pp. 63-75.
5. Lal, B.B., 1997, *The Earliest Civilization of South Asia*, Aryan Books International, New Delhi. Lal, B.B., 2002, *The Saraswati Flows On*, Aryan Books International, New Delhi.
6. Pande, G.C., *Foundations of Indian Culture*, Vols. I & II, New Delhi, 1995.
7. Gupta, S.P., 1996, *The Indus-Saraswati Civilization*, Pratibha Prakashan, Delhi.
8. Bharadwaj, O.P., 2003, *Sarupa Saurabham*, Prof. Lakshman Sarup Centenary Volume, Vol. I, (ed.) A. Agrawal, Harman Publishing House, New Delhi, pp. 267-73.
9. Pande, G.C. (ed.), 1999, *History of Science, Philosophy and Culture in Indian Civilization, The Dawn of Civilization up to 600 B.C.* , Vol. I, Part I, PHISPC, Delhi, pp. 393-442.
10. *Ibid.*, pp. 267-73.
11. *Ibid.*, p. 113.
12. *Ibid.*, pp. 200-01.
13. *Ibid.*, p. 104.
14. *Ibid.*, p. 458.
15. *Ibid.*, p. 406.
16. *Ibid.*, pp. 412-13.
17. *RV*.I.109.8; II.20.7; III.54.15; VIII.1.8; VIII.50.8.
18. *RV*.VI.25.7.
19. *RV*.I.173.10.
20. *RV*.I.189.2; VI.48.8; VII.16.10; X.101.8; I.166.8.
21. *RV*.II.11.11.
22. *RV*.I.24.12-15; V.27; I.116.16.
23. *RV*.X. 34.
24. *RV*.X. 85. 46.
25. *RV*.VIII.31.5-9; X.34.11; 85.18,19.
26. *RV*.VII.4.7.8.
27. *RV*.X.85.
28. *RV*.X.17.1.
29. *RV*.X.85.36, 38.
30. *RV*.X.85.7, 8, 10, 24-27, 42.

31. *RV*.I.1.3.10; VI. 44.8.
32. *RV*.I.124.3.
33. *RV*.X.18.2, X.173.1.
34. *RV*.VIII.2.18.
35. *RV*.X.22.8.
36. *RV*.X.117.4-6.
37. *RV*.VII.4, 7-8.
38. *RV*.I.125.6.
39. *RV*.VI.18.14.
40. *RV*.X.137.1.
41. *RV*.IX.73.7.
42. *RV*.VII.103.5.
43. *RV*.VII.17.4.
44. 2nd. Ed., Collins World 1971.
45. *The Concise Oxford Dictionary*, Tenth Edition, Oxford University Press Inc. New York, 1999.

13

Connections Between the Harappan Seals and the Vedic Literature

N.S. RAJARAM

Abstract

The connections between Harappan archaeology and the Vedic literature are so many and so diverse that no more than a survey is possible within the confines of a single presentation. Broadly speaking, they may be classified into two groups: (1) connections between the iconography depicted on the seals and the symbolism described in the Vedic literature; (2) the readings obtained by Jha's decipherment of the Indus script and their references to themes and passages in the Vedic literature. These range from the Saṃhitās, the Upanishads to the Sūtras. The text on the seals are mainly in sūtra form, and in fact are mainly sūtras that often serve as indices to Vedic passages. Of course, Vedic indices like the *Anukramanis* are well known. The seal indices are very brief and may be called the *Laghu Anukramani*.

The present article discusses mainly the connections between the Harappan iconography as found on the seals and their relation with Vedic themes from the Upanishads and the Saṃhitās. The article will also show that establishing this connection between Harappan archaeology and the Vedic literature can lead to fundamental advances in our knowledge of ancient history.

Background: The 'Āryan Invasion'

There are currently two views about the origins of the Vedic Civilization. One sees it as an indigenous development, while the other traces it to 'Āryan invaders' who originated in Central Asia, Eurasia or even Europe. The latter view came into being following the discovery of the Sanskrit language and its closeness to European languages by Sir William Jones in 1784. For almost two centuries, this formulation, which places the origin of Veda and the Sanskrit language outside India, has made Indian history and civilization subordinate to Europe. The main instrument in the propagation of this version of history has been the Āryan

Invasion Theory (AIT), now being called the Āryan Migration Theory (AMT). According to this theory, the Vedic Āryans, said to be one branch of a Eurasian people called 'Indo-Europeans', brought both the Vedas and the Sanskrit language in an 'Āryan invasion' of India in 1500 BC. There was no civilization in India prior to this.

Beginning about 1921, the work of Indian and British archaeologists revealed the existence of a vast urban civilization in India, dating to more than a thousand years before the supposed arrival of the Āryans. We know this as the Indus Valley or the Harappan Civilization. This posed a direct challenge to the idea of no civilization in India before the supposed 'Āryan invasion'. To account for this some scholars in India and the West assert that the Harappan Civilization went into decline and disappeared as a result of the Āryan invasion. This is essentially the scenario found in history books, though, recently, some textbooks are beginning to admit the possibility that the Vedic civilization was an indigenous development.

The Āryan invasion model gives rise to a peculiar situation: Harappan archaeology and the Vedic literature, both of which arose and flourished in the same geographic region, are treated as unrelated, even mutually hostile entities. According to this scenario, the Harappan Civilization (ca. 3100–1900 BC) preceded the Vedic by more than a thousand years, and fell due to the depredations of the latter. If, on the other hand, the Harappan Civilization is shown to be Vedic, the Āryan invasion/migration theory collapses. This has led some scholars, especially in the West, to deny any Vedic-Harappan connection, in order to preserve the invasion theory.

Any theory should account for all the data—both archaeological and literary. Trying to separate the archaeology from literature, both of which flourished in the same geographic region, in order to preserve an old theory is unnatural. The present article will explain how a careful study of Harappan artefacts, especially the symbolism of the seals, allows us to remove this contradiction. The rest of the article shows that the two—the Harappan and the Vedic—are but different aspects of the same civilization. Harappan archaeology represents the material remains of the civilization described in the Vedic literature. The Āryan invasion is therefore a myth. It is necessary to find an alternate historical model that does not contradict hard data.

Vedic Symbols in Harappan Archaeology

One can begin with the practice of Yoga, which is Vedic in origin. There is strong evidence suggesting that the Harappans practised Yoga. The figure (Fig. 13.1) displays several terracotta figurines in yogic postures or *āsanas*. These were found at various sites like Harappa and Mohenjo-daro.

Beyond this Vedic-Harappan connection, one can begin with familiar sacred symbols like the *svastika* signs. Harappan sites are replete with the *svastika. Svastika* stands for *svasti-ka,* meaning 'maker of welfare'. They appear singly as well as in combination with other signs. Fig. 13.2 shows a string of five *svastikas*. This is related to the sacred *pañcha-svasti mantra* found in the *Yajurveda* (25.18–19), in which the word *'svasti'* (welfare) appears five times. It may be paraphrased as:

> We invoke Him who may bring us welfare,
> May the respected Indra guard our welfare,
> May the omniscient Pushan guard our welfare,
> May the Universal Creator guard our welfare,
> May the Great Protector bring us welfare.

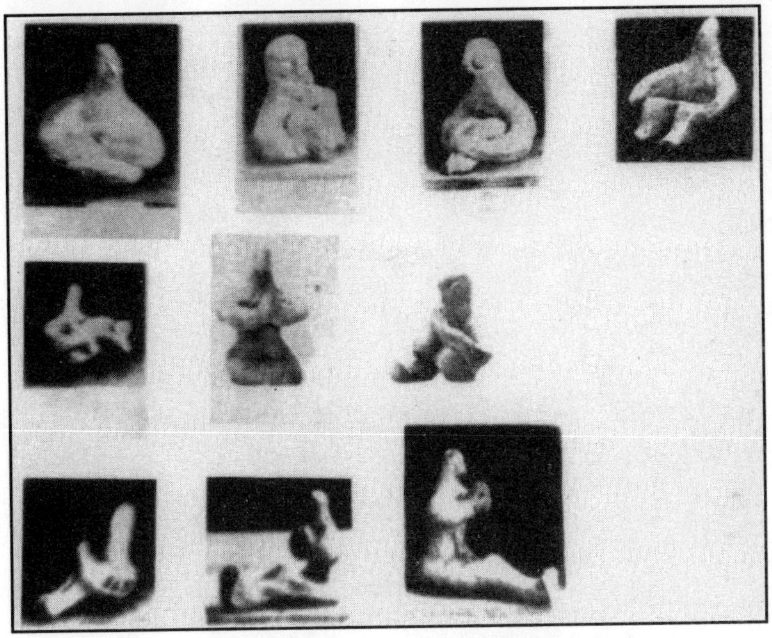

Fig. 13.1 Examples of Yoga in the Harappan archaeology.

These invocations appear also in the *Ṛigveda.* The Harappan *svastika* string is obviously related to this Vedic prayer. Such connections are not limited to the *Ṛigveda* and the *Yajurveda;* they span the whole gamut of the Vedic literature, including the Brāhmaṇas, Upanishads and others. This can be illustrated looking at the 'OM' sign, known also as *praṇavakshara.* Fig. 13.3 shows the seal known as 'Oṁkāra Mudrā' or the 'Om' seal. The same figure displays also line drawings of the seal in two positions—original and rotated by 90 degrees. The one on the right—i.e. rotated by 90 degrees—is practically the Devanāgarī 'Om'. Scripts of languages like Kannada and Telugu have retained the original orientation of the Harappan 'Om', while elongating it a little. All of them derive from the Harappan 'Om' and have deep connections with Vedic thought.

This 'bow-shaped' Harappan 'Om' is described at many places in the Vedic literature. The *Muṇḍaka Upanishad* (2.2.4) describes it as: "Praṇava (Om) is the bow, the soul is the arrow, Brahma is the target. With full concentration, aim at the target and strike, to become one with Brahma, just as the arrow becomes one with the target." This is almost a visual description of 'Om' as found on a Harappan seal.

The *'Om'*, which is adorned by *aśvattha* leaves and branches, highlights the sacredness attributed to the *aśvattha,* a Vedic idea. The *Kaṭha Upanishad* (2.3.1) describes *aśvattha* (*pipul*) tree as embodying the essence of sacredness: "This is the eternal *aśvattha* tree, with the root at the top *(ūrdhvamūlo),* but branches downwards. It is He that is called the Shining One and Immortal. All the worlds are established in Him, none transcends Him." The same idea is echoed in the *Bhagavadgītā* (15.1): "He who knows that *aśvattha* tree with its root above and branches down, whose leaves are the Vedas said to be imperishable. And, he who knows it knows the Vedas."

In all this there is the symbolism of the *aśvattha* as the seat of sacred knowledge (or Veda), and the abode of the Gods. This idea goes back to the *Ṛigveda* itself (X.97.5): "Your abode is the *aśvattha* tree, your dwelling is made of its leaves." With such explicit Vedic symbolism, there cannot be the slightest doubt that Harappan archaeology contains physical representations of Vedic ideas. What is given here is a miniscule sample of the Vedic symbolism that pervades Harappan archaeology. It is discussed in more detail in the forthcoming book *Vedic Symbolism in Indus Seals* by N. Jha and this writer.

Fig. 13.2 A string of five svastikas.

Fig. 13.3 The 'Om' seal and its two positions.

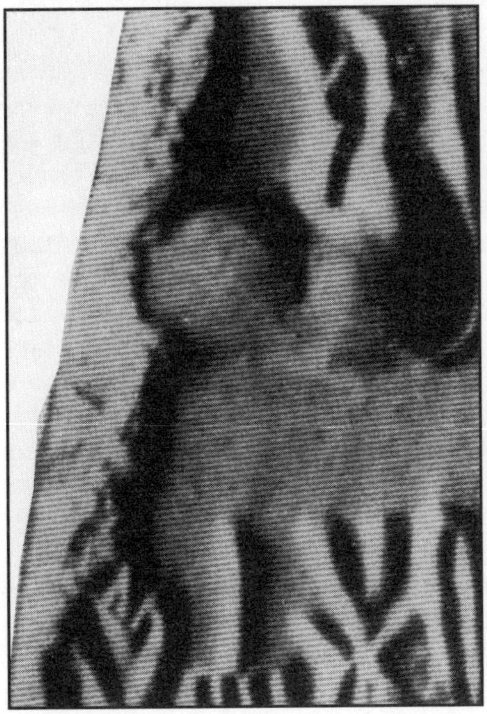

(a)

(b)

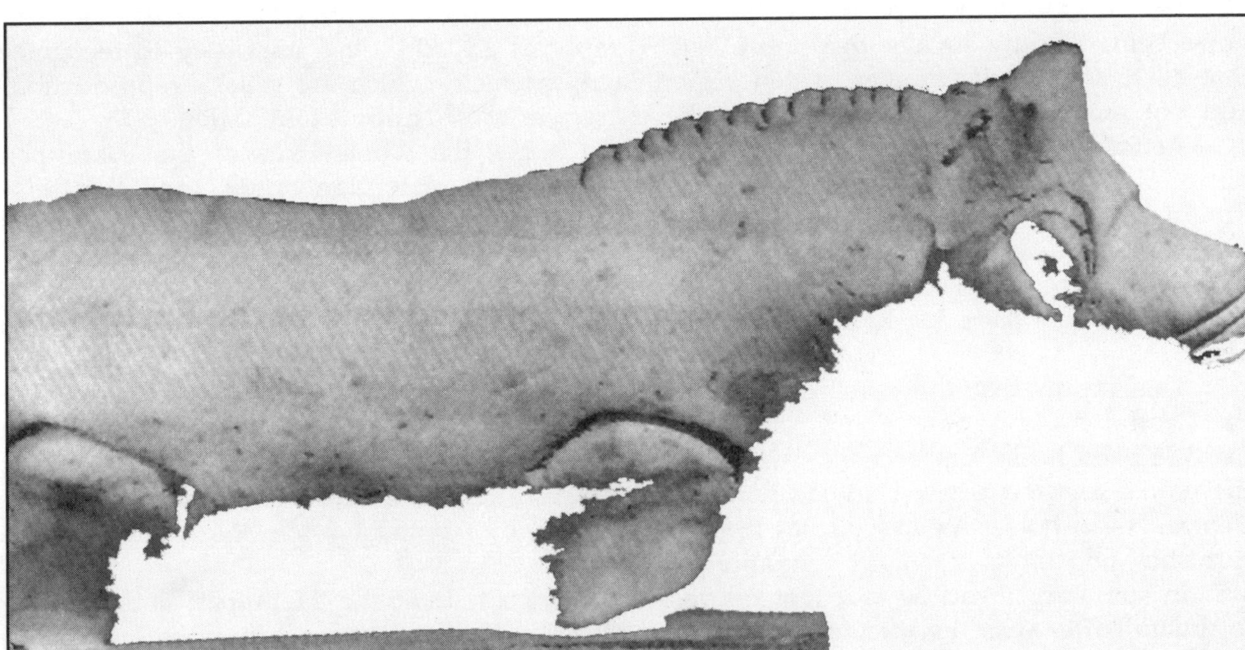

(c)

Fig. 13.4 Horse images at Harappan sites.

Fig. 13.5 Pre-Harappan vase showing Vedic themes.

Horse and Vedic Symbolism

The horse and the cow are mentioned often in the *Ṛigveda,* though they generally carry symbolic rather than physical meaning. There is a widespread misconception that the absence of the horse at Harappan sites shows that horses were unknown in India until the invading (or migrating) Āryans brought them. 'No horse at Harappa' has assumed almost the status of a sacred dogma for the upholders of the Āryan invasion. This is unfounded, for such 'argument by absence' is hazardous at best. To take an example, the bull is quite common on the seals, but the cow is never represented. We cannot from this conclude that the Harappans raised bulls but were ignorant of the cow. In any event, both horse remains and their artistic depictions are known at Harappan sites as Fig. 13.4 indicates.

More fundamentally, it is simply not true that horses were unknown to the Harappans. The recently released and authoritative *The Dawn of Indian Civilization,* Vol. 1, Pt. 1 observes (pp. 344 -45): "... the horse was widely domesticated and used in India during the third millennium BC over most of the areas covered by the Indus-Sarasvatī [or Harappan] Civilization. Archaeologically this is most significant since the evidence is widespread and not isolated."

In fact, as far back as 1931, comparing a horse specimen found at Mohenjo-daro with other specimens, John Marshall wrote (Vol. II, p. 654): "It will be seen that there is a considerable degree of similarity between these various examples, and it is probable that the Anau horse, *the Mohenjo-Daro horse,* and the example of *Equus caballus* of the Zoological Survey of India, are all of the type of the Indian 'country-bred', a small breed of horse, the Anau horse being slightly smaller than the others. (Emphasis added.)" It is important to recognize that all this is much stronger evidence than mere artefacts, which are artist's reproductions and not anatomical specimens that can be subjected to scientific examination.

Actually, the Harappans not only knew the horse, the whole issue of the 'Harappan horse' is irrelevant. In order to prove that the Vedas are of foreign origin, (and the horse came from Central Asia) one must produce positive evidence: *it should be possible to show that the horse described in the* Ṛigveda *was brought from Central Asia.* But this is contradicted by the *Ṛigveda* itself. In verse 1.162.18, the *Ṛigveda* describes the horse as having 34 ribs, *while the Central Asian horse has 18 pairs (36) of ribs.* We find a similar description in the *Yajurveda* also.

This means that the horse described in the Vedas is the native Indian breed and not the Central Asian variety. Fossil remains of *Equus sivalensis* (the 'Shiwalik horse') show that the 34-ribbed horse has been known in India going back to very ancient times. This makes the whole argument based on 'no horse at Harappa' irrelevant. The Vedic horse is not the Central Asian horse. As a result, far from supporting any Āryan invasion, the horse evidence furnishes one of its strongest refutations.

In summary it can be said that the recent controversy over the 'Harappan horse' is due to unfamiliarity with the literature and lack of attention to detail, accompanied by a stubborn attachment to a disproved theory by denying well-known facts.

The word *'aśva'* in the *Ṛgveda* often carries symbolic meaning like power, speed, and sometimes *prāṇa* (life essence). Composite animals that include the horse are described in the *Ṛgveda*. For example, the verse 1.163.1 describes a mythical horse as: "possessed with the wings of a falcon and the limbs of a deer." Fig. 13.5 displays a vase found at Mehrgarh, a pre-Harappan site, on which this mythical animal is depicted. Notice also the *aśvattha* leaves, again linking it to Vedic thought. It is a very ancient artefact from the pre-Harappan period, said to go back to 3500 BC or earlier. So, Vedic ideas were current even then. This means parts of the *Ṛgveda* must be at least that old, not brought into India by any 'Āryan invaders' in 1500 BC.

In summary, the Vedic and Harappan Civilizations were one. Harappan artefacts are material representations of ideas and thoughts found in the Vedic literature. The Harappans therefore were Vedic Harappans.

Bibliography

Jha, N. and N.S. Rajaram, 2000, *The Deciphered Indus Script: Methodology, Readings, Interpretations*, New Delhi: Aditya Prakashan.

Marshall, John (ed.), 1931, *Mohenjo-Daro and the Indus Civilzation*, 3 vols., London: Arthur Probsthain.

Pande, G.C. (ed.), 1999, *The Dawn of Civilization Upto 600 BC*, Vol. I, Pt. I, New Delhi: PHISPC.

Rajaram, N.S. and David Frawley, 2001, *Vedic Āryans and the Origin of Civilization*, 3rd (edn.), New Delhi: Voice of India.

14

आर्य और अनार्य भेद — जातिगत या कर्मगत?

वेद ओर वैदिक साहित्य के संदर्भ में

वसुन्धरा रिहानी

वैदिक संस्क ति के निर्माता और वाहक आर्यों और अनार्यों का वेदों, वैदिक साहित्य, पुराणों तथा महाकाव्यों में पर्याप्त उल्लेख मिलता है। 'आर्य' और 'अनार्य' दो परस्पर विरोधी शब्द हैं। पाश्चात्य तथा कतिपय प्राच्य इतिहासकारों का मत है कि 'आर्य' शब्द से एक जाति विशेष के लोगों का बोध होता है जो ईसा से कुछ शताब्दी पूर्व बाहर (बहुत संभवतः मध्य एशिया) से भारत में आए थे और उन्होंने यहाँ के मूल निवासी—काले रंग और चपटी नाक वाले लोगों पर, जो द्राविड़ थे, अनेक प्रकार के अत्याचार किए और उनका समूल विनाश कर उन्हें दूर दक्षिण में भगाकर अपनी सभ्यता और संस्क ति का विकास किया। दूसरी ओर 'अनार्य' शब्द से ये इतिहासज्ञ उन अनेक जातियों की गणना करते हैं जिन्होंने आर्यों का विरोध किया था और आर्य लोग इन्हें दास, दस्यु और द्राविड़ कहते थे। द्राविड़ जातीय लोग नगरों में रहते थे, समुद्री यात्रा करते हुए ये अन्य देशों से व्यापार करते थे, सुरक्षा के लिए इन्होंने बड़े-बड़े किलों का निर्माण किया था, इनके अपने दार्शनिक मूल तत्त्व थे जिनसे भारत के वैदिक दर्शन का विकास हुआ है, इत्यादि। (*वैदिक ऐज*, प ष्ठ 156) विद्वान् तो यह भी कहते हैं कि मोहनजो-दड़ो की सभ्यता, जो कि द्राविड़ सभ्यता ही है, आर्यों से पूर्व की है।

इन सब विवादों में न जाकर मुझे इस लेख में वेद और वैदिक साहित्य के आधार पर इस तथ्य का विवेचन करना अभीष्ट है कि 'आर्य' शब्द का क्या अर्थ है ? कौन 'आर्य' कहलाते हैं और कौन 'अनार्य'? तथा क्या आर्य और दास, दस्यु या द्राविड़ प थक् जातियाँ हैं।

आर्य शब्द का अर्थ

आर्य शब्द ऋ गतौ धातु से बनता है। जिसका अर्थ है 'गति-प्रापणयो'। अर्थात् गति-ज्ञान, गमन, प्राप्ति करने और कराने वाले को आर्य कहते हैं। इस धात्वर्थ के अनुसार आर्य वे हैं जो ज्ञान-सम्पन्न हैं, जो सदा सन्मार्ग की ओर गति करने वाले पुरूषार्थी हैं और जो ईश्वर तथा परमानन्द को प्राप्त करते और तदर्थ प्रयत्नशील होते हैं।

ऋग्वेद में – ''आर्या व्रता विस जन्तो अधि क्षमि''(10.65.11) कहकर आर्यों के विषय में बतलाया गया है कि आर्य वे हैं जो भूमि पर सत्य, अहिंसा, पवित्रता और परोपकार आदि व्रतों को विशेष रूप से धारण करते हैं। इसी को लेकर

संस्क त के *शब्दकल्पद्रुम* और *वाचस्पत्यब हदभिधानादि* कोशों में आर्य शब्द के निम्न अर्थ पाए जाते हैं। यथा – पूज्यः, श्रेष्ठः, धार्मिकः, धर्मशीलः, मान्यः, उदारचरितः, शान्तचित्तः, न्यायपथावलम्बी, सततं कर्त्तव्यकर्मानुष्ठाता। जैसे कि *स्म तिवाक्य* भी है

कर्त्तव्यमाचरन् कार्यम्, अकर्त्तव्यमनाचरन्।
तिष्ठति प्रक ताचारे, स तु आर्य इति स्म तः।।

अर्थात् आर्य वह कहलाता है जो कर्त्तव्य कर्म का सदा आचरण करता हो और अकर्त्तव्य कर्म अर्थात् पापादि से दूर रहता हो और जो पूर्ण सदाचारी हो। *निरूक्त* में आचार्य यास्क ने आर्य शब्द का अर्थ 'आर्यः ईश्वरपुत्रः' इन शब्दों में दिया है। 'अर्य' शब्द का अर्थ स्वामी, परमेश्वर होता है। जो उस सर्वजगत् के स्वामी परमेश्वर के सच्चे पुत्र अर्थात् उसकी आज्ञाओं का सदा पालन करने वाले हों वे आर्य कहलाते हैं। *महाभारत* के निम्न श्लोकों में भी कहा गया है –

न वैरमुद्दीपयति प्रशान्तं, न दर्पमारोहति नास्तमेति।
न दुर्गतो स्मीति करोत्यकार्य, तमार्यशीलं परमाहुरार्याः।।
न स्वे सुखे वै कुरूते प्रहर्ष, नान्यस्य दुःखे भवति प्रहृष्टः।
दत्त्वा न पश्चात् कुरूते अनुतापं, स कथ्यते सत्पुरूषार्यशीलः।।[1]

जो शान्त हुए वैर को बढ़ाता नहीं, जो न अभिमान करता है और न ही निराश होता है। दुर्गति को प्राप्त करने पर भी कभी पाप कर्म नहीं करता, जो सुख प्राप्त होने पर बहुत अधिक प्रसन्नता नहीं दर्शाता, जो दूसरों के दुख में कभी प्रसन्न नहीं होता, दान देकर जो पश्चाताप नहीं करता उसे आर्य कहा जाता है।

महात्मा गौतम बुद्ध ने धम्मपद[2] में, जैन मतावलम्बियों में तत्त्वार्थसूत्र एवं रत्नचन्द्र जैन क त *अर्द्धमागधी कोश*[3] में और पारसियों के धर्मग्रन्थ *ज़ेन्दावेस्ता*[4] में भी सज्जनों और श्रेष्ठ पुरूषों के लिए 'आर्य' शब्द का प्रयोग किया गया है। जैनों में साध्वियाँ अभी तक 'आर्या' वा 'आरजा' कहलाती हैं।

श्री अरविन्द भी 'आर्य' शब्द के अर्थ और महत्व के विषय में लिखते हैं –

The word Arya expresses a particular ethical and social order of well-governed life, candour, courtesy, nobility, straight dealing, courage, gentleness, purity, humanity, observance of social duties, eagerness for knowledge, respect for the wise and the learned and the social accomplishments. There is no word in human speech that has a nobler history.[5]

अर्थात् आर्य शब्द में उदारता, नम्रता, श्रेष्ठता, सरलता, साहस, पवित्रता, दया, निर्बल संरक्षण, ज्ञान के लिए उत्सुकता, सामाजिक कर्त्तव्य, पालनादि सब उत्तम गुणों का समावेश हो जाता है। मानवीय भाषा में इससे अधिक उत्तम और कोई शब्द नहीं है।

भारतीय संस्क ति के उपजीवी महाकाव्यों — *रामायण* तथा *महाभारत* में भी 'आर्य' शब्द उच्चकोटि की नैतिकता के अर्थ में प्रयुक्त हुआ है। उदाहरणार्थ – *वाल्मीकि रामायण* में श्री राम के उत्तम गुणों का वर्णन करते हुए नारद मुनि ने कहा है – 'आर्यः सर्वसमश्चायं, सोमवत् प्रियदर्शनः' (बालकाण्ड 1.16) अर्थात् श्री राम आर्य–धर्मात्मा, सदाचारी, सबको समान द ष्टि से देखने वाले और चन्द्र की तरह प्रिय दर्शन वाले थे। संस्क त साहित्य में राजा अथवा महाराजा को 'आर्यपुत्र' तथा 'आर्य' कहकर सम्बोधित किया जाता है।[6] इस सम्बोधन से यह भी प्रतीत होता है कि 'आर्य' शब्द केवल धार्मिक एवं आध्यात्मिक उच्चता का ही द्योतक नहीं था अपितु उसे राष्ट्रीय गौरव का भी प्रतीक माना जाता था। जिसे आर्य का गौरव दिया जाता था, उसे अपने राष्ट्रीय स्वाभिमान की रक्षा करनी आवश्यक होती थी।

'अनार्य' शब्द का अर्थ

'अनार्य' शब्द 'आर्य' का विपरीतार्थक है। यदि वेदशास्त्रोक्त साधु-आचारों का पालन करने वाला 'आर्य' है तो उसके

विपरीत आचरण करने वाला 'अनार्य' होगा। तात्पर्य यह कि सदाचार का आचरण और उसका अनाचरण ही 'आर्यत्व' और 'अनार्यत्व' की पहचान है। *महाभारत* (शान्तिपर्व 93.16,94.10) में कहा गया है कि अनार्यें के कर्मों का विद्वान् व्यक्तियों को आचरण नहीं करना चाहिए। इस आचरणगत भेद की द ष्टि से ही भारतीय संस्क ति में श्रेष्ठ और सज्जनों के लिए 'आर्य' और दुर्जन तथा अविवेकी के लिए 'अनार्य' शब्द का प्रयोग पाया जाता है। यथा – कैकयी ने जब श्री राम को वन में भेजने की माँग की थी तो *वाल्मीकि रामायण* के अनुसार राजा दशरथ ने उसके लिए 'अनार्या' शब्द का अनेक बार प्रयोग किया था जो कि 'हन्तानार्ये ममामित्रे' (अयोध्याकाण्ड 13.5) श्लोकांश में देखा जा सकता है, स्वयं वाल्मीकि ने भी कैकयी के लिए इस अनार्योचित बुरी मांग के लिए 'तदप्रियमनार्याया वचनं' (अयोध्याकाण्ड 19.19) कहकर 'अनार्या' शब्द का प्रयोग किया है। लोक में सत्कर्मों से विमुख या मूढ़ व्यक्ति 'अनाड़ी' कहा जाता है जो कि 'अनार्या' का तत्सम रूप है। इसी प्रकार *भगवतद्गीता* (2.2) में श्री क ष्ण ने जब देखा कि वीर अर्जुन अपने क्षत्रियधर्म के आदर्श से च्युत होकर मोह में फंस रहा है तो उसे सम्बोधन करते हुए उन्होंने कहा है–

कुतस्त्वा कश्मलमिदं, विषमे समुपस्थितम्।
अनार्यजुष्टमस्वर्ग्यम्, अकीर्तिकरमर्जुन।।

अर्थात् हे अर्जुन! यह अनार्यों व दुर्जनों द्वारा सेवित, नरक में ले जाने वाला, अपयश करने वाला पाप इस कठिन समय में तुझे कैसे प्राप्त हो गया?

ऐतरेय आरण्यक (3.2.5) तथा *शांखायन आरण्यक* (8.9) में आर्यों की बोली (वाच्) की विशेष चर्चा की गई है। संभवतः इसी आधार पर संस्क त साहित्य की नाटक-लेखन परम्परा में भास आदि महाकवियों ने सभ्य, सुसंस्क त और धार्मिक विद्वान् राजा प्रभ ति पात्रों से देववाणी संस्क त में संवाद कहलवाएँ हैं जबकि दास दासियाँ प्राक त भाषा का प्रयोग करती हैं। यह भाषा-भेद नाटक के पात्रों की विद्वत्ता और संस्क ति के आधार पर ही किया गया प्रतीत होता है। इन सब प्रमाणों से यही सिद्ध होता कि वैदिक संस्क ति में 'आर्यत्व' और 'अनार्यत्व' का भेद जातिगत न होकर स्वभावगत या कर्मगत था।

अब 'आर्य' शब्द के विपरीतार्थक 'अनार्य' शब्द जिसके अन्तर्गत इतिहासकार दास, दस्यु अथवा द्राविड़ आदि जातियों की गणना करते हैं, पर किंचित् प्रकाश डालना अपेक्षित है।

दास, दस्यु या द्राविड़ कौन है? क्या आर्य-दस्यु भेद जातिगत है ?

दस्यु शब्द 'दसु उपक्षये' धातु से यजिमनिशुन्धिदसिजनिभ्यो युच् (उणादि 3.20) से युच् प्रत्यय के योग से बनता है। आचार्य यास्क ने *निरूक्त* (7.25) में इस शब्द की व्युत्पत्ति और अर्थ करते हुए लिखा है "दस्यु दस्यतेः क्षयार्थात् उपदस्यन्ति अस्मिन् रसाः, उपदासयति कर्माणि"। अर्थात् दस्यु वह है जिसमे रस अथवा उत्तम गुणों के सारभाग कम होते हैं और जो यज्ञादि उत्तम कर्मों का नाश करता है अथवा उनमें बाधा डालता है। *ऋग्वेद* का एक मन्त्र –

अकर्मा दस्युरभि नो अमन्तुरन्यव्रतो अमानुषः।
त्वं तस्यामित्रहन् वधर्दासस्य दम्भय।। 10.22.8

भी दस्यु का लक्षण बतलाते हुए स्पष्ट करता है कि दस्यु वह है जो (अकर्मा) अच्छे काम न करने वाला और निकम्मा है, जो (अमन्तुः) विचारशील नहीं है, (अन्यव्रतः) जो सत्य, अहिंसा, परोपकारादि व्रतों को ग्रहण न कर इसके विपरीत आचरण करता है, जो (अमानुषः) मनुष्यता की भावना न रखते हुए क्रूर, कठोर, स्वार्थी होने के कारण मानवता से दूर है। इस मन्त्र में ऐसे दस्यु का वध करने की इन्द्र से प्रार्थना की गई है। *ऋग्वेद* के ही एक अन्य मन्त्र "विजानी हि आर्यान् ये च दस्यवो" (1.53.4) में भी दस्युओं का एक विशेषण "अव्रतान्" पढ़ा गया है जो कि उपरलिखित "अन्यव्रतः" के समकक्ष ही है। यही आर्यों और दस्युओं का मुख्य अन्तर है।

स्वामी दयानन्द ने अपनी पुस्तक *आर्याभिविनय* (1.14) में *ऋग्वेद* के उपरलिखित "विजानीह्यार्यान् ये च दस्यवो

बर्हिष्मते'' मन्त्र की व्याख्या करते हुए लिखा है कि हे ईश्वर, आप (आर्यान्) अर्थात् विद्या धर्म आदि उत्क ष्ट स्वभाव आचरण युक्त आर्यों को जानो और (ये च दस्यवः) जो नास्तिक, हिंसादि दोषयुक्त, उत्तम कर्म में विघ्न डालने वाले, स्वार्थी, वेद-विद्या विरोधी अनार्य मनुष्य हैं इन सब दुष्टों को आप समूल नष्ट कर दें। मनु ने भी –

वर्णापेतमविज्ञातं नरं कलुषयोनिजम्।
आर्यरूपमिवानार्यं कर्मभिः स्वैर्विभावयेत्।।

मनुस्म ति, 10.57

श्लोक में बतलाया है कि प्रत्येक व्यक्ति को किसी न किसी वर्ण (गुण कर्म स्वभावानुसार ब्राह्मण, क्षत्रिय, वैश्य, शूद्र) की दीक्षा ग्रहण कर उत्तम धर्मानुकूल आचरण करना चाहिए। जो किसी भी वर्ण की दीक्षा को स्वीकार नहीं करते उनमें स्वभावगत अश्रेष्ठता, कठोरता, निर्दयता होती है और धार्मिक क्रियाओं के प्रति उपेक्षा भावना रहती है, ऐसे व्यक्ति ही अनार्य या दस्यु हैं। यहाँ पर मनु के 'कलुषयोनिजम्' का अर्थ दुष्ट प्रव त्ति वाले या अनार्य अर्थ किया है। मैक्समूलर *ऋग्वेद* के एक मन्त्र ''हत्वो दस्यून् प्रार्य वर्णभावत् आदि'' (3.34.9) की व्याख्या करते हुए 'दस्यु' का अर्थ 'शत्रु' लिखते हैं। उनका कथन है कि "Dasyu simply means enemy, for instance, when Indra is praised because he destroyed the Dasyu and protected the Aryan colour."

यहाँ Aryan colour का अर्थ है आर्यवर्ण। वर्ण अर्थात् स्वभाव।

इस प्रकार हम देखते हैं कि आर्य-अनार्य अर्थात् आर्य-दस्यु भेद कर्मगत या स्वभावगत भेद है और ऐसे दस्युओं के नाश पर वेदों में बल दिया गया है, क्योंकि ये न केवल स्वयं दुष्ट होते हैं किन्तु समाज और राष्ट्र के भी विघातक होते हैं। वेद में ऐसे अनार्यो या दस्युओं को आर्य अर्थात् श्रेष्ठ बनाने की कामना से प्रार्थनाएं भी कही गई हैं। उदाहरणार्थ–

आ संयतमिन्द्र नः स्वस्ति शत्रुतूर्याय ब हतीमम ध्राम्।
यया दासान्यार्याणि व त्रा कुरू विज्रन्त्सुतुका नाहुषाणि।।

ऋग्वेद 6.22.10

मंत्र में कहा गया है कि हे इन्द्र, तुम (व त्रा दासानि नाहुषाणि आर्याणि अकरो) धर्म कार्यों में विघ्न डालने वाले और उनका नाश करने वाले दासों को भी आर्य अर्थात् श्रेष्ठ, धर्मात्मा, सदाचारी कर देते हो। सायणाचार्य भी इसी बात की पुष्टि करते हैं जब वे स्वकीय भाष्य में यह दर्शाते हैं कि उत्तम-कर्महीन मनुष्यों को श्रेष्ठ कर्मकारी आर्य बनाना इन्द्र का कार्य है। इस सन्दर्भ में एक अन्य महत्त्वपूर्ण स्थल, जहाँ ''क ण्वन्तो विश्वमार्यम्'' (ऋ 9.63.5) कहकर समग्र विश्व को आर्य बनाने का सन्देश दिया गया है, भी द्रष्टव्य है। इस वैदिक आदेश के अनुसार अनार्यों, दासों, दस्युओं को आर्य बनाने का प्रयत्न करना आर्यों का कर्त्तव्य बताया गया है।

इतना जानने के पश्चात् भी यदि कोई यह कहे कि वेद में केवल दस्युओं को मारने के लिए ही प्रार्थनाएं की गई हैं अतः ये आर्य और दस्यु दोनों भिन्न-भिन्न जातियाँ हैं; यह भी उचित नहीं हैं; क्योंकि वेद में केवल दस्युओं को ही नहीं आर्यों को भी दण्ड देने के विषय में लिखा है। तद्यथा – *ऋग्वेद* (7.83.1) में ''दासा च व त्रा हतमार्याणि'' कहकर स्पष्ट किया गया है कि व त्र यानि दास, अर्थात् स्वभाव से अच्छे कार्यों में बाधा डालने वाले पुरूषों के नाश के साथ आर्यवंशज होकर ऐसे निषिद्ध काम करने वालों का भी वध किया जाना चाहिए। इसी भांति एक अन्य मन्त्र ''त्वा तान् इन्द्र ! उभयान् अमित्रान् दासा व त्राणि आर्या व शूर । बधीः —— ।'' (*ऋग्वेद* 6.33.3) में ऋषि कहता है कि – हे पराक्रमी इन्द्र ! तू उन दोनों पापात्मा अमित्रों, दस्युओं और आर्यों को मार। वेदोक्त इन वचनों से न्यायपूर्ण समद ष्टि सूचित होती है, न कि किसी वर्ग विशेष या जाति विशेष के प्रति घ णा या द्वेष का भाव। *महाभारत* में ठीक ही कहा गया है कि –

द श्यन्ते मानवे लोके, सर्ववर्णेषु दस्यवः।
लिंगान्तरे वर्त्तमाना आश्रमेषु चतुर्ष्वपि।।

शान्तिपर्व 65.23

अर्थात् ये दस्यु सभी वर्णों और सभी आश्रमों में हो सकते हैं और उनका वध करना या नाश करना ही श्रेयस्कर होता है। अतः दासों, दस्युओं, पणियों या द्राविड़ों को आर्यों से भिन्न 'अनार्य' जातियाँ मानना अथवा इनको भारत के मूल निवासी समझना और यह कहना कि भारतीय संस्क ति या भारतीय साहित्य में उनके प्रति द्वेष का भाव रखने का उपदेश है सर्वथा अशुद्ध है। यह भेद तो गुण, कर्म, स्वभाव पर आश्रित था न कि जातीय भेद पर। दस्यु भी अपने गुण कर्म स्वभाव में परिवर्तन करके आर्य बन सकते है जैस कि *वैदिक ऐज* नामक पुस्तक के लेखकों ने भी इस प्रकार के परिवर्तन को स्वीकार करते हुए लिखा है – 'At least one Dasa Chief, however, named Balbuth had adopted Aryan culture and even patronised Brahman singers.'[7] और आर्यवंशोत्पन्न, यहां तक कि पुलस्त्य जैसे ब्रह्मर्षि के कुल में उत्पन्न होकर भी, रावण समान दुराचारी दस्यु या राक्षस कहलाते थे।

दास, दस्यु, पणि, आदि शब्दों की आध्यात्मिक व्याख्या करते हुए अरविन्द लिखते हैं कि –

एक बार नहीं बल्कि कई बार हम देख चुके हैं कि यह सम्भव ही नहीं है कि अंगिरस, इन्द्र और सरमा की कहानी में हम पणियों की गुफा से उषा, सूर्य और गौओं की विजय करने का यह अर्थ लगावें कि यह आर्य आक्रान्ताओं तथा गुफा निवासी द्रविड़ियों के बीच होने वाले राजनीतिक और सैनिक संघर्ष का वर्णन है। यह तो वह संघर्ष है जो प्रकाश के अन्वेष्टाओं और अन्धकार की शक्तियों के बीच होता है। इसके अनुरूप ही पणियों को इस रूप में लेना चाहिए कि वे अन्धकार गुहा की शक्तियाँ हैं। दस्यु हैं पवित्र वाणी से घ णा करने वाले। ये वे हैं जो हवि को या सोमरस को देवों को अर्पित नहीं करते, जो गौओं व घोड़ो की दौलत को तथा अन्य खज़ानों को अपने ही लिए रख लेते हैं और उन चीज़ों को ऋषियों के लिए नहीं देते, ये वे हैं जो यज्ञ नहीं करते। इतना तो पूर्णतया निश्चित है कि ऋग्वेद में जिस युद्ध और विजय का वर्णन हुआ है वह कोई भौतिक युद्ध नहीं बल्कि एक आध्यात्मिक संघर्ष और आध्यात्मिक विजय है[8]

आगे वे पुनः लिखते हैं कि "यह स्पष्ट है कि 'पणि' दस्यु अन त और अज्ञान की कुटिल शक्तियाँ हैं जो अपने मिथ्या ज्ञान को, अपने मिथ्या, बल, संकल्प और कर्मों को देवों तथा आर्यों के सच्चे ज्ञान, सच्चे बल, सच्चे संकल्प और कर्मों के विरोध में लगाती है। प्रकाश की विजय से अभिप्राय है – इस मिथ्या ज्ञान अथवा दानवीय ज्ञान पर सत्य के दिव्य ज्ञान की विजय"[9]। इस सन्दर्भ में एक सुप्रसिद्ध दाक्षिणात्य विद्वान प्रिंसिपल पी.टी. अय्यंगार का कथन भी बहुत महत्त्वपूर्ण है जब वे कहते हैं –

The Arya and Dasyus, Dasas are referred to not as indicating different races.... The word referred not to race but to cult.... The Dasys are without rites, fireless, non-sacrificers, without prayers, without Riks, haters of prayers. Thus the difference between Aryas and Dasyus was not one of race, but of cult.[10]

अर्थात् एक द्रविड़ लेखक ने भी आर्य और दस्युओं के भेद को जातीय भेद न मानकर गुण, कर्म स्वभाव पर आश्रित सांस्क तिक भेद ही स्वीकार किया है। इसी भांति एक अन्य दक्षिण भारतीय विद्वान श्रीरामचन्द्र दीक्षितार्, आर्यों और दस्युओं वा द्राविड़ों के जातीय भेद का खण्डन करते हुए लिखते हैं –

The fact is that the Dasyus were not non-Aryans. The theory that the Dasyus-Dravidians inhabited the Punjab and the Ganges Valley at the time of the so-called Aryan invasion of India, and overcome by the latter they fled to south India and adopted it as their home cannot stand.[11]

आगे फिर लिखा है –

In the the same way we have to look upon the theory of Dravidian race. If the Aryan race theory is a myth the theory of Dravidian race is a greater myth. The word Dravid is the name for the speakers of a group of south Indian languages—Tamil, Malayalam, Kanarese and Telugu.[12]

इन दोनो उद्धरणों का भाव यही है कि दस्यु या द्राविड़ (जातीय भेद की द ष्टि से) अनार्य न थे; अतः आर्य जातिवाद और द्राविड़ जातिवाद दोनों ही कल्पित हैं। यहाँ एक बात और ध्यान देने योग्य है कि जैसे रामचन्द्र दीक्षितार ने तमिल, तेलुगु आदि भाषाएँ बोलने वालों को 'द्राविड़' कहा है उसी प्रकार मैक्समूलर ने आर्य भाषाओं के बोलने वालों को 'आर्य' कहा है। वे लिखते हैं –

I have declared again and again that if I say Aryan, I mean neither blood nor bones, nor hair nor skull. I mean simply those who speak an Aryan language.... To me an ethologist who speaks of Aryan race, Aryan blood, Aryan eyes and hair, is as great a sinner as a linguist who speaks of a dolichocephalic dictionary of a brachycephalic grammar.[13]

इन वाक्यों द्वारा मैक्समूलर ने आर्य जाति की प थक् जाति के रूप में सत्ता का खण्डन किया है और कहा है जो ऐसा करता है वह पाप करता है।

इस सन्दर्भ में जे. म्यूर और नैसफील्ड भी कुछ ऐसा ही लिखते हैं– जे. म्यूर का कहना है कि —

I have gone over the name of Dasyus or Asuras mentioned in the *Rigveda* with the view of discovering whether anyone of them could be regarded as of non-Aryan or indigenous origin, but I have not observed that appear to be of this character.[14]

अर्थात् मैंने *ऋग्वेद* में आए हुए दस्युओं और असुरों के नाम पर इस द ष्टि से विचार किया था कि उनमें से किसी को अनार्यों या मूल निवासियों की उत्पत्ति का समझा जा सकता है, मुझे कोई नाम ऐसा नहीं मिला। इसी तरह नैसफील्ड भी लिखते है — 'There is no division of the people as the Aryan conquerors of India and the aborigines of the country.'[15] अर्थात् भारतीयों में आर्य विजेता और मूल निवासी जैसा कोई विभाग नहीं है।

द्रविड़ादि विषयक वर्णन एवं निष्कर्ष

उपर्युक्त इन सब प्रमाणों के आलोक में यह तो निश्चित होता है कि 'आर्य' और 'अनार्य' शब्द गुणवाचक हैं न कि जातिवाचक। अतः दास, दस्यु वा द्राविड़ आर्यों से प थक कोई जातियाँ न होकर उन्हीं में से हैं। *ऐतरेय ब्राह्मण* (7.19) में लिखा भी है कि दस्यु, अंध्र, पुण्ड्र, शवर, पुलिन्द, मूर्त्तव और उदन्त्य आदि विश्वामित्र की सन्तान हैं।[16] इसी प्रकार *मनुस्म ति* (10.43, 44) में भी कहा गया है कि ये पौण्ड्र, पह्लव, चीन, दरद और खश आदि जातियाँ क्षत्रिय कुलोत्पन्न होने पर भी शनैः शनैः ब्राह्मणों के सम्पर्क में न रहने तथा वैदिक क्रियाओं के लोप में धर्मभ्रष्ट हो गई तथा अलग-अलग हो गई।[17] *महाभारत* (शान्तिपर्व 65.13, 14) में भी इसी प्रकार का वर्णन मिलता है।[18] अतः यह सिद्ध होता है कि ये सभी जातियाँ एक मूल स्रोत आर्यों से निकली हैं जो अपने अपने गुण, कर्म और स्वभाव के अनुरूप 'आर्य' और 'अनार्य' इस सांस्क तिक भेद के कारण भिन्न-भिन्न होने लगी। वास्तव में ये सभी आर्य में ही हैं और यह आर्य एवं अनार्य का अन्तर कर्मों के कारण है जाति के कारण नहीं।

Notes and References

1. *महाभारत,* उद्योगपर्व, 8.82, 83.
2. *धम्मपद* 270.
3. तत्त्वार्थसूत्र, अध्याय 3 में "आर्य मलेच्छाश्च" इत्यादि सूत्र पाए जाते हैं जिनमें श्रेष्ठ पुरूषों को 'आर्य' के नाम से स्मरण किया गया है। श्री रत्नचन्द्रजैन, *अर्द्धमागधी कोश*, भाग–2, प . 82 'अरिय' या 'आर्य' पवित्र, विशुद्ध श्रेष्ठ पापरहित और High in Civilization दिया है।
4. *ज़ेन्दावेस्ता* के भाग सिरोजह 1.25 में लिखा है कि आर्यों की प्रतिष्ठा में जिन्हें मज्दा (परमेश्वर) ने बनाया। सिराजह 2.9 में लिखा है "हम आर्यों के सम्मानार्थ हवन करते हैं जिन्हें मज्दा ने बनाया।"
5. Shri Aurobindo, *Arya* (A quarterly journal) Vol. I, 1914, p. 63.
6. *वाल्मीकि रामायण* 4.17.3 और 6.16.6.
7. *Vedic Age*, p. 351 (Reference).
8. श्री अरविन्द, *वेदरहस्य*, प्रथम भाग (अनुवाद–अभयदेव) प . 308–09.
9. वही, प . 317.
10. P.T. Ayangar, *Dravidian Studies*.

11. Ram Chandra Dikshitar, *Origin and Spread of the Tamils*, Adayaar Library, Pune, 1947, p. 12.
12. *Ibid.*, p. 14.
13. Max Müllar, *Biographies of Words and Home of the Aryans*, London, 1888, p. 120.
14. J. Muir, *Original Sanskrit Texts*, Vol. II, p. 387.
15. Nesfield, *Brief View of the Caste System of the North West Provinces and Oudh*, p. 27.
16. ताननु व्याजहार अन्तान् वः प्रजा भक्षीष्टेत त एतेंध्रा पुण्ड्राः शवराः पुलिन्दा मुर्तवा उदन्त्या बहवो भवन्ति वैश्वामित्रा दस्यूनां भूयिष्ठा :।।

    ऐ. ब्रा. 7.19.

17. शनकैस्तु क्रियालोपदिमाः क्षत्रियजातयः।।
    व षलत्वं गताः लोके ब्राह्मणदर्शनेन च।।

    पौण्ड्रकाश्चौद्रविडाः काम्बोजा यवनाः शकाः।
    पारदाः पह्लवाश्चीनाः किराता दरदा खशाः।

    मनुस्म ति 10.43, 44

18. यवनाः किराताः गन्धाराश्चीना शवरबरबराः।
    शकास्तुषारा कंकाश्च पह्ल्वाश्चान्द्रमन्द्रकाः।।
    चौद्रा पुलिन्दा रमठा काम्बोजाश्चैव सर्वशः।
    ब्रह्मक्षत्र प्रसूताश्च वैश्याः शूद्राश्च मानवाः।

    महाभारत, शान्तिपर्व, 65.13, 14

सहायक पुस्तकें

1. वैद्यनाथ शास्त्री, *वैदिक युग और आदि मानव*, सार्वदेशिक आर्य-प्रतिनिधि सभा, नई दिल्ली - 1, सवंत् 2021.
2. श्री अरविन्द, *वेद रहस्य* (अनुवाद अभयदेव), श्री अरविन्द आश्रम, पांडिचैरी.
3. वैद्यनाथ शास्त्री, *वैदिक ज्योति*, आचार्य वैद्यनाथ शास्त्री, पोस्ट बाक्स - 1, राजवाड़ी, पोरबन्दर, सितम्बर 1955.
4. धर्मदेव विद्यावचस्पति, *वेदों का यथार्थ स्वरूप*, जन-ज्ञान, नई दिल्ली - 5 सवंत् 2030.
5. डा. सुरेन्द्र कुमार (भाष्यकार एवं समीक्षक) राजवीर शास्त्री (सम्पादक) *मनुस्म ति*, आर्ष साहित्य प्रचार ट्रस्ट, दिल्ली - 6. सितम्बर 1985.

15

The Sarasvatī-Sindhu Civilization and Vedic Co-relations

I.K. SARMA

The ancient Sarasvatī-Dṛishadvatī river zone was the bread basket of early civilizations. Nearly over seventy-five years of archaeological fieldwork resulted in the discovery of 1,200 sites of this civilization that were located on the dried up (now), Sarasvatī-Dṛishadvatī rivers, out of a total of 1,600 sites so far known both in India and Pakistan. Undoubtedly, Sarasvatī was a major river on whose banks the Harappans lived in largest numbers. The two major Harappan towns in Gujarat, Lothal[1] and Dholavira, opened up new channels of research on the scientific advancements and achievements in proto-historic India. More recently, Dholavira in Kutch revealed a large city consisting of formidable[2] stone fortification 11 m wide at the base, an acropolis, middle and lower towns, with impressive gateways and guard rooms and beautifully polished stone blocks and pillars exemplifying the technological excellence not only in planning but also in building great regal architectural edifices without a parallel at any other Harappan site so far. A big wooden board inlaid with ten large Indus letters, (each 37cm high, 25-27cm wide), in front of a gateway of a palace is noteworthy. This is the oldest sign-board datable to 3rd millenium BC. Recently S.P. Gupta[3] has taken stock of the entire evidence and named the Harappan as "Indus-Sarasvatī Civilization". The flourishing fortified towns of this civilization unearthed in India at Rakhigarhi and Kunal, District Fatehabad (Haryana), on the bed of Sarasvatī, Mehrgarh[4] and more recently Manda, northern-most site on Chenab river, 28 km west of Jammu; Hulas in the East Daimabad in the south (Maharashtra), apart from the ones in Pakistan, encompass a vast area. Based on the geographical extent and early horizons, this great civilization can be appropriately christened as "Sarasvatī-Sindhū" Civilization instead of merely Indus or Harappan.

Scientific Surveys in Search of River Sarasvatī

B.B. Lal[5] has observed that "During the lifetime of the Indus Civilization itself, the Yamunā owed its allegiance to the Ghagger-Sarasvatī system and flowed south-west. Besides Yamunā, the Sutlej, also seems to have fed the Ghagger system; in the Bahawalpur region of Pakistan, this river is known as Hakra. In Sindh, the river flowed southwards as indicated by the dry courses presently known as Hakra, Nara, Wahind, etc. Finally it discharged into the Rann of Kutch. The drying up and rejuvenation of the Ghaggar seem to have taken place not once but twice." It is now recognized through remote sensing and hydro-geological data that river Sarasvatī was perennially flowing from Hari-ki-dun glacier of the Himalayas in west Garhwal into the Gulf of Khambat near Lothal via little Rann and Nall lake, near Ahmedabad. Sutlej (Śatadru) originating from Mount Kailāśa was a tributory of Sarasvatī river at Shatrana, took a U-turn at Ropar and migrated westwards. The confluence of Sarasvatī at Saṅgam in Prayag is not a myth but a ground truth[6]. Gujarat was an island and it was possible to travel in the Sarasvatī river from the Gulf of Khambat to Mathura via Lothal-Dholavira, Ganweriwala, Kalibangan, Banawali, Paonta Saheb, Rakhigarhi and Indraprastha. Thus, the palaeo-channels of the river have been substantially traced using archaeological evidence, geographical information system, hydrogeology and other technologies. The scientists of the Bhabha Atomic Research Centre traced through satellite images the mighty Sarasvatī. The course has links with the dry bed of Ghaggar river (Sriganganagar District, Rajasthan) and Hakra and Nara rivers in Pakistan.

India Today, 11 February, 2002, carried an astonishing cover story (pp. 42-47) with illustrations regarding the discovery of world's oldest city submerged off the Gujarat coast. This lost civilization according to the writer (Raj Chengappa), consisted of a vast ancient city submerged 40 m under the sea. The team further reported that they had picked up over 2,000 artefacts among the ruins strung across a 9 km stretch. The structural remains resembled the Great Bath of Mohenjo-daro and a 200 m long and 45 m platform like an acropolis of Harappa. The artefacts like Neolithic axes, wood and bone fragments (fossilized ones), beads and precious stones indicated a set up of an advanced chalcolithic settlement. It may, however, be stated that these object have not shown any specific affiliation to the Indus Valley artefacts reported so far and the date range of 5500 BC (*BSIP*) to 7500 BC (*NGRI*) should be regarded as tentative. We eagerly await a more detailed report.

Dating the Civilization

The roots of this civilization are being traced to about 4500 BC at Mehrgarh.[7] In recent years we have unduely relied upon C-14 calibrations. How relevent are the observations of S.P. Gupta[8] on this issue? We reproduce his observations in a somewhat lengthy manner.

In fashion was 'Shorter Chronology' as proposed by D.P. Agrawal; he had proposed 2300-1700 BC as the 'Comprehensive' time-bracket for the urban phase of the Civilization. However, 1980s dealt a cruel blow to the so-called absoluteness of the radiocarbon dates; Agrawal knew about it, it was by then fully realised by scientists in cognate disciplines, such as Dendrochronology, that the absoluteness of the radiocarbon dates was a myth. These dates were much younger than the real ones; as we go back in time we have to add hundreds of years more in order to arrive at the absolute or near absolute dates. After a lot of trials and errors, it has now been generally agreed to follow a conversion table, called 'CALIB' programme as worked out by Stuiver and Reimer. According to this system a radiocarbon date of 2500 BC is calibrated to 3180 BC an addition of 580 years to arrive at the correct dates. And so on and so forth. The 'shorter chronology' has now been finally replaced by the 'longer chronology'. The Urban or Mature phase of the Indus-Sarasvatī Civilization is now fixed between 2700 BC and 1990 BC.

Since the proto-urban or Early Period of the Indus-Sarasvatī Civilization is now also considered as part and parcel of the Indus-Sarasvatī Civilization, we have to add at least 300 years more to it. The time-bracket for the Early Period is fixed between 3500 BC and 2700 BC divided into two phases, as noted earlier—Old Phase (3500 BC – 3000 BC) and New Phase (3000 BC – 2700 BC).

The things have, however, not stopped here. Extensive fieldwork conducted during the last more than one decade has further sharpened our understanding of the beginning of the Indus-Sarasvatī Civilization. It has added some 500 years more, pushing back the beginning to about 3100 BC or even to 4000 BC. This is called the Formative Period of the Indus-Sarasvatī Civilization (say Sindhu-Sarasvatī). The glimpses of this are available at Jalilpur, at Harappa, at Mehrgarh, at Amri, at Balakot and at about 90 sites in the Sarasvatī basin.

Religious Identity and Significance

Increasing evidence is gathering on its urban and highly religious character. Remarkable finds from Kunal (Ratia Tehsil)[9] on the left bank of Sarasvatī river consisted of a unique regalia of two silver crowns, (tiaras), necklaces of silver, gold spacers (circular *nishkas*) and some precious stones which clearly indicated the cult connected to a Rudra-like God-King.

Subhash Kak[10] has stated that the Harappans had developed specialization not only in materialistic life but religious and scientific techniques. More particularly the fire altars, both inside the houses[11] (Kalibangan, Lothal) and in public on open platform (Kalibangan, Lothal), or apsidal temples with fire altar (Banawali, Surkotda), reveal worship of Fire God and sacrifice of animals, etc., to appease the Gods of Thunder, Lightning, Sun and Agni. Seals depicting Fire God and seven chiefs are well known in Harappan context. A terracotta oval tablet from Kalibangan has on its faces depictions of seated Paśupati on the obverse, and a goat on the reverse being dragged by neck for offer to the Deity. The terracotta *liṅga* on a *pīṭha* clearly indicates the mode of Rudra-Śiva worship in a mature form at Kalibangan.

The Vedic *Gavam āyana* (sacrifice) undoubtedly, preclude an intimate knowledge of the planetary system and solar movements. Worship of Mother Goddesses (confined to Punjab and up to Banawali), sacred filters depicted on the Harappan seals[12] signified the existence of Vedic rituals like *Soma pavamāna*. Besides, depictions of *Indra dhvajas,* Horned deity (Paśupati), Pīppal trees with bearded horned *ṛishis* around clearly confirm the cults described in the *Ṛigveda,* aligned to Agni, Rudra, Śiva and Śakti. The heavy bronze *utsava* type of animal figures and the chariot yoked to a pair of humped-horned bulls driven by a robust nude male fronted by a dog kept on the tight reins in a commanding pose appears to be that of Ṛigvedic Rudra.[13]

Vedic Āryans had not migrated to India. They were autochthons around the five major rivers of Punjab and more particularly early groups among them lived on the banks of Sarasvatī-Dṛishadvatī river valleys from time immemorial. A. Ghosh's explorations along the dry beds of Sarasvatī-Dṛishadvatī clearly indicated that "the real riddle of the Harappan Civilization's origin lies in its Indianness"[14] and H.D. Sankalia proclaimed "it now appears that Indus Civilization had its roots in India — Sind, East Punjab, Haryana and Rajasthan".[15] The archaeologists' efforts in recent decades at such extensive Harappan sites as Lothal, Dholavira and Surkotda (Gujarat), Kalibangan (Rajasthan) and as far as Daimabad (Maharashtra) provided ample testimony to the physical extent of this great civilization not only in its spread but influencing various peoples in widely spread geographical zones. It had absorbed the village communities and elevated them under its cultural influence. The anthropological data has clearly shown that Harappan culture was adopted by the local population and not as a result of racial immigration and indicated the presence of composite ethnic groups in the population of that period. Another admirable feature lies in the places, persons and events connected to the Bharatas specifically. The 'Battle of Ten Kings' which finds mention in the *Ṛigveda* and the Great Epic are gaining ground. The extent of the culture to Gujarat and Saurashtra as seen from such extensive sites as Lothal, Surkotda, Dholavira and more recently Padri (a village in Bhavnagar district) and S.R. Rao's undersea archaeological probes at the submerged Dvārikā, reflecting a later phase of this civilization, fits well with the life and events of the *Mahābhārata*'s Kṛishṇa. Though born in Mathura (UP) it is well known that Kṛishṇa reached Saurashtra via Sind and Kutch and chose Dvārikā as his *Karmabhūmi*.

Finally *Ārya* does not signify race and whoever is civilized is an Ārya, may he be Indian, African, East Asian, European or American. The attempts of Western historians, earlier terming the *Āryan* and *Draviḍian* as races, confining them to certain regions, and the conflicts among them projected on a historical framework as arising out of cultural divergences no more hold good. Swami Vivekananda has appropriately said, "Āryanism meant a type of culture which pervaded the whole of India". Max Müller[16] also says "Āryan in scientific language, is utterly inapplicable to race".

Notes and References

1. Rao, S.R., *Lothal and Indus Civilization,* (Bombay, 1973), pp. 105-107, XXXII-A, B. *The Decipherment of Indus Script*, (Bombay, 1982).
2. Joshi, J.P., *Presidential Address, Indian Archaeological Society*, 24th Annual Conference (Kanyakumari, 11th-13th Nov. 1990); R.S. Bisht, "Dholavira: New Horizons of the Indus Civilization", *Purātattva*, No. 20: 1989-90 (New Delhi, 1991), pp. 70-81; J.P. Joshi and R.S. Bisht, *India and the Indus Civilization,* (New Delhi, 1994), pp. 23-31, pls. XIII-XV.
3. Gupta, S.P., "Fresh Look at the Chronology of the Indus-Sarasvatī Civilization", *National Workshop on Dating in Indian Archaeology—Problems and Perspectives,* (Mysore, Dec. 19-21, 1993) and "The Indus-Sarasvati Civilization : Some New Developments", in S.P. Gupta (ed.), *The Lost Sarasvatī and the Indus Civilization* (Jodhpur, 1995) pp. 180-199.
4. Joshi, J.P. and R.S. Bisht, *op. cit.*, pp. 2-4, *The Hindu*, dated 18th March, 1994.
5. Lal, B.B., *The Earliest Civilization of South Asia: Rise, Maturity and Decline,* (New Delhi, 1997), p. 9.
6. Kalyanaraman, S., "River Sarasvatī Civilization, Circa, 3000-1500 BC", Paper presented at the World Sanskrit Conference, (Bangalore, June, 1997), also *The Hindu,* dated 12th Jan. 1997, p. 13, *Current Science,* (Jan. 1997) and *The Hindu,* dated 18th Feb. 1997, p. 17.
7. Jarrige, J.F. "Excavations at Mehrgarh : Their Significance for Understanding the Background of the Harappan Civilization", in G.L. Possehl (ed.), *Harappan Civilization* (New Delhi, 1982) pp. 79-84.
8. Gupta, S.P., "The Indus Sarasvatī Civilization : Some New Developments", in *The Lost Sarasvatī and the Indus Civilization* (Jodhpur, 1995), p. 192.
9. Newspaper reports; *The Times of India,* dated 14th Feb., 1994, Exhibited in the National Museum, Delhi on the eve of IIIrd World Archaeological Congress.
10. Kak, Subhash, "On the Chronology of Ancient India", *Indian Journal of History of Science,* Vol. 22 (1987) pp. 222-34.
11. Joshi, J.P., *op. cit.*, also S.D. Kulkarni (ed.), *Beginnings of Life, Culture and History, Bhishma's Studies of Indian History and Culture,* Vol. I, (Bombay, 1988), Chapter VII.
12. Mahadevan, I., "The Sacred Filter Standard Facing the Unicorn! More Evidence", Paper presented at the South Asian Archaeology, (Helsinki, 1993), also see S.R. Rao, *Presidential Address, The Indian Museum,* (Calcutta, 16th Jan. 1981), pp. 26-30.
13. *Indian Archaeology: A Review*—1974-75, pp. 29-31, K.R. Srinivasan, "The Harappan and Vedic Cultures", *Bulletin of the Madras Art Museum,* Vol. XVM (Madras, 1988).
14. Fairservice Jr., Walter, *The Roots of Ancient India,* (1971) pp. 220, 228, 239.
15. Deo, S.B. and K. Paddayya (ed.), *Recent Advances in Indian Archaeology,* (Poona, 1985).
16. Majumdar, R.C., and A.D. Pusalkar (ed.), *The Vedic Age,* (Bombay, 1954), p. 205.

Bibliography

1. Joshi, Jagatpati (ed.), *Facets of Indian Civilization: Recent Perspectives – Essays in Honour of Prof B.B. Lal*, (New Delhi, 1997). Vol 1, Section-B, pp. 69-215.
2. Dhavalikar, M.K., *Indian Proto-history*, (New Delhi, 1997), Chapter 9, Archaeology of the Aryans, pp. 288-303.
3. Verma, T.P. (ed.), *Dating in Indian Archaeology: Problems and Perspectives* (Mysore, 1998), pp. 42-56.
4. Lal, B.B., *The Sarasvatī Flows On: The Continuity of Indian Culture*, (New Delhi, 2001).
5. Kalyanaraman, S., *The River Sarasvatī: Legend, Myth and Reality*, (Mumbai, 2001).

16

Need of a New Paradigm

Ascertaining Ṛigvedic-Harappan Relationship

SHIVAJI SINGH

This article has three sections. The first of these briefly reviews the three basic parities between the Ṛigvedic and the Early-to-Mature Harappan cultures: (a) that their geographical horizons coincide, (b) that their chronological horizons also overlap, and (c) that the mosaics of their cultural contents have striking resemblance. However, it is felt that though these parities point to a strong probability of the two cultures being one and the same, they do not necessarily prove their identity. What is beyond doubt, any way, is the fact that within the identical space-time limits of the two cultures, two distinct processes were at work. One was the rise, intensification, and collapse of an urban process that we call the Harappan Culture. The other was the emergence, spread, and dominance of an ideology based on a kind of sacrificial ritual and concomitant social psychology that constitutes the hallmark of the Ṛigvedic Culture. Significant is also the fact that the ideological process survived the collapse of the urban process. The possibility is that while some (or even most) of the ethnic units occupying the space-time coordinates under consideration might have participated in both the processes, some others (whatever their strength) may have been involved in only one of the two or even in none of the two processes. This makes it clear that the problem of Ṛigvedic-Harappan relationship needs a deeper probe at the level of their ethno-geographic configurations. The exercise, it is hoped, may go a long way in concretizing the Ṛigvedic-Harappan connections at specific levels of human communities and groups of communities living in various areas. Instead of talking about the Ṛigvedic and Early-to-Mature Harappan identity rather vaguely, we shall be able to say that such and such a particular Ṛigvedic social unit (*jana*)—the Bharatas or the Purus or the Matsyas, for instance—is represented by such and such a particular archaeological assemblage falling in the Early-to-Mature Harappan horizon and so on. This would evidently lead us to the identification of archaeological remains of some Ṛigvedic Āryans and non-Āryans—a problem whose solution has eluded us so far. The second section is devoted to the delineation of the Ṛigvedic and

Early-to-Mature Harappan ethno-geographic configurations. Efforts have been directed to locate the Ṛigvedic *janas* as far as possible and to ascertain the impact of emerging ideology on them. Distinguishing the Early-to-Mature Harappan social units of various areas, however, has been somewhat difficult for unlike the Ṛigvedic groups they are not known by their names. It is to tackle this problem that the need of a new paradigm involving concepts of 'palaeoethnicity' and 'cultural tradition' has been emphasized. Using these concepts, the main social groups involved in the development of the Early-to-Mature Harappan Culture have been recognized. In the third and last section of the article, a comparison of the Ṛigvedic and the Early-to-Mature Harappan ethno-geographic configurations is attempted. Juxtaposing the two configurations, it has been possible to bring out certain correspondences between the literary (Ṛigvedic) and archaeological (Early-to-Mature Harappan) ethnic units. The article ends with the conclusion that the Ṛigvedic and Early-to-Mature Harappan cultures are part and parcel of one and the same Indus-Sarasvatī cultural tradition.

I

The Geographical Parity

The geographical horizon of the Early-to-Mature Harappan Culture has been clearly demonstrated by the distribution of its sites (Lal 1997: Maps 4.1 & 6.1). The cradle of the culture is the region falling between the rivers Sindhu (Indus) and Sarasvatī (the Ghaggar-Hakra of the Survey of India maps). This also was the core area of the Ṛigvedic Culture. The Ṛigvedic people themselves designated their land as the 'Land of Seven Rivers' *('Sapta Sindhavaḥ', RV*, 8.24.27). Scholars agree that this denotes the land watered by Sindhu and Sarasvatī and the five rivers flowing in between them, namely, Jhelum (Vitastā), Chenab (Asiknī), Ravi (Parushṇī), Beas (Vipāś), and Sutlej (Śutudrī).[1] Not only the core areas but also the areas of contact and colonization of the two cultures coincide. Both extended up to Afghanistan on the one hand and up to Gujarat on the other. The discovery of a Mature Harappan site named Shortughai in north-eastern Afghanistan and the references to rivers Kubhā (Kabul), Rasā (Syr Dariya, but Panjsher, an affiuent of the Kabul, according to some), and Anitabhā (Amu Dariya), etc., provide the evidence of the contacts of respectively the Mature Harappans and the Ṛigvedic people with areas in Afghanistan. Similarly, while the Harappan sites like Lothal, Surkotada, Dholavira, etc., prove the presence of the Harappans in Gujarat, the legend of the shipwreck of Bhujyu, son of Tugra, described in the *Ṛigveda* (1.116.3-5) points to the Kutch area (Nandi 1994-95:31-33) as the south-western limit of the Early Vedic domain. Bhujyu, as his name suggests, most probably belonged to the Bhuj locality in Gujarat.

The Chronological Parity

The Ṛigvedic and Early-to-Mature Harappan chronological horizons do not coincide but they do overlap. It is accepted that the time-span of the Early-to-Mature Harappan Culture is nearly 3200 BC to 2000 BC (Possehl 1996: 9; Lal 1997: 239-54). The date of the *Ṛigveda* is not certain. However, we have a clinching evidence to fix the latest limit of the Ṛigvedic period. This relates to the drying up of the river Sarasvatī that constitutes an important line of demarcation between the early (i.e., the Ṛigvedic) and late Vedic periods. The *Pañchaviṃśa Brāhmaṇa* (25.10.6) and the *Jaiminīya Upanishad Brāhmaṇa* (4.26) clearly state that the river disappears at a place called Vinaśana, but literary and archaeological evidence shows that the river had dried up much earlier than the time of these Brāhmaṇa texts and that the two of its most important tributaries, Sutlej and Yamunā, were lost before the composition of the very next Veda, the *Yajurveda.*

The Sarasvatī was indeed flowing in its full majesty when the Ṛigvedic hymns were being composed (Singh 1997-98a: 139). It was flowing from the mountains to the sea *(giribhyaḥ āsamudrāt, RV,* 7 95.2). There is not the slightest indication anywhere in the text of any scarcity of water in it.[2] On the contrary, it is depicted as 'abounding in waters' *(Maho-Arṇaḥ, RV,* 1.3.13), 'flowing rapidly' *(Prasasre, RV,* 7.95.1), 'moving faultlessly' *(Akavārī, RV,* 7.96.3), 'possessing unlimited strength' *(Yasyaḥ amaḥ ananto, RV,* 6.61.8) and 'flowing with a roaring sound' *(Charati roruvat, RV,* 6.61.8). The *Ṛigveda* (6.52.6) informs us that the river was getting swelled by its tributaries. It had seven tributaries, as evidenced by its epithet *'Saptasvasā'* (*RV*, 6.61.10), that is, 'the one having seven sisters'. According to some scholars the term 'seven sisters' stands for Sindhu and the Sarasvatī and the five rivers of Punjab that gave the name *Sapta Sindhavaḥ.* But this interpretation is obviously incorrect for there must be seven other rivers besides Sarasvatī to be called its sisters.[3] In this context it must also be noted that the epithet *Saptasvasā* occurs in the Sixth Maṇḍala of the *Ṛigveda* and, as I have shown elsewhere (Singh 1997-98b) and other scholars also agree (e.g. Talageri 2000: 109), during the time of the composition of this *Maṇḍala* the hymn-composers were totally ignorant about the river Indus. They came to know about this river later in the Ṛigvedic period and of course settled down on its bank. The fact that Sarasvatī did have seven tributaries is confirmed by yet another epithet of the river. It is called *'Saptadhātuḥ'* (*RV*, 6.61.12) meaning 'the one constituted by seven elements'. The names of the seven tributaries of the river are not given. However, some rivers described to be in its close proximity appear to be its tributaries. Thus, along with Sarasvatī we find Dṛishadvatī (Chautang) and Āpayā mentioned at one place (*RV*, 3.23.4) and Bṛihaddivā and Rākā at another place (*RV*, 5.42.12*).* The *Nadī-sūkta* (*RV*, 10.75.5), which enumerates several rivers, situates Sarasvatī in between Yamunā and Śutudrī (Sutlej) showing their close proximity. We may not be wrong, therefore, in supposing that according to the internal evidence of the *Ṛigveda,* the rivers Dṛishadvatī, Āpayā, Bṛihaddivā, Rākā, Yamunā and Sutlej were the tributaries of the Sarasvatī. The river Giri (Puri and Verma 1998: Fig. 9) though not mentioned in the text was probably the seventh tributary. In the *Yajurveda,* however, the number of its tributaries is clearly stated to be only five *(Pañcha nadyaḥ Sarasvatīmapi yantu sasrotasaḥ, YV,* 34.11). This shows that two of its tributaries were lost by the time of the composition of the *Yajurveda.*

These literary pieces of information become very significant in the light of the archaeological and scientific discoveries made in the Sarasvatī Valley. It is now known that the rivers Yamunā and Sutlej were flowing initially into the Sarasvatī (Misra 1984, 1994), and that it was mainly the capture of these two respectively by the Gangetic and Indus systems one after the other which resulted in the drying up of the Sarasvatī. Could we surmise that the literary allusions to the two rivers lost by the Sarasvatī relate to the Yamunā and the Sutlej? It is clear enough that both, the composition of the Ṛigvedic hymns and the Harappan urbanization, came to a close by the same environmental dislocations that led to the drying up of the mighty Ṛigvedic Sarasvatī. The drying up of the river was a prolonged and gradual process whose impact in various localities or its long course must have been felt at different points of time. According to Rafique Mughal (1982/93), the process began in the upper (north-eastern) portion of the river where water supply was almost completely cut off in about the middle of the third millennium BC, but enough water was still available in its lower (south-western) part throughout the late third and early second millennium BC. 'About the end of the second, or not later than the beginning of the first millennium BC', says he, the river seems to have completely dried up. It may, however, be noted that the difficult and delicate processes of urbanization and hymn composition must have been badly jeopardized and stopped soon after the onset of environmental dislocations. They could not be expected to wait for the river to dry up throughout its course. Subsequent rejuvenations of the river from time to time also failed to restore those processes. Correlating the literary and archaeological pieces of evidence (Singh 1997-98a), it may be confidently concluded that the latest chronological limits of the Ṛigvedic and Early-to-Mature Harappan cultures perfectly coincide. Both of them came to a close in about 2000-1900 BC. The Mature Harappan settlement at Kalibangan, a site located on the banks of ancient Sarasvatī, was abandoned in about 1900 BC because of scarcity of water. On the basis of this clinching evidence, B.B. Lal has recently categorically stated that 'the river dried up some time at the beginning of the second millennium BC' (Lal 2002: 22).

Though the above conclusion can hardly be doubted, a different opinion in this connection must not be overlooked. Recently few scholars like N.S. Rajaram, David Frawley and Subhash Kak have tried to prove that the *Ṛigveda* cannot be later than 3750 BC. (Rajaram and Frawley 1995). Like K.D. Sethana (1981) they equate the Harappan and Sūtra periods and push back the Ṛigvedic period to an age much earlier than the Harappan. I have already referred to their main arguments in one of my recent papers (Singh 2001). They are: (a) the ancient Egyptian and Babylonian mathematics is derived from the *Śulbasūtras,* that deal with the construction of fire altars and, as such, constitute important appendices to the various *Śrautasūtras* and (b) this mathematical evidence is supported by astronomical considerations relating to the pole star Alpha-Draconis, Kṛittikā vernal equinox, and the time taken in the shift of the cycle of seasons from the days of the Sūtras to the present. Additional evidence for the proposed chronology provided by the stand that the Ṛigvedic period ended with the 'Battle of Ten Kings' that is calculated to have occurred in 3730 BC. There are certain logical difficulties in accepting the chronology proposed by them. I have discussed these issues in my forthcoming book *The Ṛigveda: An Archaeological Study.* Besides, the cultural levels depicted in the *Ṛigveda* such as those indicated by organized battles and sea trade do not match with those brought to light so far by the archaeological assemblages of the pre-3750 horizon. Till such an evidence is brought to light by future discoveries, an archaeologist would find it difficult to accept this early end of the Ṛigvedic period.

Regarding the earliest limit of the Ṛigvedic time-span, the opinions of scholars differ enormously. Most of the scholars of the earlier generation (e.g. B.K. Ghosh 1952/80) as several of the present (e.g. R.S. Sharma 1983, Suvira Jaiswal 1989-90) believe that the *Ṛigveda* cannot be pushed back to a date earlier than 1500 BC. This view is based on an estimation initially made by Max Müller which as B.B. Lal (1997: 286) has already shown was quite casual and rough and about which Max Müller himself was not certain at all. Nevertheless, this view gained currency and became the most received one simply because the scholars were under the spell of the Āryan Invasion Theory according to which the Ṛigvedic Āryans were believed to have destroyed the Harappan Civilization in about 1500 BC. But, this spell is now broken and the invasion has been proved to be a myth (Elst 1999). Some archaeologists like G.F. Dales (1964) and J.G. Shaffer (1984), for instance, have played a leading role in exploding this myth. Even the linguists have discarded it though they still believe in what may be designated as the 'Āryan Arrival Theory' according to which the Āryans came to South Asia from outside in small groups at different points of time. This new linguistic paradigm, however, has only a few takers among the archaeologists like A. Parpola (1988, 1995) and F.R. Allchin (1995), for example. Trying to bridge this linguistic-archaeological divide, George Erdosy (1995: 4) remarks: 'The inescapable conclusion is that while Indo-Āryan languages have an external origin, the *Āryas* of the *Ṛigveda* were not their carriers into South Asia'. Obviously, the Āryan Arrival Theory, even if incorrect, has no relevance for dating the *Ṛigveda.*

Moreover, the linguistic evidence on this point has not been definitive as shown by the estimations that vary from 1500 BC (Ghosh 1952/80) to 5000 BC (Misra 1992). Often, no distinction is made between the antiquity of the language, the antiquity of the events described and the antiquity of the composition of hymns. Commenting on the 5000 BC date of the text, Egbert Richter-Ushanas (1997: 14, fn 13) rightly remarks: 'Even if it is likely that the Āryans lived in India already at this time, that does not mean that the *Ṛigveda* is of equal age'. The West Asian inscriptional evidences confirming the presence of the Vedic-speaking people in Iraq and Turkey in about 1760 BC and 1400 BC respectively make perfect sense in the model of Āryan exodus from the Sarasvatī Valley in about 2000 BC, but this does not help us in fixing the earliest limit of the Ṛigvedic chronological horizon. The astronomical estimation of a date of at least 4500 BC for the text is significant specially because B.G. Tilak and H. Jacobi working simultaneously but independently of each other have come to the same conclusion (Winternitz 1933/91: 295-96). However, one cannot be certain about this estimation too for the hymns on which the astronomical calculations are based and interpreted variously (Singh 1997-98a: 141). In my opinion, the only way to estimate the antiquity of the *Ṛigveda* is to compare the different forms of social formations as depicted in the text on the one hand and those revealed from the pre-2000 BC archaeological assemblages of the Indus-Sarasvatī area on the other. I have developed this line of approach in my forthcoming book *The Ṛigveda: An Archaeological Study* and my impression is that the Hakra Wares Culture of the fourth millennium BC represents the earliest socio-cultural stage of the Ṛigvedic people.

The Cultural Parity

Now, let us compare the cultural contents of the Ṛigvedic and Early-to-Mature Harappan cultures. The perception that the former is rural and illiterate and the latter urban and literate is wrong. First, the rural-urban dichotomy itself is incorrect for in every culture and especially so of ancient times, the number of people engaged in agriculture far exceeds the number of those who participate in non-agricultural production and trade. Second evidence now at hand shows that the Ṛigvedic Culture too had reached the stage of urbanization. The earlier notion popularized by scholarly publications like UNESCO's *History of Mankind* that they were 'non-urbanized people and semi-barbarous' who destroyed cities (Hawkes and Wooley 1963: 406) has been brushed aside. Bhagwan Singh (1987/97, 1995) and R.S. Bisht (1988, 2000) have brought out enormous data from the *Ṛigveda* to show that some Ṛigvedic people lived in urban centres and carried on long distance land and sea trade. Undoubtedly the Ṛigvedic Āryans destroyed their enemy *purs* (strongholds or fortified towns), but they also built *purs*, and lived in them. They are seen invoking and praying their deities Agni, Maruts, Viśvedevaḥ and others not only for granting *purs* but also for helping in the construction and protection of their *purs* that have been described variously as metal-strong *(āyasī)*, multi-sided *(śatabhuji)*, spacious *(vipulā)*, broad (*urvī*), protected *(paṭṛi)*, impregnable *(adhṛishṭā)*, good-looking *(subhrā)*, auspicious *(bhadrā)*, etc. In fact, Bisht (2000: 412-13) has gleaned from the *Ṛigveda* as many as twenty-seven such adjectives qualifying *purs* and most of these have been used in the context of Āryans' own *purs.* A large number of architectural terms and descriptions found in the text, especially references to covered *(sūrmi)* and clear *(suṣira)* drains (*RV*, 8.69.12) leading discharge water to pits *(kākuda)* immediately bring to our mind the Harappan architecture.

Descriptions at several places in the *Ṛigveda* refer to business activities. The word *vaṇij* denoting a businessman or merchant is known and so are the words expressing the concepts used in the business community such as *avyaya* (capital investment), *bhāga* (share in investment and profit), *ṛiṇa* (loan), *śulka* (tax), *bali* (tribute), *samvidāna* (contract), *vasna* (value, cost), etc. (Bisht 1988: 12). Trading was done both by roadways as well as by waterways. Various kinds of land routes or roads *(pathas)* are referred to in the *Ṛigveda.* Bhagwan Singh (1996: 3-4) enumerates over two dozen words used for difficult and easy routes such as extremely dark roads *(atidhvasan patha),* underground roads *(antas patha),* toilsome roads *(vṛijin patha),* deviant roads *(vipatha),* waterlogged roads *(vārṇa patha),* and good roads *(supatha),* comfortable roads *(rajishṭha patha),* straight roads *(ṛijupatha),* illuminated roads *(jyotishman patha),* etc. Important in this connection are also the references he gives to roads leading to distant places *(prapatha, mahaspath),* and points from where roads offshoot in various directions *(vishūchī).* Trade by waterways (i.e. by rivers and sea) was well known. Bisht (1988: 13) gives the various words used in the text for denoting a boat or ship though *nau* is the general term. He provides the references to marine ships fitted with oars *(aritra),* masts *(bandhura, skambha* or *stambha)* and sails usually compared to wings of swans. I have mentioned above the event of Bhujyu's shipwreck. This, as the description shows, must have occurred while going on a sea journey for trade. Bhagwan Singh (1996: 5) provides the references to sea journeys undertaken for wealth. He quotes the Ṛigvedic verse (*RV*, 10.142.7) that reads: 'This is the reservoir of water, the home of all the waters. O Agni, now you can change your route and reach any destination you like'.

The dichotomy between the Mature Harappan and Ṛigvedic cultures on the grounds of presence and absence of literacy is also untenable. Literacy was extremely limited in Mature Harappan times. In Ṛigvedic period too it was very limited but not unknown. The well-known trading community of the time, the Paṇis, are called *'granthinaḥ'* (*RV*, 7.6.3). This epithet, according to V.S. Pathak (1986) indicates that they possessed account books. At a place in the text (*RV*, 6.53.5-8), as already noted by Bhagwan Singh, Pusha is prayed to engrave with awl feelings on the hearts of niggards to make them amicable. Bhagwan Singh (1987/97: 266-72) has many more pieces of evidence to show that the art of writing was known in the Ṛigvedic times.

Another criterion for dichotomizing the Vedic and Harappan cultures, has been the presence and absence of horse in the two cultures respectively. But, now horse bones have been found in excavations at several Harappan sites like Harappa, Ropar, Kalibangan, Lothal, Surkotada, and Malvan. Remains of horse have not been found at Mohenjo-daro and Nausharo, but the presence of the animal at these sites is attested by its terracotta figurines (Gupta 1996: 159-61; Lal 1997: 285-86).

There are many more points of convergence between the Early-to-Mature Harappan and Ṛigvedic cultures. Several characteristic pottery types like the knobbed and perforated varieties are mentioned in Vedic literature (Singh 1969). Again, and it is very significant, the archaeological evidence of post-Mature Harappan migrations tally perfectly with the literary evidence of shifting of the centre of Āryan activities in post-Ṛigvedic times. Jim G. Shaffer (1999) has discussed at length the occupational status of proto-historic sites in Cholistan, eastern Punjab, central Haryana, Sindh and Gujarat. His study shows that in response to environmental changes there occurred a significant population shift from the Indus-Sarasvatī region eastward into eastern Punjab, northern Rajasthan, Haryana, Delhi Territory and western U.P. This archaeologically attested population shift is well known from literary sources. While the centre of Āryan activity in the Ṛigvedic period was the *Sapta Sindhavaḥ* area, that is, the area between Sindhu and Sarasvatī, in the post-Ṛigvedic period it shifted to Brahmāvarta, that is, the Kuru-Pañchāla region.

II

In the light of the geographical, chronological and cultural parities between the Early-to-Mature Harappan and the Ṛigvedic cultures demonstrated above, one can hardly resist the conclusion that the two belong to one and the same cultural tradition. However, one may doubt if all the different ethnic units occupying the Indus-Sarasvatī region may have responded uniformly to the urban and ideological processes that the two cultures represent. Some of the social groups such as those represented by Kot Dijian assemblages at Rehman Dheri (Durrani 1988; Durrani, Ali and Erdosy 1991) are known to have remained unaffected by the urban revolution. Unlike Kot Diji and other sites, they did not transform themselves into Mature Harappans. Similarly, several ethnic units in the *Ṛigveda* are clearly depicted as outside the fold of expanding Āryan ideology. This necessitates a deeper probe in the congruence of the Ṛigvedic and Early-to-Mature Harappan ethno-geographic configurations.

The Ṛigvedic Ethno-Geographic Configurations

The 'Five Peoples' called Pañcha-janāḥ (*RV*, 1.89.10; 3.37.9; 59.8; etc.) are the most frequently mentioned group of ethnic units in the *Ṛigveda.* They are designated also as Pañcha-jātā (*RV*, 6.61.12), Pañcha-mānushāḥ (*RV*, 8.9.2), Pañcha-chārshaṇyāḥ (*RV*, 5.86.2; 7.15.2; 9.101.9), Pañcha-kṛishṭayaḥ (*RV*, 2.2.10; 3.53.16; 4.38.10; etc.) and Pañcha-kshitayaḥ (*RV*, 1.7.9; 176.3; 5.35.2; etc.). Some of these nomenclatures seem to refer to the developing stages of their social formation. Thus, while *Chārshaṇyah,* from root *char* (to move), may point to their predominantly nomadic pastoral condition, *kṛishṭayaḥ,* from root *kṛish* (to cultivate), may indicate their settled agricultural situation. Similarly, *kshitayaḥ,* from root *kshi* (to possess, to have power over), may express their still more developed status when these peoples had acquired territorial consciousness about the areas they occupied (Nandi 1986-87: 156-57). The names of the ethnic units constituting this group of five peoples is not explicitly stated in the *Ṛigveda* resulting in certain wild speculations by some ancient and medieval authorities (Cf. *Aitareya Brāhmaṇa,* 3.31; Yāska, *Nirukta,* 3.8; Sāyaṇa on *RV*, 1.7.9, etc.). However, on circumstantial evidence, modern scholars in general agree that the Anus, Druhyus, Purus, Yadus and Turvaśas are the Ṛigvedic 'Five Peoples'. They are clearly mentioned together in one verse (*RV*, 1.108. 8) and, substituting Yakshu for Yadu, in another hymn too (*RV*, 7.18). It is also clear that initially all these five peoples lived on the banks of the Sarasvatī (*RV*, 6.61.12) though later on in the Ṛigvedic period itself several of them moved to other areas (Singh 1997-98b: 33).

The Bharatas have received maximum notice in the *Ṛigveda* though they are not included in the group of the 'Five Peoples' mentioned above. Though pitted against these 'Five Peoples', they were themselves a branch of the most important among them, the Purus. Their relationship with the Tṛitsus is not very certain. However, the data at hand suggests that the Tṛitsus were the royal family of the Bharatas. The Kuśikas constituted another family of the Bharatas to which belonged Viśvāmitra, the former priest of the Bharata chief Sudās later replaced by Vasishṭha. The Bharatas are depicted as performing sacrifices on the banks of Sarasvatī, Āpayā and Dṛishadvatī (*RV*, 3.23.4) showing that they were living in the region between the rivers Sarasvatī and Yamunā, that is, in the Kurukshetra area.

Besides the above 'Five Peoples' and the Bharatas, there are at least thirty other ethnic units referred to in the *Ṛigveda.* We list below their names alphabetically giving one Ṛigvedic reference to each one though some of them occur in the text more than once:

1. Aja (7.18.19)
2. Alina (7.18.7)
3. Bhalāna (7.18.7)
4. Chedi (8.5.37-39)
5. Gandhāri (1.126.7)
6. Guṅgu (10.48.8)
7. Ikshvāku (10.60.4)
8. Kīkaṭa (3.53.14)
9. Kṛitvan (9.65.23)
10. Krivi (8.20.24)
11. Kuru (8.3.21)
12. Matsya (7.18.6)
13. Maujavant (10.34.1)
14. Nahusha (1.100.18)
15. Naichaśākha (7.53.4)
16. Paktha (7.18.7)
17. Pārāvata (8.34.18)
18. Parśu (7.83.1)

19. Pārthava (8.83.1)
20. Ruśama (8.3.13)
21. Śigru (7.18.19)
22. Śimyu (7.18.5)
23. Śiva (7.18.7)
24. Śṛiñjaya (4.15.4)
25. Uśīnara (10.59.10)
26. Vaikarṇa (7.18.11)
27. Varaśikha (6.27.4-5)
28. Vaśa (8.8.20)
29. Vishāṇin (7.18.7)
30. Vṛichīvant (7.27.7).

The settlements and movements of some of these ethnic units can be ascertained on the basis of the text and subsequent Vedic literature. Thus, it is known that the extreme north-west of the Ṛigvedic geographical horizon, which extended at least up to the river Kabul (Kubhā) in Afghanistan, was occupied by the Gandhāris, Pakthas, Alinas, Bhalānasas and the Vishāṇins. After their defeat in the 'Battle of Ten Kings' the Druhyus had also moved towards the north-west from the Sarasvatī Valley. Their presence in the Gandhāra region is attested to by the later tradition (Macdonell and Keith 1912/95: 1.385). The Puru leader Trasdasyu had acquired a new territory on the banks of the river Swat (Suvāstu) and he is described as ruling over there (*RV*, 8.19.37). This appears to be in addition to his original domain in the Sarasvatī Valley for he says that he has possession over two territories (*mama dvitā rāshṭram kshatriyasya, RV*, 4.42.1). In the Sindh and Punjab region were located the settlements of the Śivas, Parśus, and Vṛichīvants. The Purus and the Bharatas continued to occupy respectively the western and eastern parts of the Sarasvatī Valley down to the end of the Ṛigvedic period. The Śṛiñjayas too were located somewhere nearby the territory of the Bharatas. They were closely allied with the latter for Bharata chief Divodāsa and a Śṛiñjaya leader are celebrated together (Macdonell and Keith 1912/95: 2.469) and the Turvaśas are depicted as common enemies of both (*RV*, 7.18 & 6.27.7). During the Ṛigvedic period the Yadus seem to have migrated from the Sarasvatī region towards south and south-west finally reaching the Gujarat and Kathiawar area where, according to Epic-Purāṇic tradition, many of their lineages flourished. In their journey towards Gujarat they had to cross through large water-logged tracts in which Indra is said to have helped them (*RV*, 6.20.12). That, they became large cattle-owners and wealthy, is also attested to by the text (*RV*, 8.1.31; 6.46). To the south of the Punjab, in the region of Rajasthan and Malwa were located the settlements of the Matsyas and Chedis. In the eastern part of the Ṛigvedic geographical horizon on the banks of the Yamunā lived the Ajas, Śigrus and Yakshus who sacrificed heads of horses to Indra when the Bharata chief Sudās defeated Bheda (*RV*, 7.18.19). Another unit called the Pārāvatas also lived on the Yamunā as later attested to by the *Pañchaviṃśa Brāhmaṇa* (9.4, 11). Their location on the northern border of Gedrosia, earlier proposed by Hillebrandt, is not accepted by vedicists and as the authors of the *Vedic Index* rightly opine, the mention of the Sarasvatī river in connection with the Pārāvatas in the *Ṛigveda* accords with their position on the Yamunā (Macdonell and Keith 1912/95: 1.518-19). The eastern-most ethnic unit known to the *Ṛigveda* is that of the Kīkaṭas. They are said to be living in the Magadha area (Talageri 2000: 119). The *Ṛigveda* does not provide sufficient information about the location of several ethnic units mentioned by it. However, these too may be roughly located keeping in view the core areas of the composition of the *maṇḍalas* (books) of the text in which they occur. As I have shown elsewhere (Singh 1997-98b: 35), most of the hymns contained in the sixth and seventh books of the *Ṛigveda* were composed in the Sarasvatī Valley and the majority of hymns in the latter half of the first and fourth books in the lower Indus region, the area today known as the province of Sindh. Some other scholars (for instance, Nandi 1989-90: 37-38 and Witzel 1995: 317-18) have also tried to ascertain the core areas of various books of the text. This line of investigation may fruitfully be developed further and where no other clue to locate an ethnic unit is available, the core area of the book in which it occurs may be taken to represent its *most probable* habitat.

The Time and Area of the Emergence of the Āryan Ideology and its Impact on Ṛigvedic Ethnic Units

As far as the ideological process is concerned, the *Ṛigveda* provides us a clear indication of its rise and impact. When the ideology arose, the Ārya-Dāsa dichotomy came to represent the distinction between the populations that subscribed to the ideology and those that did not[4]. But this ideological division of the society into Ārya and Dāsa orders (*varṇas*, *RV*, 1.104.2; 2.12.4; 3.34.9) is a later development occurring sometime during the Ṛigvedic period itself. Initially there was no such differentiation. Eminent Āryan chiefs as Divodāsa and Sudās have dāsa-ending names. Some scholars, taking 'slave' connotation of 'dāsa', translate these names as 'Slave of the Gods' and 'Good Slave' respectively, but while the former rendering may have some sense, the latter is a pure nonsense since no Āryan chief would have ever liked to be called so. As a matter of fact, the word 'dāsa' originally did not mean a slave. As V.S. Pathak (1993: 91-94) has shown, initially it meant a 'man' and it was only later on in the Ṛigvedic period that the term came to denote the sense of an 'enemy', 'alien' or 'demon'. According to him, the 'slave' connotation of 'dāsa' is a post-Ṛigvedic development to be found only in the *Khila* portions of the text that are admittedly much later. Although it is difficult to accept the last part of Pathak's conclusion that the 'slave' sense of the term is totally absent in the *Ṛigveda* (Hale 1986/99: 162), the evidence does support his basic stand that 'dāsa' originally meant 'man' and later acquired a derogatory sense. As shown by him, the original 'man' connotation of the term is preserved in the *Avestā* where 'daha' invariably[5] denotes a 'man'. In Āryan names Divodāsa and Sudās, the ending 'dāsa', therefore, stands for 'man'. Pathak is right in concluding that the term *'divo'* means 'divine' as exemplified by words such as *divonara* (*RV*, 5.54.10), *divoputro* (*RV*, 1.181.4), *duhistardivaḥ* (*RV*, 1.30.22) and *divonapāt* (*RV*, 1.117.2), etc. The name Divodāsa, therefore, means a 'Divine Man' and Sudās a 'Good Man'. *Sunaraḥ* (good man) is a frequently used epithet in the *Ṛigveda* and 'Sudās' was a synonym of *Sunaraḥ* before the word 'dāsa' came to acquire a derogatory connotation. Another example of an initially respectful designation in the *Ṛigveda* later becoming hateful due to ideological differences is that of the Asura. In the early Ṛigvedic period, it meant 'the lord' and as such it has been used as an epithet of several important deities including Agni, Savitri, Mitra, Varuṇa, Rudra, and Pūshan (Hale 1986/99: 51-52). But in the later Ṛigvedic period, Asura came to denote the hateful sense of a demon. The changes in the connotations of 'dāsa' and 'asura' in the *Ṛigveda* clearly demonstrate the fact that the Āryan ideology emerged sometime during the Ṛigvedic period itself.

The ideology originated and developed in the Sarasvatī Valley and from there it spread in various directions. I have shown elsewhere (Singh 1997-98b) that by the time of the composition of the Sixth Maṇḍala of the *Ṛigveda,* accepted by several scholars as the earliest *maṇḍala,* the hymn-composers (the real torch-bearers of the ideology) were not acquainted with the river Indus. While the Sarasvatī region dominates the scene in the earlier portions of the text, in the later portions the centre shifts to the lower Indus area indicating a change in the core area of hymn compositions and implying the diffusion of the ideology towards the west. The *Ṛigveda* does not depict a comparable propagation of the ideology towards the east. This shows that for whatever reasons the various ethnic units occupying the Indus-Sarasvatī area in the Ṛigvedic period were already in a state of better interaction with each other than with the social groups living in regions east of the Sarasvatī Valley. Nevertheless, the ideology seems to have spread towards the east in the Ṛigvedic times. The legend of Videgha Māthava and his priest Gotama Rāhugaṇa described in the *Śatapatha Brāhmaṇa* (1.4.1.14-17) is rightly interpreted by scholars to indicate an eastward diffusion of the ideology from the banks of the Sarasvatī to the other side of the river Sadānīrā (modern Gandak), in Bihar. However, the scholars are not correct in concluding that this diffusion occurred in the later Vedic period at the time of composition of the *Śatapatha Brāhmaṇa* in the 8th-7th century BC. P.C. Pant (1996: 8-10) has shown that this dating goes against not only the internal evidence of the text but also against the latest archaeological findings in the area. The internal evidence of the text, as pointed out by him, makes it abundantly clear that the legend is recording a situation of hoary past and not a contemporary condition. After considering the culture sequence at excavated sites in Bihar like Sonepur, Senuwar, Manjhi, Maner, Chirand and Chechar-Kutubpur (the last one located east of the Gandak very close to its confluence with the Gaṅgā), Pant concludes that 'there was an unbroken cultural continuity, uninfluenced by any external element from about 2000 BC' to the end of the Northern Black Polished Ware (NBPW) period in 100 BC. The Saryupar region of eastern UP is the area through which any diffusion from the Sarasvatī Valley must pass through in order to reach Bihar. Pant, therefore, takes into account the archaeological culture sequence of this intervening area too that has been defined on the basis of collective evidence from excavated sites like Narhan, Dhuriapar, Imlidih, Sohagaura, etc. His conclusion is once again the same. He remarks:

> Although it is yet to be worked out whether there is any cultural continuity between the pre-Narhan (assigned approximately to the duration 1800-1300 BC) and Narhan (placed in the time-span of about 1300-800 BC) cultures, there is sufficient evidence to suggest a unilinear evolution of cultures from the period II (that is, Narhan Culture) to the NPBW culture. In this case also there is hardly any material item which can be interpreted as cultural intrusion.

This 'uninterrupted cultural continuity uninfluenced by any external stimuli from about *c.* 2000 BC in Bihar and from *c.* 1600 BC in the Saryupar plain' has been underlined by the discoverer of the Narhan Culture, Purushottam Singh (1999: 524) too.

In this connection two pieces of archaeological information, noted also by Pant (1996: 10-12), are quite significant since they indicate the eastward diffusion of Harappan elements up to Bihar through the Saryupar region. One is the introduction of the cultivation of barley and wheat along with certain other cereals at the site of Senuwar, situated in Rohtas district of Bihar that has been excavated by B.P. Singh (1988-89: 6-18). K.S. Saraswat of the Birbal Sahani Institute of Palaeobotany, Lucknow, who has collected, and examined the botanical materials from the site, informs (personal communication) that earlier the farmers at Senuwar have been growing only paddy for nearly 200 years, but after about 2000 BC they started cultivating other cereals besides paddy such as barley, wheat, pea, lentil and millets like *jawar* and *ragi*. His analysis shows that the species of barley, wheat and pulses are exactly the same that were cultivated by the Harappans. Evidently it indicates a movement of men and ideas from the Indus-Sarasvatī region to Bihar in *c.* 2000 BC The other important information is the recovery of a large number of micro beads of steatite from Imlidih Khurd, a site located on the borders of Gorakhpur and Basti districts in Saryupar plain, which has been excavated by Purushottam Singh and his team (1991-92: 120-22). Such micro beads, known only from Harappan assemblages, have been found from pre-Narhan context at the site showing once again the eastward diffusion from the Indus-Sarasvatī area. If the eastward diffusion of the Āryan ideology evidenced by the Videgha Māthava legend is related with the eastward diffusion of Harappan elements demonstrated by archaeology, as it most likely seems to be, it is an important additional point of Vedic-Harappan convergence. As far as literary evidence is concerned, it is unambiguous. Gotam Rāhugaṇa, the priest who accompanied Videgha Māthava up to the banks of the Sadānīrā, is a *ṛishi* of the Aṅgirasa family who is credited with the authorship of as many as twenty hymns of the *Ṛigveda* (1.74-93). Hence the fact that the Videgha Māthava episode, described in the *Śatapatha Brāhmaṇa*, refers to an event of the Ṛigvedic period, is beyond any doubt.

The ideology had a tremendous impact on the Ṛigvedic ethnic units for it fostered a sense of social identity among the groups that subscribed to it creating the Ārya-Dāsa dichotomy. It may be noted that there was hardly any other difference between the Āryas and Dāsas except the acceptance or non-acceptance of the Āryan ideology based on the belief in certain deities and the sacrificial ritual practice of communicating with those deities. No racial, linguistic or material-cultural line of demarcation can be drawn between the two groups. Neither 'Ārya' nor 'Dāsa' has any racial connotation. A Ṛigvedic verse (*ye manum chakrur uparam dāsaya, RV*, 6.21.11) appears to distinguish between Dāsas and Māhavas (both the words meaning 'men') by stating that 'those (gods) place Manu (the supposed progenitor of the latter) over Dāsa (the supposed progenitor of the former)'. But this distinction between the supposed progenitors of Dāsas and Mānavas has no racial significance as evidenced by other words meaning 'men' like Purushas (derived from Puru) or Nahushas (derived from Nahus). Though the ideology is couched in the Vedic language, there were some among the Āryans who were non-Vedic speakers in the sense that their first language was not Vedic (Deshpande 1995:78-80). The epithet *mṛidhra-vāchaḥ* (speaker of an unpleasant or foul language) applied generally to Dasyus and Paṇis (*RV*, 1.174.2; 5. 29.10; .32.8; 7.6.3; 10.23.5) is given to Āryan Purus (*RV*, 7.18.13) too. The Vrātyas of the later Vedic period did not subscribe to the Āryan ideology though they were Vedic-speakers (*Pañchaviṃśa Brāhmaṇa* 17.1.9). The fact that language is not a distinguishing feature of Āryanhood is maintained even by the *Manu-smṛiti* (10.45). On the socio-economic criteria too the Āryans and Dāsas of the *Ṛigveda* are indistinguishable. The text depicts a variety of social formations represented by cave-dwelling or forest camp-living nomadic hunters and food-gatherers, cattle-herding pastoralists, incipient agriculturalists, surplus-producing agriculturalists and communities engaged in land and sea trade (Nandi 1998: 153-69). No distinction between the Āryans and Dāsas is made anywhere in the text on these grounds.

The Problem of Identifying Ethnic Units in Early-to-Mature Harappan and Related Archaeological Assemblages: The Need of a New Paradigm

While the Ṛigvedic ethnic units are known by their names mentioned in the text and we have no difficulty in distinguishing them, the ethnic units pertaining to the Early-to-Mature Harappan and the immediately preceding and contemporary cultures, falling in the Ṛigvedic horizon, have to be identified by an analysis of related archaeological assemblages in various areas. Two major shifts that have occurred in the traditional paradigm governing Harappan studies partly help us in this task. First, the belief in the static uniformity of the culture has changed, diverting research emphasis on its cultural variability (Dyson 1982/93: 572-75). Archaeologists now agree that the Harappan assemblages in various areas are not alike and despite certain uniformities in the urban phase they have significant regional variations. Gregory L. Possehl (1982/93: 19-26) has distinguished as many as six Harappan 'domains'. They are: (1) Eastern or Haryana (Kalibangan) Domain, (2) Northern or Punjab (Harappa) Domain, (3) Central or Bahawalpur (Ganweriwala) Domain, (4) Southern or Sindh (Mohenjo-daro) Domain, (5) Western or Gedrosia (Kulli/Harappan) Domain, and (6) South-eastern or Gujarat (Lothal) Domain. It is further realized that there might have been several ethno-geographic configurations in each domain. The Eastern Domain, for example, has a distinct Bara Culture on the Sutlej (Sharma 1982/93: 141-65) and another equally distinct Siswal Culture on the Chautang, the dry bed of the Dṛishadvatī (Bhan 1971-72: 44-46). The second paradigm shift relates to the realization that the Harappans, though the most dominant social group of the Indus-Sarasvatī Civilization, were neither omnipotent nor the only participants in the cultural evolution that gave rise to the earliest civilization of South Asia. In fact, they were interacting with several non-Harappan peoples in various areas and it is the formation and intensification of this interaction system that led to the emergence of the civilization. Jim G. Shaffer and Diane A. Lichtenstein (1995: 137) have already shown that the Mature Harappans were, or had the potential to be, interacting with a variety of culturally similar or different peoples in different regions such as with agricultural and pastoral groups like the Kulli or Damba Sadaat on their borders in Baluchistan; with Kot Dijians, Mehrgarh VI-VII people and perhaps Amrian social groups on the Indus plain; with cattle pastoralists of Bagor in Rajasthan; with agriculturalists engaged in significant metallurgical activities of the Ganeshwar and Banas groups in the same region; with hunters and gatherers of Langhnaj in Gujarat; and perhaps with Vindhya rice horticulturists in the Gangetic plain. Several other social groups like the Neolithic people of Kashmir may be added to the list of ethno-geographic configurations given by Shaffer and Lichtenstein with whom the Harappans may have been associated. The Harappan Civilization emerged and flourished because of the close symbiotic ties maintained between the Harappans and many of these social groups living in and around the different Harappan domains.

However, though the multiplicity of the ethnic units involved in the rise and development of the Harappan Civilization is beyond any doubt, the task of distinguishing these units is still far from being complete. The absence of a clear understanding of how to recognize ethnic groups in archaeological assemblages has obstructed this task. In other words, though it is accepted that archaeological cultures spread over wide areas are generally associated with several ethnic units, there is as yet no adequate procedure for identifying ethnic affiliations in the involved assemblages. Childe (1929) had defined archaeological culture as 'a recurring assemblage of artefacts'. At present, however, this concept of archaeological culture is being criticized by archaeologists mainly on two grounds: (a) ethnographic researches have shown that assemblages of material artefacts are seldom coterminous with social boundaries (Hodder 1978) and (b) statistical analyses have demonstrated that the traits of artefacts in archaeological assemblages have widely divergent individual distributions (Shennan 1978). The settlement archaeologists have tried to approach the reality better by building models of boundaries around central places, but though this approach has helped us in getting some idea of the distribution of social groups in space, it has its own limitations. Central places represent power-wielding elite groups. These groups, though most important in any cultural process, are not the representatives of all the various other types of social groups.

The situation obviously demands the acceptance and application of a new paradigm for identifying ethnic affiliations in archaeological assemblages. It is urgently needed especially so in Harappan studies where we have to correlate literary and archaeological information on ethno-geographic configurations. Fortunately, during the last few years the problem of ethnicity in South Asian archaeology has received pointed attention of several archaeologists and a recent issue of *Antiquity* (Vol. 74, No. 285, Sept. 2000) has a special section on 'archaeology and identity in South Asia'. Elsewhere George Erdosy has criticized the undue focus on archaeological assemblages and 'underlined the importance of spatial distribution of individual traits in identifying ethnic units[6] (Allchin 1995: 92-96). Jim G. Shaffer and D.A. Lichtenstein (1989, 1995) have forcefully advocated the significance of a set of new concepts like 'cultural tradition' and 'palaeoethnicity' in South Asian archaeology. A new paradigm is, thus, emerging which promises to solve this complex problem and it deserves to be considered by archaeologists as well as vedicists working in the field of Indian proto-history.

The emerging paradigm seeks to replace the existing paradigm in which proto-historic cultures of India and Pakistan are fitted into a linear developmental model of Early, Middle (or Mature) and Late Harappan stages. As noted by Shaffer and Lichtenstein (1989: 117), this linear developmental model has affected the interpretation of Indus-Sarasvatī culture sequence in a particular way. Each and every culture complex in the area is either assigned a place in the Harappan developmental sequence, Early, Middle or Late, or else treated as totally unrelated to the Harappans. The inadequacy of the existing model is evident on both theoretical and practical grounds. On the theoretical plain, a linear developmental model presumes that cultures are closed systems, but anthropological researches have convincingly demonstrated that they are open systems constantly interacting not only with their natural environment but also with their social environment constituted by other cultures within their reach. In practice, the existing model presents difficulties when we come across a culture like that of Kot Diji. On several sites the Kot Diji Culture pre-dates the Mature Harappan stage, and it is because of this position that it has been categorized as an Early Harappan culture. However, on many other sites it is contemporaneous with the Mature Harappans. Several archaeologists have noted this position of the Kot Diji complex in different areas as, for example, Suraj Bhan (1975: 81) in the eastern Punjab and Gregory L. Possehl (1984: 86) in the northern and western Punjab. The contemporaneity of Kot Dijians and Mature Harappans is confirmed by radiocarbon dates too (Thomas and Allchin 1986, Shaffer and Lichtenstein 1989: Figure 12.1). Excavations at Rehman Dheri, a site in the Gomal Valley (Durrani 1988, Durrani, Ali and Erdosy 1991), show that the Kot Dijians at that site not only pre-dated the Mature Harappan stage but continued to exist also in the Mature Harappan and Late Harappan times (Shaffer and Lichtenstein 1995: 133). Obviously, the existing linear developmental model of Early, Mature and Late Harappan stages is inadequate to present the complexity expressed by the archaeological record.

The concept of 'cultural tradition' as developed in the emerging paradigm aims at solving the above mentioned difficulties. 'A cultural tradition' according to Jim G. Shaffer (1992: 442), 'refers to persistent configurations of basic technologies and cultural systems within the context of temporal and geographical continuity. This concept facilitates a stylistic grouping of diverse archaeological assemblages into a single analytical unit, while limiting the need for establishing the precise nature of cultural and chronological relationships that link assemblages but imply that such relationships exist'. The concept helps in developing a framework in which diverse archaeological assemblages like the Harappan, Kot Diji, etc., that appear to be related but whose relationship is not clear, may be grouped together for study and cultural and ecological variables may be integrated synchronically and diachronically to account for continuity and change. To emphasize the importance of cultural variables and to accommodate recent developments in South Asian archaeology, the definition of the concept has been slightly modified by Shaffer and Lichtenstein (1995: 141): 'A cultural tradition refers to persistent configurations of basic technologies and cultural systems *as well as structure* within the context of temporal and geographical continuity'. They clarify that the term 'structure' in this redefinition of a cultural tradition has the same meaning as that connoted by 'habitus' in P. Bourdieu's *Practice Theory* (Bourdieu 1978) and they quote G.C. Bentley (1987:36) to express the meaning: 'The habitus comprises a set of generative schemes that produce practices and representations that are regular without reference to overt rules and that are goal directed without requiring conscious selection of goals or mastery of methods of achieving them'. They remark: 'The addition of "structure" and practice theory principles to cultural tradition provides a socially dynamic framework for data analysis—one providing insights for understanding gradual and rapid cultural change, and accounting for cultural variation within a context of cultural continuity' (Shaffer and Lichtenstein 1995: 142).

The course of a cultural tradition may be sub-divided into 'eras' to mark significant changes in the nature or intensity of cultural organization. Shaffer (1992) has distinguished four eras in the Indus-Sarasvatī cultural tradition to which we shall refer to later. A significant point about a cultural tradition is that it is modelled as an 'interaction system' (Binford 1965; Singh 1985) for it is conceived to be synchronically and diachronically constituted by a series of palaeoethnic groups which are linked together in stimulus-response relationship or in an information communication network continuously interacting with each other as well as with their natural and cultural environments. The concept of 'palaeoethnicity', similar to that of 'phase' in American archaeology (Willey and Phillips 1958: 22) but implying no chronological limits, has been developed mainly on the basis of insights provided by F. Barth (1969) in his *Introduction to Ethnic Groups and Boundaries: The Social Organization of Culture Differences*, an important anthology edited by him. According to Barth (1969: 11), the basic feature of an ethnic group is that it 'has a membership which identifies itself, and is identified by others, as constituting a category distinguishable from other categories of the same order'. In other words 'ethnic groups are categories of ascription and identification by the authors themselves' (Renfrew 1978: 97). The question as to what leads to the emergence of ethnicity is debated. According to Barth, ethnicity arises because of boundary maintenance by culturally different groups. However, it is now realized that cultural differences are a necessary but not sufficient condition for the emergence of ethnic groups. 'It is more likely to support the opposite view, vigorously denied by Barth, that cultural differences emerged initially in situations of relative isolation, even, if they were subsequently amplified by boundary maintenance' (Erdosy in Allchin 1995: 94). Ethnic groups compete with each other for resources and occasionally ensure its availability by undergoing processes of segmentation and fusion (Shaffer 1989: 119). Under the pressure of decreased availability of food and other resources, some members of an ethnic group may choose to move to a new area. For some time the offshoot group may continue its association with the parent group, but sooner or later the ties are broken and the offshoot group becomes an independent ethnic unit. This is called segmentation of ethnic units. Alternatively, under constraints of certain challenges posed by natural and cultural environments requiring larger populations to meet them, several ethnic units may develop intense mutual interaction that may finally result into their merger together to form a single group. This is known as fusion of ethnic groups. Noteworthy Ṛigvedic examples of ethnic segmentation and fusion are respectively the separation of the Bharatas from the main Puru stock and the coalition of several ethnic groups to form a single group known as the Kuru-Pañchāla. In an archaeological context, the shifting boundaries maintained by ethnic groups may be recognized by material cultural symbols such as distinctive ceramic styles and other individual material traits (Shaffer and Lichtenstein 1989: 110; Erdosy in Allchin 1995: 93-96).

With the help of these new concepts of 'cultural tradition', 'palaeoethnicity', 'era' and 'interaction system', efforts have already been started to define the Indus-Sarasvatī cultural tradition. Shaffer (1992) and Shaffer and Lichtenstein (1989; 1995) have distinguished four consecutive eras in this cultural tradition. The first named the Early Food-Producing Era is represented by the Mehrgarh Phase. The second called the Regionalization Era has the Balakot, Amri, Hakra, and Kot Diji phases. The third designated as the Integration Era consists of the Harappan Phase. The fourth termed the Localization Era involves the Punjab, Jhukar, and Rangpur phases. The phases or the palaeoethnic units listed by them in the eras are not exhaustive and several others may be identified in each one of these eras. However, a promising avenue for identifying Harappan ethno-geographic configurations has been opened and these efforts need to be carried on further for fruitful archaeological-literary comparisons.

The Early-to-Mature Harappan and the Immediately Preceding and Contemporary Ethno-Geographic Configurations

As the present study is concerned with the Ṛigvedic-Harappan relationship, we need not consider ethnic groups of the periods later than 1900 BC since, as stated earlier, by about that time the Ṛigvedic period comes to a close. Again, that very time marks the end of the Mature Harappan Culture. Our ethno-geographic investigations, therefore, would be limited to what is called the Regionalization and Integration eras. Then, as the Ṛigvedic Culture originated in the Sarasvatī Valley (Singh 1997-98b), it would be proper to begin with the ethnic groups that lived in this valley.

In the Sarasvatī Valley, the earliest culture of the horizon is the Hakra Ware Culture of about 3500-3000 BC. M. Rafique Mughal (1982/93: 85-95), the first to recognize it, has mapped as many as 99 sites of this culture in the Cholistan area comprising the Bahawalnagar and Bahawalpur districts of Pakistan. None of these sites have been excavated. However, the antiquities collected from the surface of the sites, mostly single culture ones, clearly indicate that the authors of this culture were at a level of social formation which was more advanced than the Neolithic stage but had still not fully acquired a Bronze Age status. More than half of the sites (52.5 per cent) are camp sites indicating their predominantly nomadic pastoral character. Nevertheless, they have produced a good quality of red pottery both handmade and wheel-turned. Some of the pottery features, specially the tradition of coating the exterior with mud intermixed with small bits of pottery, link the culture with Amri IA levels in Sindh dated to the early part of the fourth millennium BC. Its cultural continuity in the following Sothi/Kot Diji phase is evidenced both in and outside the Sarasvatī Valley at sites including Sarai Khola, Jalilpur and Ghaligai (Shaffer 1992: 445). Hakra elements have been noticed at Burzahom in Kashmir too where, as in the Swat Valley, they seem to have persisted into the mid-second millennium BC. Probably, there were other social groups in the Sarasvatī Valley existing along with the Hakra people, but at present our knowledge about them is extremely limited. Possibility of the presence of a non-Hakra group in the earliest levels at Kunal in Haryana datable to about 3100 BC has been expressed (Gupta 1996: 52-53; Khatri and Acharya 1994-95: 84-86).

During what is presently called the Early Harappan Period, several social groups were living in the Sarasvatī Valley. They are represented by archaeological assemblages found at a large number of sites. In the Cholistan region M.R. Mughal has recorded 40 sites of this period as against 99 of the earlier Hakra stage. But compared to the Hakra Culture sites these sites are much larger in area and have thicker deposits indicating growth in population as well as increase in sedentary habits. Besides, multifunctional sites, that is, residential sites with specialized/industrial components have now increased remarkably from 2 per cent of the earlier stage to 35 per cent, a trustworthy index of significant socio-cultural changes in the period (Mughal 1992/93: 91). In the Indian segment of the Sarasvatī Valley, 137 sites of this period were recorded by J.P. Joshi, Madhu Bala and Jassu Ram (1984). Several other sites have been located since then. Some of these sites on the Indian side like Kalibangan, Banawali, Rakhigarhi, and Kunal have been subjected to excavation to various extents. The findings at these sites have been summarized by archaeologists like B.B. Lal (1997; 2002) and S.P. Gupta (1996) and there is no need to go into the details here. It is noteworthy that despite new developments and changes, these assemblages clearly manifest a cultural continuity demonstrating membership to a tradition not only by inheriting certain features (like the continuance of some ceramic styles) from the earlier Hakra phase but also by introducing significant new elements (such as the peacock and *pīpal*-leaf designs on pottery, terracotta 'cakes', the bricks with sides in the ratio of 4:2:1, etc.) to the succeeding Mature Harappan phase. The homogeneity of the assemblages is emphasized by several features especially the use of black and white colours in painting the potteries (outlines in black and infillings in white generally). This is considered to be a distinctive feature of the Early Harappan pottery not only in the Sarasvatī Valley but also outside it (Lal 2002: 30). However, it must be noted that despite the obvious homogeneity in Early Harappan assemblages, there are regional variations. Not much work has been done on the inter-assemblage variability demonstrated by the sites of the period. Anyway, the differences in the assemblages are clear enough[7] indicating the existence of several distinct ethnic units in different localities of the Sarasvatī Valley before the emergence of urbanization or what is known as the Mature Harappan phase. In fact, their individuality was not completely lost even during the peak period of urbanization which must have considerably intensified their interaction.

How did the transition from the rural to the urban phase of the Harappan Culture take place? Earlier, it was believed that it occurred somewhat quickly. G.L. Possehl (1986: 96-98) had suggested a duration of 150 years for the transition and Shaffer and Lichtenstein (1989: 123) were inclined for a still lesser time of only 100 years, around 2600-2500 BC, for it. However, after considering comparatively more recent data from Dholavira, Kot Diji, Kunal and Harappa, S.P. Gupta (1996: 68-100) assigns it a duration of at least 200 years if not more placing it roughly between 2800-2600 BC. The transition, thus, was gradual and not abrupt. The noteworthy fact about the transition is that its core area was the Sarasvatī Valley. The earliest set of Mature Harappan dates around 2600 BC are from Kalibangan, a site on the Sarasvatī (Lal 1997: Table 2, p. 246). Then, the Harappan sites in the Sarasvatī Valley outnumber those in the Indus Valley by more than six times (Gupta 1996: 3). These facts speak for themselves. Though trade, commerce and industry, the basic factors leading to any urban process, involve areas far separated from each other, the human initiative invariably comes from certain specific quarters. It can hardly be doubted that in case of the Harappan urbanization the initiative was provided by the leading social groups living in the Sarasvatī Valley. Shaffar and Lichtenstein (1989: 123) are of the opinion that the palaeoethnic group called the Harappan that dominates the Integration Era (that is, the urban stage) of the Indus-Sarasvatī Tradition was created by a fusion of Hakra, Kot Diji and Bagor ethnic groups on the Sarasvatī Valley. One may or may not agree with the inclusion of Bagor group in this fusion, but the fact remains that its locale was the Sarasvatī Valley. Here, it is worth noting that both, the urban process as well as the ideological process, referred to earlier, originated in the Sarasvatī Valley. The significance of this fact will be discussed later.

The concentration of the Harappan sites is noticed in three distinct localities of the Sarasvatī Valley. Joshi, Bala and Ram (1984: 513-16 and Map on p. 517) designate them as 'economic pockets' meaning thereby clusters of closely-knit interdependent sites developed in the process of achieving subsistence self-sufficiency. The first cluster of sites is located roughly in the area extending from Kalibangan (in District Hanumangarh, Rajasthan) in the south-west to Balu (in District Jind, Haryana) in the north-east and includes the sites of the Mansa taluk of District Bhatinda in Punjab situated along the Sirhind rivulet, a tributary of the Ghaggar. It is worth underlining that five Early Harappan and Mature Harappan sites of the Mansa area exceed 100 ha in size. The measurements given by J.P. Joshi are approximately: Lakhmirwala – 225 ha, Dhalewan – 150 ha, Gumi Kalan I – 144 ha and Hasanpur II and Baglian-De-Theh each 100 ha (Chakrabarti 1995: 89). These settlement sizes are indeed enormous for that early period. As yet, Mohenjo-daro. Harappa and Dholavira were considered to be the largest sites of the civilization. But, even the most liberal assessments of the sizes of Mohenjo-daro and Harappa are around only 200 ha and 150 ha respectively (Chakrabarti 1995: 61 & 83) and that of Dholavira comes to about 100 ha (Bisht 1991). Even more significant is the fact that all these big sites of the Mansa taluk, along with 16 others of lesser dimensions in between them, are located comparatively in a very small area measuring 1250 sq km only. Moving downstream along the Sarasvatī, the second cluster of sites is found in the Cholistan area and the third further downstream in Kutch. Though the Cholistan has the heaviest site concentration, with 174 sites as against 41 and 50 of respectively the first and third clusters (Joshi, Bala and Ram 1984: Map on p. 517), it has only one big site, Ganweriwala, which measures 81.5 ha in area, all others falling in size categories that range from less than 5 ha to not more than 20 ha (Chakrabarti 1995: 31). The concentration of sites in Kutch, where the ancient Sarasvatī joined the Arabian Sea, appears to be surprising in view of the area's minimal agricultural potentiality. Evidence at hand shows that the causes for the concentration of sites in this area must have been mainly animal breeding and cotton cultivation and to a certain extent trade. It may be pointed out that the factors leading to the formation of three distinct localities of site clusterization in the Sarasvatī Valley, the concentration of the largest sites in Mansa taluk of District Bhatinda in Punjab, the emphasis on animal husbandry in Kutch, etc., are directly linked to changing ethno-geographic configurations of people then inhabiting the Sarasvatī Valley. In absence of a detailed study of inter-assemblage variability based on specific trait distributions, these facts alone provide us a peep into the palaeoethnicity of the area watered by the Sarasvatī and its tributaries. But before coming to that problem, it would be worthwhile to have a rapid look on the Early-to-Mature Harappan settlements outside the Sarasvatī Valley.

In the Early Harappan times the lower Indus Valley was occupied by several different social groups like the Amrians, Balakotians, and others. The Amrians derive their name from a site named Amri in western Sindh where their cultural remains were clearly defined by J.M. Casal's excavations at the site in the early 1960s. The Period I at the site with four sub-divisions (I-A – I-D) belongs to them. The succeeding periods IIA-IIB represent an intermediate stage followed by III-A which is Mature Harappan. The subsequent periods III-B to V-B at Amri are irrelevant for the present study. The presence of Amrians has been noted also at Ghazi Shah and several other sites throughout western Sindh and Baluchistan. They produced a kind of distinctive pottery using black and red paints pointing to their ancestry in hilly regions of Baluchistan. According to W.A. Fairservis (1975: 208-16), agriculture, pastoralism, and fishing were three main patterns of their subsistence. Their cultural traits leave no room for doubt that they constituted a distinct palaeoethnic unit, but they were not living in isolation. The use of copper and artefacts of semi-precious stones, howsoever limited, shows that they were interacting with other peoples. Their participation in an interaction system is attested to by several other indicators too such as the presence of a few Hakran and Kot Dijian types of pottery at Amri, the findings of some Amri-style pottery at Balakot, and similarities in shapes, decorative motifs and abstract signs in the potteries of Amri, Balakot and Kot Diji assemblages (Shaffer 1992: 445). Towards the close of Period I-D at Amri, a few Mature Harappan pottery-traits including some shapes and decorative motifs begin to appear. They proliferate in Period II called the 'Intermediate', and by the succeeding Period III-A the Amri pottery is almost completely replaced by the Mature Harappan. The palaeoethnic identity of the Amrians is lost because of their subsumption in the Mature Harappans. The chronological horizon of the Amri Culture is placed roughly between 3500 and 2600 BC.

The Balakotians constitute another distinct palaeoethnic group of the pre-Harappan stage in the lower Indus Valley. They are known from Balakot, a coastal site in District Las Bela, located in Khurkera alluvial plain some 88 km north-west of Karachi. In mid-1970s, G.F. Dales conducted excavation at the site stratifying the deposits in two periods with a total of 17 phases and 42 strata. The earliest eleven phases (Phases I-XI) represent the Balakotians while

Phases XII and XIII constitute a transitional stage followed by the remaining Phases XIV-XVII that belong to the Mature Harappans. The Balakotians had affinities with social groups occupying upland areas in the north. This is indicated by the presence of specimens of a polychrome pottery called the Nal Ware (well-known from the type-site Nal in District Jhalawan) and the Togau-style decorative motifs on pottery (a feature of the Kalat-Anjira area) in the earliest levels at Balakot. Amri IC-D pottery too appears in earlier levels at Balakoi and increases in upper levels showing a developing interaction between the Balakotians and Amrians. It is interesting to find that the Balakotians were using mud bricks for constructing their houses that have side measurements in the same ratio of 4:2:1 that was soon to become typical to Mature Harappans who occupied Balakot after them. However, since there is a long gap between the two, as attested to by carbon dates as well as stratigraphy, the possibility of the Harappans borrowing this feature from the Balakotians is ruled out. The Balakotians were present on the site throughout the fourth millennium BC and for a century or so even in the third.

Moving up the Indus Valley north-east from Balakot one reaches two well-known sites, Mohenjo-daro and Kot Diji, situated at a distance of about 43 km from each other, the former on the right and the latter on the left bank of the Indus but a little away from it. The pre-Mature Harappan layers at Mohenjo-daro could not be investigated due to rise in underground-water level. However, some materials including pieces of 'Wet Ware', similar to those found at Jalilpur, recovered in borings suggest that in all probability there did exist a pre-Mature Harappan community at this site too (Lal 1997: 62-63). However, as if to compensate for the scarcity of evidence at Mohenjo-daro, Kot Diji has presented a very valuable data in this connection. The excavations carried out at the site in years 1955-57 (Khan 1965) have brought to light from its earliest levels (Layers 16-4) an important social group of the pre-Mature Harappan horizon designated after the name of the site as Kot Dijians. Their pottery, mostly wheel-turned is quite distinctive. The main pottery-type is a globular pot which is characterized by 'its fine thin body, short beaded or slightly averted rim, fugitive broad band round the neck in red, brown, sepia or warm black, varying from one to three inches in width, painted on a cream or dull red slip'. Though this feature continues throughout the Kot Dijian deposits, an evolution in pottery-production is clear enough. In earlier layers the globular pot is thinner and more squatish and has a neck-less and rim-less mouth. The paintings are almost exclusively confined to the area just below the mouth. But in the later layers, the neck and rim of the globular pot become pronounced and the designs proliferate and become complex, 'taking the embroyonic shape of such well-known Harappan motifs as fish scale, intersecting circles and linked roundels'. On one of the pots, a horned deity is painted in black and white on a dark brown glossy slip. This may have been an earlier depiction of the well-known horned deity (or deities) of the Mature Harappan times. The upper-most Kot Dijian layer is sealed by a thick deposit of burnt and charred material. The subsequent layers after a break pertain to Mature Harappans. The chronological horizon of the Kot Dijians spans roughly from 3000 to 2500 BC. The nuclear area of the Kot Dijians, however, is in the Sarasvatī (Ghaggar-Hakra) Valley where their presence is attested to at as many as 40 sites in Cholistan and over 137 sites in Indian portion of the valley (Lal 2002: 48). None of the Cholistan area sites have been excavated so far though a few of them like Gamanwala and Jalwali are quite large and appear to be promising. Fortunately, however, several of the Sarasvatī Valley sites in India have been excavated and as stated earlier, it is possible to define them stratigraphically as belonging to Kalibangan I, Banawali I, Rakhigarhi I and Kunal IA-IC. Outside the Indus Valley their presence is noticed in several areas. Besides Kot Diji (Layers 16-4) described above, several others like Harappa I, Jalilpur II, Gumla III,

Rehman Dheri II-III, Sarai Khola II and Swat Valley Period II at Ghaligai belong to the Kot Dijians (Cf. Lal 1997 and 2002; Gupta 1996; Chakrabarti 1995 for bibliography relating to the sites and Shaffer 1992: 447-48 for a brief discussion). The regional variations in pottery show that the Kot Dijians represent a large community of several distinct though interrelated social groups.

The sites in the Sarasvatī and lower Indus Valleys have been dealt with in some detail because they fall in the area that constitutes the heartland of both the processes, the one related to the Harappan urbanization and the other pertaining to the Ṛigvedic ideology as already discussed in this study and elsewhere (Singh 1997-98b). Outside this central zone, there are several palaeoethnic units whose identification is essential for a correlation of their ethno-geographic configuration with that depicted in the *Ṛigveda*.

The Kot Dijian expansion in various areas has already been referred to. In the upper Indus Valley, they had reached and settled at sites like Harappa and Jalilpur on the Ravi, at Gumla and Rehman Dheri in Gomal basin, and at Sarai Khola in Taxila area (Gandhāra). In the process of colonization, the Kot Dijians sometimes founded new settlements becoming their original settlers, but more often they overtook previously settled habitations from others. The settlement at Harappa was founded by them. Their remains have been discovered at Mounds AB and E at the site now assigned to Periods I and II (Lal 1997: 80 and f. n. 1). In Period III at the site, that continues without any break, they are seen to have transformed themselves as the Mature Harappans. However, the pattern of colonization is different at the nearby site of Jalilpur, situated just 75 km away from Harappa downstream on the same (i.e. left) bank of the Ravi. Before the Kot Dijians arrived there, it was already inhabited by a distinct social group characterized by a handmade, thick and under-fired red pottery coated with a mixture of clay and bits of pottery. The Kot Dijians joined them at the site and soon overwhelmed them. This is clearly indicated by a marked decrease in the quantity of mud-and-pottery-coated wares with a simultaneous spurt in Kot Dijian ceramics observed in Period II at the site.

A similar scenario is presented by the Gomal Valley sites. The Period III at Gumla is Kot Dijian, but the earlier social group, inhabiting the site in Period II, was a different one. As indicated by certain pottery-traits, these earlier inhabitants of Gumla had affinities with northern Baluchistan and with areas further west and north-west. There is a sterile layer between Periods II and III though some pottery-styles of the former period continue in the latter one. These facts indicate that the site was abandoned for some time and when Kot Dijians settled on the deserted site, the earlier folks came back and joined them (Lal 1997: 54). At Rehman Dheri, the earliest settlers, assigned to Period I at the site, were a distinct people characterized by a fine red pottery (ring-based bowls and cups, etc.) with paintings in black and chocolate colours. Though some Kot Diji-related pottery is present even in Period I, it is in the succeeding Periods II and III that the culture-complex becomes clearly Kot Dijian (Lal 1997: 55). The evidence at hand suggests that the Kot Dijians extended their sway further north from the Gomal Valley and colonized the Bannu basin founding some new settlements like Tarakai Qila and overtaking others like Sheri Khan Tarakai from earlier occupants.

At Sarai Khola, a site in the vicinity of Taxila, the earliest settlers, belonging to Period I, were a late Neolithic people. They produced a distinctive brown pottery that is wheel-turned and highly burnished. The shapes include mainly pans and bowls. The bowls with slightly flaring sides have mat-like impression on their bottoms. These Neolithic people, resembling their contemporaries at Burzahom, were present at this site when the Kot Dijians arrived there in Period II and gradually overtook the site from them. In the present stage of research, the Gandhāra region (districts Rawalpindi and Peshawar in Pakistan) seems to be the northern-most limit of the Kot Dijian expansion.

The work of identifying social groups in chronologically relevant archaeological assemblages must be extended to many more areas since the Early-to-Mature Harappan and Ṛigvedic geographical horizons are very large. Both of them, as shown above, extend from Afghanistan to Gujarat. For want of space, it is not possible to go into details here. However, it may be noted that a pre-Mature Harappan horizon has been distinguished even in Gujarat. A solid evidence in this regard is provided by R.S. Bisht's excavations at Dholavira in the great Rann of Kutch. The lowest 60-70 cm thick pre-Mature Harappan deposit at this site has been stratigraphically isolated on the basis of its contents that include a distinct wheel-turned red and comb-incised/reserved pottery (Bisht 1991). Though somewhat disputed (Chakrabarti 1995: 41), archaeologists like B.B. Lal give due credence to some other pieces of evidence too in this connection such as the presence of 'non-Harappan' micaceous red as well as black-and-red wares in the lowest deposits in the Lothal region, reported by S.R. Rao, the discovery of some pottery at Nagwada in the Rupen estuary that have affinities with Amri pottery in Sindh, and the pre-Mature Harappan radiocarbon dates made available for 'Pre-Prabhās Culture' at Prabhas Patan (Somnath) as also for early deposits at Rojdi in central Saurashtra and Padri in District Bhavnagar.

Jim G. Shaffer (1992) has distinguished the palaeoethnic units of Baluchistan and southern Afghanistan relating them respectively to what he designates as the Baluchistan and Helmand traditions, both sub-divided into different eras. According to his analysis, at least nine different social groups may be identified in the Baluchistan Tradition and four in the Helmand Tradition. He calls these social groups 'phases' but for convenience, we may designate them simply as 'peoples'. The Mehrgarh people (included in Indus Tradition too) constitute the earliest and the most important social group in the Baluchistan Tradition. The others are the Kili Ghul Mohammad people, Kechi Beg people, Damb Sadaat people, Nal people, Kulli people, Perano people, Bampur people and the Pirak people. In the Helmand Tradition, he counts the Mundigak people, Helmand people, Shahr-i-Sokhta people and the Seistan people. Shaffer has tried to ascertain their chronological spans and contextual positions on the sites they are found to have occupied. Though not directly related to the origin and development of the Indus-Sarasvatī Tradition, these groups of peoples do fall in what has been described above as the 'contact area' of the Early-to-Mature Harappan as well as the Ṛigvedic people. With commercial and cultural linkages, they constitute an important segment of that interaction system which is being defined as the Indus-Sarasvatī Tradition.

III

The search for Vedic-Harappan relationship should not be limited to merely demonstrating geographical, chronological and certain striking cultural parities between the two. As shown above, these parities do exist between the two cultures insofar as the Early-to-Mature stages of the one and the Ṛigvedic phase of the other are concerned. The search must proceed further to define the interrelation between the urban and ideological processes represented by the Harappan and Vedic cultures respectively. It must even go a step ahead and investigate, as far as possible, the correspondences between their ethno-geographic configurations. In short, the urban and ideological processes and the various social groups involved in the two processes need to be compared to ascertain the level of Vedic-Harappan equation.

Interrelating the Urban and the Ideological Processes

In one of my earlier studies (Singh 1997-98b), I have shown that the Vedic ideology developed initially in the Sarasvatī Valley and later on, in the Ṛigvedic period itself, it expanded and covered the lower Indus coastal areas where we find the Ṛigvedic priest-poets like Sindhukshit (meaning a resident of the Sindhu area), Sindhudvīpa and Kakshīvān praising eloquently the virtues of the river and prosperity of the area. The river, it is said, 'surpasses all the other streams in strength' and flows 'roaring like a bull'. In an enchanting imagery, its two flanks constituted by various rivers on both the sides are imagined to be two wings of an army and the river is perceived as a king as if marching on in a battle.[8] The region is said to be rich in, among other things, gold, grains, horses, wool, cloths and hemp (*RV*, 10.75.8). The flow of the ideology from the north-east to south-west is attested to also by a somewhat late inclusion of the twin-gods Aśvins, originally gods of the coastal regions, in the Soma ritual that had originated in the Sarasvatī Valley (Singh 1997-98b: 31 and f. n. 19). It is noteworthy that the urban process presents an exactly similar pattern. As shown above, it originates in the Sarasvatī Valley and diffuses first towards the lower Indus Valley and then in other areas. It cannot be taken to be just a coincidence. Occurring in the same space-time context and following the same pattern is, to my mind, a positive indication of the two processes going hand in hand.

This inference is validated by a large number of Ṛigvedic references, discussed earlier, to the construction of *purs* (fortified towns) by the Āryans themselves. Some of these Āryan *purs* had acquired the form of well-developed and refined cities with decorated public places and platforms. A verse of the *Ṛigveda* (4.32.23) refers to two slight images of unrobed girls made upon a newly wrought wooden post. Commenting on the verse, Sāyaṇa explains them as Śālabhañjikā images and Griffith likens them to caryatids (that much later decorated ancient Greek cities). The involvement of Ṛigvedic people in marine trade and commercial activities have already been mentioned. It must also be noted that even expertise in sacrificial supervision had become an important source of income. This is attested to by the details given by the so-called *dānastutis* (praise for the gifts received by the priests) found at different places in the *Ṛigveda*. The text records the names of over two dozen different priest-poets who have received guerdon from over forty donors. Very often, the wealth involved in the guerdon is enormous and may have been exaggerated. Nevertheless, it shows that the priestly profession had become quite lucrative. The case of the famous Ṛishi Kakshīvān, belonging to the family of the Pajras, may be quoted here to give an idea of the gifts received by distinguished priests for supervising sacrifices. He has himself informed (*RV*, 1.126.2-4) that he received from Svanaya Bhāvayavya, a chief who dwelt on the bank of Sindhu, a hundred *nishkas* (metallic pieces of fixed weights used as coins and often threaded to form a necklace), a hundred vigorous horses, a hundred bulls, a thousand and sixty cattle and ten horse-drawn chariots each carrying a bride (*vadhū*). He is said to have delivered all this guerdon to his father who is described as 'the parent of excellent sons, maintaining his progeny and passing life in the enjoyment of affluence' (*RV*, 1.125.1). The names of Kakshīvān's father and brother(s) are not given in the *Rigveda* but in the *Bṛihaddevatā* (4.24-25). Kakshīvān is said to have been begotten by the well-known Ṛigvedic Ṛishi Dīrghatamas on a slave woman named Uśij. This fits in with the title Auśij, considered to be a matronymic, given to him in the *Ṛigveda* (1.18.1). Another person named Dīrghaśravas, who is clearly stated to be a merchant *(vaṇij),* is also called an Auśij (*RV*, 1.112.11). Sāyaṇa, therefore, takes Kakshīvān, and Dīrghaśravas to be sons of Dīrghatamas. If this conclusion arrived at by Sāyaṇa is valid, it shows that priestly and commercial professions could be followed by persons living together in the same family.

I would like to draw attention to another significant point for consideration in this context. The factors leading to the origin of the Harappan Civilization or, to be more specific, the variables causing the transformation of the early (pre-urban) stage of the Harappan Culture into the mature (urban) stage have often been debated. Most of the scholars are of the opinion that it was trade, mainly external trade, that brought out this transformation for it resulted into the rise of an 'elite population'. However, a few scholars like D.K. Chakrabarti do not think that external trade was the main force behind this transformation. According to him, 'it is possible to argue that the long-distance external trade of the Indus Civilization was a concomitant of the Indus Civilization. This trade did not antedate it' (Chakrabarti 1990: 169). He has reiterated his stand again and postulated that 'within the framework of an ideology which cannot yet be defined in concrete social and institutional terms, an irrigation system, however simple, to cope with the problem of settling down in the riverine plains, and increased craft-specialization as seen by the presence of a large number of raw material types in the early Harappan level and the copper metallurgical area of the contemporary Ganeshwar culture, were two key variables in the emergence of the Indus Civilization' (Chakrabarti 1995: 52).

The significant role of ideology in the rise of the civilization was acknowledged earlier by G.L. Possehl (1990: 276-79) too although he gave equal importance to the contribution of external trade as well. According to him, both these factors brought about the urban revolution in what he termed 'the century of paroxysmal change'. However, as pointed out earlier, the idea of a 'paroxysmal change' has been rejected by S.P. Gupta who demonstrates that it was a gradual transition (1996: 68-100). But apart from the controversy of whether it was 'a leap' or 'a transition', Possehl's suggestion that ideology played a significant role in the transformation deserves due consideration. Unfortunately, the lack of a satisfactory decipherment of the script has prevented us from having a direct understanding of this ideology. The distinct Mature Harappan signs and symbols do represent the precepts related to the ideology, but they have not been properly explained and articulated. The uniformity in the traits of these signs and symbols over a large area clearly demonstrates a sort of 'oneness', an evidence of the emergence of a sort of social identity fostered by an expanding ideology. The question is what else this social identity was if not the Āryan? Indeed, there were Āryan and non-Āryan social groups as clearly depicted in the *Ṛigveda,* but which group at the time had an expanding ideology that diffused even beyond the frontiers of South Asia? In literature we find the optimistic and martial Ṛigvedic Āryans waging wars against their enemies and moving from the banks of the Sarasvatī towards the Indus and beyond, in archaeology we see the Mature Harappans overrunning different peoples and burning down settlements at Kot Diji in the Indus Valley and at Nausharo, Gumla and Rana Ghundai west of the Indus (Lal 1997: 91). Is this correspondence in literature and archaeology meaningless? I believe, the geograpical, chronological and cultural parities between the Early-to-Mature Harappan and Ṛigvedic cultures as well as the striking resemblance in their developmental patterns hardly leave any room for doubt regarding their identity.

Correlating the Ṛigvedic and the Early-to-Mature Harappan Ethno-Geographic Configurations

In the light of what has been said above, it is now possible to correlate those Ṛigvedic ethnic units whose locations are known from the text with Early-to-Mature and related contemporary archaeological assemblages of the respective areas. In doing so, the movements and other specific features of the social groups, if any, must also be kept in mind. This will go a long way in identifying the Ṛigvedic peoples archaeologically, a problem that still remains unsolved. To illustrate the point, a reference is made here to the archaeological assemblages of the Bharatas and the Purus, the two most important Ṛigvedic ethnic units *(janas).* For other such literary-archaeological correlations, the reader may refer to my book *The Ṛigveda: An Archaeological Study* to be released shortly.

As stated earlier, ethnic units have occasionally been segmenting and fusing to cope with the problem of maintaining availability of food and resources and to meet other natural and cultural challenges presented by their environment. The Bharatas were formed by a segmentation of the Purus though much later, by the end of the Ṛigvedic period, both of these parent and offshoot groups underwent a process of fusion along with others to create a new unit called the Kurus. It has also been noted that both, the Bharatas and the Purus, lived in the Sarasvatī Valley and that the relation between the two was somewhat strained. With these basic facts, we may now proceed further to locate them more precisely in the vast valley in order to correlate them with specific archaeological assemblages.

Since the *Ṛigveda* (3.23.4) clearly states that the Bharata chiefs performed sacrifices on the banks of the rivers Sarasvatī, Dṛishadvatī and Āpayā, it may reasonably be accepted that they occupied the region watered by these rivers. The Dṛishadvatī is identified with Chautang. Originating in the Shiwalik range, it flowed via Jagadhari, Nilokheri, Jind, Hissar, Nohar and Suratgarh and joined the Sarasvatī near Kalibangan (Sahai 1976: 37). The Āpayā was located between the Sarasvatī and Dṛishadvatī and flowed past Thanesar (Pusalker 1952/80: 242). It is Āpagā of the *Mahābhārata* (3.83.68) described as a famous river of Kurukshetra, the area between the rivers Sarasvatī and Dṛishadvatī. The geographical location of the Bharatas given in the *Ṛigveda* makes it evident that they lived in what G.L. Possehl (1982/93: 20) calls the Eastern Harappan Domain (that is, the Haryana Domain).

Then, there is a clinching evidence to infer that out of all the sites in this domain, it is Kalibangan that must be taken to be the capital of the Bharatas. As I have shown elsewhere (Singh 1997-198b), the *Ṛigveda* depicts the Bharata chiefs as the greatest performers of sacrifices. In fact, in the entire text there are only a few persons, perhaps not more than five, who are credited to have lent their names to Agni which shows their outstanding devotion and enthusiasm for sacrificial ritual. Four of these five special personalities, it may be noted, belong to the Bharata family, the fifth and the only non-Bharata being Trasadasyu of the Puru line (*RV*, 8.19.32). Agni is repeatedly called 'Bhārata' meaning 'of Bharata', or belonging to the progenitor of the Bharatas (*RV*, 2.7.1 & 5; 4.25.4; 7.8.4). Other chiefs of the Bharata lineage whose Agni has been distinguished are: Vadhryaśva (*RV*, 10.69.4 & 101), Divodāsa (*RV*, 8.103.2) and Devavāta (*RV*, 3.23.3). Looking for an indication of this special fervour for sacrifices in archaeology, attention naturally turns to Kalibangan where excavations have brought to light elaborate arrangements for performing public as well as household sacrifices (Lal 1997; 123-24 & 227-28). Many houses in the Lower Town at Kalibangan have special rooms reserved for sacrificial ritual. In the Citadel Area, atop a platform as many as seven fire-altars are found arranged in a row touching a wall oriented north-south so that persons performing the ritual could do so only facing the east. Nearby, there was a well meant in all probability for ritual bathing. In another area to the north-east of the Lower Town, called KLB-3, a group of fire-altars within a mud-brick enclosure have been discovered. Evidence even of animal sacrifice has been found at the site. Where else can the Bharatas, the greatest performers of sacrifices, be located if not at Kalibangan? The Puru chief Trasadasyu too was a great champion of sacrifices but, as we shall presently see, he was ruling in the Swat Valley, and though his territory in the Sarasvatī area was still maintained, it was to the south-west of the Bharata's realm.[9] It must be admitted that the inference that Kalibangan was the centre from where the Bharatas ruled has to be speculative even though logical. However, until future investigations bring to light some other site in the Haryana Harappan Domain producing greater evidence of sacrificial activities, the claim of Kalibangan as the seat of the Bharatan authority will have to be maintained.

Coming now to the Purus, who also lived in the Sarasvatī Valley along with the Bharatas, we find a significant piece of information in the *Ṛigveda* to isolate their location from that of the Bharatas. The text (*RV*, 7.96.2) informs us that 'in the fullness of their strength' the Purus dwelt on both the banks of the Sarasvatī. Thus, unlike the Bharatas who lived on the left (eastern) bank of the Sarasvatī in what was later to be called Kurukshetra, the area bounded by the Sarasvatī and Dṛishadvatī, the Purus occupied both the banks of the Sarasvatī. Now, anyone conversant with the distribution of Early and Mature Harappan sites in the Sarasvatī Valley will immediately recognize the Central (that is, the Bahawalpur) Harappan Domain to be the domain of the Purus wherein sites are almost equally distributed on both the banks of the river (Joshi *et al.* 1984: Map on p. 517; Possehl 1982/93: Map on p. 21; Lal 1997: Maps on pp. 33 & 103). There is yet another consideration that supports this inference. The Harappan 'domains' distinguished by settlement archaeologists are basically manifestations of power-wielding elite groups. Although several social groups occupied the Sarasvatī Valley, the Bharatas and the Purus were undoubtedly the two most dominant groups in the valley (Singh 1997-98b). Hence, if literary data lead us to assign the Bharatas to the Haryana Domain, it is only reasonable that we relate the other powerful group, the Purus, who were closely connected with the Bharatas, to the Bahawalpur Domain. Gamanwala, the largest Early Harappan site in this domain appears to be the initial capital of the Purus. According to M.R. Mughal (1982/93: 92), one of the most striking aspects of the Mature Harappan Period in Cholistan is 'a general shift of sites from the north-east to the south-west, around and beyond Derawar Fort'. While, as already noted, a north-east to south-west orientation is a general feature of the expanding Āryan ideology during the Ṛigvedic times, this shift of sites in the Cholistan area may have been partly caused by a thrust of the Bharatas on the Purus who were their adversaries. It is very likely that in the Mature Harappan times the Purus may have shifted their centre of authority from Gamanwala to Ganweriwala under such a circumstance. At present, pending excavation work at these sites, this seems to be the most reasonable inference.

The illustrious Puru chief Trasadasyu, son of Purukutsa, is known to have carved out a new territory for the Purus. At a place in the *Ṛigveda* (8.19.37), we find him ruling on the banks of Suvāstu (Swat). As noted earlier, this seems to be in addition to his original domain in the Sarasvatī Valley for he states that he has authority over two territories *(mama dvitā rāshṭram kshatriyasya, RV*, 4.42.1). This new Puru territory may also be identified archaeologically. But before we come to that, an earlier attempt at correlating literary and archaeological data in context of the Purus made by R.N. Nandi (1994-95: 13-17) must be referred to. According to Nandi, the Purus were initially non-Āryan dark-skinned indigenous inhabitants of the Swat Valley who were attacked by a group of Āryans coming from the north-west. In this invasion Purukutsa, their chief, was either killed or imprisoned. But, these very invaders helped Purukutsa's wife to perform certain sacrifices to have a son to continue her husband's lineage. The birth of Trasadasyu was thus accompanied by the Āryanization of the family. Nandi's reconstruction of the subsequent history of the Purus tries to explain how the Purus reached the banks of the Sarasvatī from the Swat Valley. To give archaeological support to his thesis, Nandi refers to the Gandhāra Grave Culture and relates the differences in the burial practices found therein to a process of acculturation between two different peoples, the invaders and the invaded. But, the Gandhāra Grave Culture cannot be dated earlier than 1700 BC (Possehl 1996: 9) and, as such, it is totally irrelevant to archaeological identification of any social group of the Ṛigvedic period since, as pointed out earlier, this period had come to a close in 2000-1900 BC. In fact, Nandi has been working under the old linguistic paradigm based on the Theory of Āryan Invasion and the late dating (1500 BC) of the *Ṛigveda,* but that paradigm has now been brushed aside.

The information that Purus were settled on the banks of the Sarasvatī comes from a family book (*RV*, 7.96.2) while the information that Trasadasyu was ruling in the Swat Valley is provided by a non-family book (*RV*, 8.19.37), and scholars unanimously opine that family books are earlier than the non-family books. It is beyond doubt, therefore, that the Purus had not come from the Swat Valley but had, in fact, reached there from the banks of the Sarasvatī. Attention may here be drawn to the site named Sarai Khola situated close to Taxila in Gandhāra area to which we have already referred to in connection with the expansion of the Early Harappans in the north-west. The culture sequence at the site makes it clear that the earliest inhabitants at this place were Neolithic folks using stone celts and flint blades besides a highly burnished brown pottery that characterizes them. These people witnessed the arrival of the Early Harappans on the site in Period II marked by a decrease in the brown burnished pottery and a simultaneous increase in the Early Harappan pottery generally designated as the Kot Dijian pottery. The newcomers lived there for a considerable duration as indicated by the thickness of their cultural deposit at the site which is about 2.15 m. In the present stage of archaeological research, it is only this Early Harappan expansion in the Gandhāra region that may be related to Trasadasyu's conquest and rule in that area.

In conclusion, I would like to emphasize that the search for Vedic-Harappan relationship needs to be carried on at the level of ethno-geographic configurations defined by literary and archaeological data in order to relate, as far as possible, the various Harappan and contemporary archaeological assemblages to specific peoples known to Vedic literature.

Notes and References

1. The word Sapta Sindhavaḥ does mean a definite country in the *Ṛigveda* 8.24.27 though at other places in the text it indicates simply 'the seven rivers' (Macdonell and Keith 1912/95: 2.424).
2. I am obliged to Prof. B.P. Sinha for drawing my attention to the famous hymn of the Third Maṇḍala of the *Ṛigveda* (3.33) in which the rivers Vipāś (Beas) and Śutudrī (Sutlej) are described as acceding to the request of Viśvāmitra to become fordable for a while to allow the Bharatas to cross through them. The description does indicate a confluence of the two rivers showing that at the time of composition of the Third Maṇḍala of the text (which is later than its Sixth Maṇḍala, see Talageri 2000: 35-93) the Sutlej had ceased to be a tributary of the Sarasvatī. But it would be wrong to suppose that the Sarasvatī by that time became 'a diminished stream deprived of its principal source of water' (Bryant 2001: 168; Witzel 1999: 337-404). This is clear from the description of the Sarasvatī as a vigorous river in the Seventh Maṇḍala which is later even than the Third Maṇḍala. In fact, as noted above, it is in the Seventh Maṇḍala of the text that, the river is stated to be flowing rapidly and faultlessly from the mountains to the sea. Moreover, the Sutlej is known to have often changed its course throughout its history down to historical times. In Arrien's time it flowed independently into the Rann of Kachchha (Macdonell and Keith 1912/95: 2385). It is not unlikely that, before being finally captured by the Indus system, the Sutlej oscillated between the Indus and the Sarasvatī systems, and the position in the Third Maṇḍala of the *Ṛigveda* may not refer to a final separation of the Sutlej from the Sarasvatī.
3. In fact, the sense of Sarasvatī being one of a group of 'seven rivers' is indicated by a different epithet 'Saptathī' (*RV*, 7.36.6) meaning 'the seventh'. But here too 'the seven rivers' do not seem to include the Indus for the enumeration of rivers in the text is generally from east to west as indicated by the famous Nadī-sūkta (*RV*, 10.75.5). Most probably, therefore, the Gaṅgā, the Yamunā and four other rivers to the east of the Sarasvatī are intended in designating it as 'the seventh'.
4. The earlier perception that the Dāsas were non-Āryan aborigines of India speaking a non-Indo-European language has now been brushed aside. They are now supposed to be Indo-Iranian-

speaking people though their dialect was somewhat different from that of the Ṛigvedic Āryans (Bailey 1959, Parpola 1988; Jaiswal 1989-90; Pathak 1993).

5. There is only one exception in the *Avestā* where 'daha' is a part of an enemy's name. In a legend found in the *Abān* (33-35), the *Gos* (13-14) and the *Ashi* (33-35) *Yasts* of the *Avestā* (Pathak 1993: 93), a three-faced, three-headed and six-eyed powerful Drug named Azi Dahāka is killed by Thraeotana. A similar legend is found in the *Ṛigveda* (10.8.8;10.99.6) and subsequent Vedic and Puraṇic literature in which a three-headed and six-eyed Dāsa named Viśvarūpa, son of Tvashṭā, is killed by Trita or by Indra. The resemblance in words Trita and Thraeotana as also in Dāsa and Dahāka shows that the Avestan legend has been borrowed from the *Ṛigveda.*
6. A noteworthy example of identifying ethnic units on the basis of spatial distributions of individual traits is provided by George Erdosy in context of the PGW assemblages. Using authentic publications on Hastinapur (Lal 1955) and Atranjikhera (Gaur 1983), he has shown that the decorative motifs on potteries from these sites have common as well as individual distributions. He hypothesizes that 'PGW saved complimentary but opposing ends. The uniformity of its manufacturing process and the use of simple geometric designs over the entire Gaṅgā-Yamunā Doab may perhaps be seen as reflecting the widespread adoption of a new ideology, while the restriction of more complex designs to individual sites may be taken as indications of the diverse ethnic affiliations of the people who subscribed to it' (Erdosy in Allchin 1995:96).
7. Despite the presence of Kalibangan I fabrics at various sites, some pottery types are found that characterize particular sites or have restricted distribution as, for instance, 'a dull chocolate-coloured burnished ware with parin marks' at Kunal (Khatri and Acharya 1994-95: 84). Besides, certain features present at one site are missing on others. Thus, the pit-dwellings found at Kunal are not reported from Kalibangan, Banawali or Rakhigarhi. Similarly, the settlements at Kaibangan and Banawali are fortified but it is not so at Kunal.
8. It may be noted that among all the rivers in the text it is Sindhu alone (that is considered to be a male, a 'nada' and not a 'nadī'.
9. In view of my further studies in the *Ṛigveda,* I have changed my earlier stand that the Purus lived to the east of the Bharatas (Singh 1997-98b: 34).

Bibliography

Allchin, F.R., 1995, *The Archaeology of Early Historic South Asia,* Cambridge: Cambridge University Press.

Bailey, H.W., 1959, "Iranian Arya and Daha", *Transactions of the Philological Society,* pp. 71-115.

Barth, F., 1969, "Introduction", in *Ethnic Groups and Boundaries: The Social Organization of Culture Differences* (F. Barth, ed.), pp. 9-38. Boston: Little, Brown & Co.

Bentley, G.C., 1987, "Ethnicity and Practice", *Comparative Studies in Society and History,* Vol. 29, pp. 24-55.

Bhan, S., 1971-72, "Siswal: A Pre-Harappan Site in Dṛishadvati Valley", *Purātattva,* Vol. 5, pp. 44-46.

——, 1975, *Excavations at Mitathal (1968) and Other Explorations in the Sutlej-Yamunā Divide,* Kurukshetra: Kurukshetra University.

Binford, L.R., 1965, "Archaeological Systematics and the Study of Cultural Process", *American Antiquity,* Vol. 31, pp. 203-10.

Bisht, R.S., 1988, "Some Glimpses of Mercantile and Maritime Activities of the Ṛgvedic Aryans", in *Marine Archaeology of Indian Ocean Countries* (S.R. Rao, ed.), pp. 12-13.

——, 1991, "Dholavira: New Horizons of the Indus Civilization", *Purātattva,* Vol. 20, pp. 71-82.

——, 1999, "Harappans and the Ṛgveda: Points of Convergence", in *The Dawn of Indian Civilization up to c. 600* BC (G.C. Pande, ed.), pp. 393-442, Delhi: Centre for Studies in Civilizations.

Bourdieu, P., 1978, *Outline of a Theory of Practice,* Cambridge: Cambridge University Press.

Bryant, E., 2001, *The Quest for the Origins of Vedic Culture: The Indo-Āryan Migration Debate,* Oxford: Oxford University Press.

Chakrabarti, D.K., 1990, *The External Trade of the Indus Civilization,* Delhi: Munshiram Manoharlal.
——, 1995, *The Archaeology of Ancient Indian Cities,* Delhi: Oxford University Press.
Childe, V.G., 1929, *The Danubey in Prehistory,* Oxford: Clarendon Press.
Dales, G.F., 1964, "The Mythical Massacre at Mohenjo-daro", *Expedition,* Vol. 6(3), pp. 36-43.
Deshpande, M.M., 1995, "Vedic Aryans, Non-Vedic Aryans, and Non-Aryans: Judging the Linguistic Evidence of the Veda", in *The Indo-Aryans of Ancient South Asia: Language Material Culture and Ethnicity* (G. Erdosy, ed.), pp. 67-84, Berlin & New York: Walter de Gruyter.
Durrani, F.A., 1988, *Excavations in the Gomal Valley: Rehman Dheri Excavation Report No. 1. Ancient Pakistan,* Vol. 6, Peshawar: Department of Archaeology, Peshawar University.
Durrani, F.A., I. Ali and G. Erdosy 1991, "Further Excavation at Rehman Dheri", *Ancient Pakistan,* Vol. 7, pp. 61-151.
Dyson R.H., Jr., 1982/93, "Paradigm Changes in the Study of the Indus Civilization", in *Harappan Civilization: A Recent Perspective* (Gregory L. Possehl, ed.), pp. 571-81, New Delhi, Bombay, Calcutta: Oxford & IBH Publishing Co.
Elst, K., 1999, *Update on the Aryan Invasion Debate,* New Delhi: Aditya Prakashan.
Erdosy, G., 1995, "Language, Material Culture and Ethnicity: Theoretical Perspectives", in *The Indo-Aryans of Ancient South Asia: Language, Material Culture and Ethnicity* (George Erdosy, ed.), pp. 1-31, Berlin & New York: Walter de Gruyter.
Fairservis, W.A., 1975, *The Roots of Ancient India,* Chicago: Chicago University Press.
Gaur, R.C., 1983, *The Excavations at Atranjikhera: Early Civilization in the Ganga Basin,* Delhi: Motilal Banarasidass.
Ghosh, B.K., 1952/80, "The Aryan Problem", in *The Vedic Age* (R.C. Majumdar, A.D. Pusalker and A.K. Majumdar, eds.), pp. 201-17, Bombay: Bharatiya Vidya Bhavan.
Gupta, S.P., 1996, *The Indus-Saraswati Civlization: Origins, Problems and Issues,* Delhi: Pratibha Prakashan.
Hale, W.E., 1986/99, *Asura in Early Vedic Religion,* Delhi: Motilal Banarasidass.
Hodder, I., 1978, "The Spatial Structure of Material Cultures", in *The Spatial Organization of Culture,* (I. Hodder, ed.), pp. 93-111. London: Duckworth.
Jaiswal, S., 1989-90, "Stratification in Ṛgvedic Society: Evidence and Paradigms", *Indian Historical Quarterly,* Vol. 16 (1-2), pp. 1-34.
Joshi, J.P., Madhu Bala and Jassu Ram, 1984, "The Indus Civilization: A Reconsideration on the Basis of Distribution Maps", in *Frontiers of the Indus Civilization* (B.B. Lal and S.P. Gupta, eds.), pp. 511-30. New Delhi: Books and Books.
Kenoyer, J.M., 1995, "Interaction Systems, Specialized Crafts and Culture Change: The Indus Valley Tradition and the Indo-Gangetic Tradition in South Asia", in *The Indo-Aryans of Ancient South Asia: Language, Material Culture and Ethnicity,* (G. Erdosy, ed.), pp. 213-57, Berlin & New York: Walter de Gruyter.
Khan, F.A., 1965, "Excavations at Kot Diji", *Pakistan Archaeology,* Vol. 2, pp. 11-85.
Khatri, J.S. and M. Acharya, 1994-95, "Kunal: A New Indus Saraswati Site", *Purātattva,* Vol. 25, pp. 84-86.
Lal, B.B., 1954-55, "Excavations at Hastinapur and Other Explorations in the Upper Ganga and Sutlej Basins", *Ancient India,* Vols. 10-11, pp. 5-151.
——, 1997, *The Earliest Civilization of South Asia,* New Delhi: Aryan Books International.
——, 2002, *The Sarasvati Flows On: The Continuity of Indian Culture,* New Delhi: Aryan Books International.
Macdonell, A.A. and A.B. Keith, 1912/95, *Vedic Index of Names and Subjects,* Delhi: Motilal Banarasidass.
Misra, S.S., 1992, *The Aryan Problem: A Linguistic Approach,* New Delhi: Munshiram Manoharlal.
Misra, V.N., 1984, "Climate, a Factor in the Rise and Fall of the Indus Civilization—Evidence from Rajasthan and Beyond", in *Frontiers of the Indus Civilization* (B.B. Lal and S.P. Gupta, eds.), pp. 461-89, New Delhi: Books and Books.
——, 1994, "Indus Civilization and the Rigvedic Sarasvati", in *South Asian Archaeology 1993* (A. Parpola and P. Koskikallio, eds.), pp. 511-25, Helsinki: Suomalainen Tiedeakatemia.
Mughal, M.R., 1982/93, "Recent Archaeological Research in the Cholistan Desert", in *Harappan Civilization: A Recent Perspective* (Gregory L. Possehl, ed.), pp. 85-95, New Delhi, Bombay, Calcutta: Oxford and IBH Publishing Co.

Nandi, R.N., 1986-87, "Anthropology and the Study of the Ṛgveda", *The Indian Historical Review,* Vol. 13 (1-2), pp. 153-65.

——, 1994-95. "Aryan Settlements and the Ṛigveda", *The Indian Historical Review,* Vol. 21(1-2), pp. 9-36.

——, 1998, "Problem of Historical Sequence in the Ṛgveda: The Text and the Context", *Journal of Studies on Ancient India,* Vol. 1(2-4), pp. 153-169.

Pant, P.C., 1996, "Archaeology and History: Some Problems of Historical Reconstruction", in *Indian Archaeology Since Independence* (K.M. Shrimali, ed.), pp. 5-15, Delhi: Association for the Study of History and Archaeology.

Parpola, A., 1988, "The Coming of the Aryans to Iran and India and the Cultural and Ethnic Identity of the Dasas", *Studio Orientalia,* Vol. 64, pp. 195-302.

——, 1995, "The Problem of the Aryans and the Soma: Textual Linguistic and Archaeological Evidence", in *The Indo-Āryans of Ancient South Asia, Language, Material Culture and Ethnicity* (George Erdosy, ed.), pp. 353-81, Berlin & New York: Walter de Gruyter.

Pathak, V.S., 1986, *Presidential Address,* 12th Annual Congress of the Epigraphical Society of India, Jabalpur.

——, 1993, "Semantics of Arya: Its Historical Implications", in *Āryan Problem* (S.B. Deo and S. Kamath, eds.), pp. 86-99. Pune: Mythic Society.

Possehl G.L., 1982/93, "The Harappan Civilization: A Contemporary Perspective", in *Harappan Civilization: A Recent Perspective* (Gregory L. Possehl, ed.), pp. 15-28, New Delhi, Bombay, Calcutta: Oxford & IBH Publishing Co.

——, 1984, "A Note on the Harappan Settlement Patterns in the Punjab", in *Studies in the Archaeology and Palaeoanthropology of South Asia* (K.A.R. Kennedy and G.L. Possehl, eds.), pp. 83-87. New Delhi: Oxford & IBH Publishing Co.

——, 1986, *Kulli: An Exploration of an Ancient Civilization in South Asia,* Durham: Carolina Academic Press.

——, 1990, "Revolution in the Urban Revolution: The Emergence of Indus Urbanism", *Annual Review of Anthropology,* Vol. 19, pp. 261-82.

——, 1996, *Indus Age: The Writing System,* New Delhi, Calcutta: Oxford & IBH Publishing Co.

Puri, V.M.K. and B.C. Verma, 1998, "Glaciological and Geological Source of Vedic Saraswati in the Himalayas", *Itihas Darpan,* Vol. 4(2), pp. 7-36.

Pusalker, A.D., 1952/80, "Aryan Settlements in India", in *The Vedic Age* (R.C. Majumdar, A.D. Pusalker and A.K. Majumdar, eds.), pp. 241-63, Bombay: Bharatiya Vidya Bhavan.

Rajaram, N.S. and David Frawley, 1995, *"Aryans" and the Origins of Civilization,* Quebec: W.H. Press.

Renfrew, C., 1978, "Space, Time and Polity", in *The Evolution of Social Systems* (J. Friedman and M.J. Rowlands, eds.), pp. 89-112, London: Duckworth.

Richter-Ushanas, E., 1997, *The Indus Script and the Ṛg-veda,* Delhi: Motilal Banarasidass.

Sahai, B., 1976, "A Note on the Old Bed of Drishadvat", in *Archaeological Congress and Seminar 1972,* Kurukshetra: Kurukshetra University.

Sethna, K.D., 1981, *Karpāsa in Prehistoric India: A Chronological and Cultural Clue,* New Delhi: Biblia Impex.

Shaffer, J.G., 1984, "The Indo-Aryan Invasions: Cultural Myth and Archaeological Reality", in *The People of South Asia* (J.R. Lukacs, ed.), pp. 77-90, New York & London: Plenum Press.

——, 1992, "The Indus Valley, Baluchistan, and Helmand Traditions: Neolithic Through Bronze Age", in *Chronologies in Old World Archaeology* (R.W. Ehrich, ed.) Third Edition, pp. 425-46, 441-64. Chicago & London: University of Chicago Press.

Shaffer, J.G., and D.A. Lichtenstein, 1989, "Ethnicity and Change in the Indus Valley Cultural Tradition", in *Old Problems and New Perspectives in the Archaeology of South Asia* (J.M. Kenoyer, ed.), pp. 117-26, Madison: Department of Anthropology, University of Wisconsin.

——, 1995, "The Concepts of 'Cultural Tradition' and 'Palaeoethnicity' in South Asian Archaeology", in *The Indo-Aryans of Ancient South Asia: Language, Material Culture and Ethnicity* (George Erdosy, ed.), pp. 126-54, Berlin & New York: Walter de Gruyter.

Shaffer, J.G., and D.A. Lichtenstein, 1999, "Migration, Philology and South Asian Archaeology", in *Aryan and Non-Aryan in South Asia* (J. Bronkhorst and M.M. Deshpande, eds.), pp. 239-60, Cambridge: Department of Sanskrit and Indian Studies, Harvard University.

Sharma, R.S., 1983, *Material Culture and Social Formations in Ancient India,* Delhi: Macmillan.

Sharma, Y.D. 1982/93, "Harappan Complex on the Sutlej (India)", in *Harappan Civilization: A Recent Perspective* (G.L. Possehl, ed.), pp. 141-65, New Delhi, Bombay, Calcutta: Oxford & IBH Publishing Co.

Shennan, S.J., 1978, "Archaeological 'Cultures': An Empirical Investigation", in *The Spatial Organization of Culture* (I. Hodder, ed.), pp. 113-41, London: Duckworth.

Singh, B., 1987/97, *Harappā Sabhyatā aur Vaidika Sāhitya,* New Delhi: Radhakrishna Prakashan.

——, 1995, *The Vedic Harappans,* New Delhi: Aditya Prakashan.

——, 1996, "Aristocracy in the Indo-Aryan Society", unpublished paper read at the 30th Annual Conference of the Indian Archaeological Society held at New Delhi on November, 24-26, 1996.

Singh, B.P., 1988-89, "Early Farming Communities of Kaimur Foot-Hills", *Purātattva,* Vol. 19, pp.6-18.

Singh, P., 1999, "Rise of Cultures in Eastern India", in *The Dawn of Indian Civilization up to c. 600* BC (G.C. Pande, ed.), pp. 509-29. Delhi: Centre for Studies in Civilizations.

Singh, P., A.K. Singh and I. Singh, 1991-92, "Excavations at Imlidih Khurd", *Purātattva,* Vol. 22, pp. 120-22.

Singh, S., 1969, "Vedic Literature on Pottery", in *Potteries in Ancient India* (B.P. Sinha, ed.), pp. 301-13, Patna: Patna University.

——, 1985, *Models, Paradigms and the New Archaeology,* Varanasi: Banaras Hindu University.

——, 1997-98a, "Dating the Ṛigveda Archaeologically", *Prāgdhārā,* Vol. 8, pp. 137-47.

——, 1997-98b. "Sindhu and Sarasvati in the Ṛigveda and their Archaeological Implications", *Purātattva,* Vol. 28, pp. 26-38.

——, 2001, "Redefining the Ṛigvedic and Harappan Connections", *Man and Environment,* Vol. 26(1), pp. 93-98.

Talageri, S.C., 2000, *The Ṛigveda: A Historical Analysis,* New Delhi: Aditya Prakashan.

Thomas, K.D. and F.R. Allchin, 1986, "Radiocarbon Dating of Some Early Sites in N.W. Pakistan", *South Asian Studies,* Vol. 2, pp. 37-44.

Willey. G.R. and P. Phillips, 1958, *Method and Theory in American Archaeology,* Chicago: University of Chicago Press.

Winternitz, M., 1933/91, *A History of Indian Literature,* Vol. 1, New Delhi: Munshiram Manoharlal.

Witzel, M., 1995, "Rgvedic History, Poets, Chieftains and Polities", in *The Indo-Āryans of Ancient South Asia: Language Material Culture and Ethnicity* (G. Erdosy, ed.), pp. 307-52, Berlin & New York: Walter de Gruyter.

——, 1999, "Aryan and Non-Aryan Names in Vedic India: Data for the Linguistic Situation, *c.* 1900-500 BC", in *Aryan and Non-Aryan in South Asia* (J. Bronkhorst and M.M. Deshpande, eds.), pp. 337-404, Cambridge: Department of Sanskrit and Indian Studies, Harvard University.

Index

Abbreviations used in the Index : *a* – author/scholar, *b* – book, *c* – country, *d* – dynasty, *de* – demon, *g* – god/goddess, *i* – institutions, *k* – king, *l* – language, *m* – mountain, *o* – ocean/sea, *p* – place, *pl* – plant/tree, *peo* – people/tribe, *q* – queen, *r* – region/province, *ri* – river, *s* – sage, *t* – technical term.